Native Brazil

Native Brazil

BEYOND THE CONVERT AND THE CANNIBAL, 1500–1900

EDITED BY *Hal Langfur*

University of New Mexico Press ❖ Albuquerque

Library of Congress Cataloging-in-Publication Data

Native Brazil : beyond the convert and the cannibal, 1500–1900 / edited by Hal Langfur.
    pages cm. — (Diálogos)
  Includes bibliographical references and index.
  ISBN 978-0-8263-3841-9 (pbk. : alk. paper) — ISBN 978-0-8263-3842-6 (electronic)
1. Indians of South America—Brazil—History. 2. Indians, Treatment of—Brazil—
History. 3. Indians of South America—Brazil—First contact with Europeans.
4. Indians of South America—Missions—Brazil—History. 5. Indians of South
America—Brazil—Government relations. 6. Brazil—Colonization. I. Langfur, Hal,
author, editor of compilation.
  F2519.N37 2014
  981—dc23

2013034139

Cover and interior design by Catherine Leonardo
Composed in Minion Pro 10.25/13.5
Display type is Minion Pro

For Kerry, Bridger, and Devon

And to the memory of John Monteiro and Neil Whitehead

Contents

Illustrations

TABLES

CHART

MAPS

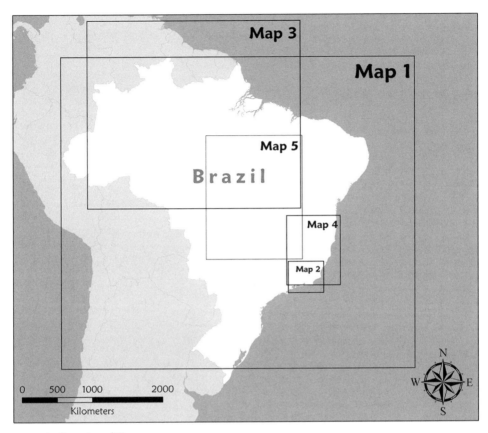

An Overview of Maps

Map 1. Brazil, ca. 1800. Source: Adapted from A. H. de Oliveira Marques and João José Alves Dias, *Atlas histórico de Portugal e do ultramar português* (Lisbon: Universidade de Lisboa, Centro de Estudos Históricos, 2003), 372–73.

Map 2. Indian *Aldeias* of Rio de Janeiro Captaincy, early nineteenth century. Source: Adapted from José Ribamar Bessa Freire and Márcia Fernanda Malheiros, *Aldeamentos indígenas do Rio de Janeiro* (Rio de Janeiro: Programa de Estudos dos Povos Indígenas, Universidade do Estado do Rio de Janeiro, 1997), 60.

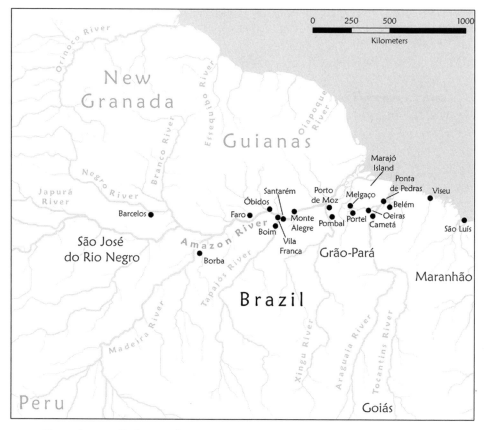

Map 3. Amazon Basin, ca. 1780

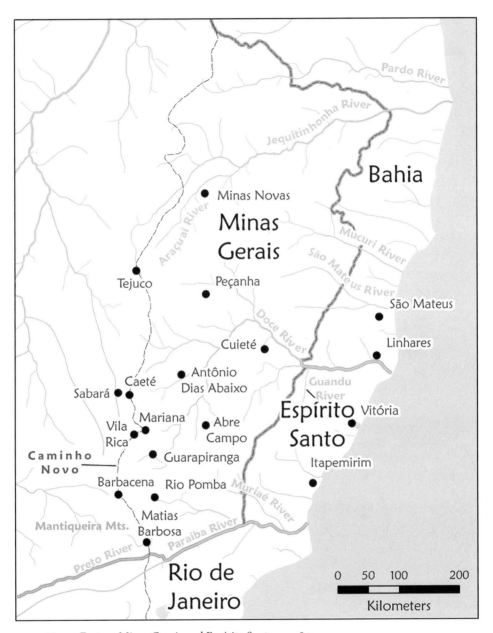

Map 4. Eastern Minas Gerais and Espírito Santo, ca. 1800

Map 5. Goiás, ca. 1840

Introduction

Recovering Brazil's Indigenous Pasts

Hal Langfur

T he earliest Portuguese account of Brazil's indigenous inhabitants contemplated their mass conversion to Christianity only belatedly. Its author, the scribe and nobleman Pero Vaz de Caminha, initially focused his attention on other matters. "They were dark, and entirely naked, without anything to cover their shame," he wrote of that first encounter after the leader of a landing party exchanged several hats for a feathered headdress and a string of white beads. To be sure, the meeting between Tupi-speakers and spellbound mariners in April of 1500 had inherent religious significance. More than a dozen priests and Franciscan friars accompanied the expedition of at least 1,200 men in thirteen ships, which veered west while retracing the voyage to India that Vasco da Gama had completed a year earlier. The clerics conducted Mass that first Sunday on the sandy shore as the explorers paused for ten days to resupply themselves with food, drinking water, and wood. Spiritual aspirations guided expedition commander Pedro Álvares Cabral to bestow the name Island of the True Cross on the tropical discovery. But with time to observe and reflect, his scribe withheld extended religious commentary until the final paragraphs of a long letter to the Portuguese monarch.[1]

Caminha devoted the bulk of his text to depicting the coastal natives and their interactions with the Portuguese, circling back to their nudity again and again, evidently unable to get used to the sight himself. The men carried bows and arrows. They approached the Portuguese without fear, setting aside their weapons when urged to do so. Pieces of bone, stones, and wooden plugs pierced their lower lips. They shaved their hair well above their ears. Some painted their bodies with a black or red dye. One, perhaps a headman, stuck feathers to his skin. Young mothers tied their infants to their breasts with lengths of cloth. Some danced in the presence of the sailors, growing particularly animated when a bagpipe player struck up a melody. But when one of the Portuguese captains caught a shark and offered it to the Indians, "they became frightened like sparrows at a feeding place." The scribe inferred that "they are bestial people and of very little knowledge; and for this reason they are so timid."[2] Yet they willingly contributed their labor to the resupply effort.

Just before departing, with mounting experience of how enthusiastically the Indians responded to inexpensive gifts, to wine served liberally at shared meals, and to time spent aboard ship with their unexpected visitors, Cabral ordered a massive wooden cross erected. A procession led by the priests, singing and in full regalia, preceded a second Mass celebrated in the presence of the natives, who helped carry the cross, kissed it, and knelt before it in the manner of the sailors. One Indian became especially spirited as the ceremony concluded. He circulated among his countrymen, conversing with them, gesturing to the cross, pointing "towards Heaven as though he were telling them something good." The ethnographic descriptions that first occupied the scribe gave way to reflections about religious conversion. "I do not doubt that they will become Christians, in accordance with the pious intent of Your Highness, and that they will believe in our Holy Faith, to which may it please Our Lord to bring them," he wrote. "For it is certain this people is good and of pure simplicity, and there can easily be stamped upon them whatever belief we wish to give them."[3] Later that day a supply ship sailed for Lisbon, carrying Caminha's letter announcing the discovery.

Upon hearing the news of Cabral's brief American sojourn, King Manuel I (r. 1495–1521) immediately dispatched another expedition to reconnoiter the coastline. Amerigo Vespucci sailed as a pilot on this voyage (1501–1502), probably his third to the Americas, although controversy surrounds his claims and even the authorship of his letters. He explored the entire Brazilian coast to the south of its easternmost protrusion, and then he sailed on almost to the tip of the continent. On a reported fourth voyage (1503–1504), he again traversed the territory between present-day Salvador and Rio

Figure 1. Jesuit missionaries first arrived in the mid-sixteenth century to spread Christianity among Brazil's diverse indigenous inhabitants, remaining active for most of the colonial period. In the mid-seventeenth century, Father António Vieira, an acclaimed orator, traveled deep into the interior to evangelize those still unfamiliar with European beliefs and practices. Source: André de Barros, *Vida do apostolico padre Antonio Vieyra da Companhia de Jesus . . .* (Lisbon: Sylviana, 1746). Courtesy of the John Carter Brown Library at Brown University.

de Janeiro (see map 1). Within a few years, labeled "America," Brazil appeared on the famed Waldseemüller Map (1507), as Europeans struggled to grasp the meaning of these feats. In addition to bequeathing his name to the New World, Vespucci provided further depictions of Brazilian Indians. His reports diverged strikingly from Caminha's sanguine images of innocents hungry for the teachings of the Roman Catholic Church.

The hunger Vespucci described was of a different sort. In August 1501 he and his fellow sailors anchored off present-day Rio Grande do Norte, coming ashore "to see if the land was inhabited by people, and of what kind." No encounter occurred that first day, as the party sought to enlist helpers to resupply their vessels. On the second, the visitors spied Indians observing them from high up a mountainside. They attempted to coax them to descend but found them distrustful. As it was already late in the day, they returned to their ships, leaving a cache of bells, mirrors, and other gifts on the sand. Once the men were out to sea, the Indians descended to collect the items. The next morning they seemed to signal the crew, lighting fires and sending up puffs of smoke. Landing again, the party sent two of its members inland, laden with trade goods. Seven days passed. The men had promised to return in five.

What happened next, as related in a passage in Vespucci's letter to Piero Soderini, head of the Florentine Republic, established the terms of an alternative view of Brazil's coastal inhabitants, a dark counter-narrative to Caminha's hopeful dispatch of the previous year. Vespucci and the others again came ashore. This time, a group of native women approached, though warily, encouraged by their men. The Europeans decided to send one of their crew, "a youth who always showed much courage," to greet the women while the rest retreated to their boats. When the young man advanced, the women encircled him, "touching him and gazing upon him in admiration." Meanwhile, another woman came down from the mountain, carrying a club:

> When she reached our Christian, she stole up from behind and raising this club, gave him such a blow that it knocked him dead on the ground. And immediately the other women grabbed him by the feet and dragged him toward the mountain, and the men leaped toward the shore to shoot at us with their bows and arrows; and they so frightened our men, who were in the boats resting with the shallow-water anchors by the land, that despite all the many arrows

they were shooting into the boats, no one managed to pick up his
weapons. Yet we fired four charges of mortars at them, and while
none of the shots hit anyone, the very sound of them was enough
to send them fleeing toward the mountain, where the women were
already hacking the Christian up into pieces, and, in a great fire
they had built, were roasting him before our eyes, showing us many
pieces and then eating them; and the men, indicating by their gestures that they had killed and eaten the other two Christians.[4]

Ordered by their captain not to retaliate, Vespucci and the others sailed away,
setting a course along the coastline to the southeast.

Starting with detractors in the early sixteenth century, Vespucci was
accused of fabrications. One or more editors likely embellished his prose.
There is reason to doubt the veracity of an author who in one letter said he
had met a man who "confessed to me that he had eaten of the flesh of more
than two hundred bodies," while in another letter increased this count to
three hundred.[5] Factual or not, Vespucci's tales of cannibalism were an early
instance of innumerable letters, reports, and histories written by explorers,
missionaries, and setters decrying the savagery of Brazilian Indians. Such
texts proliferated at the sites of interethnic contact and conflict over the
course of Portuguese America's long existence as a colony.

Caminha and Vespucci's observations, among the very first to cross the
Atlantic from Brazil, exemplify the extremes that characterized European
views of Brazil's native peoples. This volume contributes to the unfinished
task of moving beyond such polarities and dispelling the stereotypes they
fostered. Few dispute that some natives embraced Christianity. They did so
for reasons ranging from its ritual appeal to the protections missionaries
provided against the worst settler depredations. Likewise, almost no one well
versed in the sixteenth-century sources doubts that the coastal Tupi-speakers
ritually consumed enemies they captured in battle.[6] But dubious conclusions
developed from these realities. Conversion provided the ultimate confirmation for colonists that their mission was just, that the natives, given the right
conditions, might be guileless lambs, willing—even eager—to submit themselves to church and crown. Alternatively, cannibalism was only the most
disturbing of behaviors invoked to condemn them as savages, to legitimate
their slaughter, to justify their enslavement and the seizure of territory.
Neither position came close to explaining the complexity of indigenous cultures and social conduct. Both obscured the choices, ambiguities, and

contradictions inherent in native responses to colonial impositions. Both minimize the importance of changing circumstances that led distinct individuals and groups to resist, negotiate, form alliances, migrate, or enter colonial society at different times and in different places. As we will see, the convert/cannibal dichotomy had its counterpart in later scholarship. It impeded anthropologists, historians, and those who relied on their expertise when they tried to make sense of Brazil's rich indigenous past.

WHERE ARE THE INDIANS?

In most introductory college courses on Latin America's past, as in most textbooks students read in those courses, Indians dominate the scene. They do, that is, when the topic is Spanish America. Why do they so quickly vanish from historical treatments of Portuguese America? It is a question that should concern not only college students and their professors but anyone interested in the history of the Americas. It can help us come to grips with what we often neglect to teach and fail to learn about an expanse of the western hemisphere larger than the continental U.S. Indeed, the reader might pause for a moment to ask what she or he has been taught about this subject: what happened to Brazil's Indians?

As the typical Latin American survey course unfolds, progressing from conquest to the consolidation of colonial society in Spanish America, Indians are to be found everywhere. The story cannot be told without them. Columbus encountered the Taino in Hispaniola; Cortés, the Maya and Aztecs in Mexico; Pizarro, the Incas in Peru. The Caribbean crucible had by then established the patterns of conquest, coerced labor, and population collapse that ravaged the American mainland. The Spaniards met with powerful, sedentary empires in Mesoamerica and the Andes. They killed or subordinated the leaders and put the commoners to work, constructing new societies upon the old imperial foundations. The very stones once used in Aztec, Maya, and Inca palaces and pyramids became building blocks for colonial urban centers. The dense populations, intensive agriculture, draft labor rotations, and state tribute systems that once supported native royalty, priests, and warriors became the basis of colonial wealth. But no matter how virulent the diseases, or how cruel the oppression, or how determined the crown and church to transform the survivors of this catastrophe into deracinated Christian vassals, native peoples persisted and resisted, making demands on land and resources, opposing further depredations, negotiating their entrance into colonial society, and asserting their cultural practices.

Brazil, we frequently learn, was atypical. The Portuguese had to contend with more mobile, less hierarchical peoples spread out along an extensive Atlantic coastline. Unaccustomed to producing agricultural surpluses, organized by kin and clan rather than in powerful states, loosely gathered in temporary villages rather than concentrated in imposing cities like Tenochtitlan and Cuzco, Brazil's Tupi-speaking peoples, according to standard histories, quickly succumbed or faded into the forests. Their nudity, polygyny, piercings, tattoos, and tobacco use offer some authors the opportunity to comment on the challenges Europeans experienced assimilating exotic features of the New World. Their cannibalism may be mentioned as the ultimate expression of such otherness. Inland peoples may even make a few appearances later in this story, as it is conventionally told, because settlers raided the interior to replenish the collapsing coastal workforce. But as fast as they could be brought out of the forests to the cane fields, they, too, died or fled, ill-suited to the work regime on expanding sugar plantations. Certain missionaries decried this treatment, but before a thoroughgoing conversion could occur, the Indians disappeared, replaced by an influx of slaves from Africa. Accounts of Brazil's mature colonial society, its eventual break from Portugal in 1822, and its first decades as an independent nation no longer relegate all non-elite actors to the margins, as they once did, but the emphasis is on African slaves and their descendants. Native peoples almost never turn up. Indians are for Spanish America—and curious students are left to wonder why.

Disease, armed conflict, relocation, and forced labor caused severe depopulation, but the truth is that the colonization of the vast territory that became Brazil resulted neither in the effective eradication of Amerindians nor in brisk military and political subjugation. Far from vanishing quickly from the colony's Atlantic coast, native peoples comprised the primary workforce, first as dyewood harvesters, then as plantation laborers, both captive and free, throughout the first century of colonization. Outside the most profitable sugar-producing areas of the northeast, which gravitated to more expensive enslaved African labor by the early seventeenth century, a multiplicity of mission-dwelling and independent native groups continued to make their presence felt along the seaboard throughout the colonial period, though in reduced numbers.[7]

Figure 2. European artists struggled to come to terms with indigenous customs, especially cannibalism. The scenes they popularized contributed to enduring misconceptions about Brazilian Indians. Source: Hans Staden, "De voorname Scheeps-togten van Jan Staden van Homburg in Hessen, na Brazil gedaan Anno 1547 en 1549," in *Naaukeurige versameling der gedenk-waardigste zee en land-reysen na Oost en West-Indiën . . . ,* ed. Pieter van der Aa (Leiden: Pieter van der Aa, 1707), vol. 15, plate Y. Courtesy of the John Carter Brown Library at Brown University.

If Indians never disappeared, if they long continued to be important actors in every region, why have scholars disregarded this presence? The answer is complex. The intellectual origins of the all-but-absent Brazilian Indians are historical and historiographical. They can be traced to developments within the academic discipline of history, as well as to traditional disciplinary boundaries. They have to do with impediments to scholarly exchange that are surprisingly stubborn despite a globalized world. They belie unresolved tensions that separate regional from imperial and national histories, de-centered from dominant perspectives. A word about each of these issues will help clarify the nature of the problem.

ERASING INDIGENOUS HISTORY

The notion that native peoples exerted a modest influence on Brazil's early history derives some of its substance from demographic data. Indigenous pre-Columbian population figures, as uncertain and controversial as they remain, make evident key distinctions between the core areas of colonization during Spain and Portugal's first century of overseas expansion. Conservative estimates of Mexico's population on the eve of contact posit the presence of up to twenty million people. The Andean region contained as many as twelve million inhabitants. By comparison, Brazil was probably home to between two and three million.[8] Evidence for such estimates is fragmentary but suggestive, particularly when one considers Brazil's much greater size. Assuming a demographic collapse of up to 90 percent during the first hundred years after contact does little to change the picture. Simply as a consequence of their sheer numbers, the surviving peoples of the Aztec and Inca empires would exert greater sway over post-conquest society.

At the root of this demographic disparity were substantial food surpluses produced by the sedentary societies of Mexico's central valley and the Peruvian highlands. Intensively cultivating maize and other crops, Aztec and Inca commoners could provision large urban centers, including the imperial capitals Tenochtitlan and Cuzco. Inhabitants freed from the demands of agricultural labor served as artisans, traders, soldiers, priests, and government officials. They developed numerical and writing systems that preserved evidence of pre-Columbian practices. Patriarchal, hereditary nobilities arose to rule complex, centralized states organized into ethnic provinces. Once defeated in battle or coaxed into alliance, these polities could be relatively swiftly incorporated into the structures of Spanish rule. Scholars, in short, could scarcely ignore the importance of Mesoamerican and Andean peoples in post-conquest society.

By contrast, the less numerous semisedentary and non-sedentary Indians, Tupi and non-Tupi, living along Brazil's Atlantic seaboard, confounded the first European chroniclers with their linguistic diversity and political fragmentation. Counting inland peoples, anthropologists tell us that forty or more language families, grouped into three major language trunks, Tupi, Macro-Gê, and Arawak, contributed to this perplexing matrix of as many as two thousand distinct groups. Many cultivated manioc, a less intensive and protein-rich crop than maize, migrating every few years as soils lapsed. Others survived primarily by hunting, fishing, and foraging, activities which required even greater mobility. The largest of villages along Brazil's coast and great rivers may have sheltered several thousand residents. The more nomadic the group, the smaller its communities and less sharply articulated its political hierarchies. Even for the more sedentary Tupi, relocation into the vast interior long remained an option to avoid further contact. The social organization of indigenous kin groups and clans could be extraordinarily intricate, but this reality escaped observers for many centuries.

Given these characteristics, it comes as no surprise that Brazilian history has no counterpart of Cortés or Pizarro, no preeminent European protagonist, deemed hero or villain, upon which to base a narrative of initial Indian encounter, resistance, and subjugation. The absence of centralized authority meant that native polities in Portuguese America did not tend to capitulate en masse. Without wealth accumulated from agricultural surpluses or gold, with no tradition of draft labor, they presented few immediate objectives for conquest, and the task of binding them to remunerative commercial production required prolonged effort.

Differences in population densities, subsistence strategies, and social and political organization, however, go only so far in explaining the problem. National ideology and the biases of intellectual elites must also be taken into account. We now know, for example, that intensive agriculture and aquaculture did yield food surpluses in the Amazon basin, supporting larger, more stratified societies than once thought.[9] But their cultural achievements—measured in exquisite ceramics, intricate oral traditions, and matchless knowledge of the forest environment—remained unappreciated. John Monteiro, a leading figure in establishing indigenous history as a newly vital academic pursuit in Brazil, has noted that the first generation of Brazilian intellectuals who set out to write the history of their recently independent nation in the nineteenth century enshrined a vision of "noble, valiant, and (especially) extinct" coastal Indians. These thinkers sought to embrace modernity, honing a myth of their nation's founding while contending with ongoing conflicts with surviving native peoples. As a result, "the idea that the beginning of Brazilian history meant the end of the Indians became such a commonplace assumption that few historians have bothered to consider the constant presence and participation of indigenous peoples, which, to this day, continue to make Brazilian history an enormous puzzle to be solved by future generations of scholars."[10] On occasion, critics called on scholars to explore rather than devalue the indigenous contribution to Brazilian history. But only rarely did a historian make native peoples the focus of an in-depth inquiry based on primary sources.

The native peoples of Portuguese America left no early documentary record apart from a few individuals who learned to write under missionary tutelage or who engaged scribes to communicate with colonial officials. Without monumental architecture, their archaeological record is also comparatively sparse. Yet it would be a mistake to conclude that a simple paucity of sources explains the degree to which they have been left out of Brazil's history. European writers, both religious and secular, left copious descriptions of native groups beginning in the sixteenth century. Such texts might long ago have been employed to elucidate the changes these groups experienced once traders, settlers, and missionaries from across the sea appeared on Brazilian shores. Instead, historians shunned such subject matter, relegating it to ethnographers, whose findings, while often profound, contributed to a view of native societies as unable to adapt to historical change or even existing altogether outside history.

In part, historians hesitated to venture into the realm of indigenous history because the available documentary evidence, notwithstanding its extent, was dauntingly biased, disjointed, and difficult to decode. Written largely by missionaries, government officials, elite detractors, and settlers hungry for land and labor, archival and early published sources simply did not allow for a dependable reconstruction of native perspectives. Few documents even identified individual Indians by name, much less reflected their thoughts and feelings. From the outset, however, a certain disingenuousness characterized these complaints about sources. After all, documents conveying the perspectives of colonizers were also far from transparent. Literate elites not only portrayed preliterate Indians with a jaundiced eye, they also depicted themselves with great indulgence. Sources concerning Indians were not the only documents demanding skepticism. To restrict the field of analysis to those portrayed impartially in the archives would be to rule out the possibility of writing anyone's history, colonist and Indian alike.[11]

Change came slowly but scholars eventually began to apply these and other insights to well-known, neglected, and newly discovered sources. The documentary record began to suggest new meanings and themes in the face of the analytical difficulties surrounding historical subjects who were overwhelmingly non-literate. As the following chapters demonstrate, historians have learned to make use of an astonishing array of primary materials, including early chronicles, expedition records, missionary writings, military correspondence, manuscript maps, property surveys, land titles, census data, wills and testaments, post-mortem estate inventories, Inquisition cases, judicial proceedings, petitions by settlers and Indians, dispatches from native villages, ecclesiastical documents, and marriage, birth, and baptism records.

Eventually, further innovations drawn from the study of slaves, peasants, women, and other peoples whose voices archives silenced helped stir new interest in indigenous history. So did the recognition that the very search for a pristine native viewpoint, unadulterated by contact with intruders, presupposed a static view of culture that had little to do with the whirl, range, and ambiguity of historical reality. By insisting on the integrity of putatively pure and isolated Indians, scholars doubly condemned them to a changeless past. First, they helped fashion a myth of the primitive native, noble or savage, untouched by history, distinct from and a forerunner to modern society. Then, when they could not locate such dividing lines in practice, they dismissed historical Indians as corrupted by contact with the colonial world. Thus caricatured, Indians were either converts or cannibals—much as in Caminha and Vespucci's accounts—and both were of limited interest to academic historians. Only as scholars shifted their focus to colonial connections and interethnic relationships, to hybrid societies and fluid cultures, did rich stories begin to emerge at the nexus of native and non-native peoples who interacted with each other over the centuries, sometimes violently, sometimes peaceably.

It was not until the early 1990s that a few scholars, equipped with these insights and new approaches, launched what could be called a coordinated effort to address some of the most glaring misconceptions and omissions in the history of Brazilian Indians.[12] Energized by the ferment surrounding the quincentenary commemorations of Columbus's first voyage in 1492 and Cabral's official discovery of Brazil in 1500, their efforts helped propel new scholarship, especially by Brazilian but also non-Brazilian historians, ethnohistorians, and historical anthropologists. The nation's return from military rule to democracy in 1985; its new constitution of 1988, which extended long-overdue rights and protections to contemporary indigenous peoples; and a 1996 law mandating the teaching of indigenous history in primary and secondary schools further animated this scholarly activity. The accelerating professionalization of Brazil's institutions of higher learning imbued much of it with theoretical and methodological sophistication. The outpouring continues unabated in multiple forms, including monographic treatments of specific themes, ethnic groups, regions, and eras; modern editions of classic and lesser-known chronicles of discovery, travelers' journals, and early histories; primary source collections; ethnographies; accounts by indigenous peoples of their own histories; and bibliographic and archival guides.[13]

Incorporating the tools of anthropology, cultural geography, cultural studies, and literary analysis, historians of Brazil's Indians are revisiting old sources and uncovering new ones, asserting a more prominent place for native peoples both in the midst of Luso-Brazilian (Portuguese and Brazilian) society and along its territorial fringes. Their combined efforts are significantly altering conventional renderings of Brazil's past that diminished the historical contribution of the first of three peoples—Indians, Europeans, and Africans—whose labors, conflicts, and creative energies created Portugal's New World colony and the nation that emerged from it. Some have begun to classify the results as Brazil's "new Indian history," which attests to the significance of the changes in progress. However, the phrase suggests the supplanting of an "old Indian history," which in fact never coalesced. Although no single volume can convey the field's full scope and dynamism, the present collection exemplifies and extends this collective enterprise.

While most of the contributors travel to Brazilian and Portuguese archives from their posts in the U.S. academy, it should be emphasized that the crest of the wave is in Brazil. The audience there is naturally much larger, as is the number of professional historians dedicated to the task. As every experienced student of the discipline knows, however, much that seems natural is not when it comes to the writing of history. For reasons peculiar to our own national past, most U.S. students trained in Latin American history focus on the regions colonized by Spain, especially Mexico. Far more students here study Spanish than Portuguese. Of the historians who focus on Brazil, a tiny minority specializes in the colonial period, where the revisionist impulse is concentrated. A still-smaller group chooses indigenous history as a subject of research. Meanwhile, distressingly few works by Brazilian scholars are translated into English. These structural issues help account for the slow penetration of the new scholarship into textbooks and classrooms in the U.S. The predicament seems particularly unfortunate at a time when U.S. historians have called for more inclusive Atlantic, hemispheric, and transnational approaches as antidotes to parochialism and exceptionalism. Given the nature of native social organization, it makes sense to compare the semi- and non-sedentary peoples of North and South America, including the Spanish American peripheries. These groups had more in common with each other than with the great sedentary societies of Mexico and Peru. More attention paid to their similarities

and differences would yield ample returns for the comparative colonial, indigenous, and frontier history of the Americas.

Of course the very question of how Indians contribute to a nation's history
can open the door to anachronism. As we know, there were no Indians in the
Americas until Europeans labeled them as such, beginning with Columbus's
infamous mistake. Nor were there ethnic groups, per se, this designation, too,
being an imposition by outsiders who presupposed the subordination of previously autonomous peoples to a dominant society.[14] Throughout the colonial
period, with few exceptions, the distinct groups comprising the kaleidoscopic
population of lowland South America embraced no sense of common identity
vis-à-vis the Portuguese, Dutch, French, Spanish, and others who at one point
or another had designs on their territory or labor. Native struggles and aspirations centered on the local and the regional, not on the wider realm of the
colony as a whole. To emphasize ways in which individual kin groups or tribes
contributed to or rejected the colonial project is to risk misconstruing the basis
of Indian conduct. Their relations with the colonial world drew on a calculus
internal to their communities, which can often be discerned only faintly.
Native cosmology and prophecy, the ravages of epidemic disease, the claims of
competing headmen and clans, revenge, the search for food, the demands of
indigenous distribution networks for metal and other manufactured objects,
interaction with peoples of African descent, and a growing historical experience of both conflict and cooperation with settlers mattered in ways that cannot be reduced to simple dualities.[15]

Secondly, the centralized governance we associate with the modern
Brazilian state did not come into being until well after independence, when
civilian and military leaders in Rio de Janeiro quelled a string of regional
revolts. Only in the mid-nineteenth century did the nation's largely autonomous regions submit in any unified manner to federal authority.[16] Until this
consolidation occurred, much of the responsibility of interpreting, imple-
menting, and ultimately forging state policy on relations with specific indigenous groups devolved to the governors of individual captaincies during the
colonial period, then to provincial presidents after independence, or even to
their subordinates. On the Luso-Brazilian side of the equation, in other
words, relations with native peoples were similarly more local and regional
than historians once allowed, although governing elites in far-flung regions
certainly acted in greater concert than did independent indigenous groups.[17]
Such questions of proper context and scope add yet another explanation for
the belated attention to the history of Brazil's diverse native peoples by

Figure 3. Described as "civilized savages" in the original caption of this image, indigenous soldiers escort women and children taken captive in the interior. The scene serves as a stark reminder that native Brazilians never assumed a single, common identity. Source: Jean Baptiste Debret, *Voyage pittoresque et historique au Brésil, ou Séjour d'un artiste français au Brésil, depuis 1816 jusqu'en 1831 inclusivement,* vol. 1 (Paris: Firmin Didot frères, 1834). Public domain access: http://www.brasiliana.usp.br/bbd/handle/1918/624510034

scholars fixed on colonial and national matters. As we get better at grappling with these various issues, the history of Brazil's Indians—or, better, their many histories—can be perceived in ways previously obscured. This volume shines light on some of these histories, covering four key regions in roughly chronological fashion: the Atlantic coast (1500–1850), the Amazon basin (1500–1900), the southeastern territory connecting Minas Gerais and Espírito Santo (1700–1850), and the central western region of Goiás (1750–1900).

INDIGENOUS PASTS

Scholars once conventionally divided the indigenous population contacted by the first European mariners, traders, and settlers into two large groups, the Tupi-Guarani and the Tapuia. The semisedentary Tupi-Guarani occupied most of the coastal strip. The non-sedentary Tapuia inhabited the

interior or *sertão* and certain stretches of the littoral. This classificatory
scheme, borrowed from the first colonists who learned it from the Tupi,
vastly oversimplifies. The Tupi-Guarani, as their name suggests, combined
two subgroups: the Guarani, who controlled the region south of São Paulo,
including the river basins that form Brazil's southern border; and the Tupi,
who dominated the remainder of the coast north to the Amazon. The Tupi
were further subdivided into numerous village-based groups, which shared
linguistic and cultural origins but engaged in constant warfare with one
another. These wars yielded territory and captives, some of whom the victors
consumed in cannibalistic rituals that imposed cosmological vengeance and
elevated successful warriors to headmen. A pejorative term used by the Tupi
to describe dozens of inland groups that spoke Gê, Carib, Arawak, and other
languages, the designation Tapuia served colonists well in their bid to vilify
all who resisted colonization. For several decades, peaceable relations, if not
mutual understanding, characterized contacts between the Portuguese and
the coastal Indians. But as agriculture, particularly sugar cultivation, began
to replace barter, the advantage shifted to the Portuguese. The Tupi and other
groups became a barrier to efforts to clear and cultivate land. They also represented the most obvious source of agricultural labor. Thus began the drive
to conquer, assemble, enslave, and, where such subordination proved impossible, to dislodge or destroy the colony's native peoples.[18]

The Portuguese crown dispatched a royal governor-general to Brazil for
the first time in 1549. Tomé de Sousa (1549–1553) carried with him royal
orders to prevent colonists from provoking Indians to war then enslaving
those taken captive, in accordance with the medieval concept of "just war."
A precursor of future indigenous legislation benevolent in word but punitive
in deed, these orders simultaneously directed Sousa to discipline those
Indians who resisted subjection, "destroying their villages and settlements,
and killing and enslaving whatever part of them you consider sufficient."[19]
Although royal legislation made distinctions about which Indians could be
legally enslaved, settlers often did not. Over the course of the colonial period,
royal edicts prohibited generalized indigenous slavery at various junctures,
a sure sign that colonists ignored these laws.[20] Other laws, such as those
authorizing the practice of private *administração* (administration) established juridical conditions that differed little from formal slavery. By these
laws, Indians captured in the interior—or, as the euphemistic language of the
time had it, "rescued" through *resgate* (ransoming)—could be made to work
while they ostensibly received religious instruction. In practice, individuals

reduced to this status were assigned monetary values in post-mortem estate inventories, passed in wills as property to surviving heirs, and transferred to creditors to liquidate debts.[21] Even when not held captive, native peoples who lived within the colonial world found their freedom of movement and action highly proscribed.

As noted, however, previous generations of historians underestimated the capacity of peoples under siege to adapt to the disruptions of colonization and to influence the course of subsequent events.[22] Monteiro, among others, has urged us to reconsider the basic terms and categories used to describe the first century of coastal contact and conquest. Without downplaying the devastation left by disease, forced labor, and relocation, he argues that the long-established emphasis on the collapse of native polities obscures numerous instances of indigenous resistance and, even less well understood, political and cultural resilience. Ethnogenesis, which he defines as "the emergence of different and divergent forms of indigenous society," was as much as ethnocide a result of New World encounters. Indians did not simply capitulate, fade into the forest, or otherwise disappear. Instead, the radical break that conquest represented prompted creative responses to catastrophic circumstances. New ethnic and political configurations emerged. Some groups allied with the Portuguese or their French rivals, not merely as pawns but as peoples pursuing practical objectives, retaining a degree of political autonomy. Wars waged against certain ethnic groups might yield advantages for others, sometimes lasting many decades. Ethnic identities changed over time as groups fragmented, migrated, or recombined. Those who entered *aldeias* (villages supervised by missionaries, state authorities, or both) and colonial towns did not consider their customs automatically irreconcilable with incorporation into the colonial world.[23]

Such dynamics were evident from the beginning. For instance, traveling with Governor Tomé de Sousa's retinue, the colony's first Jesuit missionaries set out to instruct the Indians in Roman Catholic scripture and practice. Their efforts and the indigenous response is the subject of Alida Metcalf's essay (chapter 1). Although reluctantly conceding, as a consequence of determined native resistance, that the coastal peoples would have to be conquered militarily before they could be converted, the Jesuits stressed persuasion, residing in native villages, founding missions, learning indigenous languages, and encouraging the adoption of sedentary agriculture. They could not, however, tolerate ritual cannibalism, polygyny, and other practices deemed sinful. A rift quickly opened between missionaries and colonists who feared losing control over the supply of native labor. The crown addressed the dispute with characteristic contradiction, granting the Jesuits final authority over Indians settled in missions, which increasingly differed from traditional villages, while permitting colonists to persist in the practice of enslaving those captured in so-called just wars. Unwittingly, the missionaries served as conduits for European diseases, which they viewed as God's retribution for Indian immorality and inconstancy. Ongoing cultural resistance and further demographic decline left the growing demand for a pliable labor force unsatisfied, contributing to settlers' increasing use of African slaves.

Circumstances differed in São Paulo (or São Vicente as it was first called) far to the south, where those known as *bandeirantes* (participants in armed expeditions) concentrated. Explorers and Indian hunters, they pushed the limits of Portuguese claims westward, far beyond the line established by the Treaty of Tordesillas (1494), which had given Spain title to all newly discovered lands west of a meridian stretching approximately from the mouth of the Amazon River south to what became the settlement of São Paulo.[24] The *bandeiras* (expeditions) of the sixteenth and especially seventeenth centuries, comprising hundreds and more rarely thousands of colonists and detribalized Indians, traveled inland from the coast for months, even years, at a time. After initial attempts to locate precious metals met with failure, these ventures turned toward the capture of native laborers, known as *negros da terra* or blacks of the land. The term paired with *negros de Guiné* or African blacks, reflecting a presumption of enslavement. The southern coast's less favorable soils and greater distance from European markets left Paulistas (residents of São Paulo) at a disadvantage as sugar producers and, consequently, as importers of African slaves. Captive indigenous labor thus endured in the region as the lynchpin of production far longer than in the northeast. Indians served landowners in viticulture, cotton planting, and wheat cultivation for local consumption and export to the plantation zones. The Paulistas circumvented royal restrictions on indigenous slavery by employing the legal innovations of *administração* explained above. Portuguese men coerced and comingled with Tupi women, producing *mestiço* (mixed-race) children who sometimes passed for white, rising to prominence, becoming skilled fighters, backwoodsmen, slavers, and cultural intermediaries. Many of the women became domestic servants. Indian males newly incorporated into Paulista society became "ethnic soldiers," joining wilderness expeditions to hunt other natives, at least in part because they preferred this activity to planting and harvesting, traditionally the work of Tupi women.[25]

Up the coast in Rio de Janeiro, as in São Paulo, some of the mission villages first founded in the sixteenth century survived throughout the colonial period, and new ones formed as settlers pushed into the hinterlands. These communities endured despite continuous efforts by colonists to exploit native labor and chip away at limited communal lands granted to the Indians by the crown. Pressure to relinquish wandering and take up sedentary lives on such land led to unanticipated consequences, as Maria Regina Celestino de Almeida demonstrates (chapter 2). The inhabitants of these aldeias became Christians and, particularly in the eighteenth century, progressively mixed with Portuguese and African descendants to become multiracial mestiços. Such individuals frequently linked their ethnic identity as Indians to the lands that remained to them and their village communities. Secularization of mission villages in the 1750s, while presenting new challenges, did not dilute the sense by many that their fate depended on defending their lands and livelihoods. Some Indians successfully petitioned local and royal authorities or resorted to colonial courts to assert these principles. Others embraced opportunities to ascend to leadership positions and to earn incomes, for example, by cutting timber, selling canoes, or renting agricultural land. Their pragmatic approach to challenging circumstances should caution us against outmoded perspectives that cast Indians as unable to respond effectively, short of violence or flight, to the dislocations of colonialism.

In the north, the peripatetic bandeirantes and Portuguese missionaries were not the first to disrupt the indigenous polities of the Amazon basin.[26] Spanish explorers descended the length of the great river system from the Andes in the early 1540s, documenting the existence of large and complex societies. As Neil Whitehead explains (chapter 3), the native population was already sharply depleted by the time the Portuguese made a concerted effort to colonize the region in the seventeenth century. English, Irish, Dutch, and French colonial ventures competed to trade with the Indians at various times, seeking foodstuffs, hardwoods, dyes, and other forest products. Ethnic boundaries and European imperial pursuits were not limited by modern borders, extending from the Amazon basin to the Andes's eastern slopes and the continent's northern coast. In contrast to later preconceptions, persistent European intrusions left much of the region far from isolated, radically curtailing the autonomy of many groups. Capuchin then Jesuit evangelization, which peaked between 1650 and 1750, presented new challenges and opportunities. Resettlement in mission villages protected some Indians from being removed by slavers, but they were compelled to

Figure 4. These Guarani women headed to church on Sunday. Often referred to as "colonial Indians," many individuals of indigenous descent lived in close contact with European society, but their stories were long dismissed by those who fashioned a myth of the primitive native, untouched by history. Source: Debret, *Voyage pittoresque.* Public domain access: http://www.brasiliana.usp.br/bbd/handle/1918/624510038

labor for missionaries and colonial officials. This long experience of colonization left its mark during the following century on the peasants of indigenous descent who participated in a regionalist revolt known as the Cabanagem (1835–1840).

The end of the missionary period in the Amazon basin corresponded with major policy shifts in Lisbon. After the less-than-competent José I (r. 1750–1777) ascended to the throne, his ambitious and autocratic first minister, Sebastião José de Carvalho e Melo, the future marquis of Pombal, tightened mercantilist control over the colony. The signing of the Treaty of Madrid (1750), which systematized the borders between Portuguese and

Spanish America, incorporated many of the lands earlier explored by the bandeirantes. In the south, these changes provoked the Guarani War (1754–1756). A joint Portuguese-Spanish force overwhelmed Indians who refused to relocate from Jesuit missions to the Spanish side of the new border, which followed the Uruguay River. Convinced that Jesuit power over Indian labor threatened royal hegemony and profits, Pombal exploited this episode, as well as conflicts in the Amazon. He stripped the missionaries of temporal authority in their Amazonian mission villages, which were opened up to trade with Portuguese merchants and settlers. He promulgated a set of laws known as the *Diretório dos índios*. Governing relations with native peoples, the legislation ushered in a period historians call the Indian Directorate (1757–1798).[27] While juridically free, village Indians were to be subject to the rule of lay directors and taught the essential skills of commercial agriculture. Assimilation was encouraged through policies favoring marriages between whites and Indians. Pombal then expelled the Jesuits from the colony in 1759.

Barbara Sommer (chapter 4) narrows the focus on the region to the indigenous leaders of state-administered villages of the lower Amazon during the Directorate period. Known as *principais*, these headmen comprised what she calls a "hereditary native nobility," acting as intermediaries between the crown and numerous ethnic groups. They achieved and maintained their status by cooperating with the Portuguese in military and slaving ventures and in assembling workers for collecting expeditions and agricultural labor. For this service, the crown bestowed special privileges, honors, and other symbols of prestige, cultivating a mostly male, hereditary elite. Like all leaders, these elite pursued ambitions that sometimes led to abuses. However, they did not become passive collaborators or relinquish their concern for the welfare of their peoples, as historians once judged. Responding creatively to wrenching change, they worked to increase village autonomy and advance their own interests. When pressed to supply laborers, for instance, they often delayed, limited the numbers of workers, and helped conceal those who fled. In particularly egregious instances of unfair treatment, they used the Portuguese legal system to seek redress and, in some cases, abandoned the colonial villages with their people. Such actions bespoke a significant degree of independence despite the exigencies of colonial rule in the Brazilian north.

In the southeastern region that came to be called Minas Gerais, starting in the late seventeenth century, Paulista bandeirantes made a series of major inland gold and diamond strikes. Secondary discoveries occurred far to the west in Mato Grosso and Goiás. In the essay by Hal Langfur and Maria Leônia Chaves de Resende (chapter 5), the emphasis is on the second half of the century, when gold production declined.[28] The chapter demonstrates that Indians remained integral to the region's history, both in frontier zones and as a minority population in towns and villages. Various independent groups, most notoriously the Botocudo, inhabited the forested frontier between the mining district and the Atlantic coast. As colonists invaded, these Indians did not submit without a protracted fight, nor did they passively accept the terms of subjugation in the region's settled zones. As "colonial Indians," they and their mixed-race descendants appealed to the legal system as a defense against illegal enslavement. They asserted their indigenous origins to distinguish themselves from a growing population of people of African descent who did not enjoy the same legal protections conceded to Indians.

Tracing the subsequent history of these southeastern Indians, Judy Bieber (chapter 6) begins with the war declared against the Botocudo in 1808 by the crown as it began a thirteen-year exile in Rio de Janeiro after Napoleon's troops invaded Portugal. Determined to incorporate the fertile Doce River valley, which continued to serve various groups as a refuge, the crown mounted its military offensive and revealed the durability of colonial strategies even as Brazil moved toward national independence. Reviving the principle of just war, the crown again allowed the enslavement of those who resisted incorporation, generating a brisk trade in captives, especially children. A failure to innovate, a lack of resources, and an inability to understand indigenous attitudes toward agricultural work and material possessions prevented the state from responding adequately after Brazil broke with Portugal in 1822. The previous year João VI (r. 1816–1821, Brazil; 1816–1826, Portugal) returned to Lisbon, leaving behind his son Prince Pedro to rule the colony. Under pressure from local elites, the prince instead declared independence and as Pedro I (r. 1822–1831) assumed leadership of a newly founded Brazilian Empire (1822–1889). In the realm of indigenous affairs, the Empire's neocolonial policies meant ongoing violence and persecution, even after the state shifted its emphasis from military conquest to acculturation. Even so, Botocudo bands continued to exert considerable agency. They thwarted the state's military objectives and resisted its assimilationist plans through the first half of the nineteenth century.

To the west of Minas Gerais, the aftermath of a more modest mining boom also shaped indigenous relations in Goiás (now the states of Goiás and

Tocantins). Long since scoured by bandeirantes for precious metals and Indian slaves, this region remained a frontier on the fringe of state control and the market economy throughout the nineteenth century. Although far from insulated from the ravages of war, disease, and missionary duress, a variety of groups—including the Kayapó, Xavante, Xerente, and Canoeiro—managed to retain greater autonomy for a longer period because of the region's marginal position. Mary Karasch considers shifting official policies in Goiás (chapter 7); she and David McCreery then assess resistance to those policies (chapter 8). Colonial officials in distant Lisbon favored paternalism, seeking to civilize and Christianize groups considered heathens. As in Minas Gerais, the crown never allocated the resources necessary to achieve these ambitions. The limits of official action contributed to the survival of a number of independent groups, Karasch finds. The state focused on Indians primarily when they hampered its search for new mineral wealth. After independence, as the dream of undiscovered riches waned, the challenge of assembling agricultural workers became the predominant concern. But the state's attenuated power left a wide gap between policy and practice. The crown could not restrain colonists from mounting constant raids justified as retaliatory. Full-scale warfare resulted in the conquest of thousands of Xavante, but other military ventures failed. Certain groups, like the Kayapó, actually increased their territorial control over long periods. Effectively admitting its own impotence, the state relinquished many decision-making powers to local potentates.

The study of official policy is critical if we are to understand the way the state impinged on particular aboriginal peoples at specific times. Karasch and McCreery recognize, however, that it tells only part of the story. Cataloging the prolonged resistance of multiple groups, they demonstrate that flexible tactics were required in the face of official harassment and settler incursions. Some Kayapó, for example, survived for decades by raiding. Others migrated westward. Still others accepted relocation to state-controlled villages, often serving as soldiers, but were prepared to return to their nomadic existence when their treatment deteriorated. The Xavante and Xerente, at times allies, at times antagonists, adopted a similarly multifaceted approach, raiding when they could do so successfully, settling in missions when they could not, learning Portuguese when it served them, retreating to the forests when necessary. Their success at holding territory slowed the colonization of northern Goiás. For their part, the Canoeiro, who spoke a Tupian language, spurned interactions with both settlers and native Gê-speakers. Traveling rapidly in canoes, skillful in the use of clubs, arrows, and lances, they outmatched most expeditions deployed against them until the late nineteenth century when they were overwhelmed by expanding cattle herds.

Like the Botocudo and the Canoeiro, some of the peoples discussed in the following chapters were ultimately defeated and displaced by an implacable settler advance. Many individuals died when they were hunted down in frontier massacres, forced to labor, or sickened in epidemics. Hundreds of groups eventually disappeared as distinct entities. Yet many others found ways to enter colonial and later national society, making pivotal if constrained choices along the way. Whether favoring remote reaches of the rainforest, living on indigenous reserves, working and studying in urban areas, or lobbying for fair treatment from federal legislators in Brasília, they continue to respond to changing circumstances and struggle to shape their own futures. Today, those who self-identify as indigenous peoples officially comprise 0.4 percent of Brazil's population. Their reduced numbers make it easy to forget the extent to which their presence mattered—and continues to matter—long after their initial encounter with Europeans. Much work remains to be done to reconstruct the histories of peoples long ago reduced to stereotypes, mistakenly considered eradicated or enfeebled, and cast as irrelevant even as they altered the history of an enormous swathe of the Americas.

NOTES

1. I wish to thank Judy Bieber, Barbara Sommer, and Lyman Johnson for their insightful comments on a preliminary version of this essay. For the English translation of Caminha's letter, see Pedro [Pero] Vaz de Caminha, "Letter . . . to King Manuel," Porto Seguro, 1 May 1500, in William Brooks Greenlee, *The Voyage of Pedro Álvares Cabral to Brazil and India, From Contemporary Documents and Narratives* (London: Hakluyt Society, 1938), 3–33, quoting 8. It is now widely accepted that Cabral's expedition intentionally set out for Brazil, rather than accidentally ending up there after losing its way in the Atlantic. For the debate on this issue, see Bailey W. Diffie and George D. Winius, *Foundations of the Portuguese Empire, 1415–1580* (Minneapolis: University of Minnesota Press, 1977), 450–52. For research defending the likelihood of a planned official "discovery" based on knowledge acquired from an earlier 1498 reconnaissance voyage by the Portuguese mariner Duarte Pacheco Pereira, see Jorge Couto, *A construção do Brasil: Ameríndios, portugueses e africanos, do início do povoamento a finais de quinhentos*, 2d ed. (Lisboa: Cosmos, 1997), esp. 149–60.

2. Caminha, "Letter," in Greenlee, *Voyage of Pedro Álvares Cabral*, 22–23.

3. Ibid., 29–30.

4. Amerigo Vespucci to Piero Soderini, Lisbon, 4 Sept. 1504, in *Letters from a New World: Amerigo Vespucci's Discovery of America*, ed. Luciano Formisano, trans. David Jacobson (New York: Marsilio, 1992), 87–89. This letter was printed in Florence in 1504 or 1505. See Formisano's introduction, xxii. Disagreeing with Formisano concerning the authenticity of this text, Felipe Fernández-Armesto describes the Soderini letter as "a confection in which relatively little input can be traced to the alleged author." Felipe Fernández-Armesto, *Amerigo: The Man Who Gave His Name to America* (London: Weidenfeld and Nicolson, 2006), 132.

5. For the first figure, see Vespucci to Lorenzo di Pierfrancesco de' Medici, Lisbon, after 22 July 1502, in ibid., 30; for the second, see the so-called *"Mundus Novus"* letter in ibid., 50, purportedly written by Vespucci to Lorenzo di Pierfrancesco de' Medici and published, perhaps in Florence, in late 1502 or early 1503. For the dates of these letters and the likelihood that the second was edited by the Veronese humanist fra' Giovanni del Giocondo, see Formisano's introduction, xix–xx, xxvi.

6. For an influential treatment of conversion as a negotiation between missionaries and Indians rather than a one-sided, coercive process thoroughly controlled by the clergy, see Cristina Pompa, *Religião como tradução: Missionários, Tupi e Tapuia no Brasil colonial* (Bauru: EDUSC, 2003). For the view that cannibalism in Brazil, the early modern Americas, and the colonized world in general was a myth propagated to justify conquest and enslavement, see W. Arens, *The Man-Eating Myth: Anthropology and Anthropophagy* (New York: Oxford University Press, 1979). For works reflecting the present consensus that the Tupinambá, among others, did in fact practice ceremonial anthropophagy, see Alida C. Metcalf, *Go-Betweens and the Colonization of Brazil, 1500–1600* (Austin: University of Texas Press, 2005); Beth A. Conklin, *Consuming Grief: Compassionate Cannibalism in an Amazonian Society* (Austin: University of Texas Press, 2001).

7. For evidence of the ongoing native presence in all of Brazil's major geographic regions, see John Hemming, *Red Gold: The Conquest of the Brazilian Indians, 1500–1760* (Cambridge, MA: Harvard University Press, 1977); Hemming, *Amazon Frontier: The Defeat of the Brazilian Indians* (Cambridge, MA: Harvard University Press, 1987). Subsequent scholarship, too extensive to cite, continues to add to and refine Hemming's overviews. The following studies represent a mere sampling, emphasizing book-length, English-language works that will be accessible to most readers. For analysis of the plantation records and parish registers that document the predominance of Indian labor during the first century of coastal colonization, see Stuart B. Schwartz, *Sugar Plantations in the Formation of Brazilian Society: Bahia, 1550–1835* (Cambridge: Cambridge University Press, 1985), chap. 3. For a broader view of coastal indigenous relation

during the first century of colonization, see Metcalf, *Go-Betweens*. For the lower Amazon basin, see Mark Harris, *Rebellion on the Amazon: The Cabanagem, Race, and Popular Culture in the North of Brazil, 1798–1840* (Cambridge: Cambridge University Press, 2010). For the upper Amazon and other regions, see Robin M. Wright with Manuela Carneiro da Cunha, "Destruction, Resistance, and Transformation—Southern, Coastal, and Northern Brazil (1580–1890)," in *The Cambridge History of the Native Peoples of the Americas*, vol. 3, pt. 2, ed. Frank Salomon and Stuart B. Schwartz (Cambridge: Cambridge University Press, 1999), 287–381. For the south, see John M. Monteiro, *Negros da terra: Índios e bandeirantes nas origens de São Paulo* (São Paulo: Companhia das Letras, 1994). For the independent native peoples on the perimeter of the primary mining region, see Hal Langfur, *The Forbidden Lands: Colonial Identity, Frontier Violence, and the Persistence of Brazil's Eastern Indians, 1750–1830* (Stanford, CA: Stanford University Press, 2006).

8. John E. Kicza, *Resilient Cultures: America's Native Peoples Confront European Colonization, 1500–1800* (Upper Saddle River, NJ: Prentice Hall, 2003), 30–31; Hemming, *Red Gold*, 487–501. On the need to treat the Brazilian figures with caution, see John M. Monteiro "The Crises and Transformations of Invaded Societies: Coastal Brazil in the Sixteenth Century," in Salomon and Schwartz, *Cambridge History of the Native Peoples of the Americas*, vol. 3, pt. 1, 979–81.

9. See Neil Whitehead's essay in this collection.

10. John M. Monteiro, "The Heathen Castes of Sixteenth-Century Portuguese America: Unity, Diversity, and the Invention of the Brazilian Indians," *Hispanic American Historical Review* 80, no. 4 (2000): 710, 717.

11. Langfur, *Forbidden Lands*, 11–12.

12. The pioneering text in this revisionist effort was Manuela Carneiro da Cunha, ed., *História dos índios no Brasil* (São Paulo: Companhia das Letras, FAPESP/ SMC 1992). There were, of course, earlier individual contributions but they did not signal the broad shift in the field that occurred in the 1990s. See, for example, Alexander Marchant, *From Barter to Slavery: The Economic Relations of Portuguese and Indians in the Settlement of Brazil, 1500–1580* (Baltimore: Johns Hopkins University Press, 1942); Florestan Fernandes, *Organização social dos Tupinambá* (São Paulo: Instituto Progresso, 1948); Oiliam José, *Indígenas de Minas Gerais: Aspectos sociais, políticos e etnológicos* (Belo Horizonte: Imp. Oficial, 1965); Hemming, *Red Gold*.

13. The most comprehensive bibliographic record of this scholarship is John Monteiro's website, "Os Índios na história do Brasil: Bibliografia comentada." http://www.ifch.unicamp.br/ihb/bibcom.htm (accessed 24 Aug. 2012). Also see Stuart B. Schwartz, "The Historiography of Early Modern Brazil," in *The Oxford Handbook of Latin American History*, ed. Jose C. Moya (Oxford: Oxford University Press, 2011), 98–131, esp. 102–5.

14. Greg Urban and Joel Sherzer, "Introduction: Indians, Nation-States, and Culture," in *Nation-States and Indians in Latin America* (Austin: University of Texas Press, 1991), 4–6; John M. Monteiro, "Rethinking Amerindian Resistance and Persistence in Colonial Portuguese America," in *New Approaches to Resistance in Brazil and Mexico*, ed. John Gledhill and Patience A. Schell (Durham, NC: Duke University Press, 2012), 31–32.

15. Langfur, *Forbidden Lands*, 229; Monteiro, "Rethinking Amerindian Resistance," 25–43. On the understudied interaction of Indians and peoples of African origin, both enslaved and free, see Stuart B. Schwartz and Hal Langfur, "Tapanhuns, Negros da Terra, and Curibocas: Common Cause and Confrontation between Blacks and Natives in Colonial Brazil," in *Beyond Black and Red: African-Native Relations in Colonial Latin America*, ed. Matthew Restall (Albuquerque: University of New Mexico Press, 2005), 81–114.

16. On the belated rise of centralized authority in Rio de Janeiro, see Roderick J. Barman, *Brazil: The Forging of a Nation, 1798–1852* (Stanford, CA: Stanford University Press, 1988).

17. Langfur, *Forbidden Lands*, esp. 164, 225–29.

18. For a brief overview of Brazil's colonial period, upon which the following discussion draws, see Hal Langfur, "Colonial Brazil," in *A Companion to Latin American History*, ed. Thomas H. Holloway (Oxford: Blackwell Publishing, 2007), 89–105. For concise, regionally specific treatments of Brazil's indigenous history during the colonial period and the nineteenth century, see the essays by John M. Monteiro, Robin. M. Wright, Neil L. Whitehead, and Stuart B. Schwartz collected in Salomon and Schwartz, *Cambridge History of the Native Peoples of the Americas*, vol. 3, pts. 1–2.

19. King João III, "Regimento de Tomé de Sousa," 17 Dec. 1548, in Paulo Bonavides and Roberto Amaral, *Textos políticos da história do Brasil*, 3rd ed., vol. 1 (Brasília: Senado Federal, 2002), 159; Metcalf, *Go-Betweens*, chap. 4.

20. For legislation that repeatedly outlawed Indian slavery, see Beatriz Perrone-Moisés, "Inventário da legislação indigenista, 1500–1800," in Cunha, *História dos índios no Brasil*, 529–66.

21. Monteiro, *Negros da terra*, 129–53.

22. Among a growing number of contributions upending the older view, some particularly influential texts include Monteiro, *Negros da terra*; Monteiro "Crises and Transformations"; Ronaldo Vainfas, *A heresia dos índios: Catolicismo e rebeldia no Brasil colonial* (São Paulo: Companhia das Letras, 1995); Maria Regina Celestino de Almeida, *Metamorfoses indígenas: Cultura e identidade nos aldeamentos indígenas do Rio de Janeiro* (Rio de Janeiro: Arquivo Nacional, 2003); Pompa, *Religião como tradução*; Elisa Frühauf Garcia, *As diversas formas de ser índio: Políticas indígenas e políticas indigenistas no extremo sul da América portuguesa* (Rio de Janeiro: Arquivo Nacional, 2009).

23. John M. Monteiro, "Tupis, tapuias e historiadores: Estudos de história indígena e do indigenismo" (Tese de Livre Docência [post-doctoral thesis], UNICAMP, 2001), chap. 3.

24. Monteiro, *Negros da terra.*

25. On ethnic soldiering, see R. Brian Ferguson and Neil L. Whitehead, "The Violent Edge of Empire," in *War in the Tribal Zone: Expanding States and Indigenous Warfare* (Santa Fe, NM: School of American Research Press, 1992), 21–23; Schwartz and Langfur, "Tapanhuns, Negros da Terra, and Curibocas."

26. See, for example, Neil L. Whitehead, ed., *Histories and Historicities in Amazonia* (Lincoln: University of Nebraska Press, 2003); Anna C. Roosevelt, *Amazonian Indians: From Prehistory to the Present: Anthropological Perspectives* (Tucson: University of Arizona Press, 1994); Barbara A. Sommer, "Cracking Down on the *Cunhamenas*: Renegade Amazonian Traders under Pombaline Reform," *Journal of Latin American Studies* 38, no. 4 (2006): 767–91; Harris, *Rebellion on the Amazon*; Wright with Carneiro da Cunha, "Destruction, Resistance, and Transformation."

27. For the full text of this legislation, see "Directorio que se deve observar nas Povoaçoens dos Indios do Pará, e Maranhão em quanto Sua Magestade não mandar o contrario," (Pará, 1757), facsimile reprint in Carlos de Araújo Moreira Neto, *Índios da Amazônia: De maioria a minoria (1750–1850)* (Petrópolis: Editora Vozes, 1988), 165–203. Also see Rita Heloísa de Almeida, *O Diretório dos índios: Um projeto de "civilização" no Brasil do século XVIII* (Brasília: Universidade de Brasília, 1997); Ângela Domingues, *Quando os índios eram vassalos. Colonização e relações de poder no Norte do Brasil na segunda metade do século XVIII* (Lisbon: Comissão Nacional para as Comemorações dos Descobrimentos Portugueses, 2000).

28. For Minas Gerais, see, for example, Langfur, *Forbidden Lands*; Maria Leônia Chaves de Resende, "'Brasis coloniales': índios e mestiços nas Minas Gerais Setecentistas," in *História de Minas Gerais: As Minas Setecentistas*, vol. 1, ed. Maria Efigênia Lage de Resende and Luiz Carlos Villalta (Belo Horizonte: Autêntica, 2007), 221–51; Haruf Salmen Espindola, *Sertão do Rio Doce* (Bauru: Universidade do Sagrado Coração, 2005).

1

The Society of Jesus and the First *Aldeias* of Brazil

Alida C. Metcalf

In 1549 the first Jesuits disembarked in the Bay of All Saints with the huge responsibility of converting the indigenous peoples of Brazil to Christianity. For João III, the king of Portugal, the spreading of Christianity was the stated justification for colonizing Brazil, and hence these six Jesuits had crossed the Atlantic Ocean with his first governor appointed to rule over Brazil, Tomé de Sousa (1549–1553). A Portuguese settlement, Vila Velha, already existed right inside the entrance to the bay, and it was here that the first Jesuits, the governor, and many others stepped ashore. All around the bay and up and down the coast lay traditional indigenous villages. While the Jesuits would begin their evangelism by visiting these villages, the governor turned his attention to building a new capital, to be known as Salvador (see map 1). Within a decade, unhappy with the slow pace of evangelism, the Jesuits created a new kind of village, a mission village, where they believed their enterprise would succeed. These new mission villages replaced the traditional villages; indeed, they became the defining institution of the Jesuit project in Brazil.

The Jesuits belonged to a new religious order—the Society of Jesus— where members did not live in monasteries but rather dedicated themselves to a life in the secular world. Early Jesuit brothers and priests in Europe were known for their preaching. Standing on street corners, in plazas, in the market, or walking to distant hamlets, the first Jesuits preached out in the open air and actively sought those in need. Their proximity to João III of Portugal had opened up to them the vast world beyond western Europe explored by Portuguese sea captains and merchants. With the king's patronage, the Society of Jesus now sought to establish missions abroad in order to bring Christianity to those who had never been evangelized. The timing of their arrival in Brazil fit into this global missionary enterprise: Francis Xavier had opened a mission in India (1542) and the Spice Islands (1546–1547); the very same year that the first Jesuits arrived in Brazil (1549), a Jesuit priest took up residence in Ormuz at the entrance to the Persian Gulf, and Xavier landed on the Japanese island of Kyushu.[1]

The first Jesuits in Brazil chronicled their early missionary enterprise in dozens of letters, the majority written to members of the Society in Portugal.[2] These letters are one of the most important sources for understanding sixteenth-century Brazil, and they are especially rich if examined for what they reveal about the Jesuits themselves. Historians have used these letters to assess how the Jesuit project changed when confronted with realities in the field.[3] After thirty years in Brazil, Jesuits began to write the first histories of their efforts.[4] Between the letters and these first histories, it is clear that the Jesuits saw the creation of the *aldeia*, or mission village, as one of their most important accomplishments. Historians have noted that the mission village was not imposed from Lisbon or Rome, but evolved on the ground in Brazil.[5] How the Jesuit missionaries described their movement away from their preferred evangelism, which rested on periodic visits to traditional Indian villages, to create instead these permanent mission villages is the subject of this chapter.

EARLY VILLAGE ENCOUNTERS

The word aldeia in Portuguese is of Arabic origin and it simply means village. In Brazil, colonists and Jesuits sometimes used the term to describe autonomous Indian villages, but over time aldeia or *aldeamento* came to mean the mission villages created by the Jesuits. In this chapter, aldeia will be used to refer to the Jesuit mission villages.

Jesuits first came into contact primarily with Tupi- and Guarani-speaking groups living around the Bay of All Saints in the region known as Bahia; in the regions farther south known as Ilheus, Porto Seguro, Espírito Santo, and Rio de Janeiro (after the defeat of the French colony [1555–1560] in the Guanabara Bay); and in the southernmost colony of São Vicente (later

São Paulo). Farther north, they encountered the Caeté in Sergipe and Pernambuco. All of these native peoples were already interacting with the Portuguese, and many had been enslaved by the colonists. Beyond the Tupi villages already in contact with the Portuguese lived the Guarani to the south and west of São Vicente, and Gê-, Carib-, and Arawak-speaking groups in central Brazil and Amazonia. Those areas still under the control of indigenous groups the colonists and the Jesuits called the *sertão* (wilderness or backlands).

The first Jesuits directed their initial evangelism campaign to those still living in traditional villages relatively near the Portuguese settlements. The Tupi villages consisted of large multifamily lodges or longhouses made of straw, known as *ocas*. Manuel da Nóbrega, leader of the Jesuit mission to Brazil, described the ocas as "very large" accommodating fifty married men with their wives and children, and he noted that they slept in hammocks next to fires that kept them warm at night. In 1550, João de Azpilcueta

Figure 5. Indigenous villages could be found throughout the fertile lands surrounding Bahia's Bay of All Saints. At the plaza labeled C, natives traded goods at one of Salvador's urban markets. Indians responded to colonial intrusions in a variety of ways, including conversion to Christianity, violent and nonviolent resistance, and migration to other regions. Source: *Reys-boeck van het rijcke Brasilien, Rio de la Plata ende Magallanes, daer in te sien is, de gheleghentheyt van hare landen ende steden . . .* [Dordrecht?]: n.p., 1624. Courtesy of the John Carter Brown Library at Brown University.

explained that the villages were not fixed in location, but moved often, sometimes unexpectedly. Since the longhouses were made of straw, fire was an ever-present danger and entire villages could be easily burned. Disagreements within the village could lead to the torching of a longhouse in anger, and once one house was in flames, the fire spread, quickly engulfing the entire village. "This happened now, during a recent night," Azpilcueta wrote, adding that it "seemed like the Day of Judgment." The villages moved frequently because of slash-and-burn agriculture. Once lands wore out, new plots were cut and burned out of the virgin forest, which often required the moving of the village. Luis da Grã saw the constant relocation of traditional villages as problematic for the Jesuits. The villages in São Vicente moved when the fields wore out, he wrote, while the houses themselves, whether made from earth or straw, lasted only three or four years. As a result the Jesuit mission lacked permanence and had to be constantly reinitiated when villages split or moved.[6]

These descriptions by Jesuits match other contemporary accounts of indigenous villages in Brazil in the middle of the sixteenth century. Jean de Léry, a French Calvinist who lived in the Guanabara Bay in 1557, described the longhouses as more than sixty paces long and a typical village as having from five hundred to six hundred people. The German mercenary Hans Staden, who lived in Brazil in the 1550s, described Tupinambá villages north of São Vicente. Each village had up to seven longhouses, which formed a sort of square surrounded by a wooden palisade. Each longhouse was 14 feet wide and up to 150 feet long. The vaulted roof was 12 feet above the ground; inside the chief of the hut had his space in the center, while couples with their children strung their hammocks along the sides. Woodcuts in published books or images painted on maps provide a visual idea of these villages; the woodcuts made under Staden's direction include several representations of the palisaded villages with the longhouses. Jean Rotz, a mapmaker and sailor who had traveled to Brazil in the 1540s, painted a palisade village with four longhouses strung with hammocks forming a public square on his map of Brazil in 1542. Although represented as a single, seemingly permanent place in a woodcut or on a map, the traditional indigenous villages actually moved frequently. They were prone to fission when conflicts erupted, and therefore it was not uncommon for villages to split apart when groups broke away and established independent villages.[7]

Although we cannot know for certain the size of these villages, and indeed they most certainly varied in size, historian Warren Dean estimated the size of each longhouse in the Tupinambá region around the Guanabara Bay in 1551 as having 135 people living in each lodge. He further calculated the size of each village as having, on average, 607 persons. These estimates can serve as a rough indication of the size of the traditional Indian villages first visited by Jesuit missionaries. João de Azpilcueta described visiting a village with 150 "fires" or hearths in 1551, while another had 200. These would have been the fires kindled inside the ocas, next to which families strung their hammocks.[8]

According to the Jesuit historian Serafim Leite, there were six or seven traditional villages in Bahia where the early evangelization took place.[9] Walking on foot, the Jesuits approached them and through their interpreters began their outreach to the native peoples through speech. Seeing themselves as the spiritual intermediaries between the Indians and God, the Jesuits talked, presented arguments, preached, taught through dialogues, and recited prayers.[10] Of the original six, João de Azpilcueta acquired enough facility with the Tupi-Guarani language that was widely spoken along the coast of Brazil to model the missionary approach first envisioned by the Jesuits. Within a year, Azpilcueta had built a church near the villages he visited; there he said Mass and taught in the Indian language. He had succeeded in articulating in the Tupi-Guarani language key Christian beliefs, such as the Ten Commandments.[11]

Azpilcueta and other Jesuit missionaries developed persuasive arguments that they believed convinced many in the traditional villages to convert willingly to Christianity. Leonardo Nunes, who was entrusted with establishing the Jesuit mission farther south, in São Vicente, described in a letter that since the Indians "greatly fear death and the day of judgment and hell," he ordered his interpreter "always to touch on this in the conversations, because the fear puts them in great confusion," thus making conversions more likely. A theme stressed by Vicente Rodrigues in his conversations and preaching was that "the time of dreams had passed" and that it was time for Indians to "wake up and hear the word of God, our Lord." Also in São Vicente, Pero Correia, a Portuguese colonist who joined the Society after it arrived in Brazil, promised Indians, "if they believed in God that not only would our Lord give them great things in heaven . . . but that in this world on their lands he would give them many things that were hidden."[12]

In addition to these themes, Jesuit missionaries sought appealing ways to present Christianity, believing that music, styles of discourse, and children provided an important entrée into the villages. One Jesuit observed: "because they love musical things, we, by playing and singing among them, will win them." A group of Portuguese children, who had come to Brazil as orphans to be raised by the Jesuits, became compelling models for conversion, so the Jesuits believed. When the children went from village to village in Bahia, one brother wrote, they adopted indigenous songs and instruments, "singing and playing in the way of the Indians and with their very same sounds and songs, changing the words in praise of God." They shook rattles, beat sticks on the ground, and sang at night. This followed in the footsteps of Azpilcueta who, during the first year of the Jesuits in Brazil, had adapted the Pater Noster [Lord's Prayer] to "their way of singing" so that the Indian boys would learn it faster and enjoy it more. "We preach to them in their way," Manuel da Nóbrega wrote, "in a certain tone, walking around, and beating our chests as they do."[13]

While Jesuit missionaries were willing to incorporate indigenous music, instruments, and dancing, they insisted that certain other customs be abandoned in the Indian villages where they worked. At the top of their list was ritual cannibalism. Nóbrega referred to cannibalism as "the most abominable" custom that existed among the Tupi peoples of Brazil; he saw it as connected to their practice of war, which he saw as motivated by hatred of enemies and the desire for revenge. In a revealing statement, he wrote that for Tupi men the heart "of their happiness and desire" was to have many women and to kill their enemies (in order to eat them).[14]

Coastal Tupi groups practiced exocannibalism, which has been defined as the eating of those from outside one's group, such as enemies captured in warfare.[15] Several accounts from the sixteenth century emphasize the central role of cannibalism in the social customs of coastal villages.[16] Unlike the Portuguese colonists who often turned a blind eye to the cannibalism ceremonies in the Indian villages, the Jesuits refused to accept them and sought to persuade Indians to willingly end the practice. If Indians gave it up, Jesuits believed that they could retain other less harmful customs in their villages, such as their music, as long as it was directed toward spiritual ends.[17]

Jesuits preached constantly against cannibalism. In one letter, Azpilcueta describes how the villages where he had been preaching went to war and returned with enemies. On entering a village, he found six or seven old women dancing around a pot "looking like devils in hell." Azpilcueta then describes his response, which reveals his commitment to persuasion in his mission to the indigenous villages: "I remembered that question of the Apostles to the Lord," he wrote in a letter, then referenced the following exchange between James, John, and Jesus, as recorded in Luke 9:

> [54]And when his disciples James and John saw this, they said, Lord, wilt thou that we command fire to come down from heaven, and consume them, even as Elias did?
> [55]But he turned, and rebuked them, and said, Ye know not what manner of spirit ye are of.
> [56]For the Son of man is not come to destroy men's lives, but to save them. And they went to another village.[18]

By including this text in his letter, Azpilcueta underscored his commitment to ministering to the Tupi through persuasion. Regardless of their sin (cannibalism), he emphasized to his Jesuit companions in Portugal that he would not seek violence against them.

Just as the first Jesuits sought to challenge cannibalism through their persuasive preaching, so too did they hope to peacefully change the customs surrounding marriage.

Nóbrega wrote in his first long report from Brazil that Indian girls were not given dowries when married; instead, their husbands served their parents before they married. Once married, the women, he noted, were subject to their husbands. Later, he wrote that the Indians of Brazil did not have "true marriage" and that the men took and left women as they pleased. After many years of living in Brazil, Jesuit missionary José de Anchieta agreed that the Indians of Brazil "do not ordinarily celebrate marriage" and described their practice as polygyny. "One can have 3 to 4 women," he stated in a report written in 1584, "and if one is a great chief and valiant, one has 10, 12, or 20 women." Anchieta understood that indigenous marriage became a means through which powerful men, such as chiefs, extended and maintained their influence. Multiple wives established scores of important bonds between men. Wives produced children, and daughters could be given to powerful men, including Europeans, with the expectation that these men would serve their fathers-in-law. Anchieta noted that "by order of their fathers, young men serve their future father- or mother-in-law before they give him the girl" and observed that "he who has more daughters is more honored by the sons-in-law."[19]

It would not be easy to expect the powerful chiefs who led the traditional villages to give up polygyny, yet Jesuits frequently preached against it and required Indian men to select only one wife before baptism. Even

Figure 6. Father José de Anchieta, along with other early Jesuit missionaries, sought to persuade Indians to abandon customs he found shocking and sinful, such as cannibalism, polygyny, and cohabiting with multiple families in a single large dwelling. At the same time, Jesuits struggled to protect natives from colonists who wanted to enslave them. Source: Simão de Vasconcellos, *Vida do veneravel padre Ioseph de Anchieta* . . . (Lisbon: João da Costa, 1672). Courtesy of the John Carter Brown Library at Brown University.

when Indian men and women were willing to commit themselves to one spouse, the church's rules on consanguinity forbade marriages between related kin. Because it was so difficult for an Indian man to find a woman to whom he was not related and because the Jesuits would not baptize a man who kept a concubine, Anchieta suggested that such rules be relaxed, so that marriage at all degrees be admitted, except those between brothers and sisters.[20]

ENSLAVEMENT AND WARFARE

Cannibalism and polygyny were major obstacles to the Jesuit missionaries when they visited the traditional villages, but the Jesuits faced other problems that emanated from the Portuguese settlements. The first Portuguese settlements in Brazil predated the arrival of the Jesuits by nearly two decades; therefore, when the Jesuits arrived they encountered patterns of interaction between the Portuguese settlements and the indigenous villages that were already entrenched. Of these, the most problematic was Indian slavery. The widespread enslavement of native men, women, and children by Portuguese colonists was immediately visible to the first Jesuits. "Men who come here," Nóbrega wrote in January of 1550, "find no other way of living except to live from the labor of slaves." Virtually all of these slaves were Indians, captured in overt slave raiding along the coast of Brazil. Unscrupulous Portuguese slave traders used deception and trickery to capture men, women, and children from the traditional Indian villages. After residing in Brazil only a few months, Nóbrega believed that most of the slaves in Bahia in 1549 had been obtained through such raids.[21]

Unlike the experience in Africa, where Christian evangelism was used as an argument in favor of enslaving Africans, most of the first Jesuits in Brazil did not advocate enslaving Indians in order to evangelize them. On the contrary, Nóbrega believed that slavery impeded evangelism. Indian slaves who lived with Christian masters rarely learned anything about Christianity, according to Nóbrega. After a decade in Brazil, Nóbrega concluded that the enslavement of Indians by colonists "is not to save them nor for them to know Christ nor for them to live in justice and reason, but to rob them of their farms, their sons, their daughters, and their women." Instead, the Jesuits continually lobbied the king of Portugal to limit Indian slavery in Brazil.[22]

Brazil's first governor and judicial authorities did take some steps to place limits on Indian slavery. Even before the first Jesuits arrived, King João III had decided that slave raiding along the coast of Brazil must cease. In the Royal Instructions written for Tomé de Sousa, the king acknowledged that slave raiding had occurred and he outlawed it henceforth.[23] Following the arrival of the governor and the Jesuits, several basic rules began to be asserted for the regulation of the Indian slave trade. Enslavement of Indians was only legal if it resulted from two practices: captives acquired through a just war, or captives acquired through *resgate* (ransoming).

Jesuits fully accepted that slavery resulted from a just war because the concept derived from the writings of Christian theologians Saint Augustine and Saint Thomas Aquinas. According to Aquinas, war was just only if authorized by a sovereign and waged against peoples who deserved to be attacked, and only if the war resulted in the greater good. If a war met these conditions it could be considered just. In Brazil as elsewhere, the waging of just wars produced slaves, for prisoners taken in a just war could by killed by the victors, or they could be sold as slaves.[24]

An example of a just war is contained in the royal instructions that João III gave to his first governor of Brazil, Tomé de Sousa. The king ordered Sousa to inform himself about rebellious Indians outside of the Portuguese settlement of Vila Velha. Once Sousa ascertained which Indian groups had rebelled, the king ordered Sousa to "destroy their villages and settlements, killing and capturing those whom you deem sufficient for their punishment."[25] This fit the requirements of a just war: it was authorized by the sovereign; those to be attacked deserved it because they had rebelled; and greater good would result because rebellion would cease. But as a consequence, anyone captured in this war could be legally enslaved.

Similarly, resgate, which often meant the payment of a ransom in exchange for a captive, was linked to war and slavery. During the wars of the Reconquista in medieval Iberia, it was common for Muslims and Christians to ransom or redeem war captives following battles. War captives were commonly seen as slaves, whether the war had been declared just or not, and captives could be freed through negotiations and the payment of ransoms. The practice extended to the ransoming of captives held by pirates who attacked ships and towns around the Mediterranean Sea. But the term resgate in sixteenth-century Portuguese could also refer simply to trade and commerce. In their business dealings with Africa, the Portuguese merchants of the fifteenth century described commerce along sections of the Guinea coast as resgate. The *resgate do ouro*, for example, referred not only to trade for gold, but to the place where gold was obtained. Trading for slaves in Africa was also known as resgate. Indeed, the holder of the huge hereditary grant of Pernambuco in Brazil petitioned the king for a license to bring "some slaves from Guiné by resgate" to his colony.[26]

In Brazil, resgate was tied to the cannibalistic ceremonies of coastal Tupi groups. Following war, captives were taken to villages where they were sacrificed and eaten in an elaborate ritual. But if such captives were ransomed, they were freed from the cannibalism ceremony. Azpilcueta ransomed a beautiful youth in 1551 from an indigenous group ready to "chop him up and devour him."[27] Azpilcueta would not hold the youth as a slave, but for a Portuguese colonist, a captive so redeemed could be held as a slave. The logic was that since Tupi groups had obtained such captives from their intertribal wars and raids, they were prisoners of war. Because these prisoners were already slaves, once ransomed they could be kept legally enslaved. Moreover, since the prisoners so obtained were rescued from certain death and cannibalism, the Portuguese saw their continued enslavement to be an act of charity, infinitely better than death.

Yet, as in Africa, the term resgate also referred to trade or to what was paid for an item; in other words, the trading goods. A letter written to the king of Portugal in 1555 reported that ships only stopped at the southern end of the Bay of All Saints "to trade (*resgatar*) for hens, pigs, and slaves." In his history of sixteenth-century Brazil, the Portuguese author Pero Magalhães de Gandavo described the trade in parrots, reporting that Indians from the wilderness brought parrots to the Portuguese settlements to be exchanged for resgates, i.e., trading goods. Since slaves purchased through ransoming were known as *resgatados* (the ransomed or purchased ones), these slaves were seen as more than simply persons freed from a cannibalism ceremony. They were seen as property, acquired through trade. Eventually the entire Indian slave trade would become known as resgate.[28] As the introduction to this volume explains, many indigenous laborers obtained in this way effectively became chattel slaves, valued monetarily and transferred as property to heirs and creditors.

Initially, Jesuits in Brazil accepted resgate as a legitimate means for obtaining slaves because they believed it would reduce and eventually do away with cannibalism in the traditional Indian villages. Over time, however, Nóbrega doubted that the many Indian slaves he saw in Brazil could all be captives liberated from cannibalistic ceremonies. He came to see resgate as a commercial exchange, and one through which colonists illegally obtained slaves. In one letter he expressed his belief that the Portuguese had fomented this slave trade by teaching the Indians how to attack each other and sell the war captives as slaves. Another stratagem he denounced was when Portuguese men requested Indian women as wives, giving the women's fathers some trading goods, but then kept these women as "slaves forever."[29]

Speaking out against the illegal enslavement of Indians by colonists in Brazil and using their linguistic approach that emphasized conversion through persuasion, the first Jesuits believed that they saw concrete results from the early years of their mission to the Indian villages. Nóbrega confidently wrote that through their preaching, the fame of the Jesuits had spread through the villages, such that Indians came from very great distances to hear them. "We tell them," Nóbrega penned in 1551, "that on their account principally we came to this land and not for the whites." This clearly had resonated with the Indians, Nóbrega reflected, because the Indians showed great willingness for the Jesuits to talk to them and to teach them. With enough missionaries, Nóbrega thought that it would be easy to convert everyone. Other Jesuits similarly depicted early successes in the evangelization of Indians. "The Christians who remain with us," António Pires wrote from Pernambuco in 1551, "are so much ours that they fight with their brothers to defend us."[30]

When the first bishop appointed to Brazil arrived in the capital city of Salvador in June of 1552, the Jesuits confronted an unexpected obstacle to their mission to the indigenous villages. In a confidential letter to Simão Rodrigues, the head of the Society of Jesus in Portugal, Bishop Pedro Fernandes Sardinha questioned the Jesuits' adaptation of Indian music and dance, and he found their use of interpreters, especially in the confessional, objectionable. In his own letter to Simão Rodrigues, Nóbrega defended the strategies used by the Jesuits in their missionary work, such as relying on interpreters. But within a year, Nóbrega decided to leave Bahia and to concentrate on the Jesuit mission in São Vicente. Writing to the king, Nóbrega cited the lack of good interpreters and the unleashing of "such cruel" intertribal wars, in addition to conflicts with the bishop, as reasons why the Jesuits could no longer make headway in Bahia.[31]

In 1553, Nóbrega arrived in São Vicente in the company of Governor Tomé de Sousa, who was undertaking his visitation of all major Portuguese settlements in Brazil. In São Vicente, Nóbrega found the mission begun by Leonardo Nunes thriving—the church was well built, fifty children were in the school, and the Jesuit residence frequently supported nearly one hundred persons. As in Bahia, Jesuits in São Vicente visited autonomous Tupi villages, often travelling by canoe, where they preached and taught that customs such as cannibalism or polygyny must be abandoned. In return, other customs, such as music, could be maintained. On the plateau above the coast, Nóbrega wrote that the Jesuits created a new village on the Piratininga plateau, which would become the site of the future city of São Paulo, by joining together three indigenous villages. Brother José de Anchieta, who had arrived in Brazil in 1553 with the third group of Jesuits, and Brother Pero Correia, who joined the Society in 1549 in Brazil and was known as an excellent interpreter, described these and other missions. Beyond Piratininga, Nóbrega hoped to launch a mission among the Guarani peoples, who he believed would be receptive to Christianity. Nóbrega wrote to Lisbon that the Jesuits in São Vicente had determined it to be God's will that they enter the wilderness 100 leagues (approximately 660 kilometers) and there build a house where they would gather the children of the Guarani, teaching and joining together many in "a great city" where they would live "in conformity with reason."[32]

Governor Tomé de Sousa forbade Nóbrega's plan for a "great city" deep in the wilderness because he judged it too dangerous to allow the Jesuits to live so far away from the Portuguese settlement. The governor did allow the traditional approach of visiting villages and preaching in the sertão to continue. Nóbrega sent the Society's best interpreter, Pero Correia, to preach to villages of Indians along the coast, hoping to lay the groundwork for a future mission to the Guarani. The first reports back from Correia were enthusiastic; he had been received with "the greatest joy" and he hoped to create a large village where Indians could come and live and be taught Christianity. However, events turned against him as he proceeded deeper into the wilderness. A group of Guarani Indians, incited by a Spanish colonist, shot Correia and his companion João de Sousa to death with arrows in 1554. Pero Correia and João de Sousa became the first Jesuit martyrs in Brazil.[33]

The loss of Pero Correia was a severe blow to Nóbrega. After Correia's death, several more prominent Jesuits died, among them Leonardo Nunes, the founder of the mission in São Vicente, who drowned at sea when his ship, which was headed back to Lisbon, wrecked in 1554. João de Azpilcueta, so gifted in languages and preaching, died from a fever he contracted in 1557. A tone of discouragement can be seen in many of the Jesuit letters, as the fathers and brothers of the Society of Jesus recognized that illegal Indian slavery was becoming more common, that cannibalism and polygyny continued in the

traditional villages, and that shamans and powerful chiefs resisted and undermined the Jesuits' missionary outreach. Moreover, the first bishop of Salvador,
Bishop Sardinha, with whom Nóbrega had disagreed earlier, died on his return
to Lisbon when his ship sank off the northeastern coast. Sardinha's death was
particularly traumatic because he and many others survived the wreck only to
fall into the hands of the Caeté Indians who cannibalized them.[34]

Nóbrega returned to Bahia in 1556, and at the end of the next year Mem
de Sá, the third governor of Brazil, arrived determined to initiate a military
campaign that would force the Indians living around the capital city of
Salvador into submission. Even though this military approach directly con-
tradicted prior emphasis on conversion through persuasion in the Indian
villages, a disillusioned Nóbrega was prepared to support him.[35] Nóbrega was
no longer convinced that persuasion alone would achieve the conversion. In
a letter dated May of 1558, Nóbrega recommended first defeating the Indians
before an effective evangelism could begin. In this long and angry letter to
Miguel de Torres, who was the new *provincial* of the Society of Jesus in
Portugal, Nóbrega expressed the view that if Indians were subjugated, many
of the problems faced by the Jesuits would cease. Military campaigns would
resolve the conflict between the Jesuits and Portuguese colonists over Indian
slavery, because the governor's campaigns would require the declaration of
just wars, the defeated parties of which could be legally enslaved. Once
autonomous indigenous villages were defeated, colonists could build many
more sugar mills and cattle ranches and thereby increase the income of the
crown. Nóbrega even thought the campaigns would not be that costly, since
the Portuguese colonists would help the governor with their slaves, as would
Indians allied with the Portuguese.[36]

The level of violence unleashed by Mem de Sá's military campaigns was
devastating. "Never has another such war been waged in this land" wrote one
Jesuit in 1558, and "not only these Indians, but the whole coast will be shocked
and afraid."[37] The governor turned horses and ships into weapons, and by
targeting villages one by one, he eliminated many formerly independent and
powerful Indian chiefs living in Bahia. These chiefs had previously negotiated with some power and authority directly with the governor.

The Jesuits seem to have accepted Mem de Sá's violent campaigns. Sá
had "punished some" and "yoked all," wrote a Jesuit to Lisbon in September
1558, which had not been seen before in Brazil. Speaking through the metaphor of the vineyard, this Jesuit saw new hope. "For such a great harvest [i.e.,

Figure 7. Brazil's coastal inhabitants engaged in exocannibalism, ritually consuming enemies captured in battle. The German mercenary Hans Staden, held captive by the Tupinambá for many months, published one of the most vivid accounts of this custom, which culminated in binding a victim, clubbing him to death, and dividing his body parts among members of the community. Source: Hans Staden, *Warhaftige Historia* . . . (Marburg: Andres Kolben, 1557). Courtesy of The Lilly Library, Indiana University, Bloomington, Indiana.

of souls], it is necessary that many workers [i.e., missionaries] come," he wrote, because "this land is promising so much fruit." Afraid and obedient is how he described the Indians who "now prepare themselves to accept the faith." José de Anchieta defended the use of force, even before Mem de Sá's arrival, seeing it as laying the foundation for evangelism; subsequently, Anchieta wrote a long poem in Latin praising the exploits and sacrifices of the governor. Sá appears in the poem as a hero, a pious and magnanimous governor, a bringer of laws, and the one who put an end to cannibalism.[38]

THE NEW *ALDEIAS*

Once autonomous Indian villages were defeated, their residents were then organized by the governor into aldeias. In these large mission villages, Indians lived under the supervision of Jesuits, who not only taught them Christianity, but transformed their ways of life. Although administered by the Jesuits, the aldeias were under the authority of the governor and subject to Portuguese laws. The governor appointed an Indian bailiff, and a *pelourinho* (post) was erected in the public square. In Portuguese villages, and in the Portuguese settlements in Brazil, the pelourinho was the place where justice (i.e., punishment) was meted out. The aldeias also had stocks, where the boys were locked up if they ran away from school, or where the bailiff would detain those who resisted evangelism.[39]

Nóbrega had already articulated the need to congregate Indians into mission villages, where they would live under Portuguese law and the control of the Jesuits, before Mem de Sá arrived in Brazil. Indeed, the idea for the mission village can be seen in the creation of the Jesuit village of São Paulo on the Piratininga plateau in São Vicente and in Nóbrega's vision for a "city" among the Guarani, which he articulated in 1553. Following his return to Bahia, in August of 1557, four months before Mem de Sá landed, Nóbrega wrote to the provincial of the Society in Lisbon that he wanted to join together the Christian Indians into settlements under the rule of law. He had in mind villages where converts would advance in their learning of Christianity, where evildoers would be punished by law, and where the Indians could be protected from the colonists' incessant desire for slaves. Hence Nóbrega was prepared to support the governor's forced reorganization of the traditional villages. The changes came quickly. By April of 1558, according to a Jesuit letter, Sá had already ordered the consolidation of four

Indian villages surrounding Salvador into one large new aldeia. António Blázquez wrote on behalf of Nóbrega that this is "a new way of proceeding . . . which is by fear and submission."[40]

Four or five villages consolidated into one created the first aldeia, that of São Paulo, located near Rio Vermelho, one league (approximately 6.6 kilometers) to the north of Salvador. Mem de Sá, accompanied by elite of Salvador, attended the first Mass celebrated in the new church. Many converts were baptized, and the governor provided food for all after the conclusion of the Mass.[41] Two more large aldeias were formed in the same year: São João, three leagues from Salvador; and Espírito Santo, seven leagues from Salvador. The aldeia of Santiago was created three leagues from Salvador near the end of the next year in 1559. Santo Antonio, nine leagues to the north of Salvador, followed in 1560; Santa Cruz de Itaparica, on the Island of Itaparica at the mouth of the Bay of All Saints, in 1561; and São Miguel and Nossa Senhora da Assunção, both in Tinharé, forty-five leagues (nearly 300 kilometers) to the south of Salvador, in 1561.[42]

Jesuits recognized that force had been used to lay the foundation for the first aldeias, but they still believed that their evangelism was fundamentally based on the power of persuasion. From their letters, it seems that, in hindsight, Jesuits saw Mem de Sá's campaign as inevitable. Once this was concluded, they welcomed the new beginning that the creation of the mission villages afforded. Within the more controlled environment of the aldeias, they returned to their preferred approach: persuasion through teaching, preaching, and conversation.

The schooling of children had always been a priority and it became even more so in the new aldeias. According to Jesuit letters, São João had one hundred children in school, Santa Cruz had three hundred, and Bom Jesus had four hundred.[43] From Nóbrega's account of the São Paulo aldeia, the children followed a set routine. In the morning they fished to support themselves and their parents; in the afternoons, the Jesuits taught them for three or four hours. After school there was catechism (religious instruction) for all, which ended with a Salve Regina sung by the boys and the Ave Marias. At night, after a bell was rung, the boys taught their parents and elders.[44]

The new aldeias still had chiefs, but no longer were they independent. Nóbrega praised their "obedience" and noted that the chiefs were now required to ask for permission to leave the aldeia. If they left and visited traditional villages where they might drink, participate in cannibalism ceremonies, or have other wives, the governor's bailiffs apprehended and punished them. But on Sundays and Holy days, when the Jesuit priest said Mass and preached in the Tupi-Guarani language, the Indian chiefs of the aldeias were permitted to preach at dawn in the traditional Indian style.[45]

At least two Jesuits lived in the aldeias and undertook the day-to-day evangelism. The provincial visited the aldeias several times a year, and these rounds were when large baptisms, special masses, and processions were held. Luis da Grã, who succeeded Manuel da Nóbrega as provincial of Brazil, made a visit to at least six of the seven aldeias in Bahia in 1561. He first visited the São Paulo aldeia, which was closest to Salvador, and there he celebrated Easter Sunday. He then continued to Santiago with a Jesuit interpreter so that he could hear confessions, then it was on to São João, where he baptized some one hundred converts. The next stop, Santo Antonio, was reached only by a long journey over a poor road, through deep forest. The last two aldeias he visited were Espírito Santo and Santa Cruz. The provincial wrote that there were four more aldeias ready to be created, once Jesuits were prepared to take charge of them. He was pleased with what he saw, writing from Bahia in September that "this land is in such a peace that one could not imagine" and that the "fruit" he expected to be gained through the Jesuit mission was great. The fact that the new provincial left Salvador "not at all well, but very thin and weak," according to António Blázquez, did not dampen his enthusiasm for the missions. The new beginning had allowed the Jesuits to regain their optimism, which had wavered as their first decade in Brazil came to an end.[46]

The new aldeias were far larger than the traditional villages had been. Twenty years later, when Jesuits began writing the history of their mission in the 1580s, the aldeias were an important topic. According to one history written in 1583, each new aldeia had a population of at least two thousand, some were as large as four thousand, and mass baptisms of as many as a thousand in the first year were common. These numbers seem imprecise and impossibly high, yet the same high numbers are reported in the letters written in the 1560s by the Jesuits who visited the aldeias. Leonardo do Vale wrote that when the provincial visited the aldeias of Bahia in October of 1561, he baptized 892 at the first baptism held at the newly founded Bom Jesus aldeia and subsequently in his visit of January and February of 1562, he baptized 242 more. The first baptism in São Pedro aldeia was of 1,152, the largest ever. In Nossa Senhora da Assunção, another of the new aldeias, 1,088 were baptized in 1561 and 1562. Many couples were married during these visits—over a hundred in Santo Antonio, São Pedro, São Miguel, and Nossa Senhora da Assunção (see table 1).

Table 1. The *Aldeias* of Bahia

ALDEIA	POPULATION 1561	BAPTISMS 1561–1562	MARRIAGES 1561–1562	POPULATION 1583
São Paulo	2,000			Closed
Espírito Santo	4,000	174	86	
Santo Antonio	2,000	650	110	
Santiago	4,000	120	50	Closed
São João	4,000	549	94	
Bom Jesus	4,000	1219	144	Closed
São Pedro	4,000	1,152	150	Closed
Santo André	4,000			Closed
Santa Cruz		108	43	Closed
São Miguel	2,000	897	106	Closed
N. S. da Assunção	4,000	1088	137	Closed
TOTAL	34,000	5,957	920	2,500–3,500

Sources: Population 1561: "Informação dos primeiros aldeamentos na Bahia," 358–62. Baptisms and marriages: Leonardo do Vale to fathers and brothers of São Roque (in Lisbon), Bahia, 26 June 1562, in MB III: 469–507. Population 1583: "Informação dos primeiros aldeamentos na Bahia," 385; and Cardim, "Enformacion de la provincia del Brasil," 143–44.

The aldeias were so large because many independent villages were joined together into one large mission village. As we have seen, the first Jesuit aldeia in Bahia was São Paulo, located a league from the city of Salvador, which was created in 1558 with the joining of four or five villages where the Jesuits had formerly evangelized. But farther away from the capital, the new aldeias were even larger. When the provincial chose Jesuits Gaspar Lourenço (a skilled interpreter) and Simeão Gonçalvez (one of the orphaned children raised by the Jesuits in Brazil) to open the aldeia of São João in 1561, there were thirteen or fourteen independent villages that they intended to merge into the new aldeia. António Rodrigues who was sent to create the new aldeia of Bom Jesus wrote back to the Jesuits in Bahia that the aldeia was formed when fifteen separate villages came together.[47]

The new aldeias were envisioned by the Jesuits to be permanent, a place where they could develop a mission that would endure over time. In the new aldeias, Indians generally continued to live in their large ocas, but in the oldest aldeia, that of São Paulo, Indians began to change their houses as early as 1559. This aldeia was not only the oldest but the closest to the Portuguese settlements; this proximity, in conjunction with the new regimen, seems to have sparked this shift. António Blázquez wrote that "the Indians of São Paulo want to change all of their customs, and now that they are Christians, they are making separate houses, of *taipa* (adobe), so as to live in them permanently." This was different, he reminded his readers in Rome, than their previous custom, which was to move and remake their houses every two to three years. The Jesuits had tolerated but never approved of the ocas, which they found dark, smoky, smelly, and lacking in privacy. The move away from them to small single-family residences would have met with their approval if not overt encouragement.[48]

Not all chiefs and shamans were willing to cede their power to the Jesuits. Some deliberately resisted the Jesuits, playing on the fear of the people living under the new regimen. For example, right before the large baptism and wedding ceremony in the new aldeia of Bom Jesus in October of 1561, an unknown Indian, who might have been a shaman or chief, appeared completely painted in black. He told the Indians in the aldeia that the Jesuits had sent them there so that they could all be killed. Everyone in the aldeia was prepared to flee, wrote the Jesuit Leonardo do Vale, who describes these events in a letter, but the Jesuit missionary priest in the aldeia, António Rodrigues, quelled the rumor. The next day, the baptism began as planned, but suddenly another rumor started that the houses were all on fire. Everyone ran out of the church. Only later did the ceremony resume and continue through the rest of the day and most of the night. When the Jesuit provincial was ready to marry the first couple, and in fact was holding them by the hand, yet another rumor swept through the church. The Indians fled again, bursting through the straw walls of the church, knocking down the beams and lintels, and not knowing where they were going. Vale writes that Rodrigues pursued those in flight and again convinced them to return. Although many were wounded, and some later died, the Jesuits still judged this ceremony to have been a success. In all, 892 Indians were baptized and seventy couples were married.[49]

DISEASE, FAMINE, AND DEPOPULATION

In the two months before this ceremony, António Rodrigues had baptized eighty-five Indians *in extremis*, i.e., on the verge of death. According to Vale, these were the elderly and "innocents" (infants), who, we may infer, were not expected to live until the arrival of the provincial in October of 1561. This is suggestive of one of the most devastating consequences of the creation of the Jesuit aldeias: their facility in spreading disease. Although in the oldest aldeia Indians began to construct and live in small houses, in most they continued to live in close proximity to each other in the ocas, or longhouses, where disease could spread quickly. And, since the Jesuit aldeias joined together what were once independent villages, the larger size of the new villages concentrated more Indians together, which also encouraged the rapid spread of disease.[50]

Moreover, Jesuits themselves often were sick, opening up the possibility that they too introduced disease. A persistent theme in António Rodrigues's

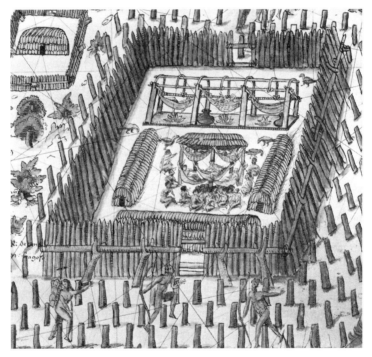

Figure 8. Palisaded as a defense against enemies, traditional Tupi villages consisted of large multifamily longhouses. The villages often moved, as inhabitants sought new places to hunt, fish, and cultivate manioc roots, a staple of their diet. As contagious disease ravaged these communities, missionaries attempted to transform the Indians into settled Christian agriculturalists. Source: Detail from Jean Rotz's map of Brazil in *Boke of Idrography* ('The Rotz Atlas'), France and England: 1542. © The British Library Board. Royal 20 E IX.

letters was his constant illness. Calls on him to personally visit the sick in the Bom Jesus aldeia had become onerous, he wrote his fellow Jesuits in Salvador, for "as you know, I am very sick and I do not have the strength that I had in times past. I sit down in a chair in the church and I have them bring the sick who can come, and I baptize them there."[51]

Jesuits who wrote about the sicknesses of their brothers emphasized their great devotion to their work; indeed they present illness as yet another burden that Jesuits must bear in their mission. Yet the consequences for the indigenous residents in the Jesuit aldeias were severe. A single Jesuit could spread disease, with shattering results. The aldeia of Espírito Santo illustrates this phenomenon. In 1558 father João Gonçalves went to the aldeia of Espírito Santo where on 8 December, the day of Our Lady of Conception, he had planned a baptism of the boys whom he had educated in the school, as well as a baptism for infants and a special Mass. In the middle of the day, he came down with a serious fever, but he continued and finished the Mass with difficulty. Thirteen or fourteen days later, having been taken back to the Jesuit residence in Salvador, he died. Following his death, nearly all of the Jesuits in Salvador became sick. Back in the Espírito Santo aldeia, other Jesuits became sick. Many, including the governor, thought that the place ought to be quarantined. But Nóbrega disagreed, writing, "I trusted in Our Lord," and sent two Jesuits, each of whom had been sick with fever, to the aldeia. He justified his action, writing, "from whence the others fled in order not to become sick, I sent the sick there to be cured." Soon after, the Jesuit João de Melo went to Espírito Santo and wrote that the entire time he was in the aldeia, from January to April 1560, "there were a great number of sick and many of them died." João de Melo himself became sick and could not participate in the Maundy Thursday procession on 11 April of that year; his fever was worsening so much that he was ordered back to Salvador. The plagues stunned the Indians, who had never before experienced such illness. António Blázquez wrote to Rome the next year that the Indians of the Espírito Santo aldeia had become so depressed from seeing so much death that they had given up singing and dancing. All that could be heard, he wrote, were cries and lamentations.[52]

It is difficult to identify these diseases, but one was certainly malaria. Jesuits frequently wrote about fevers, describing them as quartan and tertian, meaning that they recurred every four days (quartan) or every three days (tertian). António Blázquez described the Provincial Luis de Grã as returning from one of his visits to the aldeias in Bahia 1561 "very sick," adding that "at present he suffers from a quartan fever." The fever recurred every four days from mid-December to Holy Week, yet during that time he continued to preach, both in the cathedral and in the church at the Jesuit residence.[53]

As elsewhere in the Americas in the sixteenth century, the indigenous peoples of Brazil had rarely been exposed to European and African diseases. Once introduced, disease spread rapidly and brought very high mortality.[54] Although some Jesuits struggled to understand why Indians died at such higher rates than colonists, most Jesuits saw the epidemics as punishments from God. In this view, epidemics expressed God's wrath, which was directed at Indians who had refused to accept Christianity or to renounce cannibalism or polygyny. Through this representation of disease, Jesuits laid the blame for the shocking mortality of Indians in Brazil with the Indians themselves. Their deaths were unfortunate, but to be expected, Jesuits reasoned, given the natives' failure to fully embrace Christianity.

The most devastating epidemic for the Indians of Brazil, as elsewhere in the Americas, was smallpox. While smallpox appeared early in the Caribbean and broke out during the conquest of Mexico (1519–1521), no smallpox epidemic was recorded in Brazil before 1562. The first documented smallpox epidemic appeared right after the Jesuits had created their aldeias in Bahia, and given their size and the contact between them and the capital of Salvador, the epidemic spread rapidly. The results were shocking. In a long letter Jesuit Leonardo do Vale describes a plague "so odd" and so unlike any other in Brazil spreading into the new Jesuit aldeias of São Miguel, Santa Cruz, and Nossa Senhora da Assunção. In each of these aldeias one-third of the Indians died. In two months, he estimated that 1,800 died in only one of the aldeias. The plague then spread to Salvador and its environs, where it decimated the Indian and African slaves on the sugar plantations. Moving still farther north, the plague first infected and killed many Indians in the mission villages of São Paulo and Santiago. All routine ceased as the Jesuits ministered to the sick. Leonardo do Vale wrote that the Jesuits were exhausted from squatting for hours preparing the sick for baptism and confession. Although Vale describes the Jesuits as working day and night to bury the dead, they could not keep up, "for if twelve died, twenty fell sick." Soon, there was no one to dig the graves, and the bodies piled up.[55]

Jesuits attributed even this devastating smallpox plague as a punishment from God. Vale characterized it as a "whipping from the Lord" meted out against certain Indians from the aldeias who were drawn to a shaman in the wilderness. This prophet led a *santidade*, a messianic movement that encouraged Indians to flee from the Jesuit aldeias. The Jesuit José de Anchieta also saw the smallpox epidemic as a punishment sent from God: "Our Lord has visited and punished this land with many illnesses," he wrote in a letter sent to Rome in 1565.[56]

Later, Jesuit historians recognized that the population of Indians had declined at an alarming rate in the aldeias because of disease. A Jesuit history of the aldeias written in 1583 expressed astonishment at the rapid pace of destruction by disease. Its Jesuit author wrote that there had once been four-teen Jesuit aldeias in Bahia, in which the Jesuits had congregated 40,000 Indians, but that only three survived, and if these three aldeias had 3,500 living in them, "it would be a lot."[57] The Jesuit Fernão Cardim, writing in 1583 soon after his arrival in Brazil, cited the same high number of 40,000 Christian Indians who once lived in Bahia, then gave the number of remaining Christian Indians as 10,000, including those laboring on the sugar plantations as slaves.

At the time, after the epidemics ran their course, letters reveal that Jesuits proudly used the aldeias for spiritual festivals, such as large baptisms, processions, and celebrations. In 1564 the Jesuits organized celebrations at the aldeias of Espírito Santo, São Paulo, and Santiago that drew many colo-nists from Salvador, who arrived on foot, on horseback, in carts, or in ham-mocks. There was singing and dancing through the night, and confessions began at three in the morning, a procession at the eve of daybreak, and a Mass at dawn. The singing, chanting, and processing made a great impres-sion on all.[58]

Yet even as colonists attended spiritual events at the aldeias, and per-haps recognized that the Jesuits were having greater success with their evangelism in these more controlled settings, they harbored much resent-ment against the mission villages. Colonists disliked what they saw as the monopoly that the Jesuits exercised over the indigenous population. Even when Jesuits made the residents of the aldeias available for work, colonists wanted slaves to work their plantations and farms, not free laborers from the aldeias. The anger of the colonists against the Jesuits can be seen in a trea-tise written by Gabriel Soares de Sousa in 1587. A colonist, Sousa was highly critical of the Jesuits both because he believed their evangelism was ineffec-tive and because of the stance that the Jesuits took against Indian slavery.[59]

Ironically, Mem de Sá, who had been the force behind the creating of the aldeias, deeply undermined them when he declared a just war against the Caeté Indians in 1562. The Caeté were blamed for cannibalizing Brazil's first bishop, and the just war was decreed against them as a consequence of this action.[60] Certainly the Jesuits agreed with the governor that the Caeté deserved to be punished, yet the declaration of the just war against the Caeté was devastating for their aldeias. Leonardo do Vale references this decree in a letter from June of 1562, writing that the decree condemned the entire Caeté people to slavery. He expressed the fear that because there were so many Caeté in Bahia, the Indians in the Jesuit aldeias would be at risk.[61]

In the Jesuit histories written in the 1580s, Jesuit authors blame the Portuguese colonists for seizing Indians from the aldeias of Bahia and enslaving them, claiming that they were Caeté. In the wake of these attacks, many Indians fled the aldeias and made their way into the interior. Even after the governor placed captains in the aldeias to protect the Indians from the colonists, it had, according to the Jesuit historians, little effect.[62]

Famine also took a tremendous toll on the aldeias. Whereas the traditional villages were smaller and moved once lands wore out, the larger, permanent aldeias had more people to feed and less access to virgin forest. Although the queen of Portugal gave the aldeias in Bahia land grants (*sesmarias*) in 1562, the Portuguese colonists did not respect these grants. Lands set aside for aldeias were claimed by colonists or overrun with their cattle. Unable to develop sustainable agriculture, famine struck the aldeias, and when it did, many fled.[63]

Because the Jesuits viewed their aldeias as permanent, unlike the traditional Indian villages that moved every few years, they sought to maintain the population of their aldeias. By the 1570s, the Jesuits were bringing Indians from deep in the wilderness to supplement the shrinking populations of the remaining aldeias. Nevertheless, new plagues hit the aldeias, thereby reducing their size and leading to the closing of the smallest ones, as happened to the aldeia of Santiago, the residents of which were divided among the three remaining aldeias in 1574.[64]

Despite these shocking losses in the mission villages of Bahia almost immediately after they had been created, the Jesuits nevertheless saw them as the model for the newly envisioned Jesuit missionary enterprise in Brazil. At the time, Jesuits failed to recognize that the aldeia, as an institution, made the Indians more vulnerable to the colonists (because they could not protect themselves) and to the spread of disease and famine. Even in their histories written later, Jesuits defended the institution of the aldeia, claiming it to be necessary for their mission. In hindsight, the Jesuits were proud of their role in creating and administering the aldeias.

One Jesuit author cited the tremendous dedication of the missionaries during times of plagues when they cared for the sick by night and day. He lauded their work in teaching Indians "the things necessary for their salvation," as well as to read, to write, to count, and to speak Portuguese. Fernão Cardim cited the choirs, the music, and the dances (now in a Portuguese style) as aspects of the aldeias that were particularly admirable. They show, he wrote, that "such an indomitable and barbarous people have been made, through the goodness of God and the diligence of the Jesuits, rational men and Christians."[65]

The aldeias were not stable institutions, however, and as the Jesuits' own histories show, the majority did not survive even twenty years. Increasingly, aldeias were located far from the Portuguese settlements, deeper in the interior. Because the aldeias were remote and often staffed by only two Jesuits, the Society's leaders in Rome feared that Jesuits living there would lose their identity. Explicit rules were drafted to regulate the aldeias in 1586.[66]

The organization of Jesuit-administered mission villages was far from their minds when the first Jesuits stepped ashore in Bahia. Instead, they earnestly believed that the indigenous peoples of Brazil could be persuaded to convert to Christianity if they understood that baptism would allow them to enjoy eternal life. Conversion to Christianity, the Jesuits fully realized, required giving up many of the defining features of indigenous life in Brazil. But they were optimistic that they could persuade the Tupi- and Guarani-speaking peoples to do so willingly, including such entrenched customs as ritual cannibalism and polygyny.

The first Jesuits shared the conviction that conversion to Christianity should occur through persuasion, and not as a result of force. Yet after not even a decade in Brazil the leader of the Jesuit mission to Brazil, Manuel da Nóbrega, abandoned the strategy of pure persuasion and supported violence. In the wake of military campaigns led by the third governor of Brazil, Mem de Sá (1557–1572), the Jesuits created the first Jesuit aldeias. These new institutions emerged not from dictates from Lisbon or Rome, but in response to experience in Brazil. The Jesuits' own reports show that the aldeia was a flawed institution and that it could not be sustained. However, the Jesuits defended it and continued to use it as a model for future missions. As a result, many of the same problems that plagued the aldeias in Bahia would repeat themselves elsewhere in Brazil and, indeed, in Latin America.

NOTES

1. On the early Jesuits in Europe, see John W. O'Malley, *The First Jesuits* (Cambridge, MA: Harvard University Press, 1993), 93, 300; on the Jesuit missions abroad, see Dauril Alden, *The Making of an Enterprise: The Society of Jesus in Portugal, Its Empire, and Beyond, 1540–1750* (Stanford, CA: Stanford University Press, 1996), 41–60. Abbreviations used in the notes are as follows: Serafim Leite, S.J., *Monumenta Brasiliae,* 5 vols. (Rome: Monumenta Historica Societatis Iesu, 1956), (*MB*).

2. The letters have been collected and published by Serafim Leite, S.J., in *MB*. Alcir Pécora describes the format of these letters in "Cartas à segunda escolástica," in *A outra margem do ocidente,* ed. Adauto Novaes (São Paulo: Companhia das Letras, 1999), 373–414; while Cristina Pompa describes the types of letters in *Religião como tradução: missionaries, Tupi e Tupuia no Brasil colonial* (São Paulo: EDUSC, 2003), 81–84.

3. See Dauril Alden, "Changing Jesuit Perceptions of the Brasis during the Sixteenth Century," *Journal of World History* 3 (1992): 205–18; Alida C. Metcalf, "Disillusioned Go-Betweens: The Politics of Mediation and the Transformation of the Jesuit Missionary Enterprise in Sixteenth-Century Brazil," *Archivum Historicum Societatis Iesu* 77 (2008): 283–319; Thomas H. Cohen, *Fire of Tongues: António Vieira and the Missionary Church in Brazil and Portugal* (Stanford, CA: Stanford University Press, 1998), 36–37.

4. Sparked by the visit of the Jesuit visitor Cristovão de Gouveia, the most important of these histories were written by José de Anchieta, who had been in Brazil since 1553, and Fernão Cardim, who arrived in Brazil as the secretary of the visitor.

5. Pompa, *Religião como tradução,* 70; Charlotte Castelnau-L'Estoile, *Les ouvriers d'une vigne stérile: Les jésuites et la conversion des Indiens au Brésil, 1580–1620* (Lisbon: Fundação Calouste Gulbenkian, 2000), 48, 81–82, 105–8. On the first aldeais of Bahia, see Alexander Marchant, *From Barter to Slavery: The Economic Relations of Portuguese and Indians in the Settlement of Brazil, 1500–1580* (Baltimore, MD: Johns Hopkins University Press, 1942), 108–9; and Jorge Couto, *A construção do Brasil,* 2d ed. (Lisbon: Cosmos, 1997), 319.

6. Manuel da Nóbrega, "Informação das terras do Brasil," [1549] in *MB* I: 149–50; João de Azpilcueta to the fathers and brothers of Coimbra, Bahia, 28 Mar. 1550, in *MB* I: 181; Luís da Grã to Ignatius de Loyola (in Rome), Piratininga, 8 June 1556, in *MB* II: 292.

7. Jean de Léry, *Histoire d'un voyage faict en la terre du Brésil* [1580], ed. Frank Lestringant (Paris: Livre de Poche, 1994), 440; Hans Staden, *Hans Staden's True History: An Account of Cannibal Captivity in Brazil,* ed. and trans. Neil L. Whitehead and Michael Harbsmeier (Durham, NC, & London: Duke University Press, 2008), 109–11; South Atlantic Map by Jean Rotz in *The Maps and Text of the*

Boke of Idography Presented by Jean Rotz to Henry VIII [1542], facsimile edition, ed. Helen Wallis (Oxford: Oxford University Press, 1981).

8. Warren Dean, "Indigenous Populations of the São Paulo–Rio de Janeiro Coast: Trade, Aldeamento, Slavery, and Extinction," *Revista de História* 117 (1984): 6; Azpilcueta to the fathers and brothers of Coimbra, Bahia, Aug. 1551, in *MB* I: 281; Azpilcueta to the fathers and brothers of Coimbra, Bahia, 28 Mar. 1550, in *MB* I: 180.

9. Serafim Leite, *História da Companhia de Jesus no Brasil*, 10 vols. (Lisbon and Rio de Janeiro: Livraria Portugalia and Civilização Brasileira, 1938), 2: 47.

10. See Alida C. Metcalf, *Go-Betweens and the Colonization of Brazil, 1500–1600* (Austin: The University of Texas Press, 2005), 89–118, for a fuller discussion of the Jesuits as go-betweens.

11. Azpilcueta to the fathers and brothers of Coimbra, Bahia, 28 Mar. 1550, in *MB* I: 180; Nóbrega to Simão Rodrigues, Salvador, 6 Jan. 1550, in *MB* I: 159.

12. Leonardo Nunes to the fathers and brothers of Coimbra, São Vicente, 20 June 1551, in *MB* I: 233; Vicente Rodrigues to the fathers and brothers of Coimbra, Bahia, 17 Sept. 1552, in *MB* I: 410–11; Pero Correia to Brás Lourenço (in Espírito Santo), São Vicente, 18 July, in *MB* II. 70.

13. "Meninos órfãos," written by Francisco Pires, to Pero Deménech (in Lisbon), Bahia, 5 Aug. 1552, in *MB* I: 383–89; Azpilcueta to fathers and brothers of Coimbra, Bahia, 28 Mar. 1550, in *MB* I: 180; Nóbrega to Rodrigues, Bahia, end of August 1552, in *MB* I: 408. Nóbrega also disclosed that the "songs of Our Lord" were set to tunes and played with instruments that were customarily used in "their celebrations when they kill enemies and when they walk around drunk."

14. Nóbrega to Dr. Martín de Azpilcueta Navarro (in Coimbra), Salvador, 10 Aug. 1549, *MB* I: 136–37; Nóbrega to Rodrigues (in Lisbon), Bahia, 9 Aug. 1549, in *MB* I: 119–20.

15. Beth A. Conklin, *Consuming Grief: Compassionate Cannibalism in an Amazonian Society* (Austin: University of Texas Press, 2001), xxiv–xxxi, 3–15.

16. William Arens questioned the existence of cannibalism in *The Man Eating Myth: Anthropology and Anthropophagy* (New York: Oxford University Press, 1979), but for many historians and anthropologists there are too many accounts of cannibalism from too many different sources to dismiss the practice. The most famous account of cannibalism was published by Hans Staden, who claimed to have escaped from cannibalism; for a new English translation of this account see the Whitehead and Harbsmeier translation of Staden, *Hans Staden's True History*. On Staden and his story, see Eve M. Duffy and Alida C. Metcalf, *The Return of Hans Staden: A Go-Between in the Atlantic World* (Baltimore, MD: Johns Hopkins University Press, 2012). Many Jesuit letters and reports describe cannibalism. See, for example, Nóbrega to Azpilcueta Navarro (in Coimbra), Salvador, 10 Aug. 1549, in *MB* I: 136–37; Nóbrega, "Informação das terras do Brasil," [1549] in *MB* I: 152; Correia to João Nunes Barreto (in Africa), São Vicente, 20 June 1551,

in *MB* I: 227–29; Anchieta to Loyola (in Rome), Piratininga, 1 Sept. 1554, in *MB* II: 113; among many others. Besides Staden, other mid-sixteenth-century eyewitness accounts of cannibalism in Brazil are Jean de Léry, *History of a Voyage to the Land of Brazil, Otherwise Called America,* trans. Janet Whatley (Berkeley: University of California Press, 1993), 122–33; André Thevet, *Le Brésil d'André Thevet: Les Singularités de la France Antarctique* (1557), ed. Frank Lestringant (Paris: Éditions Chandeigne, 1997), 160–64; and Ulrico Schmidl, *Derrotero y viaje al Río de la Plata y Paraguay 1534–1554,* ed. Roberto Quevedo (Asuncion: Biblioteca Paraguaya, 1983), 214–15.

17. Nóbrega to Rodrigues, Bahia, end of August 1552, in *MB* I: 408.

18. Azpilcueta to fathers and brothers of Coimbra, 28 Mar. 1550, in *MB* I: 177–87; the English translation is from the *King James Version*.

19. Nóbrega, "Informação das terras do Brazil," [1549] in *MB* I: 153; Nóbrega to Loyola (in Rome), São Vicente, May 1556, in *MB* II: 277; José de Anchieta, "Informação do Brasil e de suas Capitanias 1584" in *Cartas, informações, fragmentos históricos e sermões,* Cartas Jesuíticas III (Belo Horizonte: Itatiaia; São Paulo: Universidade de São Paulo, 1988), 337; Anchieta, "Informação dos casamentos dos índios," in *Textos históricos* (São Paulo: Edições Loyola, 1989), 76–77. Other accounts of polygyny are found in Staden, *True History,* 122; Thevet, *Les Singularités,* 167–69; and Léry, *History,* 152.

20. Anchieta to Loyola (in Rome), Piratininga, 1 Sept. 1554, in *MB* II: 114.

21. Nóbrega to Rodrigues (in Lisbon), Bahia, 6 Jan. 1550, in *MB* I: 166; Nóbrega to Rodrigues (in Lisbon), Bahia, 9 Aug. 1549, in *MB* I: 121–22.

22. Nóbrega to Rodrigues (in Lisbon), Bahia, 9 Aug. 1549, in *MB* I: 122–25; Nóbrega to Rodrigues, 6 Jan. 1550, in *MB* I: 167; and Nóbrega to Tomé de Sousa (in Lisbon), Bahia, 5 July 1559, in *MB* III: 80–81. In an angry letter written in 1551, after learning that the chief Tibiriçá wanted to kill (and cannibalize) war captives in the traditional way, Anchieta expressed the view that Indians should be enslaved by Christian colonists in order for the land to be successfully evangelized; see Anchieta to Loyola (in Rome), São Vicente, end of March 1555, in *MB* II: 207.

23. "Regimento de Tomé de Sousa," 17 Dec. 1548, in Carlos Malheiro Dias, Ernesto de Vasconcelos, and Roque Gameiro, *História da colonização portuguesa no Brasil* (Porto: Litografia Nacional, 1921–1924), 3: 348.

24. Augustine argued that war was permitted when undertaken by proper authorities for a just cause, such as to establish peace and order; see Joseph F. O'Callaghan, *Reconquest and Crusade in Medieval Spain* (Philadelphia: University of Pennsylvania Press, 2003), 13. For Aquinas's classic formulation, see *The Summa Theologica,* trans. Fathers of the English Dominican Province (New York: Benziger Brothers, 1947), Secunda Secundæ Partis (Second Part of the Second Part), Question 40, 2: 1359–60. On slavery being a legitimate outcome of a just war, see José Eisenberg, "Cultural Encounters, Theoretical Adventures: The Jesuit Missions to the New World and the Justification of Voluntary Slavery,"

History of Political Thought 24 (2003): 375. Jesuits in Brazil did debate whether Indians could voluntarily sell themselves into slavery; see Eisenberg, "Cultural Encounters."

25. "Regimento," in Dias, Vasconcelos, and Gameiro, *História da colonização*, 3: 345.

26. On ransoming in the Iberian Reconquest, see O'Callaghan, *Reconquest and Crusade*, 148; on Mediterranean piracy, see Mark D. Meyerson, *The Muslims of Valencia: In the Age of Fernando and Isabela, between Coexistence and Crusade* (Berkeley: University of California Press, 1991), 71–83. On the meaning of resgate in Africa, see P. E. H. Hair, "Portuguese Documents on Africa and Some Problems of Translation," *History in Africa* 27 (2000): 96–97; and Colette Callier-Boisvert, "Captifs et esclaves au XVIe siècle: Une diatribe contre la traite restée sans echo," *L'Homme* 145 (1998): 117. Duarte Coelho [donatário of Pernambuco] to King João III, Olinda, 27 Apr. 1542, in *Cartas de Duarte Coelho a El Rei*, ed. José Antonio Gonsalves de Mello e Cleonir Xavier de Albuquerque (Recife: Imp. Universitária, 1967), 86.

27. Azpilcueta to fathers and brothers of Coimbra, Salvador, Aug. 1551, in MB I: 283.

28. Francisco Portocarrero to King João III, Salvador, 20 Apr. 1555, in Dias, Vasconcelos, and Gameiro, *História da Colonização*, 3: 377; Pero de Magalhães Gandavo, *História da Província de Santa Cruz a que vulgarmente chamamos Brasil* [1575], ed. Hue Sheila Moura and Ronaldo Menegaz (Lisbon: Assírio and Alvim, 2004), chap. 7, online version available at www.nead.unama.br. On the Indian slave trade in the 1570s, see "Asento sobre o resgate dos Indios do Brazil, 1574," in "Informação dos primeiros aldeamentos na Bahia," in Coelho, *Cartas, informações, fragmentos históricos*, 374–75.

29. Nóbrega to Rodrigues (in Lisbon), Bahia, 6 Jan. 1550, in *MB* I: 166; and Nóbrega to Sousa (in Lisbon), Bahia, 5 July 1559, in *MB* III: 79–80.

30. Nóbrega to fathers and brothers of Coimbra, Pernambuco, 13 Sept. 1551, in *MB* I: 288; António Pires to the fathers and brothers of Coimbra, Pernambuco, 2 Aug. 1551, in *MB* I: 253.

31. Bishop Pedro Fernandes Sardinha to Rodrigues (in Lisbon), Bahia, July 1552, in *MB* I: 358–60; Nóbrega to Rodrigues, Bahia, end of July 1552, in *MB* I: 369–70; 373–74; Nóbrega to King João III, São Vicente, Oct. 1553, in *MB* II: 15–17.

32. Nóbrega to Rodrigues, São Vicente, 12 Feb. 1553, in *MB* I: 420–23; Nóbrega to Rodrigues, São Vicente, Mar. 1553, in *MB* I: 457; Nóbrega to Luís Gonçalves da Câmara (in Lisbon), São Vicente, 15 June 1553, in *MB* I: 492; 496; Nóbrega to King João III, São Vicente, Oct. 1553, in *MB* II: 16; Anchieta to Loyola (in Rome), Piratininga, 1 Sept. 1554, in *MB* II: 83–118; Anchieta to Loyola (in Rome), São Vicente, end of March 1555, in *MB* II: 173–209; Correia to Belchior Nunes Barreto (in Coimbra), São Vicente, 8 June 1551, in *MB* I: 219–23; Correa to Rodrigues (in Lisbon), S. Vicente, June 1551, in *MB* I: 229–231; Correia to Rodrigues (in Lisbon), São Vicente, 10 Mar. 1553, in *MB* I: 433–48; Correa to João Nunes Barreto (in Africa), São Vicente, 20 June 1551, in *MB* I: 223–229. Following the Tietê River

downstream 660 kilometers into the wilderness would have put the Jesuits at the confluence of the Tietê and the Paraná, near the site of present day Três Lagoas, Mato Grosso do Sul.

33. Anchieta to Loyola (in Rome), Piratininga, 1 Sept. 1554, in *MB* II: 117; Anchieta to Loyola (in Rome), São Vicente, end of March 1555, in *MB* II: 200–201.

34. Grã to Loyola (in Rome), Piratininga, 8 June 1556, in *MB* II: 289; António Blázquez to the provincial of Portugal, Bahia, June 1557, in *MB* II: 394; Blázquez to Loyola (in Rome), Bahia, 10 June 1557, in *MB* II: 390. On discouragement, see Metcalf, "Disillusioned Go-Betweens."

35. Metcalf, "Disillusioned Go-Betweens." Nóbrega arrived in Salvador 30 July 1556, while Mem de Sá arrived in Salvador 28 Dec. 1557. Blázquez to fathers and brothers of São Roque (Lisbon), Bahia, 4 Aug. 1556, in *MB* II: 297; Blázquez commissioned by Nóbrega to Diego Laínez (Rome), Bahia, last day of April 1558, in *MB* II: 438.

36. Nóbrega to Miguel de Torres (in Lisbon), Salvador, 8 May 1558, in *MB* II: 445–59.

37. [António Pires?] to the provincial of Portugal, Salvador, 12 Sept. 1558, in *MB* II: 475.

38. Ibid., 469–73; Anchieta to Loyola (in Rome), São Vicente, end of March 1555, in *MB* II: 208; José de Anchieta, *De Gestis Mendi de Saa*, trans. Armando Cardoso (Rio de Janeiro: Arquivo Nacional, 1958). The title of the poem in English would be "Concerning the Deeds of Mem de Sá." On the Jesuit use of the metaphor of the sterile vine, see Castelnau-L'Estoile, *Les ouvriers d'une vigne sterile.*

39. Mem de Sá to King Sebastião, Salvador, 13 Mar. 1560, in *Documentos relativos a Mem de Sá, governador geral do Brasil* (Rio de Janeiro: Biblioteca Nacional, 1906), 100; Rui Pereira to fathers and brothers of Portugal, Bahia, 15 Sept. 1560, in *MB* III: 292–93.

40. José Eisenberg argues that the restructuring of the mission in Bahia emerged from Nóbrega's experience in São Vicente and his work with Anchieta, specifically the creation of the aldeia at Piratininga; see *As missões jesuíticas e o pensamento político moderno: Encontros culturais, aventuras teóricas* (Belo Horizonte: Ed. UFMG, 2000), 89–90; Nóbrega to Câmara (in Lisbon), São Vicente, 15 June 1553, in *MB* I: 492; Nóbrega to Torres (in Lisbon), Rio Vermelho, Bahia, Aug. 1557, in *MB* II: 401; Blázquez, commissioned by Nóbrega, to Laínez (in Rome), Bahia, last day of April 1558, in *MB* II: 438.

41. Nóbrega to Sousa (in Lisbon), Bahia, 5 July 1559, in *MB* III: 86–86; Leite, *História da Companhia de Jesu*, 2: 51.

42. Nóbrega to Sousa (in Lisbon), Bahia, 5 July 1559, in *MB* III: 86–86; Nóbrega to Torres and fathers and brothers of Portugal, Bahia, 5 July 1559, in *MB* III: 51–52; Leite, *História da Companhia de Jesu*, 2: 51–60.

43. Blázquez to Laínez, Bahia, 1 Sept. 1561, in *MB* III: 400, 408; António Rodrigues to fathers and brothers of Bahia, Aldeia do Bom Jesus (Bahia), Aug. 1561, in *MB* III: 389.

44. Nóbrega to Torres and fathers and brothers of Portugal, Bahia, 5 July 1559, in *MB* III: 51–52.

45. Ibid.

46. Grã to Torres (in Lisbon), Bahia, 22 Sept. 1561, in *MB* III: 429; Blázquez to Laínez (in Rome), Bahia, 1 Sept. 1561, in *MB* III: 414–15.

47. Pires to the provincial of Portugal, Bahia 19 July 1558, in *MB* II: 463, 465; Blázquez to Laínez, Bahia, 1 Sept. 1561, in *MB* III: 397–99; Rodriguez to fathers and brothers of Bahia, Aldeia do Bom Jesus [Bahia], Aug. 1561, in *MB* III: 389.

48. Blázquez to Laínez, Bahia, 10 Sept. 1559, in *MB* III: 137; Blázquez to Loyola (in Rome), Bahia, 10 June 1557, in *MB* II: 385.

49. Leonardo do Vale commissioned by Grã to fathers and brothers of S. Roque (in Lisbon), Bahia, 26 June 1562, in *MB* III: 473–74.

50. Fernão Cardim reports that Indians in the Jesuit aldeias lived in large houses of up to two hundred persons. Each longhouse was ruled over by a chief; see "Enformacion de la provincia del Brasil," in Frédéric Mauro, ed., *Brésil au XVIIe siècle: Documents inédits relatifs à l'Atlantique portugais* (Coimbra: n.p., 1961), 164–65.

51. Rodrigues to fathers and brothers of Bahia, Aldeia do Bom Jesus, Bahia, Aug. 1561, in *MB* III: 389.

52. Nóbrega to Torres and fathers and brothers of Portugal, Bahia, 5 July 1559, in *MB* III: 60–63; João de Melo to Gonçalo de Melo (in Lisbon), Bahia, 13 Sept. 1560, in *MB* III: 281–83. Blázquez to Laínez (in Rome), Bahia, 1 Sept. 1561, in *MB* III: 415–16.

53. Blázquez to Laínez, Bahia, 1 Sept. 1561, in *MB* III: 397, 410.

54. See my discussion of epidemic disease in Brazil in the sixteenth century in Metcalf, *Go-Betweens and the Colonization of Brazil*, 119–51.

55. Vale to Melo (in Lisbon), Bahia, 12 May 1563, in *MB* IV: 9–22.

56. Ibid.; Anchieta to Laínez (in Rome), São Vicente, 8 Jan. 1565, in *MB* IV: 178. On this santidade and on santidades as expressions of indigenous resistance, see Metcalf, *Go-Betweens and the Colonization of Brazil*, 195–34; Metcalf, "AHR Forum: Millenarian Slaves? The Santidade de Jaguaripe and Slave Resistance in the Americas," *American Historical Review* 104 (1999): 1531–59; and Ronaldo Vainfas, *A heresia dos índios: Catolicismo e rebeldia no Brasil colonial* (São Paulo: Companhia das Letras, 1995).

57. "Informação dos primeiros aldeamentos na Bahia," in Anchieta, *Cartas*, 385–86.

58. Blázquez to Diego Mirón (in Lisbon), Bahia, 31 May 1564, in *MB* IV: 59–63; and Blázquez to Mirón (in Lisbon), Bahia, 13 Sept. 1564, in *MB* IV: 72–84.

59. Serafim Leite, "Os 'Capitulos' de Gabriel Soares de Sousa," *Ethnos* 2 (1942): 217–48; see also John M. Monteiro, "The Heathen Castes of Sixteenth-Century Portuguese America: Unity, Diversity, and the Invention of the Brazilian Indians," *Hispanic American Historical Review* 80 (2000): 697–719.

60. "Informação dos primeiros aldeamentos na Baía," in Anchieta, *Cartas*, 363–64; Nóbrega to Sousa (in Lisbon), Bahia, 5 July 1559, in *MB* III: 82. Although this report traditionally has been attributed to Anchieta, current Jesuit scholars suggest that Luis da Fonseca or Quirício Caxa were the probable authors. See "Razões de um acréscimo," in Anchieta, *Textos históricos*, 31–34.

61. Vale to fathers and brothers of São Roque (in Lisbon), Bahia, 26 June 1562, in *MB* III: 489–90.

62. "Informação dos primeiros aldeamentos na Baía," in Anchieta, *Cartas*, 365–66; Nóbrega to Sousa (in Lisbon), Bahia, 5 July 1559, in *MB* III: 82.

63. "Informação dos primeiros aldeamentos na Bahia," in Anchieta, *Cartas*, 366–67; 387–90; Nóbrega to Sousa (in Lisbon), Bahia, 5 July 1559, in *MB* III: 88–89.

64. "Informação dos primeiros aldeamentos na Bahia," in Anchieta, *Cartas*, 385.

65. Ibid.; Cardim, "Enformacion de la provincia," 143–44.

66. See Castelnau-L'Estoile, *Les ouvriers d'une vigne sterile*, 121–40.

2

Land and Economic Resources of Indigenous *Aldeias* in Rio de Janeiro

Conflicts and Negotiations, Seventeenth to Nineteenth Centuries

Maria Regina Celestino de Almeida
TRANSLATED BY Thomas H. Holloway

Indigenous *aldeias* in colonial Brazil were not ephemeral, nor were they simply Christian and Portuguese spaces where defeated and helpless Indians lived in the aftermath of exploitation and cultural loss on their way to quick extinction, as is often suggested in the literature. They were also constructed in the interest of Indians who, despite their immense losses, found new opportunities for survival in the aldeias. Land and security were surely the main attractions for people whose chances of resistance in the hinterland declined due to war, epidemic disease, and mass enslavement, and they settled in the aldeias as the lesser of evils. Through intense contact with the other ethnic and social groups gathered in the same space they were able to rebuild their social networks, cultures, and identities. Indians in the aldeias lived in restrictive and oppressive conditions, subject to special laws and forced labor, but they had some rights which they made every effort to protect. Intense disputes reflected the vested interests of several colonial social categories, for whom the aldeias had different functions and meanings. Indians, colonists, missionaries, and governmental authorities confronted one another in law and in practice over issues stemming from their varying positions on how they expected the aldeias to be organized and what functions they were to serve. In their subordinate position the Indians always lost the most, but even so they continued to struggle and make small gains, as many documents reveal. The most frequent conflicts involved issues relating to their labor, which was much sought after in the sixteenth and seventeenth centuries, and involving land. Conflicts over aldeia lands increased markedly beginning in the second half of the eighteenth century.[1]

Although restricted and limited when compared to the vast expanse of the Brazilian hinterland, the common lands of the aldeias were significant for the Indians who lived there, as shown by their efforts to protect them into the nineteenth century. They had moved to the aldeias, after all, seeking better ways to survive. The basis for subsistence was land for cultivation, the tools promised in the treaties of peace and settlement previously arranged with the Portuguese, and other types of return from the land they learned to use. When they settled in the aldeias they began the process of territorialization, in the sense developed by João Pacheco de Oliveira: they began to live in a fixed territory which was given, or at times forced upon them depending on the circumstances, by an external political and administrative authority.[2] That process implied significant changes in previous ways of living for several ethnic groups who in the course of altering their daily lives managed to rebuild their cultures, values, traditions, and identities.[3] Mixing among their own people and with other ethnic and social groups, they shared new experiences, alliances, and conflicts. Broadly speaking, people in the settlements developed a generic identity given or imposed by the colonizers: aldeia Indians, Christian subjects of the king of Portugal. In doing so indigenous peoples also reconstituted their relationship with the new territory, living differently from that time forward and conforming to the exigencies of the colonial regime.

Through centuries of integration into colonial rule, living very close to or even within urban centers and connected to their productive activities, Indians developed ways of doing business with aldeia lands, such as leasing, sales, and harvesting timber. Although such activities were to contribute to an increasing loss of their territory, the Indians tried to maintain control of the land and income from it, as shown in many documents dealing with disputes involving such activities. This chapter examines those conflicts and negotiations, in a colonial setting in which the aldeias were an important space where indigenous people were able to rebuild their identity, culture, and collective memories.[4] It focuses in particular on the interests, motivations, and initiatives of the Indians themselves, through documentation resulting from disputes over land and labor in the captaincy of Rio de Janeiro (see map 2).

ALDEIA LANDS

Establishing an aldeia meant, in the first instance, defining the land allocated to it. The land could be granted by the crown, by priests, or by private parties by various means including *sesmarias* (royal land grants) as was the case of several aldeias in Rio de Janeiro. The land was usually given in the name of an applicant, or applicants, who could be Indians, priests, or lay authorities, but the territory was then considered to be the collective patrimony of the Indians in the aldeia for whom the request was made, whether or not the language of the donation made specific reference to that detail. From the sixteenth to the nineteenth centuries authorities were intent on guaranteeing aldeia lands for the Indians through legislation and several other means favorable to them, in the face of recurring land takeovers. A royal decree of 1700 clearly defined the situation of aldeia lands, ordering that each settlement be given one square league "for the sustenance of the Indians and missionaries, with the proviso that each aldeia must include at least 100 couples." If there were fewer Indian families in adjoining areas the square league of land would be divided among them, with the guarantee that if the number increased they would get the square league they were due. According to the decree the land was given to the aldeias and not to the missionaries because "it belongs to the Indians and not to them, and because when the Indians have the land the missionaries also benefit, receiving what is necessary to help sustain them and to pay for the furnishings and worship services in the churches."[5] Parish priests received plots of land like those which "any colonists ordinarily receive who are not donataries or recipients of sesmarias, and they may have the lots around their houses" for raising their animals.[6]

    In the middle of the eighteenth century the Indian Directorate reform legislation, despite having promoted the presence of whites in aldeias, reaffirmed the rights of the Indians to the lands, declaring them to be the "primary and natural lords of those lands."[7] The Regulation of 1845, the primary Indian legislation of the post-independence period, issued in a period of intense conflicts over lands, again tried to guarantee the rights of aldeia Indians, decreeing that it was the obligation of the Director General to designate lands for cultivation in common, for cultivation by individual Indians, and to be rented out.[8] The Land Law of 1850, the most important private property legislation following independence, also reserved lands for the Indians, but the regulation of that law in 1854 made the assimilationist policies of the Brazilian Empire, formed after the break with Portugal, more explicit. It secured lands for Indians in usufruct as long as they were still considered Indians, stating that such land "may not be alienated without a specific action by the Imperial government conceding to the holders full ownership of it, as their state of civilization might permit."[9]

Thus the aldeia lands were always considered to be the patrimony of the Indians, even though they were frequently threatened or usurped by various other interests. The land was granted in order to guarantee their subsistence in the colonial world through agriculture and other economic uses which the Indians learned to exploit and defend. Once they were grouped in aldeias and settled on the new lands, the Indians could choose a spot to live with their families and cultivate the farm plots from which they would sustain themselves. Not all of them, however, derived their subsistence from agriculture. We should note that the specific sociocultural features of the various indigenous groups mixed together in the aldeias led to different adaptations, even as those cultural features were surely altered by the aldeia experience itself. Groups that were originally cultivators, for example, might turn more to hunting, fishing, or other activities outside the aldeias, while groups that had not previously farmed might learn to cultivate the soil and become accustomed to farming as aldeia residents. Economic resources in the aldeias included wages earned by Indians, the sale of their farm products, leasing out their lands, or the exploitation of other natural resources such as fish, timber, and the like.

A document from 1797 tells us that all the Indians in the aldeia of São Barnabé were employed, "some in agriculture, others in fishing, and others in making baskets, mats, and other curiosities of straw and reeds, painted in different colors, and pots of clay, and with these things they engage in commerce."[10] In 1727, in addition to fish and shellfish, the Indians of São Lourenço also sold clay pots for a living.[11] Sales from craft production, employment outside the aldeias, and the leasing of land were also important sources of subsistence and income for aldeia dwellers.

According to the laws in effect, the property of the aldeias was supposed to support the Indians as well as their churches and parish priests. Some funding very occasionally came from the royal treasury, but the colonial government was not obligated to allocate any funds for such purposes. The income of

Figure 9. No less than written accounts, visual depictions of indigenous peoples conveyed European biases and must be treated skeptically. This artist exaggerated the
exotic in his rendering of a dance by inhabitants of one of the many native villages that
remained along the Atlantic seaboard long after the initial conquest era. Source: Debret, *Voyage pittoresque.* Public domain access: http://www.brasiliana.usp.br/bbd/
handle/1918/624510033

the aldeias in the late eighteenth and early nineteenth centuries came mainly
from the rental of their lands. Although it was not much, such income was
mostly spent to support the churches and Indians in need, thus relieving the
town treasury of such expenses and giving rise to many disputes with colonists
and non-Indian town councils who tried to gain control over such resources
for themselves. Since the seventeenth century aldeia Indians had learned to
view their lands in business terms, engaging in rentals and sales, despite such
practices giving rise to serious problems of land loss.

LAND TRANSACTIONS: RENTING, SALES, AND CONFLICTS

By law the lands included in sesmaria grants could be alienated (i.e., sold or
rented) only under certain conditions under which, if not fulfilled, the land
would revert to the crown. The failure of both Indians and priests to comply

with those legal requirements was a constant of the colonial era. Despite the many conflicts that resulted, one of the main sources of income of the aldeias came from renting out their lands, which was clearly in the interest of both Indians and aldeia administrators. São Lourenço and São Barnabé, aldeias which were very close to the city of Rio de Janeiro, stand out in this regard from the early colonial period. It was common for renters to unilaterally increase the area they controlled, giving rise to many legal disputes. There were laws intended to keep the aldeia lands in the hands of the Indians, but disputes were never-ending and, despite efforts to resist, the tendency over time was the persistent reduction of their patrimony. Occupation and use were always the standard means of appropriating lands in the colonial era. The law of sesmarias, which made the crown the final arbiter of land grants, and the resulting land titles secured by Indians and non-Indians were the sources of legitimacy and the main basis for judicial struggles over land. But in the society of the Old Regime, before Brazil achieved independence, judicial rulings were made, in practice, according to the specifics of each situation. The will of the sovereign, with the recommendation of his advisors, was the ultimate authority.

The Indians of São Barnabé and São Lourenço were mostly employed outside the aldeias, in the service of private individuals or the king. Thus their income was mainly from wages, the rental of their lands, and the sale of craft production, and those activities sustained the aldeias up to the early nineteenth century. Despite alienation of their lands from the seventeenth century and perhaps earlier, including rentals, sales, and trading plots of land, the record shows their interest in maintaining control over their territory and income from it, first together with the priests, and then on their own account. In São Lourenço and São Barnabé, from the seventeenth century (1659) to the nineteenth century (1828), there was always a preoccupation with measurements and surveys which the Indians, priests, governmental officials, and at times even the renters among the colonists recognized as the only legal way of trying to guarantee the boundaries of Indian land adjacent to rented land.

In 1727 the governor of Rio de Janeiro was called upon to adjudicate a request by the Indians of São Lourenço to establish the boundaries of their land. He cited the 1568 grant of the land in question to Araribóia, baptized Martim Afonso de Sousa, a famed native headman, Portuguese ally, founder of the aldeia in the sixteenth century, and its first *capitão-mor* (militia commandant). "With the approval and consent of the priests," the governor explained, "the Indians sold some land in order to build a church" and they traded other plots, as a result of which many claims emerged, to be resolved "in court to the satisfaction of the parties involved, as commonly happens in these conquests." ("Conquests," in this sense, referred generically to Portugal's overseas possessions.) The governor suggested that a formal survey be carried out to determine the boundaries of the lands in question.[12] The declaration by the governor was confirmed by the Indians and priests who also commented on the sales and rentals of land carried out on their own initiative and generally justified by the need to support the churches and worship services in them. Still, they complained of the abuses of the colonists who always expanded their holdings by taking over more land.

Other sales took place in the aldeias of São Pedro and Nossa Senhora da Guia, the latter in the region known as Mangaratiba. In the former, in 1718, a secular priest referred to the lands the Jesuits had bought from the Indians in Campos Novos.[13] And in Mangaratiba in 1806 an Indian was accused of improperly selling a farm to a white man. According to the information presented, the Indian had repossessed the farm without returning the payment to the buyer. When he was forced to return the money he did so only after stealing all the improvements on the property.[14] This case suggests that private individuals engaged in such dealings, but no clarification was provided on that point.

From these cases we can infer that the presence of outsiders in the aldeias should not be interpreted simply as land appropriation, because several of these situations resulted from initiatives by the Indians themselves and the priests who had an interest in the transaction or perhaps were charged with mediating disputes and land takeovers through these dealings. Nevertheless, they gave rise to many conflicts, which became more serious as the colony developed, the number of colonists increased, and land became scarcer. The conflicts in São Barnabé and São Lourenço began in the seventeenth century or earlier and revolved mainly around the surveys and demarcation of the lands of Indians and outsiders. They continued until at least 1828, when a survey was carried out in the aldeia of São Lourenço at the request of a non-Indian settler because the Indian capitão-mor of the aldeia objected to the boundary markers the petitioner had set out on his property. The capitão-mor in question, José Cardoso de Souza, was probably a scion of the Martim Afronso de Sousa lineage, descendants of Araribóia.[15] Now, well into the nineteenth century, José Cardoso de Souza was again involved in one of the many verifications of the boundaries of his aldeia based on the founding document of the ses-maria drawn up in 1659, which he presented as evidence in the case.[16] There were many requests for surveys and complaints filed against the usurpation of aldeia lands conveyed to the royal authorities by priests and Indians in São Lourenço and São Barnabé, reflecting the repeated disregard for the laws and the many rulings and royal proclamations issued in the aldeias' favor. In their petitions the Indians commonly invoked on their behalf their many services rendered to the king, the need to relieve the poverty of their aldeia, and their zeal to support the church.

In the early eighteenth century there were many land disputes in the aldeia of São Pedro, but the situation there seems to have been reversed— the colonists of the district of Cabo Frio, where the aldeia was located, felt

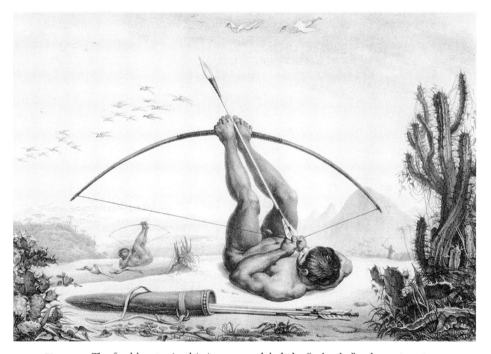

Figure 10. The fowl hunter in this image was labeled a "caboclo," a derogatory term equivalent to "half-breed." Villagers of indigenous descent who lived near the city of Rio de Janeiro did not simply cling to traditional ways of life. They participated in the colonial economy, earning wages as manual laborers, renting lands granted to them by the crown, and selling crafts. Source: Debret, *Voyage pittoresque.* Public domain access: http://www.brasiliana.usp.br/bbd/handle/1918/624510019

that their interests were hurt by the extensive territory claimed by the aldeia. They submitted a request through the town council that the aldeia lands be broken up, and accused the Jesuits not only of requesting land for an aldeia that was never formally created, but also of buying land from the Indians on which to establish a cattle ranch to support the Jesuit college. The dispute focused on Búzios point, where the Indians had for many years engaged in fishing, and where the colonists said that for several years some of their number who had received sesmarias also planted crops and fished. Both the rector of the Jesuit college and its legal advisor filed statements recognizing that the land had been granted for an aldeia that was never established. But they said the failure was due to a lack of sufficient Indians, and not the fault of the Jesuits. The two statements stressed the size of the aldeia lands, which the legal advisor said was one of the largest administered by the Jesuits and the rector said was three times larger than the town of Cabo Frio. Both mentioned the importance of the aldeia for the defense of Cabo Frio, "because the corsairs fear it."[17] The priests proposed an amicable agreement by which they would keep Búzios point and the colonists would get a half a league of land closer to the town, and open fishing rights. The rector, meanwhile, dropped his request that the Jesuits' title to Búzios point be confirmed, leaving it as public land.[18] He probably took that position as an admission that the Jesuits had no legal claim on the land in question. By all accounts, including the one submitted by the priests themselves, the Jesuits did not legally own the lands of Búzios point, where for years the Indians had fished and the priests kept some cattle. In the end all rulings in the case were favorable to the Indians, not based on points of law, but due to the relevant services rendered to the king in defense of the area, because compared to the Indians the colonists were so few, so poor, and not up to the task. A royal decree of 1727 ordered that the fishing rights be kept by the aldeia and the Indians who lived there.[19]

During the eighteenth century, conflicts over aldeia lands in Rio de Janeiro became more serious as public lands became more scarce and the demand for land increased. The expulsion of the Jesuits from Brazil and the rest of the Portuguese Empire in 1759 further complicated the situation because lands confiscated from the order by the crown were then put into play and requested as sesmarias. At the same time, the Indians lost powerful allies in their confrontations with colonists. It was a period of many conflicts and much encroachment on aldeia lands, which, although they continued to belong to the Indians, became more vulnerable due to legislation promoting the presence of non-Indians in their midst. In addition, the socioeconomic development of the captaincy led to the conquest and incorporation of distant hinterlands, the creation of new aldeias on these frontiers, and increasing threats to land in the aldeias now secularized in the wake of the Indian Directorate legislation. In the older aldeias several generations of different ethnic and social groups had settled or become territorialized, as Pacheco de Oliveira puts it,[20] in a politico-administrative space which had been given to them or imposed on them, but which had come to constitute a basic reference point for survival in a colonial world—a space where cultures, histories, and identities were rearticulated. Whether it was granted, imposed, or acquired through agreement, defeat, or capitulation, the Indians had taken over the physical space of the aldeias as their own collective patrimony, which they continued to make every effort to defend into the nineteenth century.

Despite the assimilationist nature of indigenous legislation of the Pombaline era—which prevailed from the 1750s to the 1790s, even though Pombal himself lost power in 1777—there was an effort to guarantee continuity in the rights of Indians to the land. With the introduction of the Directorate in Rio de Janeiro, care was taken to ensure that the Indians were not encroached upon, despite the incentives promoting the presence of non-Indians in the aldeias and the resulting increase in land rentals.

The establishment of businesses on the aldeias, such as taverns and mills, was permitted by the reforms, and this happened quite frequently in Rio de Janeiro. Such practices could be a significant opening for renters to encroach on aldeia lands, but they were not always successful, as several cases show. In 1773, for example, captain André Alves Pereira Vianna, a renter in the aldeia of São Barnabé, which by that time was called a *vila* (formally constituted town), claimed to be the owner of the port located there on rented land, even though the documents showed that he had "constructed only the improvements on the land, which he claims are his."[21] According to information provided by Judge Manoel Francisco da Silva Veiga, captain Vianna owned no land there but had only added the improvements, besides being an undesirable renter whose presence was detrimental to the Indians. The Directorate specified that "the lands of private individuals should be taken in order to establish Indian lands." In order to comply with that principle, the marquis of Lavradio, Brazil's viceroy and the captaincy's governor, ordered that the improvements should be appraised and the land "that this man holds in his possession in those parts" should be expropriated and "used for the establishment of the vila, because all the land there is necessary for that purpose."[22] The language of the order suggests that the land might have gone to the vila rather than to the Indians, but we have no further information on that point. There is also the compelling example of the aldeia of São Francisco Xavier de Itaguaí, located on the rich estate of Santa Cruz which had belonged to the Jesuits. After the expulsion of the Jesuits the aldeia suffered many difficulties with new administrators who wanted to extinguish it, and those problems worsened when a sugar mill was built within the aldeia. Without describing in detail the long and complex dispute that ensued, it is worth noting that despite the conflict pitting major economic interests against a handful of "miserable and degenerate Indians," the eventual ruling on the case was in favor of the latter.[23]

ECONOMIC RESOURCES: INTERESTS AND ARGUMENTS

The direct involvement of the priests in the conflicts and dealings with Indian lands might lead to the conclusion that the Indians were motivated only by the interests of "their priests," since the economic resources mainly worked in the interests of the priests and their churches. In my view that is mistaken. To be sure, the sources contain information that apparently supports that idea, such as declarations by the Indians themselves and documents from different periods confirming that income from the aldeias went primarily to satisfy religious purposes. The first priority was the church and the worship services held in it, then the parish priest, followed by the needs of the Indians such as food, clothing, care for the poor, and the education of children.[24] In 1758, for example, discussing the elevation of São Lourenço to the status of parish church, the bishop declared that all the production of the aldeia "must for now go for repairs to the church, until it is in decent condition."[25] Requests for land, in both São Barnabé and São Lourenço, were generally justified by the need to support the churches. It would be overly simplistic, however, to conclude that the resources of the aldeias were used exclusively to satisfy the interests of the priests. The suggestion that Indians were zealous supporters of the churches and worship services, it seems to me, is inconsistent with the attitudes of indifference and attempts to escape religious obligations imposed by the priests.[26] The apparent contradiction can be resolved if we examine the different meanings that could be derived from the same discourse, and the

Figure 11. Like these washerwomen in Rio de Janeiro, urban Indians comprised a minority population in many Brazilian cities and towns during the late colonial period. Only recently have historians begun to retrieve their stories. Source: Debret, *Voyage pittoresque.* Public domain access: http://www.brasiliana.usp.br/bbd/handle/1918/624510036

Indians' considerable ability to appropriate colonial legal structures and reinterpret them to serve their own values and needs.[27] One might expect that the Indians, in seeking to make their claims, would reproduce discourses consistent with what was expected of them, consistent with lived experience. With regard to the defense of their land and economic resources, as good Christian subjects and faithful servants of the king, they referred to the need to guarantee their sustenance and the income of the aldeias in order to support the churches and worship services, as well as to satisfactorily carry out their duties to the king. The symbolic significance of the churches in the aldeias, and thus what they must have represented for the aldeia Indians, also needs to be taken into account. Since the sixteenth century the churches had been the foundations on which the aldeias had been built. The names of the aldeias were commonly derived from the saints to which the churches were dedicated. Because the churches symbolized the creation and the existence of the aldeias themselves, it is not surprising that the petitions would be worded around the churches and their protection. The loss of the church could have meant the loss of the aldeia itself. It is no wonder, then, that in their legal pleas the Indians always seemed to be preoccupied with the protection of their churches.

According to Pasquale Petrone, in São Paulo the town council and the governor of the captaincy controlled the income from the aldeias and little of it reverted to the Indians or their communities.[28] I believe that in Rio de Janeiro the Jesuits or lay administrators controlled aldeia income, but all indications are that the Indians were quite involved in its disposition, as shown by several cases in which such economic resources were in dispute. In 1779, for example, when Indians rebelled against the director of São Barnabé, there were accusations that the judge who was conservator of the aldeia's economic resources neglected to use them correctly in the Indians' interest.[29] In 1799 the Indians in the same aldeia demanded the return of a parcel of their land that had been taken over by an ambitious captain.[30] They said they had a right to the land by virtue of a sesmaria grant, that it had been duly surveyed and marked out, and they had no problems with neighboring landowners or with the renters on the disputed property who paid rental to their conservatorship. They denounced the captain for usurping a plot of land which caused them "great loss, because on that land there were six renters whose lease rights have for many years passed from one renter to another, all of whom planted and cultivated well for the increase of the royal tithes and the good of the republic."[31] They concluded by saying that they had not taken their claim to the viceroy because those who had the duty to defend them supported the irregular survey of the lands taken over by the captain and, in addition, they were fearful that their petition would be misplaced in the secretariat, "because the secretary there is a brother-in-law of the defendant."[32] The Overseas Council, which ruled on such colonial disputes on behalf of the crown, suggested further investigation of the case. We do not know its final resolution, but it is clear that the Indians were interested in protecting the rental income, even if most of it might have gone mainly for administrative costs for the aldeia, as the end of their claim seems to suggest. In another case in 1794, the district judge for the city of Rio de Janeiro reported that due to the diligence of Capitão-mor Manoel Jesus de Souza the income from renting the pastures of the aldeia of São Lourenço had increased.[33]

A particularly significant example of the Indians' interest in their rental property occurred in the aldeia of Santo Antônio de Guarulhos in the eighteenth century. In a dispute with the Jesuits over who was to receive the rental payments, the Indians lost and the Jesuits won the right to collect the rents. The Indians' response, however, caused the colonists to pay rent twice: first to the Jesuits by legal decision, and then to the Indians, due to threats.[34] In this case the Capuchin Order was responsible for the administration of the aldeia, which might suggest that the Indians took action in favor of the priests and that the rents the Indians collected would go to the Capuchins. Although the available information makes it impossible to reject such an interpretation entirely, it is not likely, in view of the many examples of disobedience and disputes showing that the Indians were not easily manipulated by the priests.[35] This is not to deny that the Indians often took actions to please the priests, but it is necessary to recognize that the motives of the Indians, the bases of which are not always easy to discern, were also served in such cases. We should also consider the confrontational behavior of the Indians with respect to the missionaries, including abandoning the aldeia. Such actions do not seem consistent with taking a rebellious stance simply to please the priests. If the Indians threatened the colonists in order to obtain the rents which would serve the interests of the aldeia, as well as possibly the interests of the priests, the Indians must have expected some benefit from that action.

In addition to rental payments and wages earned by Indians, sales stemming from craft production, fishing, and timber harvesting were other sources of income that guaranteed a livelihood for the Indians, and from which they benefited. The Indians of São Pedro who, as we have seen, practiced very little agriculture, derived their income from hunting and especially fishing. In addition they engaged in the harvesting of salt and exploitation of forest resources, both of which gave rise to problems because they were prohibited activities.

Salt came from Portugal and was a monopoly of the royal treasury, and before 1801 it was prohibited to produce salt in the colony. According to Vivaldo Coaracy, in addition to the Indians who harvested salt in Cabo Frio, the colonial settlers in the area derived their livelihood "almost exclusively from the salt industry."[36] At times, due to the lack of sufficient salt coming from Portugal, merchants were authorized to acquire it in Cabo Frio. All the prohibitions, however, failed to stop "contraband in the product and its extraction in Cabo Frio."[37] The Indians of São Pedro participated actively in

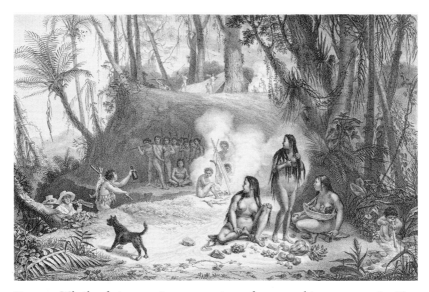

Figure 12. Whether facing ongoing pressure to conform or seeking new opportunities, many natives strengthened their ties with Brazilian society as the colonial period progressed. Others, even after being baptized and learning Portuguese, chose to keep their distance, such as those who lived in this encampment along the border separating Rio de Janeiro and Minas Gerais. The approaching visitors offer them alcohol. Debret, *Voyage pittoresque.* Public domain access: http://www.brasiliana.usp.br/bbd/handle/1918/624510020

this trade. According to Silva, "with little effort" they collected "copious amounts of salt in pits or shallow tanks where water from the sea is allowed to enter, where it soon crystallizes under the heat of the sun, and the Portuguese or Brazilian government has not discovered a way to take advantage of this, to the benefit of the Indians."[38] It is quite likely that the Indians were taking advantage of it on their own.

The harvest of timber in the indigenous aldeias was also a prohibited activity that was profitable, exploited by colonists and by Indians who were accused of working for the non-Indian residents for wages and also of selling the colonists permits to cut timber in the aldeia forests.[39] The district judge and conservator José Albano Fragoso went after the perpetrators, as the Count of Rezende had done earlier.[40] Investigation of the situation confirmed that the timber harvesters had acted with the permission of aldeia officials, "who illegally agreed to this for insignificant sums. The most notorious among them was the Indian Domingos dos Santos Ferreira who, in addition to having some education, is the owner of an establishment and some slaves."[41] His accomplice was found to be "the parish priest João de Almeida Barreto who, upon receiving considerable sums for the purchase of instruments of worship for the church, gave permission for so much devastation" of the aldeia woodlands.[42] In 1802 violators who were building two boats without permission claimed that they were contributing to the increase in shipping, to which the district judge replied that such activity did not give them the right to take what was not theirs, "as it is certain that the Indians make their living from making canoes."[43]

Among the transgressors was Plácido dos Santos who made a deal with the Indian officials of the aldeia to pay them fifty *mil-réis* (the Portuguese currency) for permission to cut timber. The Indians admitted to the arrangement, saying they had given the money to the parish priest who used it to buy "a silver censer and incense boat." The priest was severely reprimanded because instead of doing his duty to provide instruction to the Indians he set a bad example by buying needless objects at a time when the church needed repairs. The conservator was especially critical of Domingos dos Santos Ferreira, the principal Indian accused in the case, for pretending to defend indigenous interests, complaining of the theft of timber which prevented the Indians from making their wooden bowls, when the truth was that he had taken money "to let them cut trees . . . and openly sold the timber they provided to him." He was also accused of acting like a judge among the Indians, granting and taking away lands and settling disputes, for which he was ordered to be put under arrest.[44]

This case involving timber shows the individual interests of the Indians in business deals and conflicts with white people. Evidence suggests that such dealings took place according to the private objectives of the Indians involved, rather than the interests of the community, as the example of Domingos dos Santos Ferreira shows. Another Indian involved in the illegal lumber business was captain Miguel Soares Martins, who according to Silva was rich and educated and owned two slaves and two horses.[45] The Indians removed him from office in 1805.[46]

To say that most of the claims made by aldeia Indians were collective in nature is not to deny the importance of individual ambition, which was surely exacerbated in a colonial situation. We have seen the case in Mangaritiba of an Indian accused of irregularities in the sale of a farm to a colonist. To deny this sort of motivation on the part of Indians is, in my view, to return to an interpretation that tends to idealize them, considering the Indians to be pure and incorruptible and concerned only with the ideals of the community. Indians, like individuals in any other social group, obviously had their own interests, which clearly varied according to their life experiences and historical circumstances. The desire for material goods, which was strongly promoted if not originally acquired in the colonial world, clearly exercised a greater or lesser attraction on different individuals in a given group. In this regard it is no coincidence, in the case of timber harvests, that the two Indians accused of violations were among the six Indians of the aldeia of São Pedro who had acquired some property. Individual desires and ambitions on the part of some aldeia Indians, however, did not prevent the collective struggles and actions which generally characterized their behavior. While some officials, as we have seen, acted in their private interest, they did not neglect the good of the community, which was for them essential because it not only gave them their privileged status, but also the patrimony that was always considered a collective good. It is also important to note those cases in which leaders who did not take care of the interests of the community were removed from office, as in the case of captain Miguel Soares Martins in São Pedro.

This is not to assert that the Indians kept up a united front simply to guarantee access to material goods that they received collectively. Aldeia Indians derived their collective identity from living in common and using the shared lands of the aldeias, whether to plant crops or to derive income in other ways. Indigenous traditions, cultures and identities were reconstituted in the shared use of the territory the Portuguese colonial regime had set aside for them. The several uses the Indians made of that land, first together with the priests and then on their own, were an expression of their daily lives and the needs that arose over time, varying by circumstances. Through this process they established the connections of group solidarity that were manifested mainly in the struggle to maintain their collective patrimony.

AGRARIAN CONFLICTS, POLITICAL ACTION, AND INDIGENOUS IDENTITY

Living in the aldeias over three centuries of the colonial regime, different indigenous groups mixed and transformed themselves, building new forms of identification that were firmly rooted in the land that had been given to them as community property. In general they identified themselves by the aldeia where they lived, as shown in the archival record. As they sent their petitions to the king they extolled the history of efforts in defense of the Portuguese Empire and often emphasized the role of their aldeia in those struggles. Most of the aldeias, after all, were established for purposes of defense, and that fact was always mentioned in the claims the Indians submitted. The leaders of São Lourenço, for example, traced their origins to the creation of the aldeia, dating their history to the conquest of Rio de Janeiro and extolling the actions of their ancestors.

Such collective political action gave them a sense of uniting around a common objective, which helped to develop the idea of group identity and of belonging to an aldeia and to the Portuguese Empire itself. In the claims made by the Indians one can perceive two elements distinguished by Max Weber as essential for the formation of ethnic identity: political action in common and a subjective sense of community.[47] Indians went to court for a variety of reasons, but in the captaincy of Rio de Janeiro the struggle to secure the land of the aldeias seems to have been especially important as a source of unity which the Indians maintained into the nineteenth century. When they were grouped into aldeias the Indians acquired a specific juridical status, at odds with the other colonial social categories with which they interacted. The Indians were unified by the idea of belonging to the aldeias, along with sharing a common past and engaging in collective political action to secure the rights they had been granted.[48]

In addition to political action, in thinking about the constitution of a broader ethnicity in the aldeias, two other important aspects might be considered. Both were also noted by Weber and emphasized as important by Frederick Barth and Abner Cohen.[49] One is the idea of the organizational character and subjective feeling of belonging to a group. Another is the idea of contact and interaction, in contrast to separatism, as a condition for the creation of ethnic groups. According to Cohen, such groups become stronger and maintain their distinctiveness to the extent that the political and economic differences that are connected to their ethnic differences are preserved.

If we consider what happened inside the aldeias with the mixture and interaction of various ethnic groups who came to share a political, economic, and social situation defined by law specifically for them, it is not difficult to identify the elements indicated by the authors just cited. Beginning with the arrival of the Europeans, distinct ethnic groups all became Indians, mixing among themselves and with other segments of colonial society in the aldeias, sharing the common condition of being natives of the land and of having all become Indians, more specifically Indians of aldeia X or Y, and remaining in that juridical status until the nineteenth century. They mixed together in a unique space in the Portuguese colonial administrative structure, where in the condition of aldeia Indians they lived a new and common experience that put them in a situation at odds with the other social groups of the colony. We then see in the aldeias the formation of groups comprised of several other groups, which organized themselves for daily life based on a common territory assigned to them by an external power, to return to the notion of territorialization developed by Pacheco de Oliveira.[50] On that plot of land they eventually formed an organizational group, in Barth's sense, becoming unified by the subjective feeling of being members of the aldeia. They thus came together, distinguishing themselves from other groups by the condition that the law itself had imposed on them. From the sixteenth to the nineteenth centuries the aldeia Indians saw themselves and were seen by others as having that identity. In this we see the definition of boundaries (self-attributed and attributed by others) which Barth emphasizes as the fundamental issue in thinking about ethnic groups. Individual members can move about, as Barth says, but ethnic groups persist as long as their members feel themselves to be different from the rest.[51]

While Indian identities were reconstructed in the colonial aldeias, it is also important to understand the intense process of ethnic mixing that went on there, which accelerated markedly after the Pombaline reforms. By the end of the eighteenth century and the beginning of the nineteenth century, aldeia residents still presented themselves as Indians in the struggle to claim their rights. By that time it was likely impossible to differentiate them from the other ethnic and social groups with whom they interacted by criteria of language, blood ties, or specific physical characteristics. According to current theoretical and conceptual trends in history and anthropology they had all become *mestiços* (racially or culturally mixed), without necessarily ceasing to be Indians.[52]

From the mid-eighteenth century and into the nineteenth the archival record is ambiguous as to whether the residents of the aldeias should be classified as Indians or mestiços. Government authorities and colonists pointed to ethnic mixing and the disappearance of Indians from the aldeias to justify the takeover of their lands and to eliminate aldeia status. The residents themselves challenged that discourse, however, submitting claims based on the rights due to aldeia residents.[53]

According to Cohen, groups have an interest in maintaining their distinct identity as long as political and economic conditions are linked to ethnicity.[54] That seems to have been a strong motivation for the aldeia Indians to resist assimilationist policies. In Roberto C. de Oliveira's phrase, they maintained their "constrastive identity" in relation to the settlers with whom they interacted and even shared the same space.[55]

By the end of the eighteenth and beginning of the nineteenth century, in the old colonial zone, the aldeia Indians seem to have been the social actors most interested, if not the only ones interested, in maintaining the status of the aldeias. In large measure this is explained, I think, by the fact that despite all the changes that had taken place, the main function of the aldeias for the Indians persisted, i.e., they still constituted a space for survival in the unsettled and threatening world of the colonial regime. The struggles in this later period focused mainly on maintaining the patrimony to which they had rights as a group: the lands and economic resources of the aldeias. Group political action to maintain those rights was the main reason, I believe, why Indian identities were maintained and even strengthened in this period, in the face of pressure to recognize them as mestiços. Being an Indian or not meant securing or losing the collective lands of the aldeias. Conflicts over land, or even disputes over ethnic classifications, can be seen as political and social conflicts, as Guillaume Boccara has argued.[56]

The indigenous aldeias of Rio de Janeiro were extinguished in the course of the nineteenth century, ending a long and gradual process that began in the era of the Pombaline reforms and lasted to the middle of the nineteenth century, characterized by advances and retreats. The retreats—impediments to the process of extinction—were largely due to action by the Indians themselves. The dominant discourse characterized the Indians as few in number, ethnically mixed, living in poor villages, and in decline. But the residents of the aldeias, whether Indian or mestiço, continued their efforts to maintain the aldeias and community life for nearly a century after the assimilationist project launched by Pombal. Their common land was the basic element that held the aldeias together. For the Indians it meant a space for their resocialization, where they shared the common experience of struggle and survival in the colonial world and rebuilt cultures, memories, and identities. The collective aldeia land guaranteed by Portuguese law was for the Indians something of considerable value, which functioned far beyond subsistence. Indians engaged in many conflicts and negotiations over land, spurred on by their own interests and motivations, which continually changed as colonial life changed.

NOTES

1. M. Regina Celestino de Almeida, *Metamorfoses indígenas: Identidade e cultura nas aldeias coloniais do Rio de Janeiro* (Rio de Janeiro: Arquivo Nacional, 2003). I thank the Conselho Nacional de Desenvolvimento Científico e Tecnológico (CNPq) and Fundação de Amparo à Pesquisa do Estado do Rio de Janeiro (FAPERJ) for suppport of this research. I also thank the editors of the online journal *Nuevo Mundo Mundos Nuevos* for permission to publish this chapter, an expanded version of my article "Tierras y recursos económicos de las aldeas indígenas de Rio de Janeiro: Conflictos y negociaciones (siglos XVII–XIX)," *Nuevo Mundo Mundos Nuevos*, Debates (2011), http://nuevomundo.revues.org/60531. Abbreviations used in the notes are as follows: Arquivo Histórico Ultramarino, Lisbon (AHU), Documentos Avulsos do Rio de Janeiro (RJA); Arquivo Nacional, Rio de Janeiro (ANRJ); Eduardo Castro e Almeida, ed., *Inventário dos documentos relativos ao Brasil existentes no Archivo da Marinha e Ultramar* (Rio de Janeiro: Bibliotheca Nacional, 1913–1936) (RJCA).
2. João Pacheco de Oliveira, "Uma Etnologia dos 'índios misturados': Situação colonial, territorialização e fluxos culturais," in *A viagem de volta: Etnicidade, política e reelaboração cultural no nordeste indígena*, ed. João Pacheco de Oliveira (Rio de Janeiro: ContraCapa, 1999), 20.
3. Jonathan Hill, "Introduction," in *History, Power, and Identity: Ethnogenesis in the Americas, 1942–1992*, ed. Jonathan D. Hill (Iowa City: University of Iowa Press, 1996).
4. Almeida, *Metamorfoses indígenas*, 257–78.
5. "Alvará régio pelo qual se mandou dar a cada Missão uma légua de terras, em quadra, para a sustentação dos Índios e missionários," Lisbon, 23 Nov. 1700, in RJCA, vol. 6, 519.
6. Ibid.
7. "Diretório que se deve observar nas Povoações dos Índios do Pará e Maranhão," §80, in Carlos de Araujo Moreira Neto, *Índios da Amazônia: De maioria a minoria (1750–1850)* (Rio de Janeiro: Vozes, 1988), 199. The law was issued in 1757, following the expulsion of the Jesuits, to regulate the operation of the aldeias and the activities of the Indians in them. Its assimilationist policies, in large part unsuccessful, were intended to transform the aldeias into Portuguese towns and erase the distinction between whites and Indians in order to promote the settlement of whites in the aldeias, contrary to all previous legislation.
8. Decree no. 426, 24 June 1845, "Regulamento acerca das missões de catequese, e civilização dos índios," in José Oscar Beozzo, *Leis e regimentos das missões: Política indigenista no Brasil* (São Paulo: Loyola, 1983), 174.

9. "Lei das Terras de 1850, artigo 3," in *Coletânea: Legislação agrária, legislação de registros públicos, jurisprudência*, ed. Maria Jovita Valente Wolney (Brasília: Ministério Extraordinário para Assuntos Fundiários, 1983), 371; Márcia Motta, "Terra, nação e tradições inventadas (uma outra abordagem sobre a Lei de Terras de 1850)," in *Nação e poder: as dimensões da história*, ed. Sônia Mendonça and Márcia Motta (Niterói: EDUFF, 1983), 81–92.

10. "Descrição dos vários distritos da capitania do Rio de Janeiro feita por ordem do Ilmo. e Exmo. Senhor Conde de Rezende Vice Rei e Capitão General de Mar e Terra do Estado do Brasil, 1797," AHU, RJA, cx. 165, doc. 62.

11. "Requerimento do capitão mor dos índios da aldeia de São Lourenço da capitania do Rio de Janeiro, 1727," RJCA, vol. 6, 481–82.

12. "Informação do Governador Luiz Vahia Monteiro sobre a pretensão dos índios da Aldeia de S. Lourenço, Rio de Janeiro, 22 de junho de 1726," RJCA, vol. 6, 482.

13. "Requerimento do Padre Bertholomeo de Jesus, clérigo do hábito de São Pedro (anterior a 18 de setembro de 1718)," AHU, RJA, cx. 11, doc. 32.

14. Joaquim Norberto de Souza Silva, "Memória histórica e documentada das aldeias de índios da província do Rio de Janeiro," *Revista do Instituto Histórico e Geográfico do Brasil*, vol. 17, 3ª série, no. 14–15 (1854): 434.

15. In the course of the seventeenth and eighteenth centuries several of Araribóia's descendants occupied the same position, proudly making the connection to their noble ancestor and their valuable service to the king over the generations. See Almeida, *Metamorfoses indígenas*, 152–61.

16. "Auto de exame e averiguação feita, ao marco que divide a linha do sertão da sesmaria dos índios da aldeia de S. Lourenço pelo lado da Boa Viagem, e fazenda do Saco de S. Francisco Xavier que foi dos padres jesuítas," in Silva, "Memória histórica," no. 15: 339–40.

17. "Cartas sobre as terras dos jesuítas em Cabo Frio, 1722," AHU, RJA, cx. 13, doc. 79.

18. "Sobre as queixas dos moradores de Cabo Frio contra os jesuítas e suas terras, 26 de novembro de 1722," AHU, RJA, cx. 13, doc. 135.

19. Ibid.

20. Oliveira, "Uma Etnologia dos 'índios misturados,'" *A viagem de volta*, 20.

21. "Ofício do Marquês do Lavradio a Martinho de Melo e Castro, Rio de Janeiro, 20 July 1773," ANRJ, cód. 69, vol. 02, fl. 88.

22. Ibid.

23. Silva, "Memória histórica," no. 14: 182–94. In this dispute it should be noted that the aldeia Indians had the support of the settlers in the parish who wanted to elevate the aldeia/parish to the formal status of *vila* (town) in the same location, in opposition to the owner of the mill constructed in the aldeia, who wanted to move the new administrative entity. They won their case, created the vila, and organized the town council, which ended up decreeing the extinction of the aldeia using the same argument invoked earlier by the mill owner. The temporary alliance with the settlers enabled the Indians to keep their aldeia status for a

while longer, even though the opposing interests again emerged leading to its extinction. Once again the Indians lost, but the case reflects both the fluidity and complexity of the alliances and common interests among different groups involved, and the direct participation of the Indians in the confrontations where their interests came into play. See M. Regina Celestino de Almeida, "Política Indigenista e Etnicidade: Estratégias indígenas no processo de extinção das aldeias do Rio de Janeiro. Século XIX," *Anuario IEHS* (2007): 219–33.

24. Silva, "Memória histórica," no. 15: 341.

25. "Sobre o extracto das cartas do Bispo do Rio de Janeiro. 1758," AHU, RJA, cx. 62.

26. Almeida, *Metamorfoses indígenas*, 126–42.

27. Hill, "Introduction."

28. Pasquale Petrone, *Aldeamentos paulistas* (São Paulo: EDUSP, 1995).

29. "Consulta do Conselho Ultramarino sobre a representação de João Batista da Costa, 1780," AHU, RJA, cx. 22, doc. 33; and *Documentos históricos da Biblioteca Nacional do Rio de Janeiro*, vol. 95: 88–91.

30. "Consulta do Conselho Ultramarino sobre o requerimento do capitão mor e índios da Povoação de vila Nova de São José d'El Rei, 5 de dezembro de 1799," AHU, RJA, cx. 176, doc. 9.

31. Ibid.

32. Ibid.

33. "Consulta do Conselho Ultramarino sobre o requerimento de Manoel de Jesus e Souza, 7 de janeiro de 1796," AHU, RJA, cx. 162, doc. 2.

34. "Representação dos Índios da Aldeia de Santo Antônio dos Campos dos Goitacazes, capitania do Rio de Janeiro, acerca da demanda que tinham com os Padres da Companhia de Jesus, por causa das terras, que estes tinham conseguido que se lhes dessem em sesmaria, ocultando que pertenciam aos mesmos Índios," AHU, RJCA, doc. 6042–43.

35. On confrontations and negotiations between Indians and priests in the aldeias, see Almeida, *Metamorfoses indígenas*, 134–45.

36. Vivaldo Coaracy, *O Rio de Janeiro no Século XVII* (Rio de Janeiro, José Olympio, 1944), 222.

37. Ibid., 223.

38. Silva, "Memória histórica," no. 14: 214.

39. Ibid.

40. "Representação do ouvidor da comarca como Juiz Conservador dos índios José Albano Fragoso, em 16 de novembro de 1802," in Silva, "Memória histórica," no. 15: 45.

41. Ibid., no. 14: 215.

42. Ibid.

43. "Representação do Ouvidor da Comarca como Juiz Conservador dos indios José Albano Fragoso, em 16 de novembro de 1802," in ibid., no. 15: 451–52.

44. "Informação do Juiz Conservador dos indios o desembargador José Albano Fragoso, em 14 de Dezembro de 1802," in ibid., no. 15: 453–54.

45. Silva, "Memória histórica," no. 14: 216; "Descrição dos vários distritos da Capitania do Rio de Janeiro feita por ordem do Ilmo. e Exmo. Senhor Conde de Rezende Vice Rei e Capitão General de Mar e Terra do Estado do Brasil, 1797," AHU, RJA, cx. 165, doc. 62.

46. Silva, "Memória histórica," no. 14: 460.

47. "Relações comunitárias étnicas," in Max Weber, Economia e sociedade (Brasília: Editora da Universidade de Brasília, 1994), 267–77.

48. Almeida, Metamorfoses indígenas, 257–78.

49. Frederick Barth, "Os Grupos étnicos e suas fronteiras," in O Guru, o iniciador e outras variações antropológicas, ed. Tomke Lask (Rio de Janeiro: ContraCapa, 2000), 25–67; Abner Cohen, "Introduction," in Urban Ethnicity, ed. Abner Cohen (London: Tavistock Publications, 1974), ix–xxiv; Abner Cohen, "Organizações Invisíveis: Alguns estudos de caso," in Abner Cohen, O homem bidimensional: A antropologia do poder e o simbolismo em sociedades complexas (Rio de Janeiro: Zahar, 1978).

50. Oliveira, "Uma Etnologia dos 'índios misturados,'" A viagem de volta, 20.

51. Barth, "Grupos étnicos," 25–67.

52. M. Regina Celestino de Almeida, "Índios e mestiços no Rio de Janeiro: Significados plurais e cambiantes," Memoria Americana 16 (2008), 19–40.

53. This issue is notably complex, given that many Indians surely chose to abandon both their aldeia and indigenous identity, while others might have assumed the double identity of "mestiço Indians." Others might have appeared as Indians or as mestiços, according to the circumstances and their interests. There are many studies of such phenomena for Spanish America, but they have also been seen in Portuguese America. See for example Marisol de la Cadena, "Are Mestizos Hybrids? The Conceptual Politics of Andean Identities," Journal of Latin American Studies 37 (2005): 259–84; Peter Wade, "Rethinking Mestizaje: Ideology and Lived Experience," Journal of Latin American Studies 37 (2005): 239–57; João Pacheco de Oliveira, "Pardos, mestiços ou caboclos: Os índios nos censos nacionais no Brasil (1872–1980)," Horizontes Antropológicos 6 (1997): 60–83; Almeida, "Índios e mestiços," 19–40.

54. Cohen, "Organizações invisíveis."

55. Roberto Cardoso de Oliveira, "Identidade étnica, identificação e manipulação," in Roberto Cardoso de Oliveira, Identidade, etnia e estrutura social (São Paulo: Editora Pioneira, 1976), 1–31.

56. Guillaume Boccara, "Mundos nuevos en las fronteras del Nuevo Mundo: relectura de los procesos coloniales de etnogénesis, etnificación y mestizaje em tiempos de globalización," Nuevo Mundo Mundos Nuevos (2001), http://nuevomundo.revues.org/426.

3

Colonial Intrusions and the Transformation of Native Society in the Amazon Valley, 1500–1800

Neil L. Whitehead

This chapter examines the first contacts between Europeans and the indigenous peoples of the Amazon River and the region of Maranhão at its mouth (see map 3).[1] These colonial intrusions resulted in the radical transformation of native societies and their ultimate destruction as autonomous entities by the end of the seventeenth century.[2] Particular emphasis is given to the changing character of the European presence during this period and the varying consequences this had for the fate of native society. Equally the nature of indigenous responses to the challenge of colonial intrusion was not uniform, and the way in which the different political and military strategies of flight from, cooperation with, or armed resistance to the colonial intruders directly influenced the survival, or not, of native groups are stressed.[3] Native groups surviving into the eighteenth century therefore showed various kinds of continuity with the pre-colonial past that can be directly related to the character of colonial contact they experienced in this early period.

FIRST CONTACTS, 1500–1650

First contacts were often much later along the Amazon than the coastal regions of Brazil and the Guianas since neither the Spanish nor Portuguese tried to settle the Maranhão region or the upper Amazon until the 1640s. Although other colonial powers were established throughout this region, their settlements were simply fortified trading posts. Notably the first Iberian expeditions to travel the length of the Amazon departed from the Andean regions to the west. Francisco de Orellana left Quito for the "Land of Cinnamon" in the expedition of Gonzalo Pizarro in 1541 and, although it did not represent the first European intrusion into the Amazon basin, it did signal the start of a serious interest in its exploitation and discovery.[4] Until this point the interior regions of the Amazon valley were not central to Spanish colonizing efforts.

The Portuguese had first reported sighting Brazil from the fleet of Pedro Álvares Cabral in 1500 and the first Spanish discovery of the Amazon had been made by Vincent Yánez Pinzón a few months earlier. The Spaniards named the channel at the mouth of the Amazon *Santa María de la Mar Dulce*, recording that the outlet discharged so much freshwater into the ocean that it seemed to be a "sea" itself. The region around the Amazon delta was difficult for sailing ships to navigate and a coastal environment of mangrove swamps made landings difficult, with the exception of the region around São Luís de Maranhão. The captaincy of Maranhão, created by King João III in 1534, was the most northerly grant of land the Portuguese king made. The crowns of Portugal and Spain negotiated the Treaty of Tordesillas in 1494, which limited Portuguese possession in the New World to a region east of a demarcation line, variously calculated between 42°30' and 50°W, during the subsequent fifty years. Technically then almost all of the Amazon basin lay outside Portuguese jurisdiction and the Portuguese had desisted from their attempts to colonize Maranhão by 1554. Together with a lack of Spanish colonization, this situation created fertile conditions for the Dutch, English, French, and Irish trading ventures that represented the sole European occupations of the river until the 1630s.[5]

The first descent of the Amazon, by a group under the command of Francisco de Orellana that became separated from the expedition of Gonzalo Pizarro, resulted in an account by Gaspar de Carvajal that contained detailed descriptions of the native polities of the Amazon. By the time of the Portuguese colonization of the river almost a hundred years later, however, these large and complex societies had already disintegrated, partly under the onslaught of epidemic disease.[6] The disparity between the depiction of powerful overlords, vast populations, and near-urban scales of settlement and the reports of decimated populations given by the missionaries a century later have led some to doubt the probity of this early account. But much of the information given in Gaspar de Carvajal's account of the 1541 journey with Pizarro is confirmed by the only other contemporary journey down the Amazon, the expedition of Lope de Aguirre in 1560.[7] Aguirre's notoriety as mutineer, traitor, and madman does little to lend credibility to the account. Nonetheless, recent archaeological and historical research strongly suggests that many such accounts are far from fanciful.

On systematic investigation, testimony from the early documents continually stresses the great abundance of both floral and faunal resources as well as the intensity with which they could be exploited. Evidence of this abundance, as well as the great productivity of Amerindian agricultural techniques, is clearly given by the chroniclers and sometimes can be directly quantified by the study of the exchange of foodstuffs and trade goods between the Amerindians and Europeans. As the Oiapoque River colonist John Wilson bluntly expressed it, "we lived very good [and] cheap."[8]

The fact that some Amerindian economies were geared to producing such food surpluses in antiquity is also demonstrated by the existence of indigenous markets and exchange systems in fish meal and manioc flour, as well as the large scale "ranching" of turtles and iguanas. Moreover the use of seed and tuber crops other than the staple manioc was far more common than modern ethnographic experience might suggest, even in areas such as the Atlantic coast, which have been previously thought to be agriculturally unproductive. The archaeological evidence also suggests that intensive cultivators once occupied this region using mounding and irrigation techniques to control flooding, as on the Orinoco and Amazon.[9]

Although the Amazon River was to remain marginal to Spanish colonial interest, parts of the upper Amazon were eventually integrated into the jurisdiction of the Royal Audiencia of Quito. Only with the Portuguese invasion, led by Pedro Teixeira, who occupied the Amazon valley in the 1630s in defiance of the Treaty of Tordesillas, were the trading posts and forts that the Dutch, Irish, and English had established along the river swept away and the native population progressively brought under colonial control.[10]

The Amazon had been traded by the Dutch, Irish, and English for hardwoods and dyes, and they laid out profitable tobacco plantations. The Amazon basin and its numerous populations at first offered ample trading opportunities, and European knowledge of the upland routes from the Atlantic coast, in the region of Surinam and Corentyn, to the Amazon basin, grew correspondingly. The Dutch largely centered their efforts in the

Amazon valley on the lower Xingu and Tapajós Rivers while the English and Irish favored the north bank of the Amazon and the mouth of the river. The overland connections to the Guianas were to become significant again when the Portuguese were exploring the Branco and Negro Rivers in the eighteenth century, since these indigenous trade routes to the Atlantic Dutch colonies provided an escape and supply route for native resistance to Portuguese *descimentos* (slave-hunts), as in the case of the famous Manoa chieftain, Ajuricaba.[11]

As has been mentioned, the Portuguese rooted out these small settlements in the 1630s, although they had been so profitable to their owners that licenses to resurrect them were sought from both the Spanish and Portuguese crowns. Thereafter the Dutch and English concentrated their efforts on the rivers of the Wild Coast between the Orinoco and Amazon deltas, particularly Surinam, Berbice, Essequibo, and Pomeroon, as well as the Caribbean islands. It was left to the French, who belatedly occupied the Cayenne and Oiapoque Rivers in the second half of the seventeenth century, to contest with the Portuguese for control of the Amazon mouth.[12]

French interest in this region resulted from both their ejection in the 1560s from their southern colony at Rio de Janeiro, and from their broader colonial goals in South America. However, it was not until 1612 that General Daniel La Ravadière sailed with three ships to colonize the Maranhão region. Alliances with the local Tupinambá, deriving from the long history of French trading along the whole of the Brazilian coast, were sealed by their mutual antagonism to the Portuguese and their native allies, the Potiguar. French plans to expand the colony through the conquest of the Camarapin and other native populations at the Amazon mouth thus appealed to Tupinambá leaders, and a joint expedition of conquest set out in 1613.[13]

However, the Portuguese had already begun to occupy the area south of Maranhão, the captaincy of Ceará, and were already constructing forts along the coast even as the French advanced into the Amazon valley with their native allies. In 1614 the Portuguese themselves entered the bay of Maranhão and inflicted heavy casualties on the French, though without taking the fort, despite the Tupinambá having begun to desert the French cause. At the end of 1615 Portuguese reinforcements from Pernambuco finally expelled La Ravadière from Maranhão, ending forever French occupation of Brazilian territories. Over the next two decades the Portuguese slowly expanded their control over Maranhão, founding Belém on the southern bank of the mouth of the Amazon, but not without a fierce struggle with the remnant Tupinambá. In

Figure 13. François Carypyra, a Tupinambá convert to Christianity, was one of six Indians from Maranhão brought by French Capuchin missionaries to be displayed in Paris before King Louis XIII in the early seventeenth century. He died soon after arriving in France. Spanish, Dutch, Irish, English, and French traders and missionaries were active in the Amazon region, undermining the foundations of many native polities, well before the Portuguese made a determined effort to colonize the region. Claude d'Abbeville, *Histoire de la mission des pères capucins . . .* (Paris: F. Huby, 1614), 347v. Courtesy of the John Carter Brown Library at Brown University.

this campaign the Portuguese employed as military auxiliaries groups known by the generic name Tapuias, enemies of the Tupinambá. Despite a direct assault on the fortress of Belém in 1619, the Tupinambá were defeated by this same year. An outbreak of smallpox in Maranhão in 1621 then decimated even those Tupinambá who had avoided direct military conquest.

Pedro Teixeira also led a number of expeditions designed to take control of the upriver Amazon territories for the Portuguese and to integrate these northerly regions of Brazil. However, compared to the southern territories, Maranhão was poor and undeveloped. Consequently, seizing the "red gold," or native slaves, was the favored strategy for the development of the region. The legal provisions under which the slaving of the native population was organized by the Portuguese were of two kinds. The first emphasized the *resgate* (ransom) of captives who might otherwise have been sacrificed and cannibalized, a similar legal formula being employed in Spanish territories, while the second legal justification was claiming the capture of natives as a legitimate pursuit of trade. The politics of slaving also played into the rivalry between missionary orders. The Capuchin missionaries, who had reached Pará with the first settlement, in fact did little to oppose such slaving, although its brutal consequences soon became too much to ignore. As a result, the Jesuits, who successfully replaced the Capuchins in the administration of the native population, documented such abuses closely in support of their bid for the right to evangelize native populations in Brazil.[14]

When Teixeira led the first force into the Amazon in 1630, composed of over a thousand native allies and some 120 Portuguese, they summarily destroyed the Irish, English, and Dutch settlements on the lower reaches of the Amazon, and the trading posts were never reestablished, or only briefly so. The next phase in Teixeira's campaign was to move up the river with a large military expedition in 1637. The expedition reached the Spanish settlements by the end of the year and eventually even the city of Quito, well within the Viceroyalty of Peru, much to the consternation of Spanish authorities. Teixeira began his return in early 1639, accompanied by the Spanish Jesuit Cristóbal de Acuña, and Acuña's account of this journey has become a key source on the native population along the river. As they came to the territory of the Tapajós they encountered the son of the governor of Pará, Bento Maciel (named after his father), who was intent as his father had been on exploiting the labor power of the native population. Teixeira had forbidden the "ransom" (i.e., enslaving) of the Tapajoso nobles and their personal servants. Yet, as Acuña observed, "scarcely had I turned my back when . . . [Maciel] fell upon the Indians with harsh war, although they desired peace."[15] Such occurrences were to become all too familiar in the history of the occupation of the Amazon. Teixeira's brother, the vicar-general of Maranhão, claimed that "almost two million" natives had been destroyed in the course of the Portuguese occupation of this region during the 1630s and 1640s, a pattern that was to continue unimpeded as Portuguese control was extended along the whole of the river and up its major tributaries over the next century.[16]

The scale of Portuguese colonization in the Amazon valley was initially far less than that along the southern Atlantic shore of Brazil. Nonetheless, the impact of colonization on indigenous societies in this region, as elsewhere, was ultimately devastating, resulting also in a fundamental reorientation of native trade and political networks from an upland to a coastal focus, where embroilment in the colonial regimes of the Europeans appeared to offer initial opportunities. However, the resulting demographic impact, as well as overt policies concerning native groups, forced a reorganization of social and political life. Moreover knowledge of the Spanish and Portuguese occupation in the Orinoco valley, the Amazon valley, and beyond, as well as the lessons of its local consequences, was thoroughly assimilated by native leaders. This meant that native leaders often actively sought economic and military alliances with Spain and Portugal's colonial rivals, thereby hoping to impede Iberian attempts to control the region. By the beginning of the seventeenth century new native leaderships, appealing to new forms of ethnic sentiment, faced off against newly stabilized colonial regimes. These new native identities expressed these changing circumstances and so sometimes showed only a limited continuity with those that had preceded them. This social and cultural homogenization of the native population is in turn reflected in colonial missionary ethnologies in which the missionaries employed linguistic categories as a means to represent the distribution of native groups and how best to effect their conversion. The elite class of leaders, as in the case of the Tapojoso destroyed by Bento Maciel, was largely extinguished in the violence of initial colonial establishment. The power vacuum they left was filled either by the European missionaries and traders or the newly emergent trading and warring chieftaincies, such as the Manoa, Arawak, and Carib.[17] These groups, some still extant today, represent a complex historical inheritance from the ancient native polities, some being amalgams of often highly divergent cultural traditions. Politically and economically, leaders of these neoteric (newly formed) groups premised themselves on the political vagaries of colonial conflict and rivalry. However, as the colonial economies of the Amazon valley shifted from trade in forest products toward the laying out of plantations or other kinds of infrastructural activity, the importance of native allegiance declined commensurately. Additionally the economic and political infrastructure by which Europe supported the American colonies was increasingly secure, and as a result the colonies themselves also began to move toward forms of economic and political autonomy, foreshadowing the emergence of national states after 1800. Nonetheless, these new indigenous power groupings among the still autonomous native populations of the Amazon valley in the seventeenth and eighteenth centuries continued to shape colonial development for the next hundred years or so.

COLONIAL ESTABLISHMENT
AND NATIVE CONQUEST, 1650–1800

In line with their emergent role as foci for native resistance and cooperation with the colonial regimes of the region, such groups as the Carib, Manoa, or Arawak used their preferential trading relations with the Europeans to consolidate and extend their political and economic influence among the rest of the indigenous population through trade and raiding. Against a background of severe demographic decline, the domination and even incorporation of remnant populations was very successfully managed by such groups. This was particularly true where the complex rules of marriage and descent evident in the dynastic chieftaincies that had preceded them were abandoned in response to the dynamically changing conditions of sociopolitical life. It was therefore those groups who most actively sought contact with the Europeans, hoping to alter their relations with other native groups, as well as those who had already suffered *reduccion* or *descimento* (i.e., political submission to the Spanish or a forced descent downriver to Portuguese settlements), who were the primary victims of the epidemics that were to sweep this area in the eighteenth century. At the same time, where direct military conquest had failed against still independent tribes who simply fled deeper into the interior of the Amazon forests, the missionaries were often able to accomplish this end indirectly by the economic and political marginalization of regional leaders and traders. The missions were thus a source of access to the material goods of colonial economies and to sources of spiritual power and influence that challenged the authority of native leaders, especially in the context of

Figure 14. Portrayed in the center of the top row, a headman of the Maxaruna Indians (associated with the modern Matis) is depicted amid other portraits of Brazil's diverse native peoples. The Matis now live on an indigenous reserve along an upper tributary of the Amazon River, their survival a testament to their own resilience and that of many other groups that both fragmented and recombined in response to European contact. Source: Debret, *Voyage pittoresque.* Public domain access: http://www.brasiliana.usp.br/bbd/handle/1918/624510042

epidemic diseases that would have seemed to underline the power and importance of the invaders. The demographic devastation of native populations therefore directly facilitated the process of colonization and, as a result, the missions and their epidemics became the central native experience of this period. If they did not die of epidemic disease, kin, clients, and enemies alike were still trapped in a state of isolated captivity within the missions, thereby undermining the economic and social exchanges that had once supported the autonomous political authority of the native leaders.[18]

Throughout this same period the range of Dutch, French, and English trading activities with the native population diminished as the sugar plantations along the Wild Coast became more profitable than trade in dye-woods and other forest products.[19] In this context different native groups competed for the dwindling supply of European goods, promoting further conflict and disarray among native leaders. In some contexts this was very much promoted by colonial policy as a means for ensuring a trade in native slaves, but where such conflicts threatened the colonies' economic prosperity the authorities did all they could to defuse disruptive local conflicts. In both cases providing access to European goods was a way of ensuring native willingness to conform to European authority, and an informal system of ethnic ranking often emerged in regard to the distribution of these goods. Favored native leaders were formally "confirmed" in their authority by the colonial administration, who also gave them special insignia of office. As a result the native groups excluded from these arrangements were cynically targeted by native leaders themselves and "punitive" expeditions against such groups serviced both European and native ambitions. By these means the dependency of "loyal" groups was also increased, since their willingness to act as European proxies ensured that any attempts to form broad alliances among native groups, such as had occurred during the initial resistance to European incursion, would fail.

Native leaders therefore were faced with an increasingly stable colonial system, in which intercolonial rivalry itself had somewhat abated. By the end of the seventeenth century, the Spanish occupied the Pearl Coast, Trinidad, and the Orinoco, but had not advanced any further down the Amazon from their Andean colonies. The Dutch in Surinam, Berbice, and Essequibo were undoubtedly the dominant force along the Guiana coast, as Spanish governors fruitlessly warned their monarchs, and only finally abandoned their southern settlements in Brazil in 1654. The English and French held small sugar and tobacco plantations throughout the Lesser Antilles, as well as on the Atlantic coast of the Guianas, but had no further ambitions for outposts in the Amazon valley. However, the French had stabilized a colony between the Maroni and Oiapoque Rivers and had garnered sufficient native alliances to dispute the intervening zone with the Portuguese at Belém.

THE MISSION REGIME, 1650–1750

Along the Amazon and its tributaries, the period from around 1650 to 1750 marks the zenith of missionary evangelization, which was at times scarcely less violent than the military conquest that had preceded it.[20] The demographic consequences of evangelization were profound largely because evangelization usually involved the resettlement and concentration of native populations in close proximity to the European settlements, making them vulnerable to repeated epidemics. Nonetheless the missionary settlements were also a possible way to avoid being taken by slavers, particularly in the Portuguese territories. In contrast the Spanish crown's prohibition on native enslavement, dating from 1652, was largely observed, since the anarchy of slaving undermined the relative stability of the *encomienda* and, later, *repartimiento* systems of coerced Indian labor, which were the favored colonial institutions for control of the native population in the Spanish regions.

Along the Amazon, however, all the most accessible populations were continuously enslaved, despite efforts to outlaw the practice in 1680. The critical economic factor underlying this situation was the high price of imported African slaves relative to the resources of the Portuguese colonists in Pará and Maranhão. Under pressure from the colonists, the Portuguese king reintroduced slavery in 1688 as well as adjusted the terms of Jesuit control over the mission villages. In 1702 a new decree also extended slaving activities by allowing private colonists to go slaving by special royal license. In 1718 colonists were actively solicited to seek such licenses as labor needs became acute. The Portuguese royal authorities themselves had the right simply to commandeer the mission populations for royal service, such as to build forts and roads or gather forest products. However, since such services could take months to complete, it could have a serious impact on the survival of that mission population. This was not just because of the contact with potential sources of diseases such a smallpox, but also because such arbitrary demands upset the domestic economy by removing the adult males who were mostly responsible for hunting, fishing, and the heavy work of clearing garden patches.[21]

The use of native labor by the authorities in turn restricted the supply of labor available to the private colonists. Pressures both to expand access to the mission *aldeias* and to continue the enslaving of autonomous native populations therefore grew ever greater. At the same time the activities of Spanish missionaries in the upper Amazon at the end of the seventeenth century, notably those of the Spanish-sponsored Jesuit Samuel Fritz, served only to remind the Portuguese authorities of the dire necessity to control the native population, either through their evangelization *in situ* or through their removal to the immediate proximity of colonial settlements, lest their political authority in the Amazon region be usurped by Spanish missionaries. It is therefore important to appreciate that the mission was, apart from its evangelical purposes, a key institution of colonial expansion and was quite overtly used as such. In the absence of large military infrastructures, it was only through the direct control of people that a claim to territory could be made real.[22]

In the Amazon valley this situation had become critical by the beginning of the eighteenth century and this led to a series of disputes among Brazilian colonists over the control and return of "fugitives" from the missions of the Omaguas or Cambebas, or "hammerheads" as they were known due to their continuing practice of cranial deformation. By 1709 the situation had deteriorated to the point where a Portuguese force was dispatched to arrest Samuel Fritz and his companions. However, it was not until the signing of the Treaty of Madrid in 1750 that Spain and Portugal finally located a permanent boundary between the Spanish and Portuguese Amazon. However, the strategic nature of the Omagua territories, on the frontier of these colonial interests, effectively sealed the fate of the native population, particularly along the Amazon mainstream. By 1743, when the French expeditionary Charles de La Condamine travelled down the Amazon, he reported that all of the native population had either "submitted or retreated far away."[23]

Throughout the Amazon valley, the early eighteenth century was a period of increasingly frequent epidemics, due to the upsurge in missionary activity and the growing number of white colonists and their black slaves among whom the newly "descended" indigenous groups were settled. As a result the colonists fiercely opposed the missionaries' control of the dwindling native population since it threatened to even further constrain the already limited supply of native labor. Among the most effective advocates for the colonists against the Jesuit missions was Paolo da Silva Nunes, an official of the authorities at Belém. His profligate accusations against the Jesuits, suggesting that

Figure 15. The Omagua or Cambeba Indians, known for their practice of cranial deformation, as shown in this image, once presented a formidable barrier to colonization,
occupying a vast territory along what is now the border between Brazil and Peru. Of
those who entered Jesuit and Carmelite missions, many ultimately departed to reside
in still more remote areas in the eighteenth century, a reminder that Indians continued
to shape their own histories even after they initially accepted missionary protection.
Source: Louis Marie S. M. H. Prudhomme, *Voyage à la Guiane et a Cayenne: Fait en
1789 et années suivantes; contenant une description géographique de ces contrées, l'histoire de leur découverte; les possessions et etablissemens des Français, des Hollandais,
des Espagnols et des Portugais . . .* (Paris: Chez l'éditeur, Rue des Marais, No. 20, F. G.,
1798), plate 2. Courtesy of the John Carter Brown Library at Brown University.

they had usurped royal prerogatives, that they had armed natives to resist
colonists, and that they had treasonable relations with the Dutch and Spanish,
eventually forced the king to send an official to investigate. In fact the resulting report, issued in 1734, was generally favorable to the Jesuits. Tragically,
however, by recognizing the Jesuits' achievements in the creation of a viable
mission economy, the report served only to accentuate those very aspects of

their presence in the Amazon that were the source of the colonists' anxieties. Furthermore, the political ramifications of the signing of the Treaty of Madrid, which adjudicated boundaries with the Spanish regions, meant that the Jesuits and their upper Amazon missions appeared to be a substantial obstacle to the progress of demarcation. The Jesuits were also accused of failing in their obligation toward their converts. In this context and with unceasing accusations of excessive material wealth in some of the Jesuit fazendas (estates), a political climate was created that led to the removal of their control over the native population in 1755 with the promulgation of the so-called Law of Liberty, promoted by the marquis of Pombal, which deceptively declared "Indian liberty" by stripping the missionaries of all prerogatives over native labor, the real purpose of this edict.[24]

EPILOGUE: NATIONALISM
AND NEO-COLONIALISM, 1750–1900

Toward the end of the eighteenth century the native peoples of the northeastern corner of South America still showed a considerable variety of society and culture, as well as significant autonomy from the colonial regimes that had implanted themselves throughout the region. To the north of the Amazon from Trinidad to the *llanos* of the Orinoco, European dominance was unchallenged. The demographic preponderance of Europeans and Africans marginalized the native population. Indeed, native society had come to include persons of African and European descent to such an extent that groups of Afro-Amerindian "Black Caribs" or mestizo "Spanish Arawaks" had emerged. In the first instance, Amerindians intermixed with peoples of African descent; in the second, with peoples of Spanish descent. Ethnogenesis was a testament to the deep changes and dynamic responses with which native peoples had met colonialism.[25]

Along the Atlantic coast to the north of the Amazon, the Dutch and French had established stable, if not always profitable, plantation complexes. In these contexts native peoples were still valued as an informal militia that could be activated to control slave rebellions. Beyond that they were viewed with the nostalgic curiosity that set the tone of nineteenth-century ethnographic accounts and observations. The old colonial trope of the wild cannibal savage gave way to the image of the pathetic survivor of conquest eking out his last days in a mute rebuke to modernity.[26] Of course this was more than a shift in literary tastes. It did reflect a rapidly changing conjuncture at the beginning of the nineteenth century in which native peoples had to endure further crushing epidemics, as well as the ferocity of unfettered capitalist exploitation. It had been a key complaint of the anti-clericalism that produced both the Jesuit expulsions from Brazil, as well as the conflicts between civil governors and the Capuchin syndicalist mission system in Venezuela, that missionaries kept their neophytes in a state of "feudal" subjection. By this critics meant that the native labor was not freely available to them. Although there is plenty of evidence that both the Jesuits and Capuchins actually did try to accommodate the colonists' demands for hired native labor, the real source of this conflict was simply that the demands of the spiritual regime of the missionaries were not politically compatible with those of economic development, and it was this that was of interest to the colonial and metropolitan elites.[27] More generally such tensions between the ambitions of the colonial elites and the close control of metropolitan governments erupted into open conflict and led to the wars of independence throughout the Americas.

In nineteenth-century Brazil, a number of other factors, such as the late date of the abolition of black slavery (1888), the internal crises of the Brazilian state, and the sheer immensity of the Amazon region, attenuated these processes.[28] Indigenous groups like the Kayapó, the Mundurucú, and the Xavante, inhabitants of the largely unknown southern tributaries of the Amazon, mounted open military challenges to further Brazilian encroachments, just as the Caribs, Manoas, or Aruan had in earlier times. However, these groups from the interior of Amazonia lacked the kinds of external European contacts that had been integral to sustained native resistance and autonomy on the Orinoco, on the Negro River, or along the Atlantic coast. As a result it was isolation from, rather than engagement with, Brazilian society that became a key strategy for political autonomy.[29] Previously economic and political contact with the colonial regime was necessary as a means to sustain the native political economy in a given region. However, although beneficial in the short term, the negative consequence of strategies of retreat and isolation are, precisely, the consequences of retreat and isolation themselves. Such consequences included curtailment of the range of the social interaction with a corresponding tendency toward cultural conservatism. Early ethnologists, taking these nineteenth-century contexts as historically given, failed to appreciate the processes which underlay the isolation and diminution of native societies. They also ignored more complex phenomena, such as the emergence of mixed groups in the Cabanagem rebellion of the Amazon valley, so called from the *cabanos* or shacks in which the poor lived, both native and mestizo. Consequently most observers pictured the Cabanagem as evidence of the dissolution of native cultures, instead of appreciating the way in which such peoples show a historical persistence through new social means.

The advent of this kind of modernity in the Amazon valley is marked by the 1755 Law of Liberty and the policies that ensued. Prominent in these developments was the governor of Maranhão and Pará, Mendonça Furtado, brother of the marquis of Pombal, who had virtually supplanted royal power in Portugal. Governor Mendonça Furtado in 1757, after he had made an inspection of the mission villages, unilaterally decided to observe a transitional period during which those villages were put under the control of a civilian "director." This arrangement, known as the *Diretório dos índios* (Indian Directorate), persisted for the next forty years and was also extended to other regions of Brazil. The intent was to integrate the native population into a "modern" society as quickly as possible, instead of allowing them to remain socially stagnant under the "feudal" control of the friars. Indeed by 1759 the Jesuits were expelled from Portugal as well as from Brazil. The king of Spain, following the Portuguese lead, also expelled the Jesuits from his empire in 1767, and Pope Clement XIV extinguished the order utterly in 1773, it only being revived at the end of the nineteenth century. Much the same occurred with the other missionary orders in South America, particularly where they sided with royalist factions in the emerging politics of independence.

Without the mediation of the missionaries, relationships between still autonomous native groups and the colonial authorities of necessity became militarized. Even where the missionaries' *tropas de resgate* (armed bands for the "rescue" of native souls) had used the persuasion of gunfire, their activities were premised on a very different set of ideas as to the purpose of such expeditions and the destiny of the natives captured by them. Now, in the latter half of the eighteenth century, the Mura from the Madeira River and the Mundurucú from the Tapajós loomed large in the conflicts of the last decades of the eighteenth century. Just as had the Arawaks and Caribs of earlier times, the Mura and Mundurucú expanded into an arena of contact along the lower reaches of the Amazon, following Portuguese destruction and dispersion of the aboriginal native polities, especially the Tapajoso. So, too, as these emergent native forces clashed with each other and the first epidemics struck the Mura population, the Portuguese were able to negotiate a peace with the Mura. War against the Mundurucú continued into the 1790s

Figure 16. In the Amazon region and beyond, Brazilian Indians constructed many different types of dwellings, ranging from provisional shelters made from sticks and leaves to more permanent structures requiring communal labor. Source: Debret, *Voyage pittoresque.* Public domain access: http://www.brasiliana.usp.br/bbd/handle/1918/624510040

until the reasonable treatment and release of two Mundurucú captives led to a peace in 1795. Thereafter many Mundurucú were brought downstream to occupy the old mission villages of the Tapajoso.

To the north of the Amazon, and in the upper reaches of the Orinoco and Caroni, as well as in the Guiana highlands, the boundaries of the colonial regimes were as yet not delineated. As had been the case in the demarcation of the Amazon valley between Spain and Portugal, in the Guiana highlands of the Sierra Parima and Pacaraima it remained unclear who controlled what. In this context the allegiances of the interior groups were important both for the legal establishment of a claim and for its practical defense. As a result, boundary commissions for both the Portuguese and Spanish governments traveled into the interior to the north of the Amazon in order to secure control of the headwaters of the Orinoco, Negro, and Branco and to assess the extent of Dutch and French influence inland from their coastal settlements.[30]

This boundary commission represented the limit of external penetration into the interior for the next hundred years or so. The wars of independence against the Spanish crown by the Venezuelans took away any need for colonial demarcation. Further east, especially at the headwaters of the Branco, where the Pirara portage links the Amazon basin to that of the Essequibo via the Rupununi tributary, the issue of Portuguese and then Brazilian territorial claims against British Guiana remained unsettled until the end of the nineteenth century.[31] In all of these situations, as in the era of the missions, the control or allegiance of the native population was critical, both practically and legally, to demonstrate rights of possession. Consequently even very isolated groups found themselves confronted by a wave of exploratory expeditions, some with overt ethnographic purposes, but which also introduced new and virulent diseases. As a result epidemics often broke out and eventually drove native populations down to a historic low point by the early twentieth century.

The precise documentation of the overall effect of epidemics, in both this period and earlier, is fraught with uncertainty.[32] At the moment it is broadly accepted that death rates in specific cases could have been as high as eighty percent of a given population, but it is not possible to judge if this was true in all situations. Moreover, given the continuing dispute as to the ecological bases of human settlement in Amazonia, it is also difficult to derive an estimate for populations at contact, though a total of five million is currently offered as a minimum for the whole of the Amazon region (including the Orinoco basin and Guianas). The real point, however, is that there was a markedly different mortality among native and nonnatives, that this was appreciated by all parties, and that it can be shown to have had concrete political and economic effects in determining the course of conquest and colonization. One has only to contemplate the terms of colonial endeavor elsewhere, as in Africa or Asia, to appreciate the enhancement this biological factor gave to the colonial and neocolonial occupation and control of the Americas.

The colonial regimes that had initiated that occupation now also faced a rising tide of dissent, as the colonists contemplated total independence from Europe. In 1822 Prince Pedro proclaimed himself emperor of an independent Brazil, just as Simón Bolívar had declared Venezuela independent some six years earlier. The colonial regimes of the Dutch and French in the Guianas likewise underwent a reorientation to Europe, but for different reasons. The French colony in Cayenne, initially royalist, fell, as did the monarchy itself, to the forces of the new French Republic. In addition, as a consequence of the Napoleonic Wars in Europe, the British challenged both French and Dutch supremacy along the Wild Coast. Although the Dutch retained control of Surinam, the Essequibo, Demerara, and Berbice enclaves were relinquished to British control by the Treaty of London in 1814. Trinidad was unceremoniously seized from the Spanish in 1804. In 1808 a joint Anglo-Brazilian force seized the French colony of Cayenne, which the Brazilians occupied for the next eight years until the Paris Convention of 1817.

In short the effects of the changing conjuncture in Europe were felt right across the region and brought a series of consequences for native peoples.[33] In some cases native levies were used to offset the navies and armies sent from Europe, as in Venezuela, where a special regiment of Caribs was formed to support Bolívar. On the other hand, in the revolt of the Cabanagem, which engulfed the whole of the lower Amazon in 1835–1836, the role of native people was diffused in a general social revolt against the old colonial elite and its inheritors in the newly independent Brazil. The revolt was brutally crushed in 1837–1838 and was followed by the outbreak of further epidemics. Smallpox and influenza, always the companions of war, also swept through the native populations of the Orinoco in the aftermath of Venezuela's War of Independence. By the 1840s the native population was thus in very steep decline, reaching its nadir in Brazil, as noted, at the turn of the twentieth century.

In sum colonial intrusions caused a fundamental transformation of native societies in the Amazon valley, leading to their virtual destruction by the end of the seventeenth century. In this process the changing character of the European presence and the varying consequences this presence had for the fate of native society is all important in understanding the particular histories of the different indigenous groups. As a result indigenous responses to the challenge of colonial intrusion were not uniform by any means, and the different political and military strategies deployed against the intruders, from outright flight to armed resistance, directly influenced the patterns of survival, transformation, and destruction of native societies. Those native groups that survived into the eighteenth century therefore showed various kinds of continuity with the pre-colonial past, which can be directly related to the character of colonial contact they experienced in this early period, and for that reason, if no other, it remains vital to adequately appreciate the nature of those changes.

NOTES

1. For most of the seventeenth century, the Estado do Maranhão, administered from São Luís as a separate Portuguese colony, comprised most of the area located north of Brazil's Atlantic bulge, including the Amazon delta. In the 1770s, the crown divided Maranhão from Grão-Pará, which then administered the delta and the lower Amazon River region from Belém.

2. Neil L. Whitehead, "Native Americans and Europeans—Early Encounters," in *The Oxford Handbook of the Atlantic World, c.1450–c.1850*, ed. Nicholas P. Canny and Philip D. Morgan (New York: Oxford, 2011); Neil L. Whitehead, "Native Peoples Confront Colonial Regimes in Northeastern South America (c. 1550–1900)," in *The Cambridge History of the Native Peoples of the Americas*, ed. Frank Salomon and Stuart B. Schwartz (Cambridge: Cambridge University Press, 1999), vol. 3, pt. 2, 382–441.

3. Neil L. Whitehead, "Tribes Make States and States Make Tribes: Warfare and the Creation of Colonial Tribes and States in Northeastern South America," in *War in the Tribal Zone: Expanding States and Indigenous Warfare*, ed. R. Brian Ferguson and Neil L. Whitehead (Santa Fe, NM: School of American Research Press, 2000).

4. Gaspar de Carvajal, *The Discovery of the Amazon According to the Account of Friar Gaspar de Carvajal and Other Documents*, ed. H. C. Heaton, trans. Bertram T. Lee (New York: American Geographical Society, 1934).

5. John M. Monteiro, "The Crises and Transformations of Invaded Societies: Coastal Brazil in the Sixteenth Century," in Salomon and Schwartz, *Cambridge History of the Native Peoples of the Americas*, vol. 3, pt. 1, 973–1023; Manuel da Nóbrega, *Cartas do Brasil (1549–1560)* (Rio de Janeiro: Officina Industrial Graphica, 1931).

6. Carvajal, *Discovery of the Amazon*.

7. Pedro Simón, *The Expedition of Pedro de Ursua and Lope de Aguirre in Search of El Dorado and Omagua in 1560–1*, trans. William Bollaert (London: Hakluyt Society, 1861).

8. John Wilson, "The Relation of Master John Wilson . . . into England from Wiapoco in Guiana 1606," in *Hakluytus Posthumus: Or Purchas His Pilgrimes: Contayning a History of the World in Sea Voyages and Lande Travells by Englishmen and Others,* ed. Samuel Purchas (Glasgow: J. MacLehose, 1906), 16: 346–47.

9. Neil L. Whitehead, "The Ancient Amerindian Polities of the Lower Orinoco, Amazon and Guayana Coast: A Preliminary Analysis of Their Passage from Antiquity to Extinction," in *Amazonian Indians: From Prehistory to the Present,* ed. Anna C. Roosevelt (Tucson: University of Arizona Press, 1997).

10. Joyce Lorimer, *English and Irish Settlement on the River Amazon, 1550–1646* (London: Hakluyt Society, 1989); James A. Williamson, *English Colonies in Guiana and on the Amazon, 1604–1668* (Oxford: Clarendon Press, 1923).

11. Neil L. Whitehead, *Lords of the Tiger Spirit: A History of the Caribs in Colonial Venezuela and Guyana, 1498–1820* (Dordrecht: Foris, 1988).

12. Cornelis C. Goslinga, *The Dutch in the Caribbean and on the Wild Coast, 1580–1680* (Assen: Van Gorcum, 1971).

13. Claude d'Abbeville, *Histoire de la mission des pères capucins en l'isle de Maragnan et terres circoncoisines, où est traicté des singularitez admirables et des moeurs merveilleuses des Indièns habitans de ce pays, avec les missives et advis qui ont esté envoyez de nouveau* (Paris, 1614).

14. João Felipe Betendorf, "Chronica da missão dos padres da Companhia de Jesus no Estado do Maranhão [1699]," *Revista do Instituto Histórico e Geográfico Brasiliero* 72, part 1 (1909).

15. Christoval de Acuña, "A New Discovery of the Great River of the Amazons," in *Expeditions into the Valley of the Amazons, 1539, 1540, 1639,* ed. Clements R. Markham (London: Hakluyt Society, 1859), 125.

16. Quoted in Betendorf, "Chronica da missão dos padres," 72.

17. Whitehead, "Tribes Make States and States Make Tribes."

18. Robin M. Wright and Manuela Carneiro da Cunha, "Destruction, Resistance, and Transformation—Southern, Coastal, and Northern Brazil," in Salomon and Schwartz, *Cambridge History of the Native Peoples of the Americas,* vol. 3, pt. 2, 287–381.

19. Vincent T. Harlow, *Colonising Expeditions to the West Indies and Guiana, 1623–1667* (London: Hakluyt Society, 1925).

20. Acuña, "A New Discovery."

21. Neil L. Whitehead, "Indigenous Slavery in South America, 1492–1820," in *The Cambridge World History of Slavery,* ed. David Eltis and Stanley L. Engerman (Cambridge: Cambridge University Press, 2011).

22. Samuel Fritz, *Journal of the Travels and Labours of Father Samuel Fritz in the River of the Amazons between 1686 and 1723,* trans. George Edmundson (London: Hakluyt Society, 1922).

23. Charles-Marie de La Condamine, *Relation abrégée d'un voyage fait dans l'intérieur de l'Amérique méridionale: Depuis la côte de la mer du Sud, jusqu'aux côtes du Brésil & de la Guiane, en descendant la riviere des Amazones; lûe à l'assemblée publique de l'Acdémie des Sciences, le 28. avril 1745* (Paris: Veuve Pissot, 1745), 88.

24. Boris Fausto, *A Concise History of Brazil* (Cambridge: Cambridge University Press, 1999), 58.

25. Neil L. Whitehead, "Black Read as Red: Ethnic Transgression and Hybridity in Northeastern South America and the Caribbean," in *Beyond Black and Red: African-Native Relations in Colonial Latin America*, ed. Matthew Restall (Albuquerque: University of New Mexico Press, 2005).

26. Neil L. Whitehead, ed., *Histories and Historicities in Amazonia* (Lincoln: University of Nebraska Press, 2003).

27. Whitehead, *Lords of the Tiger Spirit.*

28. Wright and Cunha, "Destruction, Resistance and Transformation."

29. Jonathan Hill, "Indigenous People and the Rise of Independent Nation-States in Lowland South America," in Salomon and Schwartz, *Cambridge History of the Native Peoples of the Americas*, vol. 3, pt. 2, 704–55.

30. Laurens Storm van 's Gravesande, *Storm van 's Gravesande: The Rise of British Guiana*, 2 vols. (London: Hakluyt Society, 1911).

31. Peter G Rivière, *Absent-Minded Imperialism: Britain and the Expansion of Empire in Nineteenth-Century Brazil* (London: I. B. Tauris, 1995).

32. Whitehead, *Lords of the Tiger Spirit.*

33. Neil L. Whitehead, ed., *Nineteenth Century Travels, Explorations and Empires: Writings from the Era of Imperial Consolidation, 1835–1910*, vol. 8 (London: Pickering & Chatto, 2004).

4

The Amazonian Native Nobility
in Late-Colonial Pará

Barbara A. Sommer

New World colonizers invariably forged alliances with indigenous leaders as they sought to establish themselves in the Brazilian north. Natives, at times, instigated these alliances to help vanquish their enemies, both indigenous and European. When the French started a colony at São Luís in 1612, they found willing allies among Tupinambá leaders, who had fled north to escape Portuguese intruders. These headmen were presented at court in Paris, where they married French women, before returning to Maranhão attired in fine velvet clothing worked with gold and sporting crosses of the royal and military order of the Knights of Saint Louis.[1] Only a few years later, the Portuguese pushed up the Atlantic coast to capture the new colony. Once they ousted the French, the Portuguese developed their own alliances with the natives, who helped them eject Dutch competitors in the 1640s. In return, the crown awarded the headmen, called *principais* (singular, *principal*), gifts or payments and habits in the military orders, as well as costumes for their wives.[2] These principais and their immediate relatives soon enjoyed special legal and social prerogatives as members of a hereditary native nobility. They actively petitioned for their official posts and valued written confirmations of their titles and the distinctive European clothing, which symbolized their status.[3] During the next two centuries, such allies helped the Portuguese to occupy and defend the vast Amazon basin, to conquer and enslave Indian rivals, to establish missions and build forts, and to develop a viable economy based on agriculture and the collection of forest products for export.

As missionaries and slavers relentlessly pushed up the Amazon, their recognition of native leaders expanded. Some principais acted as ambassadors to independent Indians, whose leaders were given the choice of collaboration or enslavement.[4] As new allies became integrated into the mission system, the crown and missionaries resorted to a system of indirect rule through the principais, who would muster their followers for war and for royal and private labor assignments. Each mission, or each ethnic group (*nação*, or nation) in larger missions, had a principal, a bailiff, and a captain, as in other parts of Brazil, as well as subordinate indigenous officers "of war" whose titles corresponded to military ranks. Although in 1654 the Jesuit António Vieira recommended phasing out these lesser posts, they would survive until the nineteenth century.[5] In fact, the ranks actually increased when, in two unusual cases—both in large, unsecured peripheral areas—principais were named "governors" of their respective nations.[6]

To the extent that it suited them, indigenous leaders in the northern Brazilian captaincy of Pará (see map 3) took on these new identities and integrated themselves in colonial structures. Situated at the nexus of labor, production, and local politics, they employed the rhetoric and legal mechanisms of the colonial state to engage in local and regional power struggles, leaving a paper trail of petitions, correspondence, and legal investigations. These documents, supplemented with bureaucratic reports, show how native leaders adjusted to changing circumstances, negotiating with missionaries, colonists, and administrators and creating new strategies to protect their autonomy and advance their interests. Successful officers and their descendants maintained their status over generations and can be traced into the nineteenth century. This impressive continuity, despite staggering demographic, social, cultural, and institutional change, gives us a new perspective on the evolving narrative of Amazonian history, which has long emphasized the decimation of native peoples and the homogenization of mission Indians.

Historians have generally ignored Amazonian "colonial Indians" and the social distinctions among them, tending instead to underscore effective Portuguese conquest and the resistance of discreet ethnic groups.[7] While recent studies have presented more nuanced views, the principais remain largely unstudied, unlike their Spanish-American counterparts, the caciques and *kurakas*, who figure prominently in colonial Latin American historiography.[8] Treading a fine line between independence and submission, the principais resembled their Spanish American counterparts, generally supporting their communities though at times abusing their positions and pursuing their self-interests. The active role of the principais and other colonial Indians of Pará helps us understand the Portuguese colonial rule and the political and socioeconomic development of this understudied region.

Scholars apparently overlooked these Brazilian native leaders because of preconceived notions about primitive tropical lowland societies. If forest peoples had no familiarity with sociopolitical hierarchy, unlike the highly stratified and complex state societies of the Incas and Aztecs, then leadership was imposed—merely a co-optive tool of the Portuguese.[9] Ironically, early eyewitness accounts recorded sedentary agriculturalists on the Amazon, featuring leaders with pretensions to divine origin, similar to Peruvian models.[10] David Sweet's exceptional study recognized the significance of indigenous leaders in the Negro River region, and Carlos de Araújo Moreira Neto noted the appointment of native leaders to colonial posts and emphasized the role of the *abalizados*, a term apparently adopted by the Portuguese to distinguish Arawakan elites in the region. A more thorough treatment came only in 1991, when Nádia Farage described the principais as active colonial agents in her study of the late eighteenth-century Branco River region.[11] More recently, the principais have become full-fledged historical subjects.[12]

Another conceptual shift contributing to the reconsideration of colonial Indians comes with a more fluid view of culture. Previously, natives either joined the colony as "decultured" Indian "peasants" or risked extermination.[13] Historian John Hemming described the Indians of late colonial Pará as "pathetic creatures at the bottom of society, half acculturated, stripped of most of their tribal traditions and pride, but entirely failing to adapt to European ways or to grasp any of the finer points of European civilization."[14] The activities of the principais belie this characterization. In contrast to the old tribal versus acculturated dichotomy, historians now interpret the adoption, exchange, layering, and convergence of native and Western concepts, and the creation of new meanings and identities in colonial contexts as selective, innovative processes without a predetermined outcome.[15] While a predominance of Arawakan peoples, known for their genealogically based social hierarchies and a tendency to form interethnic alliances, may have encouraged the development of colonial Amazonian native hierarchies, a cultural predisposition to strong leadership does not seem to have determined the success or failure of individual principais.[16] Long-ignored archival sources show that Indians from diverse language groups and ethnic nations,

Figure 17. Dressed in French finery and holding fleurs-de-lis, Louis Marie, a Tupinambá leader from Maranhão, was among the Indians brought by missionaries to visit the king of France in the early seventeenth century. In the second half of the eighteenth century, Portuguese clothing and adornments became important status symbols for the leaders of former missions transformed into villages controlled by secular author- ities. Source: d'Abbeville, *Histoire de la mission,* 361v. Courtesy of the John Carter Brown Library at Brown University.

originating from the Atlantic coast to the far reaches of the Negro River, became forceful protagonists in this dynamic, interactive colonial society.

SOCIAL PRESTIGE AND THE NATIVE ELITE

Once Portuguese territorial claims in the Amazon basin were codified in the 1750 Treaty of Madrid with Spain, the powerful statesman Sebastião José de Carvalho e Melo, the future marquis of Pombal, introduced reforms to increase state authority in the region. Along with administrative reorganization, defensive measures, and the establishment of a trading company, reformers sought to end Indian slavery, eliminate the powerful Jesuits, and integrate mission Indians into civil society. While many Indians lived among the general population—some had escaped from missionary control early on, others had been urban or estate slaves—the missions were of singular importance as they represented the largest organized source of labor. As Neil Whitehead explains in the previous chapter, Pombal's own brother, Francisco Xavier de Mendonça Furtado, as governor of Grão-Pará and Maranhão, oversaw the implementation of the *Diretório dos índios* (Indian Directorate), the legislation that for a forty-year period governed over sixty Indian settlements in the captaincy of Pará comprising roughly one-third of the population (independent forest peoples were not included in the census data).[17]

Under the Directorate, the missions acquired township or village status with a nonnative director appointed to oversee administration and "civilize" the Indians, while a parish priest was to Christianize them. The legislation charged the principais with maintaining public order, overseeing labor distribution to settlers and the crown, spreading Christianity, and replenishing the workforce by attracting "heathen" from the forest.[18] A certain friction was inherent in this division of power. Directors, vicars, and native officers competed for influence with the Indians and the regional authorities, accusing each other of an array of crimes, sins, and abuses in a veritable flood of missives to the governor. While such sources are undoubtedly biased, since their authors probably exaggerated or fabricated some accusations, they nonetheless reflect local struggles in which the native leaders took an active role.

While directors and vicars were rotated every few years, probably to discourage them from acting contrary to crown interests, the principais had a local advantage over these civil and clerical appointees because the native appointments were made for life. And because some lineages endured for generations, the elite provided for continuity in many native colonial communities. The principais were initially selected by the members of their ethnic nation, which may have instigated serious debate, disagreement, and even violence, although sources rarely mention the process.[19] Leaders then petitioned the governor or king for the letters of patent that formalized their titles. Some of these men exhibited considerable longevity in office: the principal of Vila Franca in 1762 retained his position twenty-two years later; two officers of Santarém served for at least twenty-five years; and the principal and captain of Alenquer held their positions for some thirty years.[20] Anacleto de Souza served as captain of Pombal for eleven years, then as sergeant-major for over twenty.[21] In Oeiras, the remarkable Principal Manoel Pereira de Faria held his post for at least thirty years.[22] In 1784, the aged principal of Porto de Moz legally demonstrated that he had held his title since 1707.[23]

Succession followed the custom established under the missionaries when, in the seventeenth century, Padre Vieira had specified that principais should be succeeded by their legitimate sons, when these were old enough and capable.[24] During the Directorate, patrilineal succession was the norm, although a few women succeeded their fathers as leaders.[25] But strict primogeniture was not always followed, since posts were sometimes awarded to younger sons or nephews. Clearly authorities promoted cooperative leaders: Domingos Barbosa succeeded his father as principal in Monsarás because the governor had deemed his older brother too rebellious for the post.[26] Lineages could be easily disrupted, especially by periodic epidemics. Important posts went unoccupied and a few small villages were left with no officers until boys came of age.[27] But long dynastic lines developed in other settlements: in Sintra, descendants of the mid-seventeenth-century mission principal, Lope de Sousa, still ran their settlement over a century later;[28] and in Chaves on Marajó Island, another prestigious line stretched from the late eighteenth century back to mid-seventeenth-century Principal and Governor of the Aruã Nation Antonio Manajaboca.[29]

The succession of leadership in Portel, the largest Directorate town, demonstrates the potential problems of this hereditary system and highlights the complex relationships among ethnic groups within the colony. Prior to the Directorate, the principal of the Pacajá, the original inhabitants of the Jesuit mission, and both of his sons died, leaving no heirs. Faced with a succession crisis, the Jesuits named Principal Anselmo de Mendonça, leader of the Curaûm (or Ocutiatinga, as they called themselves), to act as principal of the Pacajá. Together, these two groups were known as the Tapijaras. In 1768, after

Principal Anselmo died, the Pacajá leaders discovered that the son of their legitimate principal's daughter was still alive in Belém, where he had served as an infantry soldier for nearly thirty years. In a petition to the governor, they rejected Anselmo's heir—Sergeant-Major Cipriano Inácio de Mendonça—as their leader. After all, they stressed, it was their own principal who had brought Cipriano's grandfather out of the forest in the first place.[30] As it turned out, the Pacajá did not get their legitimate leader, but neither was Cipriano ever promoted to the rank of principal. This case not only underscores problems in succession, it shows the Pacajá leadership using highly legalistic measures to defend their autonomy. It also reveals the solid historical memory of ancestry and the layering of identities within Directorate communities.

Although posts could be awarded for merit, the interests of the nobility and the directors converged to concentrate power in elite families. The native nobility actively worked to keep positions in the family, and sons and nephews of the principais generally served as lesser officers while the older men were alive.[31] Directors in turn sought to limit the total number of officers because, as the director of Porto de Moz asserted, "The more principais there are, the more they restrict the Indians, involving them in drunken bouts and hiding them when they are called for royal service. . . ." He recommended three principais' sons to fill lesser posts, reasoning that they were qualified and, because as members of the native nobility they were already exempt from labor assignments, their appointments would not decrease the number of workers on the village rolls.[32]

The Pombaline reformers encouraged the elite status of this group, and while they did not ignore the crown's Christianizing mission, the legislation emphasized the civilizing rationale of Indian policy. Simply put, the Indians would become more Portuguese, speaking the language of the mother country, as opposed to the *língua geral* (that is, the Tupi-based lingua franca) favored by the missionaries, and devoting themselves to industrious, productive activities. Native society would mirror that of Portugal. In localities with township status, the native nobility would serve on elected municipal councils (*senados da câmara*) along with qualified white settlers.[33] The reformers fortified the indigenous hierarchy, imagining this would encourage the leaders to adopt "civilized" behavior appropriate to their social standing.[34]

A paradigm of the civilizing process was clothing, and, in an era when sumptuary laws regulated who could wear what, types of cloth, adornment, and costume clearly indicated social status.[35] The royal treasury customarily advanced cloth to Indians who agreed to join the colony to mark their

Figure 18. In this idealized depiction of an Amazonian landscape, boatmen pole a wooden raft down the falls of a river. Native huts stand in neat rows before a church. Source: Christoph Gottlieb von Murr, *Reisen einiger Missionarien der Gesellschaft Jesu in Amerika* (Nuremberg: Johann Eberhard Zeh, 1785). Courtesy of the John Carter Brown Library at Brown University.

transition from savage to civilized. The commoner needed only homespun cotton to make a shirt and trousers, or a skirt, but the principal required fine material for formal attire, which like an officer's uniform signified his position.[36] In 1762, Bishop João de São José Queirós encountered a new principal from the Rio Negro, "dressed in a red suit, with a wig, sword and cane," showing "the authority of a *homem bon* [gentleman]. . . ."[37] What the headmen thought of their European costumes in private is unknown, but they were cognizant of their usefulness when dealing with the colonial authorities.

Status was also communicated by spatial hierarchies and family names. As early as the mid-seventeenth century, the place of one's grave mirrored one's social position, as in Europe. Only the principal of an entire mission would be interred within the grill that divided the main part of the church from the choir and altar; other mission Indians were buried under the nave, while slaves were banished to the churchyard.[38] Similarly, during the Directorate, the principal and native officers of towns on Marajó Island, across the bay from the capital of Belém, occupied a special bench situated in the main crossing of the church during Mass.[39]

Just as a final resting place or prominent seat in church reflected status, so did a name. Although the pre-Directorate elite had received Christian first

names at baptism, they retained their indigenous names as last names, meaning, for example, Noble Jaguar or Great Alligator, which clearly conveyed their
importance.[40] Most mission Indians, however, had two first names because
they received their parents' first names as last names.[41] Calling this "an abuse,"
the Pombaline legislation decreed that Indians, just "as if they were whites,"
should have Portuguese last names to promote cultural integration and facilitate the management of labor and taxation rolls.[42] Thus, while names were
tools of oppression, they also corresponded to social rank. Most Directorate
Indians had typical Portuguese first and last names, but native officers were
more likely to acquire double family names and some principais had particularly ostentatious names—a number were named for Governor Francisco
Xavier de Mendonça Furtado.[43] Superior social status was also conveyed by
using the term of respect *dona* for the wives and daughters of these men.[44]

In addition to European symbols, in some towns the principais continued to be honored by local custom. The women of Monte Alegre produced
elaborate drinking cups, which fascinated Alexandre Rodrigues Ferreira,
head of a prestigious scientific expedition to the Amazon in the 1780s:

> One is kept in each house reserved to serve water or their wines to
> the principal. . . . What is distinctive about it is its decoration of
> shell, adhered with a ball of wax, its encrustation of beads, and its
> sculpted green stone [*muiraquitã*] on top, which serves as the han-
> dle. . . . No matter how hard I tried to buy one of these, . . . it was not
> possible, such is the value they place on the cup from which their
> principal drinks. And the white man, to whom they offer water in
> such a cup, can be flattered by the respect and attention this merits.
> The greatest insult and discourtesy would be to reject it.[45]

Outward symbols of authority, regardless of their origin, thus identified the
principais' status.

The social prestige enjoyed by the Indian elite was further demonstrated
by their access to colonial authorities, European education, and status marriage partners. Members of the native nobility customarily conferred with
the governor in Belém, and several sailed to Lisbon to meet the king.[46] The
sons of the native nobility attended colleges, and young children were often
educated in the homes of Portuguese leaders.[47] Their education would prepare them for their future roles, and it gave them access to greater authority
among both Europeans and Indians.[48]

Although a native leader's customary right to multiple wives clashed with civil and canon law and was the subject of principal-priest conflicts throughout the period, leaders found ways of dealing with the problem: one principal told the priest that his so-called concubines were merely his servants.[49] Children and grandchildren of the elite appear to have been more likely than other Indians to marry colonists considered white. The Pombaline reformers successfully promoted intermarriage and a number of soldiers, including Captain José Antonio Salgado and the youthful Adjutant-Engineer Henrique João Wilckens, who would later be prominent in regional affairs, married Indian women, many of them daughters of the native elite.[50] The case of Lourenço Justinianno, who married a "nearly white woman," is more telling, however, because the match hinged on his noble status.[51] Similarly, Manoel Pereira de Faria, the principal of Oeiras, who in 1776 was also serving as the director of his town (apparently the first native leader to hold this post), notified the governor of his intention to marry a woman of "quality": her father seemed white (his brother was a priest), and her mother was the daughter of an Indian woman and the brother of a white regiment officer.[52]

Befitting such prestige, the Directorate continued to exempt native officers and their immediate relatives from the rotational labor imposed on commoners, such as grueling work building forts, paddling canoes, cutting lumber, or transporting cattle.[53] Granted, the laws were not always respected, but the nobility protested abuses.[54] Moreover, the Directorate introduced new measures to ensure the leaders' economic advantage. Exempt from working on the annual canoes that each town sent upriver to collect forest products for export via the General Treasury of the Indians, they were allowed, according to their rank, a specific number of men to work for them. The legislation even extended credit to the officers—if they could not pay the workers in advance, the Directorate allowed them to draw up an IOU, which they would satisfy from their share of the production.[55]

ECONOMIC AND POLITICAL PRIVILEGE AND POWER

Native officers (and their widows) used and abused their economic privileges.[56] In 1761, the director of Pombal remarked that "no Indian wants to go [on the canoe] for the principais because they do not pay. . . ."[57] Especially ambitious, Sergeant-Major Cipriano Inácio Mendonça of Portel successfully petitioned for the right to send additional men to work on the canoe, as his

Figure 19. Notwithstanding stereotypes stressing their isolation, Amazonian village Indians dedicated much of their energy during the colonial era to agriculture, lumbering, and collecting forest products, which connected them to markets and royal authorities downriver. Source: Murr, *Reisen einiger Missionarien.* Courtesy of the John Carter Brown Library at Brown University.

neighbor, the principal of Oeiras, did.[58] The principais also took advantage of their role as labor administrators. Although no Indians in the former missions were to undertake private service without license from the governor, the director of Portel accused the officers of ignoring regulations and profiting at the expense of the workers.[59]

Keenly aware of economic realities, the native leaders sought commercial opportunities and side-stepped government oversight when possible. Although the Directorate required that all commercial transactions should be overseen by the directors and export goods should be sent to the Indian treasury, the indigenous leaders often made their own arrangements. Sergeant-Major Cipriano not only got extra canoe labor, but he was involved in the manioc trade and he hired men to produce over a ton of valuable varnish (*jataiçica*), which he forwarded to the treasury.[60] After visiting Colares, quite near the capital city of Belém, however, the general intendant called the officers "great swindlers" because they "go about in suits and shoes, yet no trade has entered the treasury from this town in two years." Asked how they could afford their clothing, the men admitted to selling manioc and crabs in Belém. Not only did the director not act as an intermediary, the officers "do not inform him when they go off."[61] Even more audacious, the principal of

Monte Alegre bypassed the treasury in Belém and shipped his sarsaparilla directly to Lisbon, to take advantage of substantially higher prices there.[62] The native elite were active in the regional and Atlantic economy, and they also traded with maroons and forest communities.[63]

As a result, the principais and indigenous officers were relatively wealthy. Although the crown had denied the native nobility salaries at the turn of the eighteenth century, by mid-century some secured a monthly stipend, and many harvested more produce than the average Indian villager.[64] This affluence translated to greater purchasing power. Certainly the native elite had owned Indian slaves prior to the abolition of Indian slavery and probably acquired African or Afro-Brazilian slaves later on.[65] The officers of Boim, up the Tapajós River, were active consumers, demonstrating a penchant for displays of status goods befitting any eighteenth-century bourgeois gentleman. From the Indian treasury, they requested swords, sword belts, jackets, shoes and stockings, tools, salt, iron and steel, medical cups and a set of lancets, salt, tin plates, spoons, and forks.[66] All of the men clearly valued elite merchandise, and one of them apparently practiced western medicine.

Behind these potent cultural symbols, native officers had to negotiate their authority both externally, with the Portuguese crown, and internally, with the members of their ethnic group and other villagers. Many leaders derived strength from a large extended family that formed the inner circle of their patronage network. In 1780, the powerful Sergeant-Major Anacleto de Souza of Pombal was described as, "blind and decrepit for years now, with the temperament and custom of inciting a large circle of relatives whenever he wanted to advance false complaints against the directors . . . and whites."[67] Souza's network of relatives had served as a powerful block of support for some thirty years. Not all leaders were so active; some apparently avoided their duties.[68]

Native leaders maintained the loyalty of Indian commoners through favors, such as exemption from labor obligations, release from jail, or timely replacement on royal projects.[69] In Portel, the largest Directorate town with a population of roughly 2,500 consisting of some thirteen Indian ethnic groups,[70] leaders vied for adherents. The director accused the Ariquena principal, Basílio de Carvalho, whose people had relocated from the Negro River region, of usurping the "vassals" of the "nationals" (descendants of the original inhabitants of the mission) by promising that he would ignore the governor's labor requisitions.[71] Leaders walked a fine line, however, and could not merely cater to their followers while alienating colonial authorities, who labeled uncooperative officers *absolutos*, meaning independent or rebellious.

In extreme cases, the principais confronted censure from the governor; although verbal rebukes came first, imprisonment was a last resort.[72] Acting on orders from the governor, the director of Pombal imprisoned Principal Ascenso Rodrigues Chavez "as a pertinacious rebel." Twice the director had asked the principal for workers to assign to state service: the first time Chavez "paid no attention," and the second "he sent the messenger away brusquely to tell me he had no Indians for service." Yet according to the director, the man's house was a refuge for deserters—a fact verified by eyewitnesses and by his own domestics. Finally, the director sent the native sergeant-major to Chavez's fields, where Chavez insulted him, saying "if he wanted Indians for royal service he should get some from the forest. . . ."[73] The principal successfully maintained internal support, but he pushed the director too far and the governor authorized his arrest.

Although judicial investigations identified a number of tyrannical or even sadistic directors,[74] these men had no monopoly on local power. Everyday realities and the machinations of native leaders undermined their authority. To furnish workers for state projects the directors had to rely on the principais, who often took their time about complying, supplied only a fraction of the number requested, and then provided cover for workers who deserted.[75] Other contingencies moderated the directors' control as well. When the judge on Marajó Island ordered one native adjutant to be thrown in jail as a vagrant, the principal left the jail door unlocked. The adjutant "escaped" and, in the company of the principal, sailed off to Belém to complain to the governor. These officers sought out the crown representative for support and, what was worse for the indignant Portuguese director, who also wanted to complain, they absconded with the only canoe.[76] Such frustration appears with frequency in the directors' letters to the governor. These letters, although surely biased, reveal how power arrangements were contested at the local level.

Power sharing within Directorate towns led to the ascendancy of some local strongmen among the natives, but colonial authorities emphatically precluded any role for the *pajé*, or shaman, substituting him with the parish priest. Yet an exceptionally inventive rogue in Portel showed how it was possible, at least for a time, to elude the power of religious and civil authorities, including the principais. In the late 1750s, Raimundo Antonio avoided Mass, threatened people with witchcraft, and sang and played the maracas in a special hut where he conducted healing rites and spoke in spirit voices.

Three years later, accused of "never obeying his principal or the directors," he was sent to the governor for punishment. When he returned, he refused to undertake royal service or pay his tithe, and he flaunted the governor's authority by assuming the title of second lieutenant. Finally, he supplanted the parish priest by marrying villagers and conducting what he called Mass in the forest. He usurped the authority of the king, the governor, the priest, and the Indian leader Sergeant-Major Cipriano, who complained to the governor. Having alienated the establishment, in 1777 Raimundo was again arrested, along with his followers, for fomenting revolt.[77] Raimundo Antonio challenged all bases of colonial power. That he got away with it for two decades, despite his previous arrest, suggests lax oversight, while his ability to attract adherents indicates that the native elite did not fully represent everyone's interests.

If the organization of local power was such that principais, directors, vicars, and occasional freelancers were often at each others' throats, special circumstances made for increased tensions. In the face of an abusive director or increasing labor demands, the native leaders resorted to legal and extralegal means to protect themselves. Generally, they used legal channels, reporting abuses of the Directorate to the crown judge, although it was rumored that in 1773 the Indian Sergeant-Major Anecleto de Souza had ordered the death of his director by witchcraft.[78] Other principais, who found no redress to their grievances or who suffered personal insults, abandoned the colony altogether, taking their followers, who were valued laborers, to the forest with them.[79] Principal Mathias Caetano de Sousa of Piriá escaped both an overzealous director and the tyranny of his own uncle by moving his followers to the Atlantic coast, where he founded a new town. Such an act could only be formally sanctioned by the governor, but the principal prevailed. After five years, Governor and Captain General José de Nápoles Telo de Meneses officially recognized the de facto situation, proudly taking personal credit for the accomplishment and naming the new town Viseu.[80]

POST-POMBALINE CHANGE AND CONTINUITY

In the mid 1780s, after Pombal had fallen from power, a cabal of regional authorities ignored the elite, infringed on their rights, and mismanaged their interests at the Indian treasury. The principais of Colares and Oeiras wrote

Figure 20. As these objects drawn in the early nineteenth century attest, native peoples did not necessarily relinquish the use of traditional items such as ceremonial dress, scepters, and musical instruments even as their contacts with colonial society deepened. The cloak pictured in the upper right was made from cotton adorned with yellow and red feathers and attributed to Indians living in Pará. Source: Debret, *Voyage pittoresque.* Public domain access: http://www.brasiliana.usp.br/bbd/handle/1918/624510047

directly to Queen Maria I (r. 1777–1816) to complain.[81] Oeiras's powerful Pereira de Faria protested the appointment of José Anveres and his fifteen-year-old son as directors of the neighboring towns of Portel and Melgaço and claimed the directors and the governor were using the Indians for their personal gain. Moreover, he protested that the governor had publicly insulted him, which was strictly forbidden by the Directorate. This complaint brought a quick rebuke from the queen and the immediate replacement of the underage director.[82] When the new governor and captain general, Francisco de Souza Coutinho, assumed office in the summer of 1790, he made a clear break with the past, naming native leaders to the position of director.[83] Perhaps encouraged by the change, the leaders of the various ethnic groups in Portel united to launch a formal complaint against Anveres.[84] The governor's investigation determined the culpability of the directors of Portel, Melgaço, and Oeiras, as well as the former governor and the general intendant and magistrate.

After investigating and confirming the charges of abuse leveled by the Portel officers, the governor quickly replaced the directors and recommended ending the Directorate.[85] The corruption of state authorities was not the only justification, however. Available labor in the former missions simply could not keep up with royal demands, so the governor came up with a scheme that would incorporate more people in the state-run programs. By expanding the militias and organizing labor corps, he could still access Indian labor while shifting part of the burden to the lower strata of the general population. It may also be that the indigenous privileged class had grown proportionally large. Although the censuses did not usually list the officers separately, in 1783–1784 they totaled 192, or 3.6 percent of the native men over the age of thirteen, and in 1792, 202, or 4.0 percent, with percentages varying considerably from town to town. Along with their wives and children, this group numbered 1,064, or 5.3 percent of the total Directorate Indian population in 1792.[86] Since only some of the principais' sons and brothers and none of their daughters or sisters held offices, and yet they were all also exempt from labor assignments, the total percentage of this privileged sector would have been substantial.

Even after the Directorate was abolished in 1798, native leaders persisted as local authorities: with administrative reforms, their titles changed, but the same men occupied top posts. When the governor revoked the Directorate, he appointed native leaders to posts in the new militia. In 1799, Standard-Bearer José Antonio de Brito of the former Directorate town of Monte Alegre received the same rank in the militia of Santarém. At Ponta de Pedras on Marajó, Raimundo José Barbosa had held the rank of sergeant-major as leader of the Engaiba for nearly 40 years, when, in 1800, the governor appointed him a militia captain. The principais of Monte Alegre and Melgaço received the same post. Ethnic affiliation apparently continued to be an important aspect of community organization and identity in Ponta de Pedras and Melgaço, since their militias were organized by ethnic nation.[87]

In contrast, royal orders specified that whites and Indians should alternate as judges.[88] The long career of the native leader Sergeant-Major Amaro Pereira da Silva of Faro is well documented. He received his appointment to the post of sergeant-major directly from King José I (r. 1750–1777) during his visit to the court in Lisbon in 1764; he then served numerous times as a judge and councilman. Prominent in local affairs during the entire Directorate, Silva died in 1800, having just been appointed a lieutenant colonel in the militia.[89] Not only did directors and vicars rotate frequently while the native leaders served for life, the indigenous officers survived the administrative changes from mission, to Directorate, to post-Directorate Pará.

Even as disease and oppression ravaged the population, a hierarchy of indigenous authority descended from the original inhabitants of the missions. While ethnic identities were transformed or reconfigured—indeed, the disappearance of ethnic references should not be confused with wholesale extinction—historical memory could be called upon when needed. The survival of some leaders into the nineteenth century provides incontrovertible evidence that many indigenous residents of Directorate towns remained in them after the legislation was abolished and often retained local authority. Although the medieval arrangement wherein the native nobility controlled their vassals was replaced by a modern military structure, one more in line with expanded state powers, the same men retained leadership positions.

A profusion of newly-studied documents reveals how native leaders played essential and dynamic roles in the everyday workings of the colony, conspicuously using their economic and social privileges. Donning baroque dress and refinement, they served as judges, acted on municipal councils, wrote to, and even had audiences with the Portuguese monarch. As tenacious and inventive defenders of their own interests, they took on European ways when it suited them.

NOTES

1. John Hemming, *Red Gold: The Conquest of the Brazilian Indians* (Cambridge, MA: Harvard University Press, 1978), 198, 206–7. I gratefully acknowledge research support from the Fulbright Commission, Gettysburg College, and the Fundação Luso-Americana, Lisbon. Thanks also to my fellow contributors to this volume for being dedicated and generous colleagues. Abbreviations used in the notes are as follows: Arquivo Histórico Ultramarino, Lisbon (AHU); Arquivo Nacional, Rio de Janeiro (ANRJ); Arquivo Nacional da Torre do Tombo, Lisbon (ANTT); Arquivo Público do Estado do Pará, Belém (APEP); *Annaes da Biblioteca Pública do Estado do Pará* (*ABAPP*); Biblioteca National, Rio de Janeiro (BNRJ); *Revista do Instituto Histórico e Geográfico Brasileiro* (*RIHGB*). To

shorten document citations, I eliminated most proper names, but have retained titles, abridging "governor and captain general" to "governor," and "general intendant and magistrate" to "intendant."

2. Mathias C. Kiemen, "The Indian Policy of Portugal on the Amazon Region, 1614–1693" (PhD diss., Catholic University of America, 1954), 57–58, 70–71.

3. Kiemen, "Indian Policy," 70–71; António Vieira, "Visita," in Serafim Leite, *História da Companhia de Jesus no Brasil*, 10 vols. (Rio de Janeiro: Instituto Nacional do Livro; Lisbon: Livraria Portugália, 1943), 4: 120.

4. For more on the Indian slave trade, see David Graham Sweet, "A Rich Realm of Nature Destroyed: The Middle Amazon Valley, 1640–1750" (PhD diss., University of Wisconsin, 1974); Dauril Alden, "Indian Versus Black Slavery in the State of Maranhão During the Seventeenth and Eighteenth Centuries," *Bibliotheca Americana* 1, no. 3 (Jan. 1983): 91–142; John M. Monteiro, "Escravidão indígena e despovoamento na América portuguesa: S. Paulo e Maranhão," in *Brasil nas vésperas do mundo moderno* (Lisbon: Comissão Nacional para as Comemorações dos Descobrimentos Portugueses, 1992), 137–67; and Barbara A. Sommer, "Colony of the *Sertão*: Amazonian Expeditions and the Indian Slave Trade," *The Americas* 61, no. 3 (Jan. 2005): 401–28.

5. António Vieira to King João IV, Maranhão, 6 Apr. 1654, in *Cartas do Padre António Vieira*, ed. João Lúcio d'Azevedo, 3 vols. (Coimbra: Imprensa da Universidade, 1925), 1: 437–38.

6. Ignacio Manajaboca became governor of the Aruã in 1702; see petition filed with Inácio Coelho to king [José I], [prior to 15 Mar. 1755], AHU, Pará-013, cx. 38, doc. 3525; and Feliciano Pereira Ramalho was titled governor of the Parnaíba River region, "Língua Geral da Nação," see register of letters patent, São Luís, 3 Dec. 1748, APEP, códice 26, doc. 411.

7. For a path-breaking discussion of indigenous agents in Spanish American colonies, see Karen Spalding, "The Colonial Indian: Past and Future Research Perspectives," *Latin American Research Review* 7, no. 1 (Spring 1972): 47–76. For the second half of the eighteenth century in Brazil, see John Hemming, *Amazon Frontier: The Defeat of the Brazilian Indians* (London: MacMillan, 1987), chaps. 1–3; for independent ethnic groups, see the essays in Manuela Carneiro da Cunha, ed., *História dos índios no Brasil* (São Paulo: Companhia das Letras, FAPESP/SMC, 1992); and for resistance, see Francisco Jorge dos Santos, *Além da Conquista: Guerras e rebeliões indígenas na Amazônia pombalina*, 2d ed. (Manaus: Universidade do Amazonas, 2002).

8. Space does not allow for a summary of the Spanish American literature. Cf. Karen Spalding, "Social Climbers: Changing Patterns of Mobility among the Indians of Colonial Peru," *Hispanic American Historical Review* 50, no. 4 (Nov. 1970): 645–64; and Steven W. Hackel, "The Staff of Leadership: Indian Authority in the Missions of Alta California," *The William and Mary Quarterly* 3d ser., 54, no. 2 (Apr. 1997): 347–76.

9. John Hemming mentioned indigenous officers only in passing, noting that the 1757 *Diretório* "tried to reward or bribe the newly appointed village chiefs" in *Amazon Frontier*, 15. Rita Heloísa de Almeida dismissed the men as colonial puppets in *O Diretório dos índios: Um projeto de "civilização" no Brasil do século XVIII* (Brasília: Universidade de Brasília, 1997), a view contested in Barbara A. Sommer, "Negotiated Settlements: Native Amazonians and Portuguese Policy in Pará, Brazil, 1758–1798" (PhD diss., University of New Mexico, 2000), esp. 221; and Ângela Domingues, *Quando os índios eram vassalos: Colonização e relações de poder no Norte do Brasil na segunda metade do século XVIII* (Lisbon: Comissão Nacional para as Comemorações dos Descobrimentos Portugueses, 2000), 145n, 173. More recently, the native nobility have attracted the attention of Brazilian historians; see especially Mauro Cezar Coelho, "O Diretório dos índios e as chefias indígenas: Uma inflexão," *Campos* 7, no. 1 (2006): 117–34; and Rafael Ale Rocha, "Os oficiais índios na Amazônia Pombalina: Sociedade, hierarquia e resistência (1751–1798) (MA thesis, Universidade Federal Fluminense, 2009).

10. For a synopsis in English, see Antonio Porro, "Social Organization and Political Power in the Amazon Floodplain: The Ethnohistorical Sources," in *Amazonian Indians: From Prehistory to the Present*, ed. Anna C. Roosevelt (Tucson: University of Arizona Press, 1994), 79–94.

11. See Sweet, "A Rich Realm," esp. Appendix A; Carlos de Araújo Moreira Neto, *Índios da Amazônia: de maioria a minoria (1750–1850)* (Petrópolis: Editora Vozes, 1988), 56–57; and Nádia Farage, *As muralhas dos sertões: Os povos indígenas no rio Branco e a colonização* (Rio de Janeiro: Paz e Terra; ANPOCS, 1991).

12. Domingues, *Quando os índios*, esp. 169–76; and Sommer, "Negotiated Settlements," esp. chap. 5. For Rio de Janeiro, see Maria Regina Celestino de Almeida, *Metamorfoses indígenas: Indentidade e cultura nas aldeias coloniais do Rio de Janeiro* (Rio de Janeiro: Arquivo Nacional, 2003), esp. 150–68.

13. See Colin MacLachlan, "The Indian Directorate: Forced Acculturation in Portuguese America," *The Americas* 28, no. 4 (Apr. 1972): 357–87; Moreira Neto, *Índios da Amazônia*; and Eric Ross, "The Evolution of the Amazonian Peasantry," *Journal of Latin American Studies* 10 (Nov. 1978): 193–218.

14. John Hemming, "Indians and the Frontier," in *Colonial Brazil*, ed. Leslie Bethell (1987; repr., Cambridge: Cambridge University Press, 1991), 189.

15. See, for example, Serge Gruzinski, *The Mestizo Mind: The Intellectual Dynamics of Colonization and Globalization*, trans. Deke Dusinberre (New York: Routledge, 2002).

16. For more on Arawakan culture, see Jonathan D. Hill and Fernando Santos-Granero, eds., *Comparative Arawakan Histories: Rethinking Language Family and Culture Area in Amazonia* (Urbana and Chicago: University of Illinois Press, 2002).

17. The *Diretório* is published in facsimile as "Directorio que se deve observar nas Povoaçoens dos Indios do Pará, e Maranhão em quanto Sua Magestade não mandar o contrario" (Pará, 1757), in Moreira Neto, *Índios da Amazônia*, 165–203. References to *Diretório* articles are based on this facsimile.

18. *Diretório*, art. 78.
19. See [intendant], Veiros, 21 Dec. 1766, APEP, cód. 160.
20. See lists, Vila Franca, 28 Feb. 1762, APEP, cód. 113, doc. 31; 1 July 1776, APEP, cód. 301, doc. 21; 1 July 1784, APEP, cód. 408, doc. 69[r]; captain-major to governor, Santarém, 12 May 1759, APEP, cód. 71, doc. 6; list, Santarém, 1 July 1784, APEP, cód. 408, doc. 69[z]; director to governor, Alenquer, 20 Aug. 1764, APEP, cód. 141, doc. 41; and list, 1 July 1784, APEP, cód. 408, 69[u].
21. Register of letters patent, 30 Oct. 1752, 16 Aug. 1763, APEP, cód. 58, docs. 108, 634a; [director?] to governor, Pombal, 30 July 1780, APEP, cód. 127, doc. 79; and list, Pombal, 1 July 1784, APEP, cód. 408, doc. 69[j].
22. [Principal] to governor, Oeiras, 28 Sept. 1767, APEP, cód. 71, doc. 125; petition, principal to king [José I], prior to 17 June 1771, AHU, Pará-013, cx. 67, doc. 5752; director [and principal] to governor, Oeiras, 26 Feb. 1774, APEP, cód. 272, doc. 66; and 13 May 1776, APEP, cód. 298, doc. 110.
23. João Vasco Manoel de Braun, "Roteiro Corographico," *RIHGB* 12 (1849), 327. Probably Principal Francisco Xavier de Mendonça Furtado.
24. Vieira, "Visita," in Leite, *História da Companhia*, 120.
25. See register of letters patent, 9 Sept. 1780 and 6 Oct. 1781, APEP, cód. 368, docs. 50, 153.
26. [Director] to intendant, Monsarás, 14 Feb. 1785, APEP, cód. 325, doc. 32.
27. Director to governor, Penha Longa, 21 Apr. 1774, APEP, cód. 271, doc. 48; and 11 Sept. 1775, APEP, cód. 284, doc. 43.
28. Overseas Council to King João V, Lisbon, 30 Apr. 1732, AHU, Maranhão-009, cx. 19, doc. 1977; Sebastião Joseph de Carvalho e Melo [Pombal] to [king], Paço, 15 Mar. 1755, and petition filed with Inácio Coelho to king [José I], AHU, Pará-013, cx. 38, doc. 3525; principal to governor, 13 Jan. 1765, Sintra, APEP, cód. 151, doc. 35; and principal to [overseas secretary], Pará, 24 June 1765, AHU, Pará-013, cx. 58, doc. 5219.
29. Register of letters patent, 26 June and 6 Oct. 1752, 19 Sept. 1758, 14 Aug. 1764, APEP, cód. 58, docs. 64, 100, 255, 670, and 671; governor to [overseas secretary], Pará, 26 Nov. 1753, AHU, Pará-013, cx. 35, doc. 3307; petition, AHU, Pará-013, cx. 38, doc. 3525; list, Chaves, 1 July 1776, APEP, cód. 301, doc. 10, and 1 Jan. 1784, APEP, cód. 408, doc. 48a; and register of letters patent, 3 Aug. 1791, APEP, cód. 368, doc. 770.
30. Sergeant-major et al. to [governor], [n.p.], [1768], APEP, cód. 189, doc. 75; director to [governor], Portel, 14 Sept. 1771, APEP, cód. 236, doc. 15; and petition, sergeant-major to queen [Maria I], Pará, [prior to 7 Sept. 1779], AHU, Pará-013, cx. 83, doc. 6839.
31. Director to [governor], Portel, 18 May 1778, APEP, cód. 331, doc. 50; Pombal, 26 Oct. 1761, APEP, cód. 108, doc. 14; and list, Pombal, 1 July 1784, APEP, cód. 408, doc. 69[j]. Generational disputes were not unknown, see [director] to governor, Souzel, 17 Aug. 1764, APEP, cód. 141, doc. 36, and 1 July 1776, APEP, cód. 301, doc. 20.
32. Director to governor, Porto de Moz, 2 Aug. 1764, APEP, cód. 141, doc. 1.

33. For letters from the municipal councils to the governor, see APEP, cód. 69.
34. *Diretório*, art. 9.
35. Ibid., art. 15. For legislation prohibiting slave women from wearing silks, velvets, or cloth with gold or silver threads, see governor to King João V, Belém, 3 Aug. 1734, AHU, Pará-013, cx. 16, doc. 1516.
36. See the Royal Treasury records in APEP, cód. 110.
37. Bishop João de São José Queiroz [Queirós], "Viagem e visita do sertão em o Bispado do Gram-Pará em 1762 e 1763," *RIHGB* 9 (1847), 69.
38. Vieira, "Visita," in Leite, *História da Companhia*, 118.
39. To [overseas secretary], [n.p.], [post 1759], AHU, Pará-013, cx. 45, doc. 4139.
40. "Jaguará Abaité," in Procurador Geral [Attorney General of Maranhão] Jorge de Sampaio e Carvalho, 24 July 1662, in João Renôr Ferreira de Carvalho, *Momentos de História da Amazônia* (Imperatriz: Ética, 1998), 72; and "Jauarucú," [Jaguar açu], "Vacará Vosú," [Jacaré açu?], sergeant-major et al., APEP, cód. 189, doc. 75.
41. Girls often received their mother's name, boys their father's. See Arlene Marie Kelly, "Family, Church, and Crown: A Social and Demographic History of the Lower Xingu Valley and the Municipality of Gurupá, 1623–1889" (PhD diss., University of Florida, 1984), 94.
42. *Diretório*, art. 11.
43. See town rolls, APEP, cód. 301, 408.
44. See, for example, commandant to governor, Fort N. Senhora de Nazaré, 16 Feb. 1784, APEP, cód. 408, doc. 19; and petition, Maria Matildes Barboza, [Monsarás], [3 Feb. 1785], APEP, cód. 325, doc. 31.
45. Alexandre Rodrigues Ferreira, *Viagem Filosófica pelas capitanias do Grão Pará, Rio Negro, Mato Grosso e Cuiabá* (Rio de Janeiro: Conselho Federal de Cultura, 1974), 38.
46. Petition, Lisbon, [prior to 4 July 1764], AHU, Pará-013, cx. 57, doc. 5143.
47. Braun, "Roteiro Corographico," 313; list, Fragoso, 21 Aug. 1777, APEP, cód. 312, doc. 24, no. 44; and Domingues, *Quando os índios*, 120–24.
48. In 1783, Rodrigues Ferreira described the septuagenarian Sergeant-Major Severino dos Santos of Monforte as "civilized, or at least with the civility of having learned to read, write, and count. . . . He speaks quickly and understands Portuguese and so I had no scruple about subscribing to his information." Ferreira, *Viagem Filosófica*, 99. Natives at Veiros supported a literate leader, [intendant], Veiros, 21 Dec. 1766, APEP, cód. 160.
49. Chaplain to governor, Serzedelo, 8 Feb. 1784, APEP, cód. 408, doc. 13[16].
50. [Director] to governor, Portel, 10 May 1759, APEP, cód. 95, doc. 39; judge to governor, Monforte, 30 Jan. 1774, APEP, cód. 276, doc. 9; and commandant to governor, Santarém, 6 Feb. 1778, APEP, cód. 277, doc. 74. Historians do not mention Wilckens' marriage, although it may have influenced his development as a political figure in late eighteenth-century Amazonia. See [governor] to [overseas

secretary], Pará, 31 July 1759, AHU, Pará-013, cx. 45, doc. 4100; and Henrique João Wilckens to governor, Barcellos, 10 Aug. 1800, in *Relatos da fronteira amazônica no século XVIII: documentos de Henrique João Wilckens e Alexandre Rodrigues Ferreira*, eds. Marta Rosa Amoroso and Nádia Farage (São Paulo: NHII-USP; FAPESP, 1994), 63–67.

51. Captain-director to governor, Salvaterra, 25 Aug. 1787, APEP, cód. 365, doc. 58.

52. Director [and principal] to governor, Oeiras, 13 May 1776, APEP, cód. 298, doc. 110.

53. *Diretório*, art. 15; and royal letter, 3 Feb. 1701, "A Junta das Missões do Estado do Maranhão," in "Documentos sôbre o índio Brasileiro (1500–1822)," ed. Leda Maria Cardoso Naud, *Revista de Informação Legislativa* 8, no. 71 (1971), 2: 250–52. For the quality and quantity of work performed by natives, see the impressive list in Aluisio Fonseca de Castro, "Manuscritos sobre a amazônia colonial: Repertório referente à mão-de-obra indígena do fundo Secretaria do Governor (Colônial e Império)," *Anais do Arquivo Público do Pará* 2, no. 1 (1996): 9–121.

54. See, for example, petition and intendant's investigation, APEP, cód. 325, docs. 28–33; and [director?] to governor, Pombal, 30 July 1780, APEP, cód. 127, doc. 79.

55. *Diretório*, arts. 9, 46–58, 71.

56. See lists, APEP, cód. 141, 312; lists, Boim, 23–24 Oct. 1760, APEP, cód. 107, doc. 81[a].

57. Director to [governor], Pombal, 26 Oct. 1761, APEP, cód. 108, doc. 14. See also director to [governor], Alter do Chão, 21 Nov. 1761, APEP, cód. 108, doc. 31; and [intendant], Conde, 18 Jan. 1765, APEP, cód. 160.

58. Petition, sergeant-major of Portel to queen [Maria I], [prior to 7 Sept. 1779], AHU, Pará-013, cx. 83, doc. 6839.

59. *Diretório*, arts. 62, 69; and director to [governor], Portel, 3 Oct. 1759, APEP, cód. 95, doc. 119.

60. Director to [governor], Portel, 22 Aug. 1769, APEP, cód. 202, doc. 58.

61. [Intendant], Colares, 30 Jan. 1765, APEP, cód. 160.

62. General intendant of commerce to [secretary of commerce], Pará, 31 Dec. 1777, AHU, Pará-013, cx. 78, doc. 6508.

63. See, for example, padre to governor, Santa Anna de Macapá, 15 Apr. 1759, APEP, cód. 17, doc. 12.

64. Petition, AHU, Pará-013, cx. 57, doc. 5143; lists, APEP, cód. 141, 312.

65. List, Monte Alegre, 24 July 1761, APEP, cód. 107, doc. 51. In the 1790s, Indians owned African or Afro-Brazilian slaves, although admittedly very few—only 35 in 1792 and 47 in 1797. Although censuses did not specify who owned the slaves, the native nobility's relative wealth points to them. See censuses, 1 Jan. 1792, BNRJ, I-17, 12, 2; and 1797, ANRJ, cód. 99, vol. 20, fol. 50.

66. Lists, Boim, 24 Oct. 1760, APEP, cód. 107, doc. 81[a].

67. APEP, cód. 58, docs. 108, 634a; [director?] to governor, Pombal, 30 July 1780, APEP, cód. 127, doc. 79.

68. One director, not a disinterested observer, described a "rustic" principal who preferred fishing. [Director] to [governor], Monte Alegre, 28 Feb. 1778, APEP, cód. 331, doc. 24.

69. Director to [governor], Portel, 14 Dec. 1762, APEP, cód. 115, doc. 67; and 2 Mar. 1764, APEP, cód. 137, doc. 62. One principal requested the release of an imprisoned Indian because he was related to another officer, in director to [governor], Pombal, 24 Aug. 1771, APEP, cód. 232, doc. 59.

70. Queiroz, "Viagem," 491.

71. Director to [governor], Portel, 10 May 1759, APEP, cód. 95, doc. 39.

72. In response to complaints about the principal of Barcarena, the governor hoped a sharp reprimand would solve the problem. Director to governor, Barcarena, 7 Apr. 1776, APEP, cód. 298, doc. 83; and governor to director, Pará, 20 May 1776, APEP, cód. 291, doc. 436. Also see judge to governor, Monforte, 30 Jan. 1774, APEP, cód. 276, doc. 10; and governor to regiment commander-director, Pará, 23 May 1776, APEP, cód. 291, doc. 448.

73. Director to [governor], Pombal, 23 Dec. 1763, APEP, cód. 131, doc. 109.

74. Abusive directors are highlighted in Hemming, *Amazon Frontier*, 52–55.

75. [Director] to governor, Ponta de Pedras, 10 Aug. 1764, APEP, cód. 141, doc. 26; Portel, 30 Oct. 1764, APEP, cód. 140, doc. 40; Monsarás, 20 Feb. 1765, APEP, cód. 151, doc. 77; [intendant], Monsarás, 25 June 1765, APEP cód. 160; director to [governor], Pombal, 24 Aug. 1771, APEP, cód. 232, doc. 59, and 30 Sept. 1771, cód. 236, doc. 44; judge to governor, Monforte, 30 Jan. 1774, APEP, cód. 276, doc. 10; and director to governor, Porto de Moz, 14 Apr. 1776, APEP, cód. 298, doc. 91.

76. Captain-director to governor, Monforte, 17 Sept. 1787, APEP, cód. 365, doc. 59.

77. Summary depositions, 27 Sept. 1758, Portel, ANTT, Inquisição de Lisboa, maço 1073, no. 12,886; director to governor, Portel, 13 Sept. 1761, APEP, cód. 107, doc. 89; 20 Mar. 1775, APEP, cód. 285, doc. 77; and sergeant-major to governor, and director to governor, Portel, 24 June 1777, APEP, cód. 314, docs. 22, 23.

78. Friar to [governor], Pombal, 14 Jan. 1773, APEP, cód. 224, doc. 56. See also, [intendant], Santarém, 30 Jan. 1767, APEP, cód. 160; intendancy scribe, transcript of investigation, Santarém, 21 Feb. 1775, APEP, cód. 286, doc. 14[b]; and captain to governor, Veiros, 16 Feb. 1792, APEP, cód. 472, doc. 28.

79. Directors to governor, Pinhel, 29 Nov. 1762, APEP, cód. 115, doc. 52; Portel, 17 Apr. 1765, APEP, cód. 151, doc. 131; and Pombal, 21 Feb. 1772, APEP, cód. 241, doc. 33.

80. Commandant-director to [governor], Serzedelo, 5 Feb. 1776, APEP, cód. 298, doc. 12; governor to commandant-director, Pará, 23 Feb. 1776, APEP, cód. 291, doc. 311; and governor to [overseas secretary], [Pará], 27 Jan. 1781, ANRJ, cód. 99, vol. 3, fol. 12r.

81. Petition, principal [of Colares] to queen, in bishop to Queen Maria I, Pará, 1 Aug. 1787, AHU, Pará-013, cx. 96, doc. 7663; and regiment commander-principal to queen [Maria I], Pará, 1 Mar. 1785, AHU, Pará-013, cx. 94, doc. 7484 (copy in APEP, cod 77, doc. 75).

82. Queen to governor, Lisbon, 25 Oct. 1785, APEP, cód. 77, doc. 72; and registry of letters patent, APEP, cód. 368, docs. 405, 465.

83. Register, 17 June 1790 and 29 July 1790, APEP, cód. 368, docs. 674, 683.

84. Copy of principais' petition, governor to [overseas secretary], Pará, 31 July 1790, ANRJ, cód. 99, vol. 11, fols. 174r–75v; another copy, Palace, 1 Aug. 1790, APEP, cód. 471, doc. [30].

85. Governor to [overseas secretary], Pará, 31 July 1790, ANRJ, cód. 99, vol. 11, fols. 174r, 202r–3r; register of letters patent, 4 Oct. 1790, APEP, cód. 368, docs. 698, 699, 700; Alexandre Rodrigues Ferreira to [overseas secretary], Pará, 6 Feb. 1792, in D. A. Tavares da Silva, *O Cientista Luso-Brasileiro: Dr. Alexandre Rodrigues Ferreira* (Lisbon: 1947), 144–46; chart, governor, 1792, ANRJ, cód. 99, vol. 13, fols. 222r–25r; Governor Francisco de Souza Coutinho, "Plano para a civilização dos indios na Capitania do Pará," ANRJ, cód. 101, vol. 2, fols. 54r–81v; and prince, Palacio de Queluz, 12 May 1798, ANRJ, cód. 101, vol. 2, fols. 48v–52r.

86. Censuses, 1783/84, ANRJ, cód. 99, doc. 6, fol. 23r; and 1792, BNRJ, I-17, 12, 2.

87. Register, APEP, cód. 368, docs. 403, 693; book 13, APEP, cód. 568, docs. 16, 167, 77, 171, 281; and petition, militia captain to prince regent [João], [post 18 Oct. 1804], AHU, Pará-013, cx. 131, doc. 10029.

88. Prince to governor, Queluz Palace, 12 May 1798, ANRJ, cód. 101, vol. 2, fol. 45v.

89. Petition, Lisbon, [prior to 4 July 1764], AHU, Pará-013, cx. 57, doc. 5143; João de Palma Muniz, "Limites Municipaes do Estado do Pará," *ABAPP* 9 (1916): 248–51; and book 13, APEP, cód. 568, doc. 130.

5

Indian Autonomy and Slavery in the Forests and Towns of Colonial Minas Gerais

Hal Langfur and Maria Leônia Chaves de Resende

First christened the Minas dos Cataguases (the Cataguá Indian mines), the mineral-rich inland territory that became known as Minas Gerais (the general mining district) did so only later, as the eighteenth century unfolded (see map 4). The original name assigned to the region by the Portuguese explorers who traversed its mountains and river valleys bespoke a colonial history set in motion by encounters with native peoples. For generations, scholarship devoted to its fabled history contributed little to our understanding of the process by which its indigenous inhabitants responded. Even though their presence was the topic of countless contemporaneous administrative and ecclesiastical discussions, the mining district's Indians remained virtually unstudied until quite recently.[1] Although a few historians noted native participation in the early history of Portuguese America's primary gold- and diamond-producing zone, they almost always did so in the most restricted fashion, reducing the role of Indians to preliminary interactions, without considering their subsequent importance as historical agents who contributed to the captaincy's social and cultural formation. Even when their persistent presence was noted, Indians were treated as a mere afterthought and assigned an inferior status.

A primary justification for this gap in the historiography was the alleged genocide perpetrated by paramilitary expeditions of conquest, known as *entradas* (entrances) and *bandeiras* (flag-bearing troops), toward the end of the seventeenth and beginning of the eighteenth centuries. According to this narrative, the first colonists penetrated the region's *sertões* (backlands), advanced indiscriminately through indigenous territory, and decimated the native population.[2] Indians were presumed to have been all but exterminated, leaving them no active role in the construction of regional society.

Our objective in this essay is to refute this interpretation. We are not the first to recognize the survival of native peoples in the mining district long after the onset of Portuguese exploration, conquest, and settlement.[3] However, our analysis of an extensive corpus of neglected archival sources has allowed us to offer a significantly more complete rendering of this chapter of Brazil's indigenous history.[4] In this text we emphasize a particular aspect of our collaborative research: the prominent, simultaneous, and connected presence of Indians not only in the region's remote, unsettled sertões, but also in its towns and villages. We propose, first, to gauge the degree to which seminomadic native peoples confronted the aggression of soldiers and settlers in the surrounding forests and, second, to elucidate the struggle against enslavement of those who came to live within the colony's rural and urban communities.

By examining the characteristics and conduct of these indigenous peoples and their mixed-race descendants, our aim is to contribute to a revised understanding of Minas Gerais during and immediately after its gold cycle (ca. 1700–1770), and of the wider colony during its final century of Portuguese rule. Like the other chapters in this volume, our findings help dispel a tenacious myth of the vanishing Indian.[5] Indians surviving to the end of the colonial period thereby become more visible, no longer presumed to have died off, to have lost their cultural identity, or to have fled deep into the continental interior.

The ongoing colonization of Minas Gerais linked forest Indians to those living in settled areas. By necessity, we have employed distinct sets of sources to reveal this connection. Military dispatches, expedition accounts, and frontier settler petitions detail the consequences of Portuguese incursions into native territory, discussed in the first part of the essay. Baptismal registries, marriage records, and judicial documents trace the trajectories of Indians absorbed into colonial domain, examined in the second part. The very different nature of these sources and experiences makes for a less-than-seamless story. In compensation, a more comprehensive portrait can be drawn of an indigenous population living simultaneously in more than one world. At the outermost reaches of settler society, bloody clashes with farmers, ranchers, and miners presented a constant challenge for still-independent natives, provoked outrage among frontier colonists, and preoccupied state authorities, who mobilized troops to secure distant homesteads, trails, and river routes. Some Indians resisted with surprising success over many decades. Others entered colonial society, sometimes willingly, often coerced, abandoning their wandering existence to reside in *aldeias*, towns, and villages under the supervision of the church and crown. While violent conflicts continued at the edge of the settled zone, new kinds of tensions developed within it, as Indians and their descendants struggled against those who sought to make them slaves. Rejecting invisibility, they asserted their indigenous identity in the face of attempts to define them as deracinated, generic members of a growing population of peoples of color. Throughout the eighteenth century, both in the mining district's surrounding forests and in its thoroughly colonized areas, the region's Indians remained historically significant.

"THEY AMUSE THEMSELVES BY SETTING OUT TO HUNT INDIANS"

The hunting of Indians was on the mind of poet Tomás Antônio Gonzaga and his readers, when in the captaincy capital of Vila Rica he pseudonymously circulated stanzas that included the line quoted above. The disturbing image comes from Gonzaga's *Cartas Chilenas*, which satirized royal administration on the eve of the anti-colonial intrigue known as the Inconfidência Mineira (Minas Conspiracy).[6] The plot was discovered in 1789, before its participants, including Gonzaga, could put their planned rebellion into action. At that moment, Governor Luís Antonio Furtado de Mendonça, the viscount of Barbacena (1788–1797), also thought of Indians. Having discovered that local poets, priests, military personnel, and indebted plutocrats planned his assassination and the declaration of an independent republic, the governor set in motion a plot of his own. The alleged sighting of hostile Indians along the captaincy's main road and primary escape route, the Caminho Novo, provided Mendonça the excuse he needed to reinforce troops on patrol. Scheming to avoid the "suspicion that any extraordinary movement of troops would cause," the governor calculated that residents of the mining district, accustomed as they were to seeing soldiers deployed to control unsettled Indians, would remain ignorant of his true motives. What he really sought—and successfully secured—was the swift arrest of the rebellious cabal.[7]

The Inconfidência Mineira has preoccupied generations of historians seeking to understand the demise of colonial rule in Portuguese America, but the governor's deception involving Indians has rarely prompted a second scholarly thought. Although a minor incident in the foiled conspiracy, the actions of Indians, real or imagined, at this decisive historical moment raise an important question about the broader contours of life in the mining district during the eighteenth century. Why was it, counter to almost everything that existing scholarship tells us about the region, that the policing of Indians supplied the governor with his most plausible excuse for the movement of Portuguese troops?

The answer is clear. Residents of Minas Gerais would have readily believed that Indians could be spotted along the Caminho Novo. They knew that many Indians and their descendants lived in the captaincy's towns and villages. They knew that countless others remained hidden in its unincorporated forests. Most, they believed, were savage cannibals. By the second half of the eighteenth century, moreover, an increasing number of Mineiros (inhabitants of Minas Gerais) had become convinced that the presence of Indians on the periphery of settled mining, farming, and ranching zones was thwarting the discovery of new deposits of gold, emeralds, and diamonds. They believed that the conquest of these outlying lands through the use of armed expeditions would restore Minas Gerais to a grandeur fast fading with the progressive exhaustion of its great alluvial mineral strikes.

The height of the violence that pit soldiers and settlers against Indians in the Mineiro sertão occurred not at the onset of the gold rush in the 1690s, as might be assumed, but during the second half of the eighteenth century in the eastern third of the captaincy. During the sixteenth and seventeenth centuries, numerous indigenous groups had retreated inland away from coastal colonization. During the early eighteenth century, the mining boom established a consolidated line of settlement to the west of these groups. The result was the creation of a refuge zone in the captaincy's eastern forests. A royal prohibition on settlement in the area, prompted by concerns about smuggling from the mines to the coast, helped sustain the relative freedom of movement independent Indians experienced in these forests. The systematic conquest of this zone, known as the Eastern Sertão, began only after the mining boom subsided around midcentury. As the original gold discoveries began to run out, colonists pushed eastward into the forests. Some searched for new sources of mineral wealth, while others sought agricultural, pastoral, and commercial alternatives to the waning mining economy.[8]

On the surface, the cause of the resulting conflict appears obvious, representing simply another episode in what John Monteiro has described as the "chronicle of extinction" that characterizes the greater part of the historiography pertaining to Brazilian Indians.[9] Beneath that surface, however, many complexities emerge when evaluating the origin and extent of this interethnic violence. Hence the need for a more detailed, historically specific account of the deteriorating relations between the Portuguese and the eastern seminomads as an antidote to sweeping generalizations about the fate of the captaincy's Indians.

Some tightly focused questions provide a starting point. When tensions in this frontier zone degenerated into violent confrontation, who initiated the ensuing attacks—Indians, settlers, or the colonial state? What was the link between the numerous violent encounters found in the documentation and the increased activity of state-sponsored wilderness expeditions during this period? Did Indian attacks prompt the deployment of these armed expeditions, as officials claimed, or did the persistent, antagonizing presence of the troops themselves provoke confrontation? Were reports of Indian aggression fabricated by captaincy authorities to justify invasion of this zone, or were the reports accurate and thus evidence of determined Indian resistance? On an even more basic level, is it possible to appraise the degree to which the surviving sources, all of them drafted by colonial intruders, exaggerate or, conversely, underreport the number of violent clashes in the Eastern Sertão? Such questions will better prepare us to consider why some Indians opted to cross the frontier and enter into colonial society.

The aggressive seizure of land from the aboriginal inhabitants of the Eastern Sertão undermines the claim, advanced by colonial officials and settlers, that the Portuguese entered the wilderness as heralds of civilization, forced into violence only in self-defense when attacked by incorrigible, ungrateful natives. As Governor Luís Diogo Lobo da Silva (1763–1768) explained the issue, Portuguese soldiers simply sought to "reduce" the Indians "to peace and civil conformity" in accordance with royal orders. Only when the state's benevolent methods failed to sway these Indians were soldiers permitted to "submit them to the stated obedience by means of force."[10] This assertion proves to be as false in the case of Minas Gerais as it does in the innumerable other instances in which colonists made similar claims elsewhere in the Americas. In our haste to dispel this myth, however, we must guard against the opposite view, no less distorted and reductive, that the natives were invariably blameless victims. To reject the view that Indians always initiated violent confrontations only to conclude that they never did so brings us no closer to a balanced understanding of the motives and behavior of either native or colonist. The image of a reactive, defenseless indigenous population misconstrues the chain of events that led to the eventual subjugation of the Indians of eastern Minas Gerais, underestimates the role of frontier violence, and strips the natives of the initiative they took, including their prolonged resistance to conquest.

It is true that the various peoples of the region—including the Coroado, Puri, Botocudo, Kamakã, Pataxó, Panhame, Maxakali, among others— found themselves in the end outnumbered and outgunned, stricken by disease, and displaced in the face of dwindling land and resources. Throughout their long struggle for survival, however, they, like the colonists they fought against, acted not only in self-defense. Particularly in the case of the Puri and Botocudo, they also staged numerous aggressive forays into territory recently settled, and, in some cases, territory long-since considered securely under colonial control. The Indians, in short, were both victims and perpetrators of violence. Of course even the closest scrutiny of sources written by colonists can only begin to explain how this struggle was perceived by the Indians. Nevertheless, such analysis suggests that they conducted themselves in a fashion at odds with what the colonists portrayed as the random and irrational nature of indigenous resistance.

Between 1760 and 1808, the year in which Prince Regent João declared open war against the Botocudo, culminating a half-century of increasing conflict, eighty-six violent engagements involving Indians in the Eastern Sertão were reported in the records of the captaincy government (see table 2).[11] During this time, only one five-year period (1785–1789) passed without at least one denunciation of violence, although the frequency of such reports proved to be highly erratic. Almost one-half of the incidents occurred between 1765 and 1769, the period during which military operations against the Indians in the sertão reached their peak under governors Lobo da Silva and his successor José Luís de Meneses Abranches Castello Branco, the count of Valadares (1768–1773).

The sources that reported these many clashes, however, did so in terms that make even this kind of rudimentary quantitative analysis a challenge. In some cases, only the vaguest mention of violence appeared. We learn from Captain Paulo Mendes Ferreira Campelo, then the region's top military commander, for instance, of an attempt by settlers to farm fields that former colonists had abandoned for fear of Indian attacks at the remote settlement

Figure 21. The Puri and Coroado were among the many groups occupying the forested mountains separating the inland mining district of Minas Gerais from coastal settlements in Rio de Janeiro and Espírito Santo. Many Puri mounted fierce resistance to colonial incorporation, while most Coroado chose the path of greater accommodation. In some instances, the two groups themselves clashed; in others, they cooperated. Source: Hermann Burmeister, *Landschaftliche Bilder Brasiliens und Portraits einiger Urvölker als Atlas seiner Reise durch die Provinzen von Rio de Janeiro und Minas Geraës* (Berlin: Druck und Verlag von Georg Reimer, 1853). Public domain access: http://www.brasiliana.usp.br/bbd/handle/1918/003612–011

of Cuieté, halfway down the Doce River valley.[12] The implication was that such fear derived from experience, and many sources reported other attacks at the settlement. The document cited, however, remains opaque. The formal letter to the count of Valadares in which the commander describes his frustrations at the slow pace of settling the sertão can be dated to the period soon after the governor took office in 1768. The flight of settlers it mentions,

Table 2. Violent Engagements with Indians in Eastern Sertão, 1760–1808[*]

YEARS	NUMBER OF ENGAGEMENTS
1760–1764	3
1765–1769	42
1770–1774	1
1775–1779	12
1780–1784	5
1785–1789	0
1790–1794	7
1795–1799	1
1800–1804	11
1805–1808[*]	4
TOTAL	86

SOURCES: APM, CC, cód. 1156; APM, SC, códs. 118, 224, 260, and 277; BNRJ, SM, II-36, 5, 32 and cód. 2, 2, 24, cód. 19, 3, 39, and cód. 3, 1, 35; BNRJ, SM, CV, cód. 18, 2, 6; *RAPM* 1, no. 4 (1896): 781; Diogo P. R. de Vasconcelos, *Breve descrição geográfica, física e política da Capitania de Minas Gerais* (1807; reprint, Belo Horizonte: Fundação João Pinheiro, 1994), 147–48; Diogo [Luís de Almeida Pereira] de Vasconcelos, *História média de Minas Gerais*, 4th ed. (Belo Horizonte: Ed. Itatiaia, 1974), 203; Cambraia and Mendes, "Colonização," 142.

[*]Not including incidents after the crown's declaration of war against the Botocudo on May 13, 1808, when violent incidents again increased significantly for several years. Counts as two all engagements described in sources as multiple but whose total number is not specified. When multiple locations are mentioned, counts each as a single engagement.

however, occurred at some unspecified point in the past, perhaps even before Campelo was named to his command by Governor Lobo da Silva in 1765. The letter did not indicate what sort of violence occurred, whether, for example, the alleged attacks were directed against soldiers or settlers, against persons or property, or whether they took place in the surrounding forest or within the confines of the town of Cuieté itself. Nor did Campelo state how many Indian raids occurred before settlers chose to flee. Probably it took more than just one. In such cases—and there are many—in which the ambiguity of the source rules out an accurate identification and quantification, we have not included the incident or implied incident in our count of violent engagements.

Many reports cite multiple attacks but do not tally how many occurred. In such instances, we have adopted the most conservative approach, assuming one violent incident per location cited, two if described in the plural, that is, as "attacks" in a single place. Thus a series of military expeditions deployed by Governor Lobo da Silva in the 1760s responded not simply to a single Indian attack, or a series of single attacks in several places, but against attacks that he said were occurring "year after year" at sites throughout the Eastern Sertão.[13] The frequency of such reports of numerous but unspecified incidents provides the first piece of evidence for surmising that substantially more interethnic violence occurred in the Eastern Sertão than suggested by the eighty-six cases that can be dated and linked to a particular location with enough precision to include them in our count.

Further evidence concerning the origin and extent of the violence surfaces when comparing the data on reported attacks with those on the armed expeditions dispatched to the Eastern Sertão. We have identified nearly one hundred military and paramilitary expeditions that marched into the wilderness of colonial Minas Gerais to pursue a variety of objectives related to territorial conquest and incorporation. Frequently referred to as entradas and bandeiras, but known also by other terms such as *expedições, escoltas*, and *tropas* (expeditions, patrols, and troops), these military and paramilitary ventures set out to neutralize native resistance, to secure land, to search for new sources of mineral wealth, to clear new trails and roads, to reconnoiter rivers, to pursue runaway slaves, to extend state authority over areas sparsely populated by subsistence farmers and unsupervised prospectors, and to track down smugglers. Most combined more than one of these objectives, although their primary aim was the pacification of Indian territory. This bandeira activity became especially intense during the second half of the eighteenth century in the eastern forests. Of these many documented bandeiras, seventy-nine traversed the forests and river valleys of the Eastern Sertão between 1755 and 1804, after which early mobilization for the 1808 war transformed these expeditions into more conventional crown-ordered military operations.[14] Although further research will likely uncover still others, the peak years of this activity will surely remain the two decades between 1765 and 1785, precisely that period during which the economic dislocations of the post-boom era became most severe.[15]

A comparison of the archival data reveals an exceedingly close correspondence between reported Indian attacks and the deployment of bandeiras (see chart 1). The spate of attacks documented between 1765 and 1769 occurred amid two separate assaults, the first coinciding with expeditions deployed during the final two years of Governor Lobo da Silva's rule, the second with similar activity during the second year of the count of Valadares's tenure. Both governors were particularly avid in their attempt to rejuvenate the captaincy by way of expansion into the sertão. Together, the peak in violence during this five-year period and the absence of aggressive acts during the nine-year span between 1782 and 1791 corresponded with the periods of greatest and least bandeira activity, respectively. The same correspondence held true, on a relative scale, for virtually every other period of intensification or diminution of bandeira activity.

A number of explanations suggest themselves for the direct relationship between violent incidents and bandeiras. First, the most skeptical hypothesis: that in most or at least many cases violence did not really occur at all but was invented by authorities as a pretext for dispatching troops to explore and occupy the sertão. Because the crown had restricted access to the Eastern Sertão early in the century in an attempt to block the passage of smugglers in and out of the mining district by promoting the survival of Indians considered to be hostile, captaincy governors needed some sort of justification for venturing into this territory imagined to be rich in mineral wealth.[16] The call to retaliate against Indian atrocities provided precisely the required excuse. Even so, especially in the case of the specific accounts that have been included in our tally, there were simply too many cases providing too many details over too long a period to support the conclusion that authorities invented these incidents.

A pair of alternate possibilities explaining the correlation of bandeiras and violence is less easily assessed. The first assumes that violent incidents in almost every case provoked the government or local settlers to form retaliatory bandeiras. The converse possibility is that whenever and wherever bandeiras roved the wilderness they provoked native resistance. Anecdotal evidence can be assembled to support both hypotheses.[17] Thus a third possibility suggests itself, a middle position, which assumes that both types of events occurred: violence prompted expeditions, and expeditions stirred up violence. All three possibilities share the supposition that in almost every case and every place a direct relationship existed between frontier violence and the presence of bandeiras.

On closer examination, however, the data suggest still another interpretation (see tables 3 and 4). In an overwhelming majority of cases (92 percent), Indians were reported to be the aggressors. In only a handful of cases (8 percent) were soldiers said to have initiated hostilities. Of the entire eighty-six

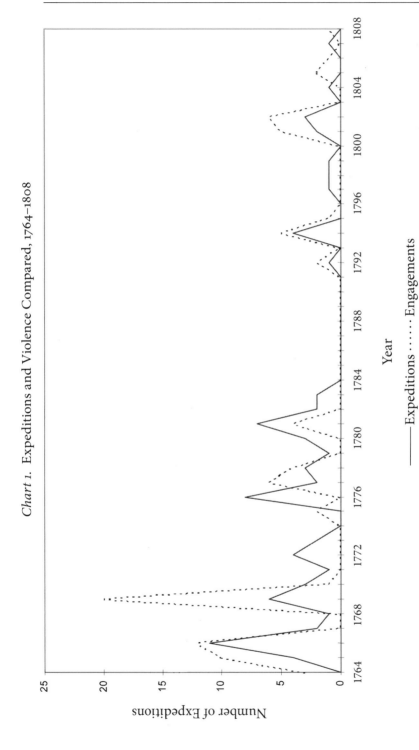

Chart 1. Expeditions and Violence Compared, 1764–1808

Source: Langfur, *Forbidden Lands*, chap. 6.

instances of violent conflict, not a single incident was attributed to the actions of settlers, a point to which we will return.

As for the victims of Indian attacks, settlers were named in almost three of every four cases (72 percent), soldiers in about one of five (20 percent), and settled Indians living in aldeias (state- or church-supervised villages) in just a few (5 percent). Adding the sixteen attacks against soldiers to the seven attacks they initiated, the total number of clashes between Indians and soldiers amounts to twenty-three, or slightly more than one-fourth of the total eighty-six. The violence in the Eastern Sertão, it thus becomes clear, stemmed from a conflict that seethed primarily between Indians and settlers, not Indians and soldiers, even though the sources highlight the connection between native violence and military deployment, even though officials touted soldiers as the vanguard of the drive to subdue the natives of the Eastern Sertão, and even though settlement of the region was supposed to be forbidden by the crown.

The direct correlation between the data on violence and bandeiras conceals the bloodiest aspect of the conflict, which took place at far-flung farms and mining operations in the eastern forests, out of the immediate reach of the roving wilderness expeditions. Bandeiras may have stirred up Indian

Table 3. Identity of Aggressor

AGGRESSOR	NUMBER	%
Indians	79	92
Soldiers	7	8
Settlers	0	0
Total	86	100

Table 4. Identity of Victims of Indian Attacks

VICTIM	NUMBER	%
Settlers	57	72
Soldiers	16	20
Settled Indians	4	5
Unknown	2	3
Total	79	100

Sources: See table 2

resistance, but they did so in an indirect way. They were deployed when hostilities between Indians and settlers, in the opinion of the ruling governor and his commanders, merited resorting to the use of military force. The link between violence and bandeira activity, in short, can be attributed to the nature of the sources themselves. These sources necessarily documented the attacks that prompted the government to act and warranted the accompanying expense and recruitment efforts. Such documents also provided a written rationale for the decision to flout, in an official and conspicuous fashion, the royal prohibition on the settlement and exploration of the Eastern Sertão. For the same reason, furthermore, it seems likely that many violent episodes went unreported. When government officials were too preoccupied by other matters, when financial resources were too limited to contemplate a response, or when an incident because of its isolated nature went otherwise unattended, no documents were generated by the bureaucratic machinery set in motion by the mounting of a retaliatory bandeira.

The elimination of military expeditions as the primary source of violence makes sense from the perspective of the Indian side of the conflict, as well. After long experience dealing with colonists encroaching on their territory, Indians recognized the folly of engaging a well-armed military expedition in the field, even through the use of hit-and-run tactics. Rather, they chose their targets cautiously from among the isolated homesteads, farms, ranches, and even villages and towns along the shifting frontier between Portuguese and native territory. The use of bandeiras was an essential tactic of the state, as it moved to incorporate the Eastern Sertão into the colonial domain. For the Botocudo, Puri, and other indigenous groups, however, soldiers on the march posed less of a threat than frontier settlers. Settlers were far more numerous, their presence was far more disruptive to nomadic ways, and they were far more vulnerable to attack than the armed soldiers who passed through native territory on intermittent expeditions and then disappeared. As Mineiro settlers repeatedly and increasingly crossed the boundaries established by the crown between settled zones and Indian territory, they became victims, as well as perpetrators, of interethnic violence. Only an elite minority of these settlers possessed the power and influence to gain the attention of public authorities when Indians attacked. These incidents, and these alone, were the ones that surfaced in the documentation pertaining to military expeditions sent out in response. Many other incidents, it seems prudent to conclude, went unrecorded, whether because they involved impoverished, illiterate settlers

Figure 22. During the eighteenth and early nineteenth centuries, the Botocudo were cast as archetypical savages. The German naturalist Maximilian, Prince of Wied-Neuwied, traveled through their territory not long after the Portuguese crown declared war on them, justifying the action with accusations of cannibalism. Source: Wied-Neuwied, *Travels in Brazil in the Years 1815, 1816, 1817* (London: Henry Colburn, 1820). Courtesy of the John Carter Brown Library at Brown University.

with little recourse to official aid, or because the captaincy government itself was unable to attend to every appeal.

Of all the quantitative characteristics of the documents describing inter-ethnic violence in the sertão, the one that most clearly highlights how the very production of sources both molded and reflected the way officials understood the conflict is the utter absence of reported attacks initiated by settlers against Indians. The imbalance is simply impossible to credit. Having surmised that many individual attacks between settlers and Indians never appeared in government records, we can better determine why those that did were consistently blamed on Indians. In issuing orders to bandeiras entering the sertão, Governor Lobo da Silva warned that those engaging in acts of unjustified aggression against the Indians would be punished. Violence was to be used only in self-defense to repel Indians who proved uncooperative.[18] One suspects, however, that it required little effort either to conceal the use of such violence or to provoke Indians to actions that justified retaliation. For example, the settler Manoel Pires Farinho, who was both a bandeira organizer and a settler, led an unauthorized expedition into the southeastern reaches of the captaincy, attacking a group of Puri and killing ten. When the news reached Governor Rodrigo José de Meneses, he drafted a forceful rebuke, describing himself as "very displeased." He condemned the "impetuosity" with which the bandeira had attacked the Indians, even though the Puri had given no "immediate motive for being treated as enemies." He warned against waging similar attacks "in any case other than natural defense."[19] Under such conditions, it seems fair to conclude that settlers learned to conceal their own aggression against Indians by attributing it to self-defense or failing to report it.

The denial of colonial responsibility for clashes with indigenous peoples became a trope of conquest throughout the Americas. The Portuguese version of the conflict in the Mineiro sertão comes as no surprise. But the sources teach us something more. Subjected to careful analysis, their lacunae and biases made evident, they reveal that strife between settlers and Indians proliferated to an extent even greater than that suggested by the dozens of violent engagement documented in the Eastern Sertão during the second half of the eighteenth century. Inadvertently the sources and their silences illustrate how much remained hidden from official view. For the Portuguese, the violence endemic in the eastern forests assumed the form of an ageless contest between civilization and barbarism, which required an organized, government-led military advance on unincorporated territory to combat the random acts of irrational cannibals. Nonetheless, the reported incidents, while blamed virtually without exception on Indian savagery, contained evidence of settler culpability, although to exactly what degree is, in the end, difficult to assess. Despite crown restrictions, settlers of all classes were pushing slowly but relentlessly into Indian territory. Some sought gold, others simply subsistence. The prominent presence of the state in the form of military expeditions and troops garrisoned at frontier presidios should not distract us from the basic fact that violent clashes occurred overwhelmingly between Indians and settlers, not between Indians and soldiers. It is also clear that native opposition to Portuguese territorial expansion persisted in a sustained, meaningful, and exceedingly disruptive fashion throughout the second half of the eighteenth century. If Luso-Brazilian behavior did not conform to the peaceful, civilized intentions colonists claimed for themselves, neither was the native response characterized by the passive acceptance of defeat.

FROM *MESTIÇOS* TO COLONIAL INDIANS

Confronting settlers and clashing with bandeiras in the Eastern Sertão, Indians also waged their struggle in the towns and villages of Minas Gerais. In these colonized zones, they turned their determined resistance against the practice of slavery. While violent conflict predominated in the forests, official channels and the legal system provided openings for challenging oppression from within colonial society.

The presence of Indians and their descendants in settled areas can be attributed to several factors. Some of these Indians were *carijós* (detribalized natives) who arrived from other regions in the company of Paulistas (inhabitants of São Paulo). Paulistas accounted for most of the famed *bandeirantes,* expeditionaries who began to settle the area after striking gold toward the end of the seventeenth century. Among the carijós were many taken prisoner in bandeirante slave-hunting raids.[20] Another segment of the native population was taken captive by subsequent expeditions, those manned by Mineiro settlers and often financed by the captaincy government. As we have seen, the Mineiro expeditions continued throughout the eighteenth century. In contrast to standard depictions, the conquest of Brazil's Indians—the colony's "red gold"—did not cease with the early discoveries of mineral wealth, only later to erupt again in the declared war against Botocudo in 1808.[21] The primary motivation to participate in wilderness expeditions during the second half of the century was the discovery of new sources of precious minerals and, by extension, the acquisition of land grants, official appointments, and other rewards and honors. But one should not underestimate the ongoing lure of capturing natives. Indians seized in confrontations with colonists were used as mining, agricultural, and domestic laborers.

As the historian A. J. R. Russell-Wood notes, there has been a scholarly tendency to exaggerate the degree to which Paulistas ceased to "molest indigenous communities after the discovery of gold." For him, the distinction between those known as the Emboabas (Portuguese settlers newly arrived in the mining region) and the Paulistas, who fought unsuccessfully to retain control of the mineral-rich lands they discovered, was not limited to their different places of origin. The Paulistas were also distinguished by a standard of comportment and way of life that emphasized "a high prevalence of relationships with Indian women." They constructed "a culture that was neither entirely European nor entirely indigenous, but an amalgam." Although their "ambivalent" relationship with Indians was essentially predatory, it also implied the incorporation of the Indian "into the context of the domestic economy," leading to a preference for Indians who were young, "easy to domesticate," and, in the case of women, "desirable as sexual partners."[22]

This legacy carried over into Minas Gerais and appears to have impelled the participants of the wilderness expeditions discussed in the first part of this essay. A good example was the situation that developed in the parish of Guarapiranga in the southeastern portion of the captaincy. As early as 1720, Domingos Dias Ribeiro appealed to the governor for permission to arm an expedition that would head out from Vila Rica to a new mineral strike at the headwaters of the Piranga River. There, the expedition would "conquer any wild heathens." The governor's response was supportive on the condition that Ribeiro keep careful records of any conquered Indians "in accordance with the law and royal dispositions."[23] In 1729, Francisco Melo Coutinho de Souto Maior announced the results of a subsequent expedition, proposing to "sell in the public square" the Indians he captured. After paying the requisite royal taxes, he intended to divide what remained among the men that accompanied him. "Their self-interest," he wrote, would encourage them to apply "greater effort in the conquest of the heathen."[24]

By midcentury, this region was still a final outpost of mining exploration bordering the barrier established by the presence of "wild Indians," such as the Botocudo, Puri, and Coroado, who impeded the advance of colonists in what to this day is still referred to as the Zona da Mata (Forest Zone).[25] In 1746, reacting against the Indian obstacle, local inhabitants filed a petition lamenting the "oppression" resulting from "infidel" attacks. They called on the Portuguese king to provide a "swift remedy" and requested "permission to be able to enter into those sertões with bandeiras, and to conquer those wild heathens, and to discover gold, because they were in possession of the best lands." To repay expenses, the expeditionaries proposed retaining any Indians who "made war and were apprehended as captives." Such Indians would be made to serve them and "instructed in church doctrine."[26] To provide legitimacy to the proposal, they alleged that it derived from the principles of "just war."

Little changed over the ensuing years. Settlers continued to complain. Indians continued to be transferred forcibly from forests to homesteads and fields. In 1750, settlers petitioned for help in purchasing "gunpowder and shot to force the heathens to retreat" from their farms, where they were committing "murders and thefts." Again, settlers asked the king to allow them to make any captured Indians "serve as slaves" while they received "the benefit of our sacred faith."[27] From Lisbon, came the royal response: "to use kindness if [the Indians] became tame"; otherwise, not to hesitate to wage "war, continuing until they become tame or flee or are extinguished."[28]

Many other requests of this sort were registered in the colonial archives. A great number of Indians were unquestionably taken prisoner beginning in

Figure 23. This image of a Puri family portrayed the isolation of life in the eastern forests. Although dozens of military and paramilitary expeditions crisscrossed the forests even before the 1808 declaration of war, the increasing presence of encroaching settlers caused even greater disruption, interfering with seminomadic hunting and gathering practices in a shrinking territory. Source: Wied-Neuwied, *Travels in Brazil.* Courtesy of the John Carter Brown Library at Brown University.

the 1760s, when captaincy governors implemented the policy of invading indigenous lands that produced the peaks in violence and bandeira activity registered in table 2 and chart 1. As noted, one wilderness expedition after another set out during the second half of the century. The captivity of Indians increased accordingly, based on the principles of what was known in Brazil as the Indian administration system or *administração*. The system is conventionally associated with an earlier period.[29] However, many Indians were taken captive in the growing number of wilderness confrontations and transferred to towns and villages as "administered Indians" or *administrados*.

In a letter sent to the governor in 1772, Captain Paulo Moreira da Silva reported on Indians captured in the "Conquest of Cuieté," the remote expanse of the eastern forests centered on the town by that name in the Doce River valley. They had been placed under the authority of local settlers "in order to give them the necessary guidance and doctrines and to teach them the skills to provide for their sustenance and civilization, and to instruct them in the dogmas of the sacred faith."[30] This incident suggests the means by which Indian "administration" became formalized. Once a petition to capture Indians received official approval, colonists were required to present the names of those taken prisoner to the local municipal council. The council was responsible for delegating to colonists the task of administering Indians. The first responsibility of an administrator was the consecration of baptism. From that point on, he was to accompany the "nurturing" process (*criação*). Officials were to verify whether these Indians had learned "a skill or occupation in some sort of lawful work," had been "instructed in [church] dogmas," and had been "freed of [their] nature."[31] Every three months, administrators were called before the municipal council to account for how much progress their Indians had made.[32] As one might expect, the system served as a pretense for removing Indians from the forest and inserting them into the civilized, Catholic world under the auspices of their masters, resulting in the indiscriminate appropriation of native labor.

Bewildered and threatened by the numerous expeditions crossing their lands, many Indians simply fled to the nearest towns. In these cases, too, they were systematically received by town councilors and, after certain preliminaries, were placed under the care of colonists.[33] Dispersed in the archives are numerous requests for assistance by Indians from a full range of ethnic groups who appeared "voluntarily."[34] To cite just one example, Governor Lobo da Silva stated that "more than twenty wild Indians called Coropós,

Gavelhos, and Croás" presented themselves to authorities soon after he took office in 1763. He arranged for them to be dressed and provided them with tools. A few days later, thirty more arrived "with the same commitment [to be baptized], possibly having been informed of the friendly reception that the first group received."[35]

One should also not overlook those Indians from officially established aldeias who were fugitives, deserters, or abducted.[36] Some escaped from aldeias in Rio de Janeiro; others came from Jesuit missions in Ceará and Pernambuco; others from the aldeias of São Miguel and São José in São Paulo; and still others from the Rio Pomba aldeia in southeastern Minas Gerais.[37] These do not include additional carijós who arrived from Taubaté, a town in the interior of São Paulo.[38] Such mobility was a common behavior during this period. As historian Sheila Faria has noted, itinerancy in frontier regions was a strategy to escape privation adopted by the poor, whom she calls "survival wanderers."[39] It is likely that the same logic prevailed among many of the captaincy's Indians.

All of these Indians—whether they arrived from São Paulo during the gold rush, were survivors or captives of raids in the sertão, or were in flight from supervised aldeias—came to live in Mineiro towns and other localities under the tutelage of colonists. They can be designated "colonial Indians," that is, Indians and their descendants, detribalized for diverse reasons, of various ethnic and/or geographic origins, brought to live in or born into colonial society and thereby incorporated in the social and cultural life of Minas Gerais during the eighteenth century.[40]

IN SEARCH OF LIBERTY

The restrictions on the enslavement of Indians articulated in a series of royal laws[41] encouraged colonists in Minas Gerais to reproduce the secular practice of Indian administration. Settlers assumed private responsibility for the conversion and religious indoctrination of Indians, treating them as neophytes in all aspects of the Christian faith. Under the pretext of administering catechesis, the religious instruction that was to lead to baptism or confirmation, colonists obtained the prerogative to control Indians in ways that otherwise would have been characterized as slavery and a violation of legal principles. By way of this expedient, they bypassed problems of a juridical and moral nature. However, this practice was not employed without resistance. In legislation issued between 1755 and 1758, as other contributors have explained, Sebastião José de Carvalho e Melo, the future marquis of Pombal, affirmed the freedom of Brazil's Indians. The move only deepened the impasse over the emancipation of Indians in Minas Gerais.

Luís Diogo Lobo da Silva, then still governor of the northeastern captaincy of Pernambuco, ordered the new laws made known to the public so that the "scandalous abuses" suffered by Indians would be "extirpated and abolished." He sought to "uproot such practices once and for all," practices by which "Indians were enslaved under impious pretexts." The crown had insisted upon the "incontestable liberty" of Brazil's Indians, ordering that this principle be obeyed "without apology, interpretation, or modification of any kind." When Lobo da Silva assumed the governorship of Minas Gerais in 1763, he again invoked this legislation, ordering freedom to be restored to Indians and mixed-race mestiços of European and indigenous descent, so that they could live according to the same civil code that governed the colony's nonnative population.[42]

This measure set a significant precedent for Indians and their descendants. Having until then suffered an uncertain juridical status, caught between slavery and freedom, they could now appeal to the colonial legal system in defense of their right to liberty. Many colonial Indians initiated legal proceedings against their administrators in various regions of the captaincy.[43] Considering the ongoing violence in the eastern forests, these developments may seem contradictory. The new laws, in fact, helped justify the conquest of the sertão, whereby Indians could allegedly receive the liberty that was due them once the state "convey[ed] the law of God to the barbarous nations, reducing them to the Catholic faith and to the true knowledge of His Holy Name."[44] Yet the same laws provided a mechanism by which Indians who migrated to towns and villages could defy colonists' attempts to keep them in bondage.

In 1764 a family claiming to be of "carijó conception" petitioned the governor in Vila Rica, basing their petition on this new legislation. Leonor, her three children (José, Manoel, and Severina), and her grandchildren (Felix, Mariana, Narcisa, and Amaro) asked to be "free and exempt from the slavery in which they were held" by Domingos de Oliveira, whom they accused of maltreating them and inflicting "harsh work and beatings." According to Leonor's deposition, their administrator maintained the entire family under strict surveillance. One of Oliveira's sons spied on them "so that they would not complain." Upon official investigation, several

Figure 24. The German naturalist Maximilian witnessed rival Botocudo clans practicing a highly ritualized form of combat. A very different kind of military practice, relying on ambush and hit-and-run tactics, was required for successful warfare against advancing colonial adversaries. Source: Wied-Neuwied, *Travels in Brazil.* Courtesy of the John Carter Brown Library at Brown University.

individuals confirmed these claims, and the governor ordered a patrol sent out to free the carijós.[45]

Another petition along these lines came from Maria Moreira, the descendant "of *gentio da terra* [heathens of this land; i.e., Indians], having been born of free parents who were straight-haired carijós." Such individuals, she affirmed, had been "declared free by repeated orders of His Majesty." Appealing to the governor, she requested permission to leave the home of Lieutenant Francisco Xavier, where she had been "deposited by the orders of her master." Prevented from passing through the streets, she maintained that she could not "tend to her interests" in securing her liberty. After it was determined "by way of visual inspection" that "her status as an Indian was evident," a favorable official ruling resulted.[46]

Not all such individuals had the same luck. Many encountered difficulties in proving their indigenous ancestry. Administrators sought to conceal the ethnic origin of these Indians, labeling them with names that corresponded with generic mixed-race categories. They employed terms such as *caboclo* (detribalized Indian rustic), *curiboca* (Afro-native mestizo), and *cabra da terra* ("goat"; i.e., mestizo of this land), among many others, all of them pejorative labels roughly equivalent to "half-breed." By thus engendering the "invisibility" of these peoples, they created a loophole in royal legislation, since the crown did not prohibit the captivity of mestiços whose racial mixture derived in part from enslaved mothers of African descent. With this tactic, they legitimized indigenous slavery. Had it not been for the insistence of colonial Indians, resolute in setting the justice system in motion in order to guarantee the recognition of their indigenous origins, these individuals surely would have remained enslaved.

Apparently this was the unfortunate fate of Violante, labeled a "cabra," and her mother Josefa dos Prazeres, who sued for freedom sometime around 1769.[47] They reasoned that they were "free" because they had "descended from Indian origins." Their owner appealed, calling on ecclesiastical authorities to verify descent through baptismal records, and alleging that the petition was false and "malicious" because "only on the paternal side was there this ancestry." In fact, by way of testimony given in the case, we know that Violante was the daughter of an African slave named Josefa, who had married a carijó who was called both "freed" and "administered." Violante was the child, grandchild, and great-grandchild of carijós, but only on her paternal side. We do not have the final ruling in the case, but in view of the testimony provided by several witnesses the petition likely did not succeed. This conclusion is based on the sole exception to the laws granting freedom to Indians, established since 1755, which excluded those who were also the children of *negras escravas*, female slaves of African origins. Given that slave status was transmitted through the mother's womb, *partus sequitur ventrem*, many mestiços who were descendants of an indigenous father and an enslaved mother ended up being considered slaves. Thus, for Violante, slavery seems to have been inescapable.[48] However, the case was controversial because, as one judge wrote, some "laws declared the freedom of Indians and heathens, and others demanded the preservation of the possessions and rights of owners."[49]

Precisely for this reason, those masters who were most resistant to granting freedom to the colonial Indians under their administration claimed that they were children of enslaved mothers. Caterina Florência, her son, and her two grandchildren suffered this misfortune.[50] In 1766 Dr. Francisco Pais de Oliveira Leite filed a petition, refusing to recognize her claim to be descended from the "Indian nation." To her advantage, her master did not present her baptismal record but merely insisted that she was the "daughter of a legitimately captive womb." In conformance with the law, faced with a lack of documentation, it fell to the judge to conduct a "visual inspection" to determine ethnic ancestry. In this case, the judge was convinced that Caterina's "quality" was that of an Indian, destroying "any presumption that she was the daughter of an enslaved black" mother.[51] The judge ruled that she could no longer "be aggrieved by captivity."[52] One can deduce from this finding that mestiços could turn indigenous physical traits to their own advantage. If characteristics of phenotype were among the many variables that classified certain individuals as mestiços of ambiguous origins, in other situations these same characteristics made possible the passage from mestiço to colonial Indian.

That said, attempts to turn Indians back into slaves were not uncommon, and many Indians failed to evade the schemes of the most stubborn colonists. One of the tools employed was the system of *coartação*, which made manumission possible under certain conditions through self-purchase contracts between slaves and their owners.[53] Widely used among slaves of African descent, this mechanism was a means to forestall the right to liberty of many colonial Indians. Such was the case of Isabel de Souza [Guimarães?], who in 1769 presented manumission papers received from Lieutenant Manoel Funchal on the occasion of his death. To her dismay, her manumission "could not take effect" until its "conditions were fulfilled," indicating that the sum for her self-purchase had not been paid.[54] Accordingly, we can glean that the enslaved status of many colonial Indians was tacitly recognized. So common was this assumption that even when one such individual, Valentim, presented his baptismal records, he was ordered by a parish priest to show his manumission papers as well, given that "in the baptismal records it was evident he was a captive." In fact, those records stated that his mother, "Micaela, a carijó, was the slave of Captain João de Monteiro Santiago." As such, the priest had to be reminded that Valentim "was demonstrably free, for being the son of a carijó mother."[55]

In another incident in 1769, Bárbara Moreira de Castilho, the wife of a renowned *sertanista* (backwoodsman), Bento Furtado, appealed to the governor, the count of Valadares. Castilho claimed that she had "possessed this half-breed" for more than thirty years "in full view of everyone, without any trouble, and always as a legitimate slave who had been part of a dowry given by her parents." She had "never heard anything" about her slave Caterina being of Indian descent. Furthermore, she complained that because of Caterina's initiative yet another one of her children, Felizardo, had left to join his mother. For this reason, she feared that Caterina's remaining three children, who were still living in her home, would take the same action. Caterina was asked to provide clarification. She claimed to be a "cabocoula" (perhaps a misspelling of cabocla, the female counterpart of a caboclo) and was prepared to prove this by presenting her baptismal records once she obtained them from the town of Taubaté in São Paulo. In the face of this impediment, Castilho offered a new explanation. Her husband had followed His Majesty's orders "not to hold *Tapuias* [wild Indians] in captivity, since they were born free, sending away those he had in his company." As for Caterina, she had only called attention to "the status of being a carijó," "freed and free," as a result of "the insinuations of ill-intentioned persons and the scheming of one of her daughters, a half-breed." These individuals were seeking to take advantage of Castilho, "seeing the extreme poverty and defenselessness in which she lived." In addition, she insisted, if Caterina had "vestiges of a Tapuia," they appeared to be strictly from her father's side. But to demonstrate her benevolence, Castilho made an opportune suggestion: "In the event that this captivity was found to be unjust, she would not cast doubt on the need to give [Caterina and her daughter] days off as required by law or any days they wanted, provided that this concession not apply to more children and descendants, since they must remain in the power of the claimant."[56] We do not know the outcome of this case, but many other suits of this sort indicate the difficulties encountered by Indians while attempting to secure their freedom.

Near the end of the century, in 1797, the fate of the Cardoso family exemplified this struggle. The justice system in this case moved slowly and methodically. Members of the family had to deal with threats, followed by arbitrary imprisonment. Such incidents served to intimidate colonial Indians who claimed their right to be free. Perpétua and Ângela Cardoso were the daughters of Quitéria Cardoso. Francisca was the daughter of Lucrécia Cardoso. All three were the "natural children" of Lieutenant Miguel Raposo de Camargos. That is, they were born out of wedlock, their mothers described as "Indian women of this America" from São Paulo. Camargos later moved to Rio das Mortes, the southernmost *comarca* (county) of Minas Gerais, bringing with him his "administered Indian women." There, he became indebted to the Captain André Alvares da Silva, who quickly sued for payment. Camargos's possessions, including the "mothers of the suplicants, a brother, and other

Indian women of that family," were seized and put up for public auction. The Indians did not even have "a chance to cry out," due to their "poverty and distress." When they pleaded for their rights before a judge, they were held captive by court officials. According to the claimants, they had been "stifled by the utter rigidity" and "unchecked ambition" of the attorney Antônio Gonçalves Figueiredo," who condemned them with the "help of justice officials" to imprisonment in the town jail "for his own advantage." Objecting to these actions, convinced of the women's just cause, the head of the local municipal council ordered the Indians freed. Nevertheless, acting according to the "cunning and violent methods that were his custom," Figueiredo insisted on auctioning off the Indian women. At this point, they appealed to the governor. They pleaded for royal protection against their "intended oppression and obliteration." The governor finally demanded that the earlier order mandating their freedom be fulfilled to the letter of the law "with due punishment for anyone who challenged his ruling."[57]

In the same year, another petition by a "mestiço [and] American Indian" named Antônio similarly revealed the reluctance of administrators to respect royal orders and government dispatches.[58] After requesting his "simple freedom from [his] master, the Sergeant-Major Antônio de Castro e Souza," Antônio was imprisoned for ten months, despite receiving a favorable ruling from the district court before which he was unable to appear "because he was in prison and without money." After receiving a provisional release, he was again thrown in jail, where he remained "in chains, receiving whippings," due to the "vengeance" of his master, who accused him of "desertion." All of this had been concealed, Antônio charged, by reports issued by the local notary. "Help!" he pleaded in his petition, crying out to the crown. As a vassal, he sought "the favor of the sovereign law," asserting his "right . . . to be free from imprisonment and the torments of cruel vengeance." An official ruling placed him in the power of a competent person for the time necessary to clarify "the motives for what had occurred while the claimant was imprisoned." Antônio's misfortune apparently had not yet reached its conclusion.

As administrators, their accomplices, government authorities, and court officials attempted to interfere with the Indians' right to liberty, so too did representatives of the Catholic Church. The story of the Indian João Colomis reveals this aspect of their struggle. Colomis accompanied a committee that brought Bishop Frei Manoel da Cruz from the northeastern captaincy of Maranhão to the town of Mariana, where he served as the first bishop of Minas Gerais between 1748 and 1764. Still a minor, Colomis was turned over to the Reverend Canon Francisco Ribeiro da Silva to "instruct him in the Christian doctrine and the sacred dogmas of the faith."[59] After years of captivity, Colomis finally achieved his freedom, but not without fighting a long judicial battle.

We do not know his ethnic origin, but it is likely that he had come from one of the Jesuit aldeias along the bishop's route.[60] Another possibility is that he was taken prisoner during encounters with the Gueguê and Acroá Indians. These encounters forced the committee to field "many troops of men" in order to pass safely through the "dangerous sertão."[61] Against the bishop's recommendation, the reverend sent the "heathen" Colomis to a fazenda (farm or estate), "where he was reputed to be a slave, subject to the rigors of captivity." According to the deposition of the Sargeant-Major João Teixeira da Costa, to whom Colomis complained, he was "mistreated and despised, whipped and put in irons, the food he lived on as wretched as the clothes he wore." Colomis recounted the harsh punishments administered on the orders of Dona Quitéria, the reverend's strict niece. She kept him bound with "handcuffs and cunning" after he had been caught attempting to escape with a Brazilian-born slave named Isabel. Making use of his labor, "just like the rest of the slaves," the reverend forced Colomis to work for two years in a mining operation in which he had an interest, and another four or five years in the fields. At this point, the fazenda and its slaves were sold to Cipriano Pereira de Azevedo, who did not pay what he owed for the purchase. When the property was seized by the government, an official questioned the reverend about listing the Indian João Colomis as one of the property's slaves, which was prohibited by law. A month later, with the approval of the count of Valadares, an official ruling declared that the Indian was "free" and that the reverend was obligated to compensate him for the daily pay he had done without "for the entire time in which he was enslaved."[62] Furthermore, in accordance with the penalty stipulated in legislation that had forbidden the sale of Indians since 1680, the priest was to be sent to Lisbon's Limoeiro Prison. It was there that he eventually ended up, not for this violation, but because he was "considered rebellious and one who disturbed the public peace" and "truly evil."[63]

Many other Indians accompanied the same expedition that brought Bishop Frei Manoel da Cruz to Minas Gerais. In addition to Colomis, we have information about the Indian Inácio Xavier, who also submitted an appeal to end his enslavement.[64] Aiming to deflect responsibility for the matter from the Bishop of Mariana, a number of priests conspired to claim that it was customary to enslave Indians. Yet it was the bishop himself who, in compliance with royal orders, acknowledged forwarding to the governor in 1760 an "authentic collection of pontifical briefs, royal laws, instructions, and other papers" pertaining to the execution of the legislation that "restored to the Indians of Brazil their primitive and natural liberty." All of this documentation had been zealously safeguarded "in a chest with three keys in the diocesan archive."[65] As one can see, the bishop cast a blind eye to these laws, about which he had clear knowledge. In one form or another, these and many other appeals testify to the colonists' reluctance to concede freedom to Indians and their descendants.

FINAL CONSIDERATIONS

Colonial Indians, as these cases indicate, did not stop challenging their uncertain juridical and social status that placed them between freedom and slavery. Using the laws imposed by their colonizers, they forced even the most obdurate to give ground. By reaffirming their indigenous origins, they rejected the ambiguous mestiço status and, as such, captivity. Despite their "invisibility," colonial Indians reconstituted their alterity by asserting their "Indianness." In Minas Gerais's slave-based society, in which freedom was an essential mark of social differentiation, to evoke indigenous origins as gentios da terra, irrespective of ethnic differences, was to assume the shared status of the free. In this way, the actions of colonial Indians helped to deepen all of slavery's complexities and contradictions and to shift its boundaries. These changes resulted not from the concessions of colonial society, but from the conquests of Indians struggling to contend with their restrictive daily lives. In the region once known as Minas dos Cataguases, the mines of the Cataguá Indians, colonial Indians recreated themselves as beneficiaries of an indigenous past, making the slave system more flexible.

In light of native conduct in both the unsettled and settled regions of colonial Minas Gerais, the history of the captaincy, one of the most thoroughly studied in Brazilian historiography, takes on a different aspect with its indigenous peoples restored. Minas Gerais was deeply marked by native resistance to the seizure of ancestral lands, to detribalization, and to the dissolution of cultural ties resulting from colonization. Indians stood firm in the forests, mounting long-term challenges to colonists who maneuvered to seize their land. Although official sources portrayed them as aggressors, much evidence points to settler culpability. When imprisoned by wilderness expeditions and taken to the region's towns and other settlements, or when they chose to enter colonial society on their own, Indians did not become passive. They used the colonial justice system to affirm their indigenous origins in order to secure their freedom under the prerogatives of the law.

Our objective in this text was to consider the place that indigenous peoples occupied in the history of Minas Gerais. Their history is rarely mentioned. When it is, they are usually cast as subordinate social actors. Our research demonstrates their determined participation in colonial Mineiro society, both at its territorial fringes and at its core. In this sense, it was no coincidence that the region entered colonial consciousness at the end of the seventeenth century under the name Minas dos Cataguases, and that its colonial period ended more than a century later following a declaration of war against the still-unincorporated Botocudo.

NOTES

1. On this "void" in the historiography, see Crisoston Terto Vilas-Bôas, "A questão indígena em Minas Gerais: Um balanço das fontes e bibliografia," *Revista de História* (Ouro Preto) 5 (1995): 42–55. All translations from the Portuguese are by Hal Langfur, including the portion of this chapter written by Maria Leônia Chaves de Resende. Abbreviations used in the notes are as follows: Arquivo da Cúria de Mariana (ACM), Processo Matrimonial (PM); Arquivo Histórico Ultramarino, Lisbon (AHU), Projeto Resgate (PR); Arquivo Público Mineiro (APM), which houses a portion of the dispersed Arquivo Casa dos Contos (CC), the Seção Colonial (SC), and the Secretaria do Governo (SG); Biblioteca Nacional, Rio de Janeiro (BNRJ), Seção de Manuscritos (SM), Arquivo Conde de Valadares (CV); Banco de dados Campanha da Princesa: Guia de fontes para a história do Sul de Minas (BD), which uses data from the Livro de Batismo de Campanha (1748–1762), a project coordinated by Marcos Ferreira de Andrade and Maria Tereza Pereira Cardoso; *Revista do Arquivo Público Mineiro* (*RAPM*).

2. For an analysis of this approach to the region's indigenous history, see Hal Langfur, *The Forbidden Lands: Colonial Identity, Frontier Violence, and the Persistence of Brazil's Eastern Indians, 1750–1830* (Stanford, CA: Stanford University Press, 1996), 21–23.

3. See, for example, Renato Venâncio Pinto, "Os últimos carijós: Escravidão indígena em Minas Gerais: 1711–1725," *Revista Brasileira de História* 17, no. 34 (1997): 165–81; Paulo Mercadante, *Os sertões do leste; estudo de uma região: A mata mineira* (Rio de Janeiro: Zahar Editores, 1973); Celso Falabella de Figueiredo Castro, *Os Sertões*

de Leste: Achegas para a história da Zona da Mata (Belo Horizonte: Imp. Oficial, 1987); Ricardo de Bastos Cambraia and Fábio Faria Mendes, "A colonização dos sertões do leste mineiro: Políticas de ocupação territorial num regime escravista (1780–1836)," *Revista do Departamento de História-FAFICH/UFMG* (July 1988): 137–50; Maria Hilda Baqueiro Paraíso, "O tempo da dor e do trabalho: A conquista dos territórios indígenas nos Sertões do Leste" (PhD diss., Universidade de São Paulo, 1998); Oiliam José, *Marlière, O Civilizador: Esboço biográfico* (Belo Horizonte: Ed. Itatiaia, 1958); and José, *Indígenas de Minas Gerais: Aspectos sociais, políticos e etnológicos* (Belo Horizonte: Imp. Oficial, 1965).

4. Texts resulting from our research include Maria Leônia Chaves de Resende, "Gentios brasílicos: Índios coloniais em Minas Gerais setecentista" (PhD diss., UNICAMP, 2003); Resende, "Devassa da vida privada dos índios coloniais nas vilas de El-Rei," *Estudos Ibero-Americanos* 30, no. 2 (Dec. 2004): 49–69; Resende, "Minas dos Cataguases: Entradas e bandeiras nos sertões do Eldorado," *Vária História* 33 (Jan. 2005): 186–202; Resende, "Brasis coloniales: Índios e mestiços nas Minas Gerais Setecentistas," in *História de Minas Gerais: As Minas Setecentistas*, ed. Maria Efigênia Lage de Resende and Luiz Carlos Villalta (Belo Horizonte: Autêntica, 2007), vol. 1, 221–51; Hal Langfur, *Forbidden Lands*; Langfur, "Uncertain Refuge: Frontier Formation and the Origins of the Botocudo War in Late Colonial Brazil," *Hispanic American Historical Review* 82, no. 2 (May 2002): 215–56; Langfur, "Moved by Terror: Frontier Violence as Cultural Exchange in Late-Colonial Brazil," *Ethnohistory* 52, no. 2 (Spring 2005): 255–89; Langfur, "The Return of the Bandeira: Economic Calamity, Historical Memory, and Armed Expeditions to the Sertão in Minas Gerais, Brazil, 1750–1808," *The Americas* 61, no. 3 (Jan. 2005): 429–62. Earlier versions of this essay have appeared in Brazil and Portugal. See Resende and Langfur, "Minas Gerais Indígena: A resistência dos índios nos sertões e nas vilas de El-Rei," *Tempo* (Universidade Federal Fluminense) 12, no. 23 (July–Dec. 2007): 15–32; Resende and Langfur, "Minas Expansionista, Minas Mestiça: A resistência dos índios em Minas Gerais do século do ouro," *Anais de História de Além-Mar* (Lisbon) 9 (2008): 79–103.

5. For the counterpart of this myth in North American historiography, see Brian W. Dippie, *The Vanishing American: White Attitudes and U.S. Indian Policy* (Lawrence: University of Kansas, 1991); Jean M. O'Brien, *Firsting and Lasting: Writing Indians out of Existence in New England* (Minneapolis: University of Minnesota Press, 2010).

6. Tomás Antônio Gonzaga, *Cartas Chilenas*, ed. Tarquínio J. B. De Oliveira (São Paulo: Ed. Referência, 1972), carta 10ª, linhas 307–8.

7. Governor to viceroy, Cachoeira do Campo, 6 May 1789, *Anuário do Museu da Inconfidência* 2 (1953): 49; Governor to colonial secretary, Vila Rica, 11 July 1789, ibid., 72. Kenneth R. Maxwell mentions this incident in his history of the Minas conspiracy, *Conflicts and Conspiracies: Brazil and Portugal, 1750–1808* (Cambridge: Cambridge University Press, 1973), 154.

8. Langfur, "Uncertain Refuge"; Langfur, *Forbidden Lands*.

9. John M. Monteiro, "The Heathen Castes of Sixteenth-Century Portuguese America: Unity, Diversity, and the Invention of the Brazilian Indians," *Hispanic American Historical Review* 80, no. 4 (Nov. 2000): 718.

10. Governor, "Instrução que hade seguir o Cap.[am] Antônio Cardozo de Souza," [Vila Rica], [ca. 1767], BNRJ, SM, CV, cód. 18, 2, 6, doc. 293.

11. For a more detailed discussion, see Langfur, *Forbidden Lands*, 216–26.

12. Campelo, "Representação," s.d., BNRJ, SM, CV, cód. 18, 2, 6, doc. 198.

13. Governor, "Lista das pessoas que devem e tem obrigação de concorrerem para embaracar o corso com que o gentio Sylvestre esta todos os annos entrando pelas fazendas e sesmarias da Beira do Rio Doce . . . ," Vila Rica, 9 May 1765, APM, CC, cód. 1156, fl. 4.

14. See Hal Langfur, *Forbidden Lands*, 165; Resende, "Gentios Brasílicos," anexo; Resende, "Minas dos Cataguases," 186–202.

15. On the gradual economic recovery beginning in the early 1780s, see Laird W. Bergad, *Slavery and the Demographic and Economic History of Minas Gerais, Brazil, 1720–1888* (Cambridge: Cambridge University Press, 1999), 163–66.

16. Langfur, "Uncertain Refuge."

17. See, for example, governor, "Portaria para Joaquim Correya Mosso commandar hum Esquadra para afugentar os Indios Bravos," Vila Rica, 9 July 1792, APM, SC, cód. 259; Antônio Veloso de Miranda to governor, [Presídio dos] Arrepiados, 23 Nov. 1781, APM, SC, cód. 224, fls. 79v–80v.

18. "Requerimento de Antonio Cardozo de Souza, morador no Rio Pardo da Comarca de Serro Frio, respectivo sobre a rodução de Indioz que circulão a Otinga," [1766], APM, SC, cód. 60, fl. 86; Governor to Souza, Vila Rica, 29 Aug. 1766, ibid., fls. 86–86v.

19. Governor to Francisco Pires Farinho, Cachoeira, 13 Nov. 1781, APM, SC, cód. 227, fls. 13–13v.

20. See various account of this practice in Luciano Raposo de Almeida Figueiredo and Maria Verônica Campos, eds., *Códice Costa Matoso: Coleção das notícias dos primeiros descobrimentos das minas na América que fez o doutor Caetano da Costa Matoso sendo ouvidor-geral das do Ouro Preto, de que tomou posse em fevereiro de 1749, & vários papéis* (Belo Horizonte: Fundação João Pinheiro, 1999), 2 vols. See also Muriel Nazzari, "Da escravidão à liberdade: A transição de índio administrado para vassalo independence em São Paulo colonial," in *Brasil: Colonização e escravização*, ed. Maria Beatriz Nizza da Silva (Rio de Janeiro: Nova Fronteira, 2000), 30.

21. John Monteiro, for example, maintains that the exodus of residents from São Paulo to the mining district led to the suspension of bandeirante slaving. John M. Monteiro, *Negros da terra: Índios e bandeirantes nas origens de São Paulo* (São Paulo: Companhia das Letras, 1994), 210.

22. A. J. R. Russell-Wood, "Identidade, etnia e autoridade nas Minas Gerais do século XVIII: Leituras do Códice Matoso," *Vária História* 21 (July 1999): 101–2.

23. APM, SC, cód. 11, p. 262.

24. AHU, PR, 13563, cx. 15, doc. 30.

25. Pinto, "Os últimos carijós," 173.

26. APM, SC, cód. 10, fot. 808–11.

27. AHU, PR, 4515, cx. 55, doc. 25.

28. BNRJ, SM, Papéis Vários Manuscritos, 1, 4, 1, doc. 20.

29. See, esp., Monteiro, *Negros da terra*, 129–53.

30. APM, SC, cód. 179, fot. 1768–1769.

31. APM, SC, cód. 179, fot. 1774, 1775.

32. APM, SC, cód. 182, rolo 25, fot. 2303; APM, SC, cód. 167, fot. 862–63.

33. According to the historian Diogo de Vasconcelos, a policy adopted in 1758 and confirmed in 1768 sanctioned the distribution of clothes, tools, and other goods to Indians who arrived in the captaincy's settlements and presented themselves to authorities. Diogo [Luís de Almeida Pereira] de Vasconcelos, *História média de Minas Gerais*, 4th ed. (Belo Horizonte: Ed. Itatiaia, 1974), 205.

34. See, for example, in 1766, eleven Coroado Indians, APM, SC, cód. 152, fot. 287, 288; in 1767, another eight Coroado, APM, SC, cód. 152, fot. 448, 449; and in 1776, seven Coroado, APM, SC, cód. 152, fot. 357.

35. AHU, PR, 6728, cx. 83, doc. 16.

36. During the early stage of the gold rush, Indian labor was used in the mines, which led many to "abduct" Indians settled in aldeias, according to a complaint made in the mining town of Mariana. See APM, SC, cód. 9, fot. 53. M.T. Ferreira discusses three types of dislocation experienced by aldeia Indians: "absence" by permission of the village director or his agent in order to work or learn a trade for a period of one month or one year; "flight," which consisted of unauthorized absence; and "desertion." M. T. C. da R. Ferreira, "Os aldeamentos indígenas no fim do período colonial" (MA thesis, Universidade de São Paulo, 1990), 52.

37. On the flight of Indians from the aldeias of Rio de Janeiro, see Maria Regina Celestino de Almeida, "Os índios aldeados no Rio de Janeiro colonial: Novos súditos cristãos do Império Português" (PhD diss., UNICAMP, 2001), 140. On Indians from Ceará and Pernambuco, see ACM, PM, no. 1989 (1735) and ACM, PM, no. 2904 (1743); on those from the aldeia of São Miguel, see ACM, PM, no. 4042 (1750). Various baptism records from the city of Campanha da Princesa in southern Minas Gerais reveal the presence of Indians from the aldeia of São José, such as José Antunes (1749), Geraldo Dias (1754), and Lucas Dias (1758), as well as José Domingues (1775) from São João de Atibaia in São Paulo. See BD, Livro de Batismo de Campanha (1748–1762). On Indians from the aldeia of Rio Pomba, see ACM, PM, no. 2808 (1791).

38. Ana Cardoso and Pedro Dias, also identified as Clara Aguiar and José de Oliveira, were recorded as "carijós from the town of Taubaté" when they baptized their son

in the parish of São Gonçalo in Campanha in 1761. See BD, Livro de Batismo de
Campanha (1748–1762).

39. Sheila de Castro Faria, *A colônia em movimento: Fortuna e família no cotidiano
colonial* (Rio de Janeiro: Ed. Nova Fronteira, 1998), 102.

40. On native participation in colonial society elsewhere in Portuguese America, see,
in addition to the other chapters in this collection, John Monteiro, "Rethinking
Amerindian Resistance and Persistence in Colonial Portuguese America," in
New Approaches to Resistance in Brazil and Mexico, ed. John Gledhill and
Patience A. Schell (Durham, NC: Duke University Press, 2012), 37–40.

41. See Beatriz Perrone-Moisés, "Inventário da legislação indigenista, 1500–1800," in
História dos Índios no Brasil, ed. Manuela Carneiro da Cunha (São Paulo:
Companhia das Letras, FAPESP/SMC, 1992), 529–66.

42. BNRJ, SM, cód. 5, 2, 2, p. 1–3. On the application of this law in Minas Gerais, see
Langfur, *Forbidden Lands*, chap. 2. Concerning the laws known as the Indian
Directorate, the basis for indigenous policy between the 1750s and 1790s, see Rita
Heloísa de Almeida, *O Diretório dos índios: Projeto de "civilização" no Brasil do
século XVIII* (Brasília: Universidade de Brasília, 1997).

43. Elsewhere in the colony, commissions set up to hear these cases were composed
of authorities occupying the following positions: *ouvidor geral, juiz de fora,
procurador dos índios, prelado diocesano,* the captaincy governor, and
high-ranking representatives of the Jesuit, Carmelite, and Capuchin missionary
orders. Final verdicts were issued by the Mesa de Consciência e Ordens. See
Carlos de A. Moreira Neto, *Índios da Amazônia: De maioria à minoria (1750–1850)*
(Petrópolis: Editora Vozes, 1988), 162. In Minas Gerais, it fell to a *juiz ordinário*
to issue the final verdict.

44. "Providencias tomadas para a catechese dos Indios no Rio Doce e Piracicaba,
Vila Rica, 1764–1767," APM, CC, cód. 1156, fols. 1–2, 4.

45. APM , SC, cód. 59, fol. 103–104v.

46. APM, SC, cód. 59, p. 101v–102.

47. APM, SG3, cx. 6, doc. 39 (6/12/1769).

48. Almeida, *O diretório dos índios*, 199.

49. BN, SM, cód. 18, 3, 3, p. 188.

50. APM, SC, cód. 60, fot. 2123–2124.

51. APM, SC, cód. 60, fot. 2086.

52. APM, SG3, cx. 6, doc. 39.

53. On freed slaves in eighteenth-century Minas Gerais, see Núbia Braga Ribeiro,
"Cotidiano e liberdade: Um estudo sobre os alforriados em Minas no século
XVIII" (MA thesis, Universidade de Sao Paulo, 1996), 79; Laura de Mello e Souza,
Norma e conflito: Aspectos da história de Minas no século XVIII (Belo Horizonte:
UFMG, 1999), 166.

54. BN, SM, cód. 18, 3, 3, p. 82.

55. ACM, PM, no. 7862 (1769).

56. BN, SM, cód. 18, 3, 3, p. 75–79.
57. APM, SC, cód. 260, fot. 772–74. A similar case occurred in the town of Pitangui in 1760. In this instance, several Indian women were not released from prison when local officials failed to act on an order to grant them their freedom. See APM, SC, cód. 130, fot. 1837–1838.
58. APM, SC, cód. 260, fot. 783–86.
59. PR, AHU, 8078, cx. 103, doc. 6. This was the same canon who ordered published the panegyric *Áureo Trono Episcopal* in Lisboa in 1749, which recounts the committee's voyage from Maranhão to Mariana. See Iris Kantor, "Um visitador na periferia da América Portuguesa: Visitas pastorais, memórias históricas e penegíricos episcopais," *Vária História* 21 (July 1999): 441.
60. See Figueiredo and Campos, eds., *Códice Costa Matoso*, 917–42.
61. Iris Kantor, "Um visitador," 443.
62. AHU, PR, 8078, cx. 103, doc. 6.
63. AHU, PR, 8086, cx. 103, doc. 87.
64. APM, SC, cód. 184, fot. 2134.
65. AHU, PR, 6163, cx. 75, doc. 54. Knowledge of such legislation had been widespread in Minas Gerais since the beginning of the eighteenth century. See, APM, SC, cód. 9, fot. 64.

6

Catechism and Capitalism

Imperial Indigenous Policy on a Brazilian Frontier, 1808–1845

Judy Bieber

In 1808 Portugal's Prince Regent João, who would assume the throne as João VI in 1816, declared a "just war" against the Botocudo Indians of the Doce River basin of Minas Gerais and Espírito Santo (see map 4). This measure did not represent a departure from late colonial policy, as Hal Langfur and Maria Leônia Chaves de Resende demonstrate in the preceding chapter. Rather, it provided formal sanction to nearly a half-century of local-ized militarization initiated by royal governors in Minas Gerais.[1] Dom João's formal declaration of war also suggested the backward-looking approach to indigenous policy that would be followed well into the nineteenth century. In Joanine (1808–1821) and Imperial Brazil (1822–1889), lawmakers were more likely to replicate colonial models of native administration than to innovate. Following independence in 1822, policy shifted toward peaceful accultura-tion although military forces continued to play a decisive role in the crafting and implementation of indigenous policy. Imperial initiatives remained self-consciously derivative of two colonial precedents discussed previously in this volume: the Jesuit *aldeia* system and its secular successor, the Directorate (1757–1798).

Nineteenth-century indigenous policy ultimately failed largely due to the crown's inability or unwillingness to explore alternative administrative models. The government attempted to apply institutions that had been developed in the colonial period for Tupi-speaking, semisedentary tribes to seminomadic, small-scale, primarily Gê-speaking peoples located in isolated settings, the so-called Botocudo. Moreover, the government devoted inadequate resources to indigenous pacification and settlement. During the post-1808 period of militarization, the several hundred Portuguese troops that were scattered throughout eastern Minas Gerais were no match for the tens of thousands of Indians that still populated the region.[2] Within a few years, as the focus of policy shifted from aggression to acculturation, military commanders continued to administer native populations, but their divisions remained undermanned and undersupplied. These limitations enabled the Botocudo to exert considerable agency in their dealings with authorities and with settlers who attempted to establish themselves in indigenous territory.

In so doing, the Botocudo effectively thwarted the prince regent's plans for the Doce River basin. He envisioned pacification of the Indians as the first step in a plan of regional integration that would strengthen economic ties between Minas Gerais, Rio de Janeiro, and Espírito Santo. In order to provide security for prospective settlers in the presumably rich and yet uncultivated forested lands to the east, frontier forces were divided among seven military divisions which were assigned the Herculean tasks of opening and maintaining trade routes through the dense forests, transforming the Botocudo into productive workers and loyal vassals and maintaining the peace. Their mandate included transforming indigenous foragers into farmers by fostering dependence on consumer goods and introducing them to the benefits of settled agriculture. Within the policy of *catequese* (literally catechism or religious conversion), an emphasis on capitalist accumulation predominated as a means of acculturation and assimilation. However, accumulation of private property was incompatible with Botocudo cultural preferences as well as subsistence practices. Acquisition of material goods made little sense for peoples who carried their possessions on their backs when moving from place to place. Private ownership of land was of limited perceived utility for people who foraged for a living. The inability of policymakers to recognize vital differences like these contributed to the failure of indigenous policy to achieve state goals in eastern Minas Gerais during the first half of the nineteenth century.

COLONIAL AND IMPERIAL INDIGENOUS LEGISLATION:
CONTINUITIES AND DISCONTINUITIES

Most of the legislation concerning indigenous peoples passed during the first half of the nineteenth century targeted the Botocudo, an ethnic group that was more imagined than real. Dom João and his advisors envisioned the Botocudo as ferocious cannibals who wandered aimlessly and irrationally through the forests in search of subsistence. They could be readily distinguished by their use of *botoques*, large wooden disks worn in their pierced ears and lower lips. However, Botocudos were defined more by whether or not they resisted Portuguese expansion than by cultural, material, or linguistic criteria.[3] The eastern *sertões* (backlands) of Minas Gerais, the forested region separating Brazil's inland mining district from the Atlantic coast, were home to a multitude of small-scale, often mutually hostile indigenous societies who practiced diverse cultural, subsistence, and migration patterns. The majority spoke dialects of Macro-Gê. Military commanders, Indian directors, settlers, and priests recognized a number of subgroups (not all of whom used botoques) including the Borun, Bacuê, Guakines or Guatexi, Guanaã, Giporok, Jurupi, Kopoxó, Kumanaxó, Kutaxó, Krenak, Kamakã-Mongoió (also referred to as the Menian or Canarin), Kutatoi, Malali, Makoni, Menhame, Monxoco, Panhame, Pataxós, Pojixá, Punxó, Puri, and Taititûs.[4] Generic names were also applied to tribes according to settler or official perceptions regarding their relative ferocity or intransigence. For example, more tractable tribes often were labeled Maxakalis or Naknenuks to distinguish them from the more hostile Botocudo and Puri.[5]

The effective meaning of these ethnic markers is not entirely clear. In some cases tribal groups seem to have taken their names from their leader, like the Zamplan.[6] In other cases, labels were descriptive terms often applied by other tribes such as Maxakali (meaning "reunion of tribes"), Naknenuk ("not of the land"), Giporok ("bad"), or Puri ("thieves").[7] To further muddy the waters, contemporaneous observers often confused or conflated the categories Naknenuk, Maxakali, Puri, and Botocudo. Although most of these groups were small-scale and autonomous, many admitted common linguistic or cultural origins with other tribes.[8] Some sparse documentary evidence also exists of temporary military alliances among individual peoples to combat the Portuguese.[9] However, it seems quite clear that the Portuguese crown did not face a unified enemy even if they portrayed the "Botocudo" as such. In the interests of stylistic simplicity, I will use the term as if it were

Figure 25. Like many aboriginal inhabitants of the eastern forests, the Pataxó Indians portrayed in this image deftly handled both European tools and indigenous weapons. Although colonizers cast Indians as either savage or civilized, native cultural and technological versatility defied such categorization. Source: Wied-Neuwied, *Travels in Brazil.* Courtesy of the John Carter Brown Library at Brown University.

self-evident in the remainder of this essay, while retaining awareness of its problematic and complex origins which are enumerated above.

Regardless of the ethnic, cultural, and material realities lived by the indigenous populations of the eastern sertões, Portuguese and Brazilian policymakers imagined them as irredeemably vicious, bestial, and incapable of civilization. Many stereotypes that affirmed the supposed rapaciousness of Gê-speaking peoples came from Tupi-speaking tribes who had allied with the Portuguese during the early period of contact.[10] Maria Hilda Paraíso has even argued that the descriptions of cannibalism recorded in the nineteenth century by one German naturalist are so strikingly similar to sixteenth-century chronicles that either he or his Botocudo informant had been directly influenced by those sources.[11]

During the colonial era, the primary point of reference for Portuguese settlers in their dealings with native peoples was the semisedentary Tupi-speaking peoples of the coast and the Amazon basin. Although the Portuguese did not find complex indigenous states or civilizations (or at least ones that they recognized), the Tupi populations they encountered practiced sedentary agriculture supplemented by hunting and gathering.[12] Early chronicles described fortified Tupi villages, the cultivation of corn, manioc, and cotton, and the production of craft goods such as cotton textiles and ceramics.[13] Archaeological evidence from present-day Minas Gerais suggests that the cultivation of maize dates back at least 3,900 years before the present era.[14] However, the practice of slash-and-burn agriculture required periodic migration as land became less fertile over time. Large villages incorporated approximately seventy square miles of territory. By about AD 1000, competition for land along the coast became intense.[15]

Being well versed in agriculture and extractive activities, the semi-settled Tupi speakers proved useful to the Portuguese. For several decades following the first landfall in 1500, Tupi-speaking men willingly cut and hauled timber for Portuguese traders. Although *pau-brasil* (brazilwood, *caesalpina echinata*), a dyewood, was especially prized, old-growth hardwoods were in demand as well. The Indians also bartered cotton as well as exotic and expensive ritual goods in order to forge relations of reciprocity with the newcomers. Supplying the Portuguese meant merely an expansion of activities that were already part of indigenous material and cultural life. In return, they accepted a variety of simple trade goods from the Portuguese.

Contemporaneous observers judged the Indians to be irrational in their willingness to exchange expensive and heavy timber for trinkets, fish hooks, knives, and axes. From the indigenous point of view, however, the availability of metal tools represented a substantial saving in labor expenditures. Imagine the impact of metal tweezers for a people that ritually plucked all body hair including eyebrows and lashes; the importance of steel fish hooks for a people accustomed to spearing fish and then swimming after them; and the ease with which trees could be felled with a metal ax.[16]

The economic rationality of the Tupi in exchanging backbreaking labor for trade goods of nominal value was first examined seriously by Alexander Marchant in his pathbreaking thesis, *From Barter to Slavery*.[17] Unlike most of his scholarly contemporaries, Marchant entertained the possibility that Indians responded logically to economic incentives. However, he emphasized material factors at the expense of cultural motivations. Stuart Schwartz subsequently refined and qualified Marchant's depiction of the Tupinambá as "economic men," arguing that the entry of iron tools into indigenous society functioned not so much as a stimulus for increased production, but rather useful items that permitted more leisure time.[18] Schwartz also suggested that labor patterns of Tupinambá males were shaped by their notions of appropriate sexual division of labor. Cutting brazilwood was an adaptation of the male task of land-clearing whereas plantation agriculture was perceived as women's work. Not surprisingly, when the Portuguese began to shift to sugar cultivation they found few indigenous men willing to subject themselves to what they saw as demeaning work and low pay associated with the plantation regime. Moreover, native economies probably had reached market saturation in durable goods like metal tools, especially as their numbers began to decline due to disease. So the Portuguese resorted to slavery, first indigenous and then African, to meet their labor needs. Simultaneously, Jesuit missionaries began to organize structured communities, aldeias, to convert the Tupi to Christianity and European habits and customs.

As others in this volume have noted, in 1757 the Portuguese crown placed indigenous administration under secular authorities. The Directorate system (1757–1798), however, retained many essential organizing principles of the Jesuit aldeia system. Converted Indians who resided in Directorate communities were expected to subject themselves to work discipline, including communal agriculture, labor contracts with private individuals, and forced labor on state projects. Directors were compensated in proportion to the production of the Indians under their tutelage and were also expected to make their charges available to work for settlers.[19] Although the Directors are generally believed to have been more abusive than the Jesuits in exploiting their charges, under both clerical and secular tutelage, Indians faced unremunerated work obligations and expropriation of the profits of their labors.[20]

The Directorate was abolished in 1798; thereafter, the crown authorized interested individuals to provide "tutelage" for unincorporated tribes. From the abolition of the Directorate to its modified reintroduction in 1845, Brazil lacked a coherent, national indigenous policy. Although statesman and royal advisor José Bonifácio de Andrada e Silva proposed a general policy at the Constituent Assembly in 1823, it was not incorporated into Brazil's 1824 Constitution. Bonifácio's vision was directly inspired by the Jesuit aldeia system and blended religious tutelage and economic imperatives.[21] He favored the stimulation of consumer wants and a "love of property" (*amor à propriedade*) among newly settled Indians through the distribution of gifts and the scheduling of regular market days in the aldeias. Bonifácio also recommended that Indians be put to tasks consistent with their level of civilization including clearing forest, transporting timber, building roads, and working as mule traders, foot soldiers, fishermen, farmhands, and shepherds. He believed that displays of Portuguese affluence and abundance eventually would convince Indians to opt for farming. To further that goal, fields would be cleared, tools distributed, and instruction given. In addition to promoting subsistence agriculture and ranching, Bonifácio also advocated the cultivation of cash crops such as cotton, tobacco, castor seed, peanuts, coffee, linen, and hemp.[22] Women would be taught to spin and weave and interested men would receive training in the mechanical trades. To prevent nomadic peoples from backsliding, he advised that villages be situated far from abundant hunting or fishing grounds.

Instead of a general policy like José Bonifácio's, the government passed a series of individual laws that targeted specific native groups, principally the Botocudo. Gê-speaking groups, in contrast to the Tupi, had comparatively little contact with the Portuguese. Known as Tapuias or Aimorês in the colonial era, they were vilified for their primitivism and retained a reputation for cannibalism, a trait formerly shared with the Tupi. As the Tupi had expanded demographically along Brazil's coasts, Gê tribes were pushed further into the interior. Consequently, they were able to avoid contact with the Portuguese to a much greater extent than the Tupi-speaking groups. Their language was a further means to isolation as it was distinct from the *língua geral*, a missionary dialect invented by Jesuit missionaries that was based on Tupi. Finally, although Gê tribes might have also practiced agriculture at some time, by the era of Portuguese contact their subsistence seems to have derived primarily from hunting, fishing, and foraging.

During the first two centuries of Portuguese rule, the eastern sertões of Minas Gerais and the contiguous frontiers of Espírito Santo, Ilheus, and Porto Seguro, which at times were autonomous captaincies and at times administrative dependencies of Bahia to the north, received comparatively little attention. The Jesuits limited their activities in Espírito Santo to the creation of four small aldeias near the coast.[23] A sparse European population coupled with demographic decline of the coastal indigenous population transformed the eastern sertões into a viable haven for eastern Brazil's remaining seminomadic indigenous tribes. However, following the discovery of gold in central Minas Gerais in the 1690s, Indians from the interior were enslaved in sizeable numbers.[24] Within a few decades, African captives replaced them.[25] As the authors of the preceding chapter explain, the crown created "forbidden lands" to the east of the primary mining zones in order to inhibit contraband trade of gold via the lightly populated coasts of Espírito Santo and southern Bahia. The presumably hostile Indians served as a convenient deterrent to would-be smugglers. However, as known gold supplies in Minas Gerais began to decline by the mid-eighteenth century, the crown and its local representatives began to view the east as an untapped resource to be exploited and violence intensified.

Many of Prince Regent João's advisors advocated the use of violence to subdue Indians expansively defined as Botocudo. Some even openly supported outright extermination or the systematic destruction of indigenous forest habitat.[26] Underpinning this aggressive policy lay the interrelated economic goals of opening the Doce River region to Portuguese settlement and gaining access to indigenous labor. Pacification of the Botocudo would provide the minimal conditions necessary to attract settlers to invest in and populate the eastern frontier. A military presence would also facilitate the transformation of indigenous nomads into sedentary producers and consumers who would recognize the sovereignty of the Brazilian state. Although the most striking aspect of João's *carta régia* (royal decree) of 13 May 1808 is the monarch's revival of the custom of "just war" and the sanctioned enslavement of native Brazilians "for as long as their ferocity endures," this and subsequent legislation also contained detailed economic directives for transforming the Botocudo into "useful vassals."[27]

In fact, in 1808 the prince regent issued no less than three decrees that addressed frontier settlement in the Mineiro east.[28] As a group, they provided compelling inducements for potential settlers including debt forgiveness, freedom from paying the *dízimo* (a royal tax) for ten years, and liberal distribution of *sesmarias* (royal land grants) consisting of territory that was "rescued" from the Botocudo. In so doing, these decrees uniquely perpetuated colonial privileges that were being eliminated in other parts of Brazil. In addition to maintaining the sesmaria exclusively in the Doce River region, *fazendeiros* (large landholders) who successfully sponsored stable native settlements of acculturated Indians acquired the archaic title of *senhor e donatório* (master and donatary) over their charges. Frontier settlers also were given labor rights to any Indian children that they were willing to raise for an eight-year period.

Many settlers were quick to take advantage of this windfall. By 1811, within the territory associated with the first military district, a total of 381 sesmarias were granted. The *sesmeiros* (land-grant recipients) were people of wealth and stature if the size of the slave population is any indication.

Figure 26. The traveling French artist Jean Baptiste Debret, who admitted to finding his subjects "repugnant," informed viewers that this scene depicted Botocudo, Puri, Pataxó, and Maxakali Indians, all of them targets of the state's aggressive moves to incorporate their territory in the nineteenth century. Evidently intended to shock, the composition tells us more about the European imagination than about native conduct and appearance. Source: Debret, *Voyage pittoresque*. Public domain access: http://www.brasiliana.usp.br/bbd/handle/1918/624510024

Afro-Brazilian captives made up 41 percent of this frontier community of just over 3,000 souls, and dependent laborers constituted nearly 22 percent.[29] In the town of Itapemirim, across the border from Minas Gerais in Espírito Santo, Afro-Brazilian slaves comprised 45 percent of the population by the mid-1820s.[30]

To protect these frontier settlers, the crown created a network of seven infantry divisions consisting of Brazilians and "tame" Indians (*mansos*) to protect them; these forces were expanded to eight larger units by 1820.[31] Although referred to as the Doce River Divisions, the units spread northward into other major river basins and from Minas Gerais to the borders of the neighboring captaincies of Espírito Santo and Bahia. Military commanders were empowered to distribute land, to direct road construction, and to apportion indigenous laborers to both civilians and the state. Bonuses were awarded for effectively protecting Portuguese lives and property or for imprisoning or destroying the greatest number of Indians.

To create and maintain these divisions the state resorted to conscription of criminals and vagrants, typically poor and of Afro-Brazilian descent. Most of these reluctant recruits came from the humblest ranks of society and the pejorative terminology used to describe these soldiers was typically indistinguishable from language applied to Indians. Division soldiers did double duty as farmers, carving out small plots to feed themselves and to attract wandering Indians to the settled life through their example. Criminals who had been incarcerated in more centrally located towns were also sent to Botocudo territory as were Eufrasia María Joaquina, sentenced to sew, launder, and cook for an indigenous aldeia, and María Carneira who was to cook for a military division and provide "additional services suited to her intellectual faculties."[32] Male convicts also were pressed into division service. Additionally, a small number of indigenous men were willing to serve as soldiers, guides, interpreters (*línguas*), and cultural go-betweens.[33]

However, the crown quickly modified its approach toward the natives of the eastern sertões. A subsequent carta régia of 28 July 1809 laid out markedly different guidelines to govern aldeias of the Puri and Xamixuna of Minas Gerais.[34] Why the Puri were singled out as deserving of benign treatment is unclear as in the late colonial period they were often conflated with the Botocudo and typically deemed to be hostile. Nevertheless, the decree offered them and the obscure Xamixuna protection from the enslavement and labor extortion that undermined the formation of stable native communities. The directive put native self-sufficiency first and the labor needs of settlers second, at least on paper. Indians were not to hire themselves out at the expense of their own production. It also set a minimum wage: a paltry sixty *réis* per day, which was, nonetheless, 50 percent more than that paid to indigenous military recruits.

The 1809 decree sought to instill a love of property by offering the necessary instruction and tools for agriculture, animal husbandry, and the manual trades. Women and girls were to be provided cotton and the tools necessary to spin and weave cloth. In addition to curing Indians of their "laziness and indolence" through work, property accumulation would "serve as a stimulus to those that are dispersed throughout the forest to come and seek out in the villages the temporal pleasures that their brethren enjoy and to flee from the misery and barbarity that they have lived in until now." The authors of these regulations also recognized the lure of alternative forms of subsistence and forbade aldeia Indians to leave the community to work or hunt unless a blood relative remained in the aldeia and the director granted written permission. Mobility would be "conceded only to those who have something to lose."

By 1811, lawmakers began to make distinctions between "tame" and "wild" Botocudos (*mansos e bravos*), the former seen as potential allies in the war with the latter.[35] However, regulations concerning economic roles were not articulated until 1824, and then the Botocudo did not warrant the same protections that had been granted to the Puri and Xamixuna. Secular Indian directorates, similar to those that had been in effect between 1757 and 1798, were created and their directors were instructed to use nonviolent means to encourage Indians to settle down near frontier forts. Although provisions were made for demarcating aldeias, the state set no minimum wage nor did it enjoin directors to protect their charges from unscrupulous traders or settlers. The 1824 regulations stipulated that day laborers were to be hired for the first year of settlement in order to ensure an adequate food supply for the inexperienced Indians, who were to be given tools, food, and cotton clothing until they were capable of obtaining these goods through their own labor. The most detailed economic instructions pertained not to the Botocudo but to the military forces stationed along the Doce River. Their duties included farming, construction of houses, barracks, and roads, manufacture and repair of tools, making canoes, cutting timber, and transporting supplies.[36]

The cartas régias that had declared war against the Botocudo were abolished in 1831.[37] The end of legalized indigenous enslavement coincided with legislation prohibiting the African slave trade. Although neither measure was enforced, these laws signaled at least a discursive preference for free labor. For Indians, however, this did not translate into economic independence. The law stipulated that the treasury would support former indigenous slaves until they obtained salaried work or learned a manual trade. But all native peoples were defined as juridical minors and, as such, they lacked autonomy to make independent economic decisions. Administration of their property was placed in the hands of the *juiz dos órfãos*, a local judicial official. Moreover, illegal indigenous enslavement flourished well into the mid-nineteenth century.[38]

In 1845, the Brazilian state finally adopted a national indigenous policy inspired by José Bonifácio's 1823 recommendations which, in turn, derived heavily from earlier colonial policy. Secular directors were appointed in each province to administer native populations. Their mandate included keeping detailed statistical and fiscal records, establishing land rights, determining the viability of existing aldeias, establishing new settlements for "wandering hordes," providing for moral and practical education, and placing missionaries to best advantage.[39] Directors were to protect indigenous cultivators' usufruct rights to land provided that they were "well behaved and demonstrated an industrious way of life."[40] This implied that such claims to land could be easily lost if Indians "misbehaved." Legal title was limited to Indians who cultivated land for an uninterrupted span of twelve years. Lands that were "abandoned" (occupied sporadically rather than continuously) or underutilized could revert to the state. The law reflected nineteenth-century economic liberal principles by advocating and encouraging an eventual shift from communal to private property. Directors were also to continue the policy of distributing tools, clothing, medicine, and other items to Indians to "attract their attention, excite their curiosity and awaken in them a desire for social life."[41] Provisions were even made to defend pacified aldeia Indians militarily and to protect their economic interests by regulating trade and work contracts.

POLICY IN PRACTICE: WORKING THE *ALDEIA* SYSTEM

From the point of view of the policymakers of the Joanine and early Imperial periods, indigenous legislation directed toward the Botocudo failed. Indians of the eastern sertões continued to be maddeningly mobile. At best they expressed temporary enthusiasm for state-sponsored aldeias. Those who experimented with agriculture often abandoned their fields or harvested the crops before they ripened fully. Even more so than the *ausentes* (absentees) described in Barbara Sommer's work on late-colonial aldeias in Pará, the Botocudo refused to settle down and work for a living.[42]

Portuguese failure to control and regulate indigenous labor and settlement patterns probably had as much to do with Portuguese misperceptions as with indigenous recalcitrance. Portuguese and European observers proved unable to understand why indigenous peoples would prefer "poverty" and uncertainty over a means of subsistence that would provide wealth and security.[43] They concluded that this preference was proof of indigenous irrationality, childishness, or inability to progress. José Bonifácio was more perceptive than most commentators in evaluating the characteristics of simple material existence, writing:

> In effect, man in his savage state, and principally the wild Indian of Brazil, *should be lazy*; because he has few or no necessities. Being a vagabond, he can set up and dismantle his hut at will in lands abundant in game or fish or even wild and spontaneous fruits. Living every day exposed to the weather, he doesn't need houses or comfortable clothing or the affectations of our definition of luxury. Finally he has neither an idea of property, nor a desire for social distinctions or vanities that are the powerful motives that propel the civilized man into action.[44]

The pursuit of a foraging lifestyle privileges leisure time over possessions, a choice that Portuguese policymakers failed to appreciate. The amount of time expended to meet subsistence needs by agriculture generally exceeds that needed for hunting and gathering. For example, in her study of the !Kung tribe of Botswana, Marjorie Shostak estimated that women could meet the caloric needs of their families by foraging two days out of the week, even in the harsher environment of the Kalahari desert.[45] It is doubtful that meeting subsistence would have taken longer for the Botocudo in the exuberant *mata atlântica* (Atlantic forest).

Portuguese economic preferences also demanded a substantial reorientation of labor responsibilities found within foraging indigenous societies. Contemporary anthropological accounts that have studied hunter-gatherers have determined that male hunting provides only between 20 and 40 percent of the calories necessary for survival of the group. Women provide the balance through their gathering activities that generally provide a more reliable return than the pursuit of game.[46] In asking indigenous men to give up hunting and adopt agriculture, the Portuguese probably did not fully understand the gender implications of what they were demanding. In addition to requiring steady and constant labor, potentially they were also shifting more of the burden onto the men.

Hunting and gathering, however, requires low population densities in order not to compromise the environment's ability to provide. It necessitates migration to take advantage of seasonal resources such as fruits, vegetables, fish, and game. Foraging also places limits on the accumulation of nonessential possessions that have to be lugged from place to place. Simply put, this way of life was inconsistent with European notions of private property. Portuguese officials often argued that foraging Indians had no notion of land ownership because they did not live permanently in a fixed location. However, it is likely that most Gê tribes confined their hunting, fishing, and gathering to particular areas in order to not invite conflict over resources with other indigenous groups.

Foraging should not be romanticized. Brazil's hunting and gathering peoples experienced seasons of abundance and want, and in periods of drought or scarcity people died. Demographic pressures could and did compromise this way of life. Portuguese settlers systematically began to intrude upon eastern indigenous territories by the 1760s. However, the timing and extent of population pressures and associated environmental change is difficult to determine with any precision due to source limitations. The location of land grants, much less the extent to which they were occupied or exploited, remains vague.[47] However, many sources attest to extensive land speculation by enterprising sesmeiros in the Doce River region, rapid turnover in ownership, and frequent abandonment of sesmaria grants in the face of Botocudo armed resistance.[48] Speculators often left their lands uncultivated or "improved" them by burning the forest before selling their property to unsuspecting buyers.[49] Land disputes also arose between indigenous claimants and newly arrived settlers.[50] However, without more specific and detailed information, the demographic effect of sesmeiros on native subsistence patterns remains a matter of informed speculation.

Accounts by European travelers reported intensifying competition for hunting and provision grounds by the 1810s and 1820s, thereby contributing to the violence that had already been set into motion by the militarization of the frontier. The presence of the army in eastern Minas Gerais also pushed many Botocudo to migrate into Espírito Santo and Bahia where they competed for environmental resources with the pre-existing, semisedentary indigenous populations.[51] The German naturalist Maximilian, Prince of Wied-Neuwied, attributed conflicts between tribes in southern Bahia to invasion of hunting grounds and also noted that truces were called when certain forest products became ripe enough to harvest. He reported similar conflicts over usufruct rights to land in Minas Gerais.[52]

Road building associated with settlement almost certainly compromised subsistence patterns although, again, the magnitude of change is hard to measure. Destruction of forest cover probably altered migratory routes of game. It certainly created more areas of standing water where disease-carrying mosquitoes could breed.[53] Road projects such as the Mariana-Itapemirim-Vitória road also made heavy use of the labor of coerced Indians and soldiers of humble origin.[54] Yet when the road was finally completed, it was little more than a narrow track that became all but useless in the rainy season. By 1830, the route had already begun to fall into disrepair.[55] Many traders and soldiers preferred to transport their goods by canoe.[56]

Finally, sanctioned enslavement of the unpacified indigenous population also profoundly disrupted Gê cultural and material survival. First and foremost, it compromised a central Gê characteristic—mobility. Additionally, increased demand for labor motivated tribes to war with one another in

Figure 27. A racially mixed crew built this road in the early nineteenth century, one of several that cut through the forests separating Minas Gerais from the coast. Disruptive to hunting and gathering practices, such projects affected wildlife migration, provided greater access for colonists, and depended on coerced indigenous labor. Source: Wied-Neuwied, *Travels in Brazil.* Courtesy of the John Carter Brown Library at Brown University.

order to capture prisoners to sell.[57] Settlers preferred captive children, and kidnapping children often inspired retaliatory attacks. In foraging cultures, children are typically spaced through post-partum sexual taboos and late weaning so that women do not have to carry more than one child at a time when on the move.[58] The loss of one or two children to a family or small-scale tribe would be all the more devastating when so much time and emotional commitment had been invested in each child. Many documented cases of violence against settlers arose because children had been stolen.[59] Theft of children could also motivate Indians to quit the aldeias.[60] Curiously, Portuguese authorities often expressed wonder at the capacity of Gê parents to mourn the loss of their children. As one director observed, "One cannot remove a single child from them because as parents, although savages, they adore their children as we do."[61]

Demand for slaves also disrupted indigenous subsistence. The theft of even a few women or children could result in significant shortfalls within a small-scale group. The loss of men who were captured as prisoners-of-war or who were killed in battle also weakened the ability of the group to survive. So, too, did the absences of men who were forced to work for private individuals or the state for months or years at a time. Many officials assumed that Botocudo men would not succumb easily to wage incentives and coerced or enslaved them accordingly. However, it is not clear whether the Botocudo would have participated if wages had been better or more reliably paid. Clearing forest to open roads was consistent with traditional male roles and might have been considered an acceptable means to acquire valuable trade items. Many indigenous men showed interest in signing on for military service but balked if they were not compensated accordingly. Indian foot soldiers were paid only one-third the wage received by Luso-Brazilians, and more often than not their salaries were paid tardily, if at all. One director reported that day laborers and soldiers in the employ of the military often went six to ten months without receiving a cent, and unless Indian employees were paid quarterly, they deserted.[62]

INDIGENOUS STRATEGIES: WORKING THE *ALDEIA* SYSTEM

The aldeia system potentially offered some benefits to indigenous hunter-gatherers. It included the cultivation of lands for their benefit, distribution of valuable metal tools, and a more secure food supply. The fact that some

Indians opted to settle in an aldeia suggests that in some areas traditional subsistence means had been compromised severely by ecological change and population pressures. Documentary evidence left by aldeia directors, however, suggests that most Indians who entered the aldeias did so as a temporary solution during periods of scarcity or disease. Rather than adapting to Portuguese economic imperatives, they incorporated aldeias and settler properties as additional resources to support a mobile subsistence strategy.

The Botocudo were interested in many of the goods that the Portuguese directors had to offer. In particular, they prized metal implements. To underscore the point, one ethnohistorian has made the somewhat dubious and unsubstantiated claim that metal tools were so highly regarded that Indians were willing to trade children for them.[63] For the Coroados of southeastern Minas Gerais, pocket knives were the most valued "presents" they received.[64] Knives, axes, scissors, nails, and fish hooks figured prominently in José Bonifácio's list of recommended trade goods.[65] The desire for such items was poignantly expressed in an account describing the capitulation of the Naknenuks before the Indian Director Guido Tomás Marliére in 1824. The tribe sent their women first, hoping to inspire pity (and presumably handouts) by brandishing their "miserable" stone axes.[66]

Gifts to Indians typically consisted of practical items that would enable them to adopt Portuguese work patterns. These included agricultural tools, saws, knives, rifles and other weapons, ammunition, unworked steel and lead, kettles and cauldrons, clothing, and sewing implements. On occasion, luxury and symbolic goods were also included as was the case with an Indian named Innocencio who negotiated a peace in 1825. In addition to the abovementioned items, he and his entourage also received a cocked hat with a gold buckle, a police uniform, some gold braid trim, epaulettes, a sword, an English saddle, a pair of high, laced shoes, and a portrait of the king in a gilded frame, presumably to impress upon them the authority of their new sovereign. The women received dresses, shawls, hat ribbons, two dozen mirrors, sixteen necklaces of colored crystal, and four hundred assorted needles.[67]

Trinkets also found takers among indigenous populations. Although they may have been seen as relatively inconsequential items by Portuguese merchants, making traditional ornamentation could be a time-consuming business. Native forms of decoration incorporated natural vegetable dyes, feathers, and beaded necklaces. Boring holes in shells and animal teeth was labor intensive, especially without recourse to metal tools. The ownership of European notions, trims, clothing, and jewelry may also have given indigenous leaders a certain status. Indians also used European articles for purposes not intended by their makers. For example, one Indian director complained that his charges did not wear the shirts, pants, and hats given to them but instead used them as sacks to carry manioc flour.[68] When Guido Marlière gifted some Puri "virgins" with some glass rosary beads, they reworked the simple strings into a large, showy necklace.[69]

Indigenous populations of the eastern frontier were certainly interested in Portuguese trade goods, but they did not become dependent upon them as officials and policymakers had hoped. Their response ran counter to the expectations of a prominent Austrian mining engineer in the service of the Portuguese crown who saw salutary effects in the inculcation of a "certain sense of luxury" among the Indians. He predicted (wrongly) that "Luxury produces vices that are capable of reducing a civilized nation to a state of barbarism, but also can produce the opposite effect in a barbarous nation. What was in the beginning a luxury will become in short time a necessity."[70]

Moreover, the Botocudo did not embrace agriculture in order to acquire prized goods. Rather they resorted to a variety of strategies including trade, theft, and handouts. They were willing to engage in extractive activities that did not disrupt their traditional subsistence patterns. For example, Gê-speakers became actively involved in the extraction and sale of *poaia* (*ipecacuanha preta*; scientific name, *psychotria emetica*), the active ingredient in the widely used nineteenth-century emetic, ipecac. In the early decades of the nineteenth century, it became a leading export from Minas Gerais.[71] The organization of the poaia trade was dominated by settlers, traders, or Indian directors. Marliére encouraged the Indians under his care to engage in its extraction in order to make the state-sponsored aldeias self-sustaining.[72] However, he and other directors were also accused of coercing Indians to gather the plant at the expense of their own farming.[73] This may have been the case but may also reflect indigenous choice.[74] Gathering forest products was consistent with traditional subsistence strategies and could have been combined with other activities like tracking and hunting. One would expect that women would have been involved in collecting the plant but extant documentation does not mention female participation.

In any event, the trade was said to be extremely profitable; one military officer from the third division claimed that it had yielded the staggering sum of thirty *contos* in the final years of the 1820s.[75] It is unlikely that much profit accrued to the Indians who gathered poaia. Competition among settlers and traders for a share in the trade also contributed to the intensification of conflict in the Doce River region.[76] The Brazilian government sought information about other indigenous medicines, but poaia was the only commercially viable medicinal plant identified in the eastern sertões.[77] However, indigenous men also bartered other extractive products including game, pelts, parrots, monkeys, honey, wax, and tropical flowers.[78]

It seems clear that Indians approached the aldeias not to embrace agriculture's supposed benefits but to receive free trade goods from aldeia directors and military officers who believed that an initial offering of "presents" was required to attract the Indians to settled life. Unfortunately, the government's late or nonexistent shipments of promised goods hindered efforts to gain the confidence of curious Indians.[79] When supplies ran out, Botocudo men were likely to abandon the aldeia or attack military posts while the women and children stole what they needed.[80] Frustration was also apparent higher in the administrative hierarchy as is evident in the words of the provincial president of Espírito Santo, who complained about the long-term financial drain involved in sustaining an indigenous population "that does not subject itself to any kind of work, always inclined to predation which causes great losses for the farmers."[81]

It also appears obvious that raiding would be preferable to the life of daily toil and strict supervision that the aldeias offered. Legislation passed in 1824 for the Doce River region gave indigenous raiders virtual impunity. The law forbade settlers to retaliate violently to avenge attacks against property. Instead they were to be compensated for their losses by the state.[82] The indigenous peoples on the Espírito Santo frontier were likely aware of this protective legislation as they raided settler crops and livestock frequently but generally stopped short at violence against settlers.[83] One captain who resided on the Minas Gerais–Espírito Santo frontier reported being attacked on the road by a group of Botocudos who fired arrows at his horse and cattle but left him unharmed.[84] Another captain and landowner, João Dias Pacheco Guimarães of Itapemirim, was turned down by a group of sixty Botocudo when he invited them to settle on his land where he would provide them with subsistence in exchange for their labor. They declined, telling him that they easily could meet their needs in the forest.[85] However, they supplemented their foraging by continually raiding his property in the amount of 800$000 *mil-réis*.[86]

Agricultural predation was a logical strategy to expand an indigenous group's subsistence base. Killing domesticated animals that were enclosed and did not run away was much easier than hunting. Stealing crops that one didn't cultivate oneself was more efficient than procuring vegetable foods dispersed about the forest. Yet, much of the time, reports of raids on agricultural property reveal that Indians often did not destroy to consume. Officials reported numerous incidents of unacculturated Indians uprooting unripe crops and leaving them on the ground.[87] Similarly they killed cattle, horses, and mules without eating them. In one instance some Portuguese settlers subsequently claimed and ate the carcasses that the Indians had left on the roadside.[88]

What are we to make of this behavior? The simplest explanation is economic sabotage. Further evidence to support this view comes from settler reports of indigenous attacks on black slaves, a strategy which also threatened the intruders' means of production.[89] Yet some admittedly sparse evidence also suggests that these foraging Indians might have been engaging in a form of symbolic rejection of agriculture. For example, one report also offers the intriguing possibility that indigenous people killed livestock as a means to avenge death from disease which they attributed to the ill intent of settlers who employed indigenous workers.[90] Another source suggests that the Botocudo found repugnant the transformation of the landscape that agriculture required. Reputedly, the Botocudo version of the afterlife for evildoers was an exposed, open plain under a hot sun with no game.[91] A contemporaneous article written by Indian Director Guido Marlière also documented the planting of crops at grave sites, suggesting a possible connection between agriculture and death.[92] '

The notion that the Botocudo might have rejected agriculture for cultural reasons is supported by more contemporary ethnographic studies of Gê-speaking peoples.[93] These sources must be used cautiously; obviously we cannot project uncritically the cultural and material customs of mid-twentieth-century savannah dwellers from Goiás and Mato Grosso onto early nineteenth-century forest peoples of eastern Minas Gerais. Only fragmentary evidence of migration links the two population groups and cultural divergence spanning time and place is all but certain.[94] However, as nineteenth-century sources are relatively opaque regarding indigenous motives and cultural preferences, later sources offer some potential insights about work habits and patterns that may have been distinctly Gê.

Figure 28. While the French artist Debret discussed the general characteristics of the Kamakã Indians, he offered no specifics about the woman who modeled for this portrait. Contemporary anthropologists have found that women in hunter-gatherer societies supply more than half of their peoples' caloric intake through foraging. Conquest of the eastern forests meant domestic slavery for many indigenous women. Source: Debret, *Voyage pittoresque.* Public domain access: http://www.brasiliana.usp.br/bbd/handle/1918/624510016

The Xerente and Xavante studied by British ethnographer David Maybury-Lewis in the 1950s and 1960s demonstrated behavior that was markedly similar to the Gê tribes of eastern Minas Gerais at a similar phase of Portuguese contact. They lived in dispersed villages and maintained tense, often hostile relations with neighboring subgroups. For months at a time, they abandoned their villages on sustained foraging treks. The sexual division of labor was similar: men hunted and fought while women foraged and cooked, carried everything on trek, set up temporary camps, and tended children. Some continuity in ritual practices is also observable.[95]

Of particular interest is Maybury-Lewis's analysis of hunting as the basis for masculine identity and ceremonial life. Although agricultural products like corn were also necessary for certain rituals, field labor was held in the utmost disdain. The Xavante, he writes, "are inefficient cultivators because they are bored by the drudgery of agricultural work, and because they have no pressing need for crops to supplement their abundant diet. Aboriginally they planted maize, beans, and pumpkins, which are hardy crops that require virtually no tending."[96] Despite the modest effort required, Maybury-Lewis observed, Xavante men perceived field work as a major imposition. He adds, "When they return from the plantations, having done the minimum of agricultural labour, the same men who can perform feats of endurance on the hunt complain of stiffness and pains all over."[97]

Maybury-Lewis also observed that despite shrinking access to land, Xavante life "was so well adapted to their environment that as late as 1958 a visitor got an impression of abundance and efficiency in their villages which was in striking contrast to the feeling of poverty and inadequacy conveyed by Brazilian settlements in Central Brazil."[98] Like the Botocudo before them, the Xavante demonstrated a seemingly insatiable desire for gifts and were willing to linger around state-sponsored aldeias only as long as the goods held out. Maybury-Lewis concluded, "The influence of the Indian agent seemed to be directly proportional to his supply of gifts."[99]

However, the Xavante were motivated not simply by greed but by complex notions of reciprocity. What was most important was not the acquisition of gifts per se but social relationships defined by ongoing exchange. Some limited documentation suggests that reciprocity also governed exchange of goods among some Gê tribes of Minas Gerais.[100] These cultural norms differed from capital accumulation strategies advocated by state agents, be they operating in nineteenth- or twentieth-century Brazil.[101]

CONCLUSIONS

Indigenous responses to the availability of aldeia settlement suggest that they adapted Portuguese policy to extend the viability of hunting and gathering as a means of subsistence when it was under threat by population pressures and environmental change. Many Brazilian indigenous myths maintain that hunting and gathering or selecting native technology over imported methods were active choices.[102] It is plausible that the Botocudo were behaving in a similarly proactive way through their selective and temporary residence in aldeias and their practice of agricultural raiding. If the crown and settlers viewed the eastern sertões as a region of unlimited resources that could be most efficiently exploited through predation, as Paraíso contends, the same might be said of the Indians in their view of the colonists.[103] However, such strategies were not sustainable over the long term. Population pressures steadily increased over the course of the century as did patterns of land use incompatible with foraging.

As long as indigenous groups were able to mount symbolic attacks on livestock or crops they probably were not yet experiencing a subsistence crisis. However, by the late 1830s, reports of raids increasingly refer to Indians "devouring" what they killed or stole, suggesting that population pressures and environmental change had begun to compromise their material survival.

The agricultural solution that Brazilian settlers, soldiers, and officials presented to foraging Indians was not necessarily more secure. In the late colonial period and well into the nineteenth century, officials and naturalists alike lamented the wasteful practice of *rotina*, slash-and-burn agriculture.[104] According to the French naturalist Auguste de Saint-Hilaire, the method had originated with the now extinct Tupi and subsequently was adopted by the Luso-Brazilians.[105] Regardless of its origin, Brazilian settlers habitually burned fields in order to clear them and enjoyed only a few years of abundant harvests before they fell victim to weeds, pests, and declining fertility. The method required ample forest reserves to be burned in subsequent years and enough land to permit letting fields lie fallow long enough to acquire secondary growth. As population pressures increased, this strategy would have become increasingly difficult to sustain, especially for small-scale farmers or aldeias with limited lands. Many settlers also let their stock roam freely, leaving unfenced aldeia fields vulnerable to being trampled and destroyed.[106]

The enthusiasm for free royal land grants along the Doce River following Prince Regent João's declaration of just war against the Botocudo was motivated in large measure by a shortage of arable land.[107] For decades, land exhaustion continued to be cited as a justification for removing indigenous groups from their traditional territories who "deserved" to be expelled from potentially fertile farmland.[108] Yet most farmers do not seem to have prospered on lands that were expropriated from Indians. Ironically, settlers who fared the best economically were those who exploited native practices, like poaia extraction.

New forms of land exploitation had a negative impact on indigenous habitats. During the colonial period, the crown had monopolized the extraction of certain kinds of wood like pau-brasil and other *madeira de lei* (state-monopolized woods) and regulated their extraction. These laws were gradually repealed over the course of the nineteenth century. Sawmill machinery was imported to Brazil in the 1820s and 1830s, facilitating the commercial exploitation of hardwoods for timber. Some Indians were employed as sawyers to selectively cut desirable specimens of valuable trees scattered through the forest.[109] Increasing deforestation did not go unnoticed by learned societies that sprang up in the early nineteenth century. Many of them began to discuss issues related to forest loss including its effects on rainfall, watercourses, and temperature variation, and of the availability of fuel wood for urban populations.[110]

Still, as late as midcentury, enough viable territory remained for indigenous groups to avoid the aldeia solution. Settler populations continued to fluctuate, and the effects of disease on native tribes, although impossible to quantify, must have contributed to the demographic decline of indigenous communities. By the mid 1840s, the provinces of Minas Gerais and Espírito Santo each boasted only one remaining aldeia. In Minas Gerais, some fifty kilometers northeast of Rio Pomba, the aldeia at Guidowald established by former Indian Director Guido Marliére housed about fifty settled Indians. Espírito Santo's only aldeia, Imperial Afonsino, located on the road linking the province to Minas Gerais, had only fifty-four Indians.[111] However, land reform laws passed in 1850 and 1854 eventually succeeded where previous legislation had failed. The new legislation acknowledged land rights only of Indians who were willing to settle in aldeias, demarcated land that generally was inadequate in both quantity and quality, and introduced mechanisms to deny acculturated Indians access to aldeia lands.[112] For the Botocudo, this was the beginning of the end of their way of life. Although isolated bands managed to remain autonomous until the turn of the twentieth century, for most the only option for material survival became settled agriculture and the cultural compromises it entailed.[113]

NOTES

1. The last "just war" had been declared in 1739 but *entradas* and *bandeiras* (armed expeditions) that were more limited in scope were sanctioned in Minas Gerais for nearly a half-century prior to the 1808 edict. On just war, see Beatriz Perrone-Moisés, "Índios livres e índios escravos: Os princípios da legislação indigenista do período colonial," and "Inventário da legislação," in *História dos índios no Brasil*, ed. Manuela Carneiro da Cunha (São Paulo: Companhia das Letras, FAPESP/SMC, 1992), 115–32, 529–66; Hal Langfur, *The Forbidden Lands: Colonial Identity, Frontier Violence, and the Persistence of Brazil's Eastern Indians, 1750–1830* (Stanford, CA: Stanford University Press, 2006); Maria Hilda Boqueiro Paraíso, "O tempo da dor e do trabalho: A conquista dos territórios indígenas nos sertões do leste" (PhD diss., Universidade of São Paulo, 1998). Ricardo de Bastos Cambraia and Fábio Faria Mendes date the militarization of the mineiro frontier somewhat later, in the 1780s, in "A colonização dos sertões do leste mineiro: Políticas de ocupação territorial num regime escravista (1780–1836)," *Revista Departamento de Historia* 6 (June 1988): 137–50. Abbreviations used in the notes are as follows: Arquivo Estadual de Espírito Santo, Vitoria, ES (AEES); Arquivo Histórico do Exército (AHEX); Arquivo Público Mineiro (APM), which houses the Seção da Província (SP); Biblioteca Nacional, Rio de Janeiro (BNRJ); Câmara Municipal (CM); presidente da província (provincial president, PP [of Minas Gerais, MGPP; of Espírito Santo, ESPP]); *Revista do Arquivo Público Mineiro* (*RAPM*); *Revista do Instituto Histórico e Geográfico* (*RIHGB*).
2. Langfur, *Forbidden Lands*, 193–96; Diogo L. A. P. Vasconcelos, *História Antiga das Minas Gerais* (Rio de Janeiro: Imprensa Nacional, 1948); Diogo L. A. P. Vasconcelos, *História Média de Minas Gerais* (Belo Horizonte: Imprensa Oficial, 1918); Oiliam José, *Indígenas de Minas Gerais: Aspectos Sociais, Políticos e Etnológicos* (Belo Horizonte: Imp. Oficial, 1965). Recently Brazilian and North American scholars have begun to examine more systematically the indigenous history of eighteenth- and nineteenth-century Minas. See the following papers presented at the 2001 Latin American Studies Association congress (6–8 Sept., Washington, D.C.): Izabel Missagia de Mattos, "Descanibalização e Expropriação da Língua "Botocuda": Vale do Mucuri, século XIX"; Judy Bieber, "Cannibalism or Commerce? Economic Relations among Indians and Settlers in Minas Gerais, Brazil, 1808–1850"; Maria Leônia Chaves de Resende, "Brasis coloniales: O gentio da terra nas Minas Gerais setecentista (1730–1800)"; and Hal Langfur, "Sources of Conflict: The Evidence of Indian Resistance in Eastern Minas Gerais, 1760–1808."
3. Paraíso, "O tempo da dor," 9–10, 23–26.
4. José, *Indigenas de Minas Gerais*, esp. 11–19; Paraíso, "O tempo da dor," 4–5, 93; Langfur, *Forbidden Lands*, 172; "Botocudos ou Aymores," *RAPM* 2 (1897): 28–36; Wilhelm Ludwig von Eschwege, *Jornal do Brasil, 1811–1817, ou relatos diversos do*

Brasil, coletados durante expediçõs científicas por Wilhelm Ludwig von Eschwege, trans. Friedrich E. Renger, Tarcísia Lobo Ribeiro, and Günter Augustin (Belo Horizonte: Fundação João Pinheiro, 2002), 75–76.

5. Paraíso contends that documents often erroneously conflated the Naknenuks with the Botocudo and that the two were distinct groups. Paraíso, "O tempo da dor," 150.

6. Auguste de Saint-Hilaire, *Viagem pelas províncias do Rio de Janeiro e Minas Gerais,* trans. Vivaldi Moreira (Belo Horizonte: USP/Itatiaia, 1975), 95–96.

7. Paraíso, "O tempo da dor," 176; Mattos, "Descanibalização e Expropriação da Língua Botocuda," 2; Eschwege, *Jornal do Brasil,* 90.

8. European travelers often highlighted tribal connections. Saint-Hilaire, for example, reported that the Malali admitted a common origin with the Monoxó despite the fact that their languages had little in common. The Panhame, Malali, Pindi, Monoxó, and Coroado also claimed common ancestry and shared cultural customs. Saint-Hilaire, *Viagem pelas províncias,* 181–82. Spix and Martius reported cultural similarities among the Maxakali, Malali, Makoni, Lopoxó, Panhame, Jumanaxó, and Monoxó of the region around Peçanha in J. B. von Spix and S. F. P. Martius, *Viagem pelo Brasil* (São Paulo: Melhoramentos, 1976), 55. Eschwege also claimed that the Coroado and Puri were descended from a common ancestor and spoke mutually intelligible dialects. Eschwege, *Jornal do Brasil,* 101. All of these travelers shared a common informant, Indian Director Guido Tomás Marlière.

9. Hal Langfur cites a document from 1794 that describes an unusual attack of two thousand Botocudo against a small Portuguese settlement. This suggests that temporary alliances for military purposes occurred on rare occasions. Langfur, *Forbidden Lands,* 242. Paraíso also reports a group of six hundred Indians who attacked fazendas along the Mucuri River in 1809, "O tempo da dor," 229.

10. Paraíso, "O tempo da dor," 44; Warren Dean, *With Broadax and Firebrand: The Destruction of the Brazilian Atlantic Forest* (Berkeley: University of California Press, 1995), chap. 5; John M. Monteiro, "The Heathen Castes of Sixteenth-Century Portuguese America: Unity, Diversity, and the Invention of the Brazilian Indians," *Hispanic American Historical Review* 80, no. 4 (2000): 703–5.

11. Paraíso, "O tempo da dor," 270.

12. Dean, *Broadax and Firebrand,* chap. 2; Anna Curtenius Roosevelt has documented the social and material complexity of Brazil's lowland Amazonian Indians in "Arqueologia Amazônica," in Cunha, *Historia dos índios no Brasil,* 53–86.

13. See "The letter of Pero Vaz de Caminha," in William Brooks Greenlee, *The Voyage of Pedro Alvares Cabral to Brazil and India from Contemporary Documents and Narratives* (London: Hakluyt Society, 1938); Jean de Léry, *History of a Voyage to the Land of Brazil,* trans. Janet Whatley (Berkeley: University of California

Press, 1993); Hans Staden, *The True History of His Captivity, 1557*, trans. Malcolm Letts (London: Routledge and Sons, 1928).

14. Dean, *Broadax and Firebrand*, 25.

15. Ibid, 30–33.

16. The importance of fish hooks and tweezers is described by Léry in *History of a Voyage*, chaps. 8 and 12. On trade relations in general, see Dean, *Broadax and Firebrand*, chap. 3.

17. Alexander Marchant, *From Barter to Slavery: The Economic Relations of Portuguese and Indians in the Settlement of Brazil, 1500–1580* (Baltimore, MD: Johns Hopkins University Press, 1942).

18. Stuart B. Schwartz, "Indian Labor and New World Plantations: European Demands and Indian Responses in Northeast Brazil," *American Historical Review* 83 (1978): 43–79.

19. John Hemming, *Red Gold: The Conquest of the Brazilian Indians, 1500–1760* (Cambridge, MA: Harvard University Press, 1978); Hemming, *Amazon Frontier: The Defeat of the Brazilian Indians* (Cambridge, MA: Harvard University Press, 1987); Carlos de Araujo Moreira Neto, *Índios da Amazonia: De maioria a minoria (1750–1850)* (Petrópolis: Editora Vozes, 1988).

20. On the transition from Jesuit to secular administration see Manuela Carneiro da Cunha, ed., *Legislação indigenista no século XIX: Uma compilação (1808–1889)* (São Paulo: EDUSP, 1992), 9–17; Rita Heloisa de Almeida, *O Diretório dos índios: Um projecto de "civilização" no Brasil do século VXII* (Brasília: Editora UNB, 1997). For a revisionist interpretation of the Directorate, see Barbara Ann Sommer, "Negotiated Settlements: Native Amazonians and Portuguese Policy in Pará, Brazil, 1758–1798," (PhD diss., University of New Mexico, 2000).

21. José Bonifácio de Andrada e Silva, "Apontamentos para a civilisação dos índios bravos do Império do Brasil," in Cunha, *Legislação*, 347–60.

22. Bonifácio also recommended distributing milk to children and cheese and butter to adults to interest them in raising cattle, a suggestion that did not take into account a tendency toward lactose intolerance among Native Americans.

23. Auguste de Saint-Hilaire, *Viagem ao Espírito Santo e Rio Doce*, trans. Milton Amado (Belo Horizonte: Editora da USP/Livraria Itatiaia Editora, 1974), 7–10.

24. Diogo Pereira Ribeiro de Vasconcelos, *Breve descrição geográfica, física, e política da capitania de Minas Gerais*, ed. Carla Maria Junho Anastacia (Belo Horizonte: Fundação João Pinheiro, 1994), 55–56; Saint-Hilaire, *Viagem ao Espírito Santo e Rio Doce*, 84. Also see preceding chapter in this volume.

25. Wilhelm Ludwig von Eschwege, *Pluto brasiliensis*, trans. Domício de Figueiredo Murta (Belo Horizonte: USP/Itatiaia, 1979), 1:28; Charles R. Boxer, *The Golden Age of Brazil, 1695–1750: Growing Pains of a Colonial Society* (Berkeley: University of California Press, 1969).

26. "Itinerario da viagem que fez por terra, da Bahia ao Rio de Janeiro, por ordem do principe regente, em 1808, o Desembargador Luiz Thomaz de Navarro," *RIHGB*

7 (1845): 443–44; Paraíso, "O tempo da dor," 182, 184; María Hilda Boqueiro Paraíso, "Os Botocudos e sua trajetória histórica," in Cunha, *História dos índios no Brasil*, 416.

27. Cunha, *Legislação*, 59.

28. Cartas régias of 13 May 1808, 24 Aug. 1808, and 2 Dec. 1808 in Cunha, *Legislação*, 57–61, 66–69.

29. BNRJ, I-33, 30, 22; Conde de Linhares to the Junta das divisões in Vila Rica, 29 Jan. 1811.

30. AEES, cód. 239, p. 310, Capitão Mor João Dias Pacheco Guimaraens, Itapemirim, 7 Apr. 1824; Antonio Luiz da Cunha, *mapa* dated 16 May 1827.

31. Cartas régias of 13 May 1808, 24 Aug. 1808, 2 Dec. 1808, and 12 Sept. 1820 in Cunha, *Legislação*, 57–61, 66–69, 101–2.

32. See "Direção Geral dos Indios de Minas Gerais: Golpe de Vista sobre o estado atual da civilização dos mesmos (1827)," *RAPM* 12 (1907), 535.

33. The most celebrated of these was Guido Pokrane, an interpreter who worked closely with Guido Marlière, the most celebrated official of the divisions, who served from 1813–1829. "Apontamentos sobre a vida do indio Guido Pokrane e sobre o Francez Guido Marliere," *RIHGB* 18 (1855): 426–34; Oiliam José, *Marlière, O Civilizador: Esboço biográfico* (Belo Horizonte: Ed. Itatiaia, 1958).

34. Carta régia of 28 July 1809, http://www2.camara.leg.br/legin/fed/carreg_sn/anterioresa1824/cartaregia-40089-28-julho-1809-571822-publicacaooriginal-94951-pe.html.

35. "Aviso sobre as reflexões a respeito das Divisoes do Rio Doce, especialmente da 7a. e civilização dos Botocudos," 11 Dec. 1811, in Cunha, *Legislação*, 79–80.

36. "Decreto no. 31—Império—Dá regularmento interino para o aldeamento e civilisação dos Indios do Rio Doce, e ordena a concessão de sesmarias aos indivíduos civilisados que as pedirem, 28 Jan. 1824," in Cunha, *Legislação*, 111–14.

37. Lei Imperial of 27 Oct. 1831, http://www2.camara.leg.br/legin/fed/lei_sn/1824-1899/lei-37625-27-outubro-1831-564675-publicacaooriginal-88614-pl.html.

38. *Relatório da repartição dos Negocios do Imperio apresentado á Assembléa Geral Legislativa na 3ª. sessão da 6ª. legislatura, pelo respectivo ministro e secretario d'estado, Joaquim Marcellino de Brito* (Rio de Janeiro: Typ. Nacional, 1846), 25; Avisos of 9 Aug. 1845 and 2 Oct. 1845, in Cunha, *Legislação*, 199–202; "Noticia sobre os selvagens do Mucury, em uma carta do Sr. Theophilo Benedicto Ottoni," *RIHGB* 21 (1858): 173–218.

39. Decreto 426, 24 July 1845, in Cunha, *Legislação*, 192.

40. Cunha, *Legislação*, 192.

41. Decreto 426, 24 July 1845, in Cunha, *Legislação*, 192.

42. Sommer, "Negotiated Settlements," 113–23, and chap. 4.

43. Portuguese perceptions about indigenous *"miséria"* or impoverishment in abundant physical landscapes were similar to those voiced by English settlers in seventeenth-century New England in William Cronon, *Changes in the Land:*

Indians, Colonists, and the Ecology of New England (NY: Hill and Wang, 1983), 33, 54–81.

44. Cunha, *Legislação*, 348, emphasis mine.

45. Marjorie Shostak, *Nisa: The Life and Words of a !Kung Woman* (New York: Vintage, 1983), 12.

46. Frances Dahlberg, ed., *Woman the Gatherer* (New Haven, CT, and London: Yale University Press, 1981), 14–15; Shostak, *Nisa*, 12–14.

47. Langfur, *Forbidden Lands*, 122–26.

48. Eschwege, *Jornal do Brasil*, 78.

49. APM, SP PP 1/15, cx. 90, p. 22, Cel. Miguel Teotonio de Toledo Ribas to MGPP, 29 Nov. 1830; APM SP PP 15 cx. 91, doc. 6, Quartel Geral das Divisões, S. João do Madureira, Felipe Joaquim da Cunha e Castro M. Centerno to MGPP, 9 Nov. 1832.

50. "Guido Thomaz Marliére," *RAPM* 10 (1905): 391; 393–94, 415, 423–25, 454, 474; "Guido Thomaz Marlière (Noticias e documentos sobre a sua vida)," in *RAPM* 11 (1906): 79; "Direção Geral dos Indios de Minas Gerais," 510, 512, 516, 548–49; Eschwege, *Jornal do Brasil*, 77.

51. AEES, Livro da Capitania do Espírito Santo (cód. 163), 1, 6, 27, 31v; Conde de Linhares to Manoel Vieira de Tovar e Albuquerque, 22 July 1811, AHEX, RJ, cód. 21, Capitania do Espírito Santo, 1808–1824, 31–31v.

52. Maximilian, Prince of Wied-Neuwied, *Viagem pelo Brasil* (Belo Horizonte: Itatiaia/USP, 1989), 61, 232–38, 310–13.

53. Ironically, many scientists believed that forests were the cause of diseases like malaria and favored cutting them down. See Dean, *Broadax and Firebrand*, 102–3.

54. Saint-Hilaire, *Viagem ao Espírito Santo e Rio Doce*, 32, 69.

55. Ibid, 92–93; 108–9.

56. For examples of soldiers using canoe portage, see AEES, Série Accioly 67, João Antonio Lisboa to ESPP—p. 147, 14 Mar. 1829; p. 167, 1 Sept. 1829; p. 198, 1 Feb. 1830; AEES, Serie Accioly, Governadoria, cód. 30, p. 902. João Antonio Lisboa to ESPP, 1 Sept. 1831. On the river trade more generally, see AEES, Serie Accioly, Governadoria, cód. 30, 682–756.

57. Saint-Hilaire, *Viagem pelas províncias*, 272–77.

58. José Bonifácio improbably maintained that indigenous women nursed for up to seven years and urged missionaries to curtail breast feeding to two years at the most. "Apontamentos," in Cunha, *Legislação*, 357–58.

59. AEES, Serie Accioly, cód. 30, p. 24, 28 July 1824; AEES, Série Accioly 67, p. 124, 13 Dec. 1826; p. 218, 2 Oct. 1827.

60. AEES, Série Accioly 67, p. 187, 12 Jan. 1830.

61. Ibid, p. 150, 2 Apr. 1829.

62. Ibid, p. 81, 3 Dec. 1825; p. 83, 22 Dec. 1825; AEES, Serie Accioly, cód. 30, p. 822, 7 Mar. 1831; p. 825, 8 Mar. 1831.

63. Paraíso, "O tempo da dor," 272. She does not cite a primary source to back this claim.
64. Saint-Hilaire, *Viagem pelas províncias*, 33.
65. José Bonifácio, "Apontamentos," in Cunha, *Legislação*, 352. He also included various trinkets including mirrors, beads, red caps, gilt braid, ribbons, and brightly colored or striped scarves; comestibles such as tobacco, sweet, mild wines, and sugar; and useful items like blankets and hunting dogs.
66. Saint-Hilaire, *Viagem ao Espírito Santo e Rio Doce*, 95–96.
67. "Guido Thomaz Marlière (Noticias e documentos sobre a sua vida)," *RAPM* 11 (1906): 30–31.
68. AEES, Serie Accioly, Governadoria, cód. 30, p. 217, João Antonio Lisboa to ESPP, 1 Oct. 1827.
69. Eschwege, *Jornal do Brasil*, 91.
70. BNRJ, 8, 1, 8, no. 66, f. 135 (1811), Copia de uma carta de Sgto. Mor. Eschwege sobre os Botocudos com notas pelo deputado da junta militar.
71. Dean, *Broadax and Firebrand*, 130–31; Cunha, *Legislação*, 8–9.
72. "Guido Thomaz Marlière (Noticias e documentos sobre a sua vida)," *RAPM* 11 (1906): 36.
73. APM SP PP 1/15, cx. 90, p. 33, Miguel Teotonio de Toledo Ribas to MGPP, 7 Mar. 1831.
74. APM SP PP 1/15 cx. 91, doc. 14, Interim Director das Divisões to MGPP, 28 Feb. 1833.
75. APM SP PP 1/15 cx. 90, p. 14, Ofício do Cap. Mor Esteves Lima to MGPP, 6 Feb. 1830; Marliére to MGPP, 13 Feb. 1819, in "Guido Thomaz Marliére," *RAPM* 10 (1905), 423–25.
76. Paraíso, "O tempo da dor," 228–29.
77. "Decreto no. 33—Guerra—Pediu uma declaração circunstanciada dos productos medicinaes indigenas de cada uma das Capitanias, 28 July 1813," in Cunha, *Legislação*, 87–88.
78. Dean, *Broadax and Firebrand*, 130, 162–63; BNRJ II-36, 7, 5, 45, no. 1, 1797, Informações por Henrique Vicente Sousa da Magalhaes sobre a industria dos indigenas do Rio Paraiba do Sul, RJ (Coroados), Registro de Parahibuna, João Pacheco Lourenço e Castro to Vice Rei Sr. Conde de Rezende, 12 Aug. 1797; APM SP PP 15 cx. 91, doc. 6, Quartel Geral das Divisões in S. João do Madureira, Felipe Joaquim da Cunha e Castro M. Centrno to MGPP, 9 Nov. 1832.
79. Coronel Julião Fernandes Leão, AEES, Serie Accioly, cód. 30, p. 9, 8 June 1824; p. 17, 3 May 1824; and p. 22, 14 July 1824; and his successor, João Antonio Lisboa: AEES, Serie Accioly, cód. 30, p. 157, 17 Feb. 1827; p. 223, 1 Dec. 1827; p. 258, 1 Mar. 1828; p. 849, 31 Dec. 1831; p. 858, 8 Apr. 1831; p. 871, 22 June 1831; p. 876, 1 July 1831; and p. 902, 1 Sept. 1831.
80. AEES, Serie Accioly, cód. 30, p. 251, 21 Nov. 1828; AEES, Serie Accioly, cód. 30, p. 850, 2 Apr. 1831.

81. Decisão no. 85 of 24 May 1823, in Cunha, *Legislação*, 106.
82. Decreto no. 31, 28 Jan. 1824, in Cunha, *Legislação*, 111–14.
83. APM SP GA¹ cx. 3, p. 27, 22 May 1824, Governador das Armas to MGPP; APM, SP PP 1/15, cx. 90, p. 20, Miguel Ribas to MGPP, 11 June 1830; APM SP PP 15, cx. 91, doc. 14, Interim Director das Divisões to MGPP, 28 Feb. 1833; BNRJ, II-36, 4, 44, 17 Oct. 1827, Representaçao de S. Miguel, termo de Caeté, ao D. Pedro II; APM, SP 827, 14 Apr. 1860, CM of Serro to MGPP.
84. AEES, Accioly 239, 13 Oct. 1824; ibid, p. 350, 12 Oct. 1824.
85. Ibid, p. 342, 29 Aug. 1824.
86. Ibid, p. 345, 20 Sept. 1824; p. 348, 7 Oct. 1824.
87. AEES, Serie Accioly, cód. 30, p. 217, 10 Oct. 1827; p. 220, 1827; p. 902, 9 Sept. 1831; p. 910, 10 Oct. 1831; p. 916; 19 Oct. 1831; p. 923, 2 Nov. 1831; p. 931, 16 Jan. 1832; AEES, Accioly 31, p. 21, 1 Mar. 1833.
88. "Guido Thomaz Marliére (Noticias e documentos sobre a sua vida)," *RAPM* 11 (1906): 418–20.
89. Saint-Hilaire, *Viagem ao Espírito Santo e Rio Doce*, 22.
90. BNRJ II-36, 7, 5, 45, no. 1. 1797, Informacoes por Henrique Vicente Lousa da Magalhaes sobre a industria dos indigenas do Rio Paraiba do Sul, RJ (Coroados), Registro de Parahibuna, João Pacheco Lourenço e Castro to Vice Rei Sr. Conde de Rezende, 12 Aug. 1797.
91. "Guido Thomaz Marlière (Noticias e documentos sobre a sua vida)," *RAPM* 11 (1906): 81–82.
92. Guido Marlière, *O Universal* (Ouro Preto, Minas Gerais), 21 Nov. 1825, 219–20. *O Universal* was a newspaper published between 1825 and 1842.
93. David Maybury-Lewis, *Akwe-Shavante Society* (Oxford: Clarendon Press, 1967); Seth Garfield, *Indigenous Struggle at the Heart of Brazil: State Policy, Frontier Expansion, and the Xavante Indians, 1937–1988* (Durham, NC: Duke University Press, 2001). Contemporary orthography has substituted an X for Sh for the Xavante and Xerente tribes, hence the inconsistent spelling.
94. Garfield records a Xavante oral tradition that first contact between the Xavante and the Europeans took place "near the sea," *Indigenous Struggle*, 3. Indian Director Musqueira documented migration from eastern Minas Gerais to the borders of São Paulo and Goiás in *Relatório que ao Illmo. e Exm. Sr. Dr. Manoel Teixeira de Souza apresentou no dia 16 de corrente O Exm. Sr. Dr. José Maria Corrêa de Sá Benavides por occasião de passar-lhe a administração desta provincia* (Ouro Preto: Typ. do Minas Gerais, 1870).
95. Eschwege, Garfield, and Maybury-Lewis report a number of like practices including the ritual use of corn, marriage practices involving prepubescent girls, and ritual rape. Eschwege, *Jornal do Brasil*, 85, 99, 105, 108–9; Maybury-Lewis, *Akwe-Shavante Society*, 26, 44–48; Garfield, *Indigenous Struggle*, 70, 121, 129.
96. Maybury-Lewis, *Akwe-Shavante Society*, 47.
97. Ibid, 47–48.

98. Ibid, 61.

99. Ibid, 27.

100. Eschwege cites several examples of gift giving and the reciprocal expectations it engendered in *Jornal do Brasil*, 88, 91, 96.

101. Similar observations about Xavante interactions with government agents and missionaries are documented in Garfield, *Indigenous Struggle*, chaps. 2–3.

102. Manuela Carneiro da Cunha, "Introdução a uma história indigena," in Cunha, *História dos índios no Brasil*, 19.

103. Paraíso, "O tempo da dor," 20–21, 132–34.

104. Emblematic is José Vieira Couto, *Memória sobre a capitania das Minas Gerais: Seu território, clima e produções metálicas* (Belo Horizonte: Fundação João Pinheiro, 1994), 35–36.

105. Saint-Hilaire, *Viagem ao Espírito Santo e Rio Doce*, 61.

106. BNRJ, II-34, 17, 5, Aldeias de S. Fidelis e Pedras. José Libanio de Souza, ouvidor da Comarca do Espírito Santo, 3 Oct. 1824.

107. BNRJ, 8, 1, 8, no. 66, f. 135, Copia de uma carta de Sgto. Mor Eschwege sobre os Botocudos com notas pelo deputado da junta militar, 1811; APM SP PP 1/33 cx. 142, p. 82, Antonio José da Costa and others to the CM, n.d.

108. APM SP PP 1/33 cx. 142, p. 82, Antonio José da Costa and others to the CM, n.d.

109. Dean, *Broadax and Firebrand*, 165–66.

110. Ibid, 221–38.

111. *Relatório da repartição dos Negocios do Imperio apresentado á Assembléa Geral Legislativa na 4ª. sessão da 6ª. legislatura, pelo respectivo ministro e secretario d'estado, Joaquim Marcellino de Brito* (Rio de Janeiro: Typ. Nacional, 1847), 31–34.

112. Lei do Império 601, 18 Sept. 1850; Decisão 92, 21 Oct. 1850; Decreto n. 1,318, 30 Jan. 1854.

113. William John Steains, "A Exploração do Rio Doce e seus afluentes da margem esquerda," *Revista do Instituto Historico e Geografico do Espírito Santo* 35 (1984): 103–27. On the recent resurgence of indigenous identity in eastern Minas Gerais, see Jonathan W. Warren, *Racial Revolutions: Antiracism and Indian Resurgence in Brazil* (Durham, NC: Duke University Press, 2001).

7

Catechism and Captivity

Indian Policy in Goiás, 1780–1889

Mary Karasch

[Thus has] our very excellent General the satisfaction of having freed the peoples of this Captaincy of so many wild animals . . . and at the same time the incomparable glory of having brought to the Church [an] equal number of children, with so many other vassals to the Portuguese Empire.   —*José Rodrigues Freire, 1790*

So ended *The Narrative of the Conquest of the Xavante People*, attributed to José Rodrigues Freire in 1790.[1] In one sentence Freire captured the Portuguese ideal of Indian policy in the captaincy of Goiás in the late eighteenth century, that is, to free the people of the captaincy from conflicts with autonomous Indians, while at the same time bringing them under the authority of church and state as "sons" and loyal vassals of the Portuguese monarchs (see map 5). The 1790 image of the Xavante as both *feras* (wild animals) and *filhos* (sons) summarizes the contradictions in late colonial and nineteenth-century Indian policy in Goiás, located near the geographic center of Portuguese America. While paternalistic officials in Lisbon or their governors in Vila Boa de Goiás, the capital of the captaincy, decreed Christianization and "civilization" to persuade the Indians to settle in

Christian missions, local militias, *bandeiras* (armed expeditions), and settlers tried to "disinfest" the captaincy of those they termed feras and enslave
their women and children. Whatever colonial officials dictated from Lisbon,
however, the search for mineral wealth, land for cattle, and indigenous slaves
drove Indian policy in Goiás, leading to violent resistance or flight by those
attacked and enslaved.[2]

Upon independence, we can discern some continuities with colonial
Indian policy, but nineteenth-century decision makers turned away from
paternalism to a greater stress on economic concerns: the transformation of
the Indian into an agricultural worker, symbolized by the placement of the
Indians under the authority of the Minister of Agriculture. Although the
national government sponsored European missionaries from France and
Italy in an attempt to continue the missionary tradition in Goiás, some
nineteenth-century Indians enter the historical record as petitioners, seeking missionary presence in their *aldeias* (villages) from a government that
was no longer as interested in financially supporting Christianization. The
contradictory governmental motives of the late colonial period had given
way to singular capitalist concerns for Indians as labor units. Meanwhile,
new settlers and cattle ranchers continued to disinfest the province of its
autonomous Indians, to enslave those they could (i.e., women and children),
and to destroy the forests that sheltered them. Either Indians became subject
to the new invaders, or they fled across the Araguaia River to find refuge
west of the river; others died in the bitter wars of the period. That so many
survived the long years of Luso-Brazilian rule in Goiás is a testament to the
strength of indigenous sociopolitical structures that made it possible for
some of them to endure in spite of warfare, conquest, and enslavement.

The narration of Indian policy in Goiás is a one-sided affair in historical
documentation. Rarely does the Indian perspective appear in official records.
One exception is a provincial report of 1856, cited by Rita Heloisa de Almeida
Lazarin, of an attempt to contact the Xavante in the Mortes River region in
eastern Mato Grosso. When a small group of soldiers directed by the missionary Segismundo de Taggia entered the Xavante village, they were
received by an elderly Indian, who with gestures of hostility demonstrated
their aversion to a new relationship with whites. He explained that "the
Christians are very bad," and when the Xavante were in [the mission aldeia
of] Carretão, they suffered the "*palmatória* [a paddle with holes], *tronco*
[stocks], chain, whip, and collar."[3]

The evolution of Indian policy can be traced from the late colonial period to the fall of the Brazilian Empire, which began with independence in 1822 and ended in 1889. Considered alongside the preceding discussion of developments in the neighboring captaincy of Minas Gerais to the east, this and the following chapter highlight those features that were constant and those that were distinctive in separate regions of the colony. The very failure of Luso-Brazilian Indian policy (i.e., to commit significant financial resources and administrative talent to official efforts to settle down, civilize, and Christianize the Indians) in part permitted their survival as a people. In late colonial Goiás, Indian policy was a minor concern of the royal officials who sat on the Overseas Council or who worked in the royal treasury; their principal objective, as judged from the volume of documentation in Lisbon, was to acquire the gold of Goiás. Indians entered the Portuguese records when they threatened existing gold mines or mining towns; and after those mines had declined by the 1780s, attention shifted to the exploration and conquest of new lands still held by autonomous native peoples in order to enrich the Portuguese Empire through new mineral wealth. Once the explorers of the period 1780–1822 failed to find gold mines, and with the economy of Goiás in what colonists deemed a state of decadence, official attention shifted to new development efforts designed to populate Goiás with settled Indian agricultural workers. Since few new enslaved Africans and even fewer European immigrants entered Goiás in the nineteenth century, lack of labor for the expanding agro-pastoral economy led Goiano officials to seek so-called wild Indians as agricultural workers and slaves.

COLONIAL INDIAN POLICIES

The first Indian policy in Goiás was unofficial. Bandeiras from São Paulo penetrated southern Goiás and enslaved the Indians at the same time that Jesuits from Belém explored the Tocantins River area and established missions in northern Goiás. The violence of the initial contact with the Paulistas destroyed many tribes in southern Goiás and led to a continual state of warfare with others, such as the southern Kayapó, as gold miners penetrated Goiás and established mining towns in the 1720s and 1730s. In order to protect the miners, governors organized local forces in repeated expeditions to conquer the Kayapó but failed. The gold rush hindered missionary activity as priests took up mining with their own enslaved Africans, acquired fortunes in gold, and returned to Lisbon to claim *mercês* (honors) and comfortable clerical offices in Portugal. The priests that remained in Goiás largely served resident Luso-Brazilian communities and Indians attached to them as slaves and household dependents (*agregados*). In this period, missionaries barely played any role in the Christianization of autonomous nations, except to baptize and indoctrinate war captives, usually women and children. When priests went out on the frontier, it was usually to serve as chaplains or participants in bandeiras, assisting in the conquest of hostile nations and afterward sharing in the division of war captives. The only significant missionary activity was that of the Jesuits in the north until 1759, when, in spite of indigenous rebellion, they were forcibly expelled from Goiás.[4] Thereafter, former mission Indians in the north petitioned for missionaries to provide religious services in their communities and for protection against enslavement by neighboring Luso-Brazilian settlers and ranchers. As late as 1880, the governor of Goiás admitted that there were "rare periods" in the history of Goiás in which "there was a serious interest in catechizing [converting] them by the means of humanity and civilization."[5]

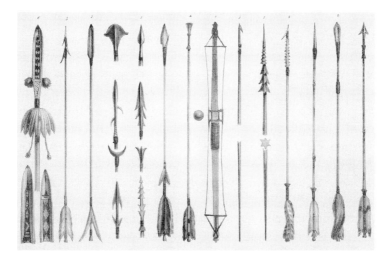

Figure 29. In Goiás, as elsewhere, native peoples faced a prolonged military conquest, but their arms could not defend them against the relentless spread of contagious disease. Colonial incursions intensified after gold was discovered in the region in the early eighteenth century, then persisted as the regional economy turned to ranching and agriculture. Source: Debret, *Voyage pittoresque.* Public domain: http://www.brasiliana. usp.br/bbd/handle/1918/624510050

Pombaline reformers and Portuguese officials in the 1750s sent lay directors into the mission villages and encouraged the Indians "to farm, gather forest plants, and trade in the cities," but this system failed in its objectives in Goiás as the Indians resisted the forced labor of the Directorate system (1757–1798),[6] fled into the forests, and resumed cattle raids and warfare on the frontier settlements and mining towns. In retaliation, governors authorized expeditions to pursue wars of conquest in regions "infested with hostile Indians." But warfare did not achieve a key goal of the Directorate system, which was to convert Indians into settled agriculturalists, nor did it protect settlers and miners from repeated raids and incursions by the Kayapó or Xavante. The unresolved situation on the frontier of Goiás led crown minister Martinho de Melo e Castro to send instructions to the new governor of Goiás, José de Almeida Vasconcellos (1772–1778), later Baron of Mossâmedes. On 1 October 1771, he wrote that "without population" there would be no hope of any utility from Goiás, and since it was impractical to populate that captaincy without "Americans," and since all the *sertão* (backlands) was filled with Indians, they must be the principal ones to populate the places, towns, and cities, for without them there would not be any culture, commerce, opulence, or security that would not be precarious. He stressed the "civility of the Indians" as a more important object than all other riches and counseled officials to gain the confidence of the Indians by means of "suavity and gentleness" and by giving them gifts "of the goods that most please them . . . until they come of their free wills and establish themselves on the banks of the rivers."[7]

The governor responded to these instructions in typical frontier fashion: he ordered the conquest of the Indians. The objective of the official bandeiras of this period was "to pacify the forest Indians" and "discover new mines."[8] Afterward, the Indians were to be settled in aldeias under lay directors, usually military officers, and attended to by nearby parish priests. Gifts of textiles, ironware, and foodstuffs for pacified groups were paid for by the royal treasury. The first Indians to be contacted by the expeditions of the Baron of Mossâmedes were the Akroá, who lived in the vicinity of Natividade in the Tocantins region and in the aldeia of São Francisco do Duro. In 1775 they were brought south to be established in the new model aldeia of São José de Mossâmedes, near Vila Boa.[9] The Xacriabá, Karajá, and Javaé also went to live in São José and swore "fealty and alliance." As Governor José de Vasconcellos wrote, the objective was to create there "a regular and permanent establishment, that would make all the forest Indians envious." After seeing São José, they would leave their villages for the new aldeia that would serve like "a university for those who wanted to be in an aldeia"; it was to be in an "agreeable" place of fields, good waters, and many forests.[10]

In addition to the Akroá and Xacriabá, the Xavante had often attacked settlements in the north. When bandeiras failed to stop the warfare, the governor was given royal authorization to make war against them. The result was the "celebrated" conquest of the Xavante by Governor Tristão da Cunha Menezes's expedition that in 1788 returned with three thousand to four thousand Xavante to settle in the aldeia of Carretão about twenty leagues from Vila Boa. In his report to Lisbon, Governor Menezes (1783–1800) viewed the entry of the Xavante into Carretão as an occasion of "great jubilee" in which three thousand persons entered into the same "vassalage." After taking them to the church, the governor gave them hospitality and assurances of "our good faith, with all the signs of trust and reciprocal friendship." He promised them royal protection and the security of "our friendship" in consequence of which they would be helped while they were unable to maintain themselves. He sent a garrison to guard the aldeia and asked the parish priest of Pilar to administer the sacrament of baptism to the Xavante. In conclusion, he summarized the advantages to the Portuguese of the conquest of the Xavante: it brought security to the vassals of Her Majesty Queen Maria I (r. 1777–1816), it "disinfested" vast *sertões* (backlands)—the most fertile and richest in gold—and augmented the number of the "sons of the church." From the governor's perspective, only positive good flowed from this conquest. The only problem he foresaw would be the expense of supporting three thousand Xavante as well as the rest of their nation that planned to come to the aldeia in the next dry season.[11]

The perceived success of settling the Xavante in the aldeia of Carretão led to another attempt at conquest: that of the Canoeiro in the Tocantins River region, where they harassed settlers, often threatening São Félix, the site of the Foundry House, where gold was processed and taxed. Although an expedition managed to destroy many of the Canoeiro villages in 1796, they were not subdued. Throughout the nineteenth century, they refused to receive missionaries and resisted all efforts to conquer them, continuing to attack and kill settlers. As late as 1880, the governor of Goiás considered them to be "the most ferocious of the province."[12]

Another region of official concern and policy was that of Bananal Island in the Araguaia River. The Karajá and Javaé had forcibly retarded settlement in the area until 1775 when an expedition under José Pinto da Fonseca finally made peace. The mission of Nova Beira was created for them, and a garrison at the *presídio* of São Pedro do Sul helped keep the peace but did not survive long. In 1780 some 800 of the Karajá and Javaé were transferred to the aldeia of São José de Mossâmedes, where their descendants remained into the nineteenth century.[13]

In summary, although official policy in Lisbon might prohibit warfare against the Indians and recommend kind treatment of them, the governors in Goiás or Goiano settlers resisted Indian attacks with force and formed aggressive expeditions to "disinfest" regions threatened by them. While a few were settled in aldeias and were supported by the royal treasury, the majority escaped official control. Writing in 1801 from the General Accounting Office in Rio de Janeiro, a critical official called attention to the 245,000 *cruzados* that had been spent over thirty years on the "civilization of the Indians" that was "without fruit." He argued that the reason for the decadence in Goiás was the lack of population (i.e., Luso-Brazilian settlers and miners). As a remedy, he suggested that the then governor of Goiás follow the policies of the Baron of Mossâmedes; and he should try to win "by suave ways" the confidence of the inhabitants of the sertões, introducing them to tools and helping them embrace Portuguese customs so that in place of "savage men" the monarch would have "vassals" useful for the future. After taking up the issue of financing these proposals, he noted that all moderation be used in persuading the Indians to do different types of work and in showing them the utility of such works. By associating with local settlers, he argued, they would gradually break away and leave their native lands, forgetting their "barbarous customs" and becoming domesticated to the uses and exercises of the Europeans; and by embracing "with gusto" this way of life, they would attract still other nations, who would voluntarily come to join them under Portuguese dominion.[14]

GOIANO INDIAN POLICIES

By the early nineteenth century, these assimilationist policies faced a major difficulty: assimilation implies the cultural change of a so-called inferior people in the direction of adopting the superior culture of a colonial power. In Goiás, however, there was a shortage of colonizers due to the exodus of the Portuguese from the eighteenth-century mining towns once dominated by them. People of color—enslaved Africans, mestizo and mulatto descendants of Portuguese miners and Indian or African slave women, and "domesticated Indians"—increasingly formed the population of Goiás. Given the lack of Portuguese officers of "good quality," the authorities turned to the inhabitants of Goiás to "solve the Indian problem," as they perceived it. They commissioned *sertanistas* (frontiersmen) to take over responsibilities once allotted to Portuguese officers.

The most famous of the sertanistas of the early nineteenth century was the Kayapó woman Damiana da Cunha, who lived with her soldier-husband at the aldeia of São José de Mossâmedes. Commissioned by the governor, she led expeditions into the sertão to persuade her people to settle with her in São José. Traveling as far as the upper Araguaia River, she succeeded in attracting small groups who then stayed for a while in São José before returning to the forests and resuming warfare against the settlers on the road heading west to Cuiabá, which became the capital of Mato Grosso in 1835. For more than fifty years, the government's policy to reduce all the Kayapó to settled aldeia life had failed. With the progressive withdrawal of the Portuguese from Goiás and diminished financial support to the aldeias for the type of goods that had attracted them in the first place, the Indians abandoned the aldeias.[15] Meanwhile, the Kayapó and other indigenous nations grew stronger on the frontier—strength as measured in the number and severity of attacks on farmers and ranchers—and for a time it seemed as if the Indians and not the Goianos would claim Goiás from the Portuguese, especially in the north.

In the early nineteenth century, protective legislation ended and paternalistic Portuguese governors lost their influence over Indian policy as the Goianos took more control over setting Indian policy. In the colonial period, Indians might petition Lisbon and have grievances attended to by royal officials who had no personal interest in perpetuating land loss and enslavement. In 1821, for example, five Indian nations who lived on the banks of the Tocantins River protested to the crown about being treated like "Ethiopian slaves" and the robbery of their lands. They also pleaded for the building of a church dedicated to the saint of their devotion, Saint John the Baptist, and for baptism.[16] The arrival of the royal family in Rio de Janeiro in 1808, however, did not bring protection to the Indians of Goiás. Instead, royal letters authorized war against the Indians of Goiás. As a reward, settlers received the right to their services and exemption from payment of the *dízimo* (tax on agricultural crops). For the first time since 1755 when Pombaline reforms had abolished Indian slavery—in law if not in practice—the government gave official permission to fight hostile Indians, who then had to labor for their captors. One reason for the shift to Indian labor was the precipitous decline in the number of enslaved Africans in Goiás. Without gold to buy new Africans, slaveholders turned to Indian captives. Increasingly, Indian policy reflected local settler interests—the unrestrained seizures of land, especially after the Land Law of 1850, and Indian slavery. In response, the Indians retaliated in frontier wars or withdrew across the Araguaia River, while others never had a chance to resist and died of diseases imported with new settlers who took possession of their lands. Since Indian policy was often set by Goiano-born governors and powerful ranchers on the frontier, it is more difficult to characterize nineteenth-century Indian policies, since so much of the treatment of the Indians was determined by local elites.[17]

One important influence on local Indian policy was whether settlers raised crops or cattle. According to Julio Cezar Melatti, farmers required lots of manual labor; therefore, they pursued policies of coerced labor; but pastoralists, on the other hand, needed little labor to care for cattle and horses and perceived the Indians as another predator on their livestock. As cattlemen killed off wolves in North America or jaguars in South America, so too they exterminated or drove off the natives they regarded as wild animals. The capacity to absorb labor, Melatti notes, determined the mode of action with Indians: preservation along the Araguaia River, which was an agricultural area, and extermination along the Claro and Tocantins Rivers, which were cattle frontiers.[18]

Policies also varied from region to region, with the north being more independent of policymakers in the southern part of the province and subject to continuing attacks by the Xavante and Canoeiro. In the south, the Luso-Brazilians had conquered, enslaved, civilized, or exterminated the Indians, settling "pacified" survivors among themselves, while in the north most Indians remained unconquered. Since the local government was "impotent to dominate them," the royal letter of 5 September 1811 affirmed the "necessity of pacifying the Karajá, Apinayé, Xavante, Xerente, and Canoeiros"; but if pacification was impossible, then war would be legal, since "there does not remain presently another way to follow except to intimidate them, and even destroy them, if it be necessary, in order to avoid the damages that they cause."[19]

With official authorization to wage offensive war once again, the government and local settlers established presídios (small garrisons), organized expeditions, and killed and enslaved Indians. A trade in Indian captives

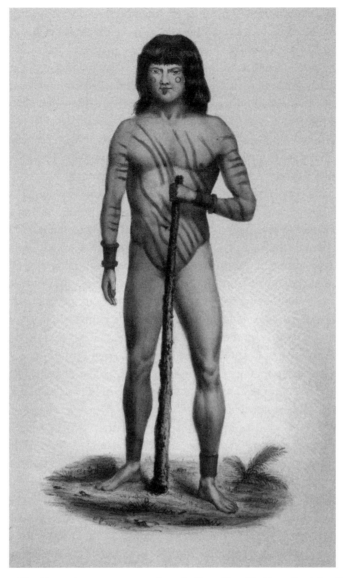

Figure 30. Karajá warriors were among those Indians identified by colonial authorities as requiring pacification. Where efforts at persuasion failed, official policy sanctioned extermination. Source: Francis de Castelnau, *Expedition dans les parties centrales de L'Amérique du Sud, de Rio de Janeiro a Lima, et de Lima au Para; exécutée par ordre du gouvernement français pendant les années 1843 à 1847,* Part 2, *Vues et Scènes. (Les Planches Lithographiées par Champin)* (Paris: Bertrand, 1853). Courtesy of The Catholic University of America, Oliveira Lima Library, Washington, D.C.

flowed to the north to Belém, while others, especially children, entered baptismal and death records as adopted agregados in towns, such as Natividade. Retaliation by the Xavante, Xerente, and Canoeiro quickly followed, and the north remained in a state of constant warfare. Especially adept at fighting in 1813 were the Xavante who had fled from Carretão, where they had learned Portuguese, the use of European weapons, and settler customs, which they took advantage of to attack at the most advantageous times for the success of their "criminal intentions." Often joining them were the Xerente, and they caused "many evils," attacking the inhabitants of the towns of Pontal, Carmo, and Almas. Therefore, this "nation" was declared "our enemy" to be "disinfested" from that territory.[20] In 1819 Ouvidor (superior judge) Joaquim Theotonio Segurado organized "a crusade" against the Canoeiros; but his brutality only contributed to Canoeiro anger and resistance, and the Tocantins River continued to be a dangerous region because of Indian attacks.[21]

In order to further trade on the Tocantins River, officials aimed to remove Indians deemed hostile from its banks, a policy that was incompatible with other official objectives of civilizing the Indians in settled aldeias so that they would provide a reliable labor supply to the settlers. When the traveler Johann E. Pohl explored the region, he found that few settlers lived there in 1819, and only Porto Real (later Porto Imperial, then Porto Nacional) prospered. Another attempt to resolve the warfare along the Tocantins River was to make peace with the Xerente and establish them in the aldeia Graciosa in 1824. Located to the north of Porto Real, it was attacked by the Xavante in 1824. The Xavante were still fighting settlers in that region in 1836, when another bandeira was organized against them. The Xerente soon abandoned Graciosa.[22]

In the early nineteenth century, the Araguaia River also had few Luso-Brazilian settlers. In an effort to secure the river and control trade to the north to Belém, authorities erected a small presídio, Santa Maria do Araguaia, in 1812. The Indian reaction to this invasion of the Araguaia was violent: an armed coalition of four nations attacked and destroyed it one year later.[23] The governors of Goiás did not give up on the construction of presídios, however, and another important one was built at São Pedro de Alcântara (now Carolina) on the Tocantins River in 1820. Two others were constructed in the Araguaia region: one named Leopoldina and the other Santa Isabel do Araguaia. The objectives of these presídios were to protect the navigation of the Araguaia River and attract settlers to its banks. Ten years later the presídio of Monte Alegre reinforced security in the region. By 1856 the presídios of Santa Barbara, Santo Antônio, and Santa Cruz guarded the left bank of the Tocantins River. On the whole, the presídios were few in number for the vast sertão, and the frontier was never well garrisoned. In most cases a few badly supplied soldiers could defend an essential road or river route, but seldom did they have the numbers of men capable of leading offensive expeditions against hostile indigenous nations.[24]

Since the government then supported few troops or missionaries in that area, conquest was in the hands of frontier adventurers who were supported in their efforts by local settlers, who rewarded successful conquerors with gifts of cattle. In 1813 José Pinto de Mangalhens bragged about his conquest of the Macamecran for which he received offerings of cattle from local ranchers. He also retained for his own use, or so he was accused, the official gifts designated for the Indians.[25] In other words, furthering warfare could yield handsome profits and indigenous captives. Such policies were reflected in the following critique: those who took up arms against the Indians did so to "sell them in a public market, in the quality of a perpetual slavery."[26]

In other words, Indian policy in the north was not to assimilate Indians in religion or culture but to enslave them. One market for the Indians of northern Goiás and Maranhão was Belém at the mouth of the Amazon River, and shipments of indigenous "captives," especially of women and children, ran to the north via the Tocantins River.[27] Another use of indigenous labor in the 1820s was in a newly founded textile industry in Vila Boa. In 1820 a factory for the production of cotton cloth and stockings was established. Along with slaves, one Kayapó man labored at carding and spinning, while three indigenous women were carders.[28]

The early nineteenth-century imperial policies of permitting aggressive warfare and indigenous slavery were legally revoked in 1831. This was followed by another law, which placed the Indians under the civil protection of the so-called judges of orphans (*juiz dos órfãos*) in their respective districts.[29] The Indian wars did not end, however, as governors' reports of 1837–1842 reveal.[30] Expeditions against the Canoeiro, Xerente, and Xavante further inflamed their hostilities, resulting in no security for settlers, who abandoned ranches and settlements. In 1838 the governor recommended continued financing of bandeiras against them, while at the same time giving gifts to the Karajá and other nations. The violence was so widespread by 1839 that the governor described the warfare as "a black page" of "horrors" and "atrocities" practiced against "us" by the "Savage Indian." As a consequence, settlers had fled their lands in the north. His solution was to appeal to the Minister of War in Rio de Janeiro for a military force. He also recommended making the "ferocious Savage [a] useful friend" by attracting them with presents and sending two missionaries to them. However, the violence continued, and so the governor wrote in 1842:

> I must speak clearly, it is necessary, Senhores, to strike strongly all
> the Indians that attack us, and render all help not only to those who
> live in peace with us, but also those with whom, I suppose, we do
> not yet have relations . . . : only thus will the Province [of Goiás] be
> able to be lifted up.[31]

A shift in imperial policy from encouraging war and slavery to more paternalistic protection and Christianization may also be perceived in the decrees of 1843 and 1845, although in 1847 the governor recommended that a military force be kept in every aldeia in Goiás.[32] The decree of 24 July 1845 handed over the Indians to directors, who were usually government officials and military men, or to their delegates, who, according to the Minister of Agriculture in 1865, abused them "scandalously." These men viewed the aldeias as "colonial centers," where nationals, including military men, would live along with Indians who cultivated some agricultural commodities needed for trade. The effective result, however, was debt peonage, because the Indians were held against their will for enormous debts. Many fled the forced labor of aldeia life. To remedy these abuses, the minister argued that the aldeias should be subordinate to the religious element. The decree of 25 April 1857 passed the direction of the aldeias to the religious, but the shortage of priests led the imperial government to seek foreign missionaries for Brazil—and for Goiás.[33]

NEW MISSIONARY EFFORTS

In theory, the new aldeia policies were to be centered on the missionaries and stressed the following approach: the first objective was to make the Indians leave their nomadic way of life. Afterward, the European missionary was to teach them Christian doctrine. By the 1850s another official concern was the establishment of schools in the aldeias. As new "civilized" converts, the Indians were to labor at removing forests and cultivating cash crops, such as coffee and sugar. Still others were to learn trades, herd cattle, work in river transport, or provide firewood for the new steamships. The missionary was once more central to what was then perceived as "successful" Indian policy, but he would still be subordinate to lay directors in Goiás—such as Joaquim Barros Pitaluga Caiapó, appointed in 1860, and José Vieira Couto de Magalhães—and ultimately to the Minister of Agriculture.[34]

A revived missionary effort and the arrival of Italian Capuchins led to the founding of new aldeias in the mid-nineteenth century. The following mission villages were established for Christian Indians between 1841 and 1872: São Vicente of Boa Vista do Tocantins (1841), São Joaquim (or São José do Jamimbu, 1845), Santa Maria do Araguaia (1845), São Pedro Affonso (1849), Thereza Christina (Piabanhas, 1851), and the mission of the Chambioás (Xambioás, 1872). The government also continued to support the old aldeias of Graciosa (1824), Carolina, and Carretão (1788), which was then in decadence due to Xavante flight. No longer under government support was the famous aldeia of São José de Mossâmedes, which had become a village of about two hundred non-Indians living about the old church, where the Kayapó had once worshipped. In 1832, the last of the Kayapó had been transferred to the settlement of Arinos in Mato Grosso. The aldeia Maria I, which had also housed the Kayapó, was extinct by 1856, while the aldeias of Graciosa and Carolina no longer appeared in official reports. Also missing from them was São José do Duro (1755), although some Xerente and Xavante continued to live there until the end of the century.[35]

From the 1850s on Indian policy tended to focus on the two regions of the Araguaia and the Tocantins Rivers. Of lesser concern was the Rio Claro–Rio Bonito area to the south, where settler-Kayapó conflicts erupted in the 1880s, threatening the road to Cuiabá. Although most officials stressed the Christianization effort along the Araguaia and Tocantins Rivers, when the Kayapó attacked in the 1880s, officials again turned to the missionaries.[36] Indian policy was then deemed inseparable from the missionary enterprise, but as before, the imperial or provincial governments devoted few of their financial resources to it.

In the immense region of the Araguaia River, catechesis (instruction in Christian doctrine) was under the direction of Brigadeiro José Vieira Couto de Magalhães with its base at Leopoldina (now Aruanã). Financial affairs were handled by a treasurer appointed by the imperial government, which also supported the Colégio Isabel, founded for indigenous students in 1871. The aldeias of São José do Jamimbu and Santa Maria do Araguaia and the mission of the Chambioás were under this administration. Two of the responsibilities of the administration were to distribute iron tools to the mission Indians and pay the salaries of the missionaries.[37]

Figure 31. The São José de Mossâmedes Mission, founded in the 1770s, dated from a period during which the governor of Goiás favored nonviolent means to encourage Indians to enter colonial society. By the early nineteenth century, it had fallen to ruins, abandoned by most of its native residents after years of official neglect. Source: São Paulo, Biblioteca Mário de Andrade, Seção de Obras Raras e Especiais, Mss.b.65, Planta da Aldeya de S. Jozé de Mossamedes . . . , Estampa 2 . . . , Tirada por Joaquim Cardozo Xavier Sargento do Regimento de Infantaria de Melicia [sic] de Villa boa de Goyas, 24 Jan. 1801. Courtesy of the Biblioteca Mário de Andrade, São Paulo.

The policies of the 1870s returned to the old Jesuit idea of catechizing the Indians in their own languages. As one 1874 report proclaimed, the "catechesis of the Indians" would not otherwise be so quick or efficacious. The best persons, therefore, to bring the message of Christianity to the forests were "the children of the aboriginal families, educated since infancy in the ideas, customs, and institutions of our society."[38] The children who were at the *colégio* in 1874 were mostly Kayapó and Karajá. Besides learning to be interpreters, they studied "first letters," mechanical trades, and ironworking. By 1877 only thirty-six boys and nine girls of at least seven nations attended the colégio. Such small numbers led the Minister of Agriculture to complain that the colégio "had still not given a notable result." Four more schools were located in the aldeias of São José do Araguaia, Chambioás, Santa Maria, and Piabanhas.[39] Obviously, the education effort reached comparatively few

Indians as late as the 1870s, although it was an integral part of Indian policy. As the Minister of Agriculture explained in 1877: "It leaves to the savage the liberty of his customs and . . . limited official intervention to education of the minors, to the furnishing of instruments of work, and to the spiritual help and councils of a chaplain and two missionaries."[40]

As a consequence, he reported that the number of Indians "conquered by religion" exceeded four thousand, while the civilized population established on the banks of the Araguaia with ninety-two fazendas (ranches) reached 3,170. All this had happened because the conflicts provoked by the Indians had ended. The "deserts of the Araguaia begin to be populated by nationals, and the number of docile Indians augments day by day." Due to the growth of fazendas in this area, he also authorized the establishment of a fazenda north of Leopoldina to serve as a practical school in pastoral industry for the students of the Colégio Isabel.[41]

One reason for the emphasis on the role of the Indians in the regional economy of Goiás was the perceived need by Goiano settlers and government officials to turn to the indigenous population to populate and develop Goiás. The reports of the Minister of Agriculture from 1862 to 1892 reveal the imperial government's neglect of the economic development of the province. There were only a few development projects in Goiás, such as steamship transportation on the Tocantins and Araguaia Rivers, the construction of roads and bridges, and the granting of mineral concessions. Rather than fund more economic development or new methods of agriculture that might empower Indians, the ministers of agriculture looked to the past—to the eighteenth-century programs of establishing mission villages and pacifying hostile Indians to convert them into "sons of the church"—and through Christianization to make them into useful workers, supporting themselves and "civilized" society by agricultural labor and the river trade.

"RELIGION AND WORK"

The governors of Goiás echoed imperial policies. In 1880 Governor Aristides de Souza Spinola gave a brief historical summary of past Indian-Portuguese relations and described the "death or captivity" mentality of the colonial era. There were, he concluded, "two systems of terror and of kindness, of extermination and of catechesis, of civilization and of barbarism." He contrasted such policies with those of the Baron of Mossâmedes, when the

Christianization of the Indians had entered a period of "growth and splendor, not known in the annals of the captaincy." Reflecting upon Portuguese colonial policy, he stated that, "indigenous colonization is one of the most important subjects which challenges the attention of the governor." Moreover, it is "a sacred duty" because, he admitted, we are in possession of the lands taken from their relatives."[42]

In late nineteenth-century Goiás, government officials once again developed an Indian policy that stressed "religion and work." As Governor Spinola wrote, "religion and work are two powerful agents for indigenous civilization." When catechesis was simply limited to the teaching of Christian doctrine, or when the Indian was obliged to work before being accustomed "to the habits of civil life," the results of catechesis were often discredited.[43]

In addition to requiring cultural change of the Indians, Governor Spinola was unique in recommending that Brazilian nationals be taught Indian languages. But there was little emphasis on cultural change by nationals in official policies of the 1880s. Rather, bureaucrats tended to focus on one or more of these methods of resolving "the Indian problem." One suggestion was to provide security on the frontier via the construction of presídios along the Araguaia and Tocantins Rivers; second, to populate the banks of the rivers with settlers so that the Indians could no longer retard the free flow of trade and commerce; third, to colonize Indians in Christian aldeias, so that they would be educated in religion, Portuguese, and agricultural labor; and finally, to convert them using foreign missionaries.[44]

In 1880 the Minister of Agriculture, Manoel Buarque de Macedo, also stressed the relationship of religion and pacification. He viewed aldeias directed by "zealous missionaries" as "intermediaries of the society with the savage, making evident practically that the civilized man is not his enemy. . . . The fact is that where regular aldeias exist, indigenous attacks have diminished or ceased." Thus, he believed that aldeias under missionary direction were the best way in which to pacify hostile Indians. What is of even greater interest in this report, however, is that Manuel Buarque de Macedo argued that the number of the indigenous individuals that had assimilated to national culture was "greater than one thinks." As an example, he cited the valley of the Araguaia, where the indigenous inhabitant was "the principal collaborator" and where the Karajá and Kayapó furnished wood to the steamships in the river trade to Pará.[45] Thus, a notable "success" of the aldeia efforts in the north and the Tocantins and Araguaia River valleys was to make the Indians essential to the river trade rather than a hindrance. In exchange for tools, axes, firearms, and other articles, the Indians supplied the firewood that powered the steamships. In 1884 the governor bragged that the change in relations was so amicable that the ships' crews and passengers could travel peacefully all the length of the rivers.[46]

In contrast, however, the Colégio Isabel had failed to achieve its goals. By 1880 it had only twenty-six students, who were employed in "useful works," having acquired "the habits of civilized men," including marriage. Although this primary school was viewed positively as an instrument of assimilation, few Indians attended. By 1886 the number of students had declined still further to seventeen, supported by ten staff members, leading the Minister of Agriculture to complain that its students presented "little or no advantage."[47]

NUMERICAL ASSESSMENTS

Government officials also kept records on the aldeias they funded; and, in the 1880s, they measured their progress (or lack thereof) over a century of existence. According to the government reports, the aldeia policy had yielded very mixed results. One of the oldest aldeias, founded in 1764 near Pilar, was almost extinct in the 1880s. The Xerente and Xavante had once populated Carretão after 1788, but the vast majority had fled because of forced labor and slavery. As of 1849, the seventy or eighty remaining Xerente and Xavante were obligated to plant crops for their own consumption and for the supply of travelers. They also had to serve as paddlers for the river trade to Pará. By 1880 the aldeia had only eighteen inhabitants (ten adults and eight children), who lived by field labor. According to Estevão Gallais, who visited it, the aldeia had once sheltered some ten thousand Indians of different tribes and had a church and a governor's house with a large back-yard. Only a wooden bridge over the river and ruined houses remained in 1888. One man and two women populated the aldeia, but around it lived *caboclos*, the racially mixed descendants of Indian women who had married black men. The forest had reclaimed the fields once cultivated by the Xavante. Other Xavante, however, about two hundred, lived at the aldeia of Estiva with some Karajá and two Canoeiro.[48]

Three other aldeias (Piabanhas, Pedro Affonso, and Boa Vista) were located in the Tocantins River region. In the early 1880s they were subject to Antônio Fleury Curado.[49] Piabanhas, founded for the Xerente in 1851, was still a somewhat successful aldeia in 1880. In 1852, the missionary Frei (Friar) Rafael de Taggia recorded 2,139 Xavante and Xerente at the aldeia; twenty-two years later it sheltered three thousand Xerente and Krahô. Another six years later only two thousand Xavante and Xerente were counted, living in 220 houses with thatched roofs. They supported themselves by fishing, agriculture, and riverboat navigation. The aldeia had a primary school with thirty-one children, a chapel, and a resident missionary, Frei Antônio de Gange. In 1886, however, there were only one hundred households with 1,500 "souls." Of that number about half (or seven hundred) had been baptized by 1882. At the end of the century some hundreds of Xerente remained; the Xavante were "extinct."[50]

Another new aldeia was Pedro Affonso, founded in 1849 by Frei Rafael de Taggia in the parish of Porto Imperial to house three hundred Krahô from the banks of the Farinha River in order to remove them from the cattle ranches near Carolina. Ranchers had complained about their stealing cattle. Indian removal was also designed to facilitate communication and trade along the Tocantins River to Porto Imperial. Shortly after the Krahô settled in the aldeia, epidemics broke out in 1849–1850. By 1852 there were only 620 Indians. Adding to the population were three hundred *sertanejos* (backlanders) from Bahia and Piauí, who settled there in 1857. As late as 1880, one thousand Krahô lived at Pedro Affonso, supporting themselves by fishing, agriculture, and pastoralism; they also traded their cattle to Maranhão. Frei Rafael de Taggia still served as their missionary; he died at age eighty in 1892. By 1886 only two hundred Krahô still lived at the aldeia, which by that time had evolved into a backlands village of sertanejos.[51]

Other Krahô lived at the aldeia of Boa Vista, founded in 1841. In 1870 six hundred Apinayé had worked in agriculture, cattle raising, and river navigation to Pará. Other Apinayé and Gradau lived in nearby villages. When another accounting was done ca. 1880, the Apinayé numbered 1,362; the Guajajara, 92; and the Krahô, 200; or more than 1,600 under the lay director João Francisco Baptista. Besides raising cotton, manioc, corn, and other food crops, they also worked as day laborers in the service of individuals, who paid them in money or commodities. In spite of a measles epidemic that lasted over three years, the governor's report of 1881 still recorded 1,564 Indians living at Boa Vista.[52]

In contrast to these large aldeias, São Joaquim (also São João) do Jamimbu seems to have sheltered no more than five hundred Indians in 1856. Founded by Frei Segismundo de Taggia in 1845 for the Xavante and Karajá,

Figure 32. By the late nineteenth century, long since decimated by disease, many of the Apinayé had relinquished their traditional seminomadic ways and adopted a sedentary life, raising foodstuffs for their own subsistence and local markets. Source: Castelnau, *Expedition.* Courtesy of The Catholic University of America, Oliveira Lima Library, Washington, D.C.

it had declined to only one hundred Karajá (three hundred in 1877) and Xavante by 1880. The Xerente had also lived at the aldeia shortly after its founding. In 1863 Couto de Magalhães transferred the Indians at Jamimbu to São João do Araguaia to facilitate river commerce. By 1880 they not only cultivated cereals, raised cattle, and fished, but they also sold their goods to river travelers. They had a chapel and primary school with seventeen students of both sexes under a lay director, Casimiro Caetano Linhares. The 1884 governor's report listed only two hundred Indians at the aldeia: Xavantes and Caracutás, of which 119 were baptized; but shortly thereafter only 136 Xavante, all of whom were baptized, remained at the aldeia in 1886.[53]

The last aldeia listed in 1880 was the mission of the Chambioás, founded in 1872 and directed by the Capuchin Frei Savino de Remini. However, its director and school were at São Vicente. Described in 1877 as "the most remote from civilized population," the mission was in the center of still "fierce tribes." Consequently, a military force of ten soldiers was assigned to guard the mission. In 1886, six hundred Indians lived at the aldeia and supplied firewood to passing steamships.[54]

IMPERIAL CRITIQUES OF INDIAN POLICIES

In surveying the results of more than one hundred years of Indian policy focused on government-funded Christian aldeias, imperial officials in the 1880s addressed the reasons for the abandonment of aldeias by disaffected Indians. In 1882 Minister of Agriculture José Antonio Saraiva clarified reasons for the failure of Indian policy in Goiás: the lack of money committed to it, the inadequate organization of the aldeias, the lack of missionaries, and the Indians themselves, because the adult Indian is rarely subjected to instruction and work. The minister then gave his views of what should be done. He argued that

> the essential is to inspire confidence in them and persuade them
> more by example, than by any obligation that is imposed on them;
> to utilize their aptitudes for the industries that they exercise or they
> are connected to, which are extractive, rudimentary agriculture,
> and further some industrial arts; and by the exchange of products
> and services mold them into civilized people until they are resolved
> to confide [their] children to be educated, and to cultivate the land

and exercise any profession. For this end the catechesis ought to help them with the foundation of a nucleus of civilized people, who are put in communication with the savages, offering them incentive for work and commerce, and constituting the place not of aldeamentos, but of settlements, which can guard the peaceful Indian, utilize the services, and modify the habits of those that prefer the errant life, and above all educate their children.[55]

In 1881, the Minister of Agriculture Manoel Alves de Araujo admitted that the service of catechesis had been directed to the adult Indian, trying to subordinate him to rules and practices "contrary to the indolence of savage life, . . . when the greatest and most active force should be to focus on the indigenous child: a natural intermediary and interpreter, who would be most useful to the catechetical effort." However, it would be an error, he noted, to judge all the aldeia efforts as sterile, for there are in the population "numerous Indians" that catechesis has brought to the "bosom of society." These Indians did not remain long in the asylum of the aldeia, a truth measured by the continuous decline registered in official records. The civilized and Christianized Indians were no longer counted because they had mixed with the rest of the population. Only by listing the numbers of the "civilized Indians" could officials measure the real success or failure of the catechetical effort. After criticizing the employment of foreign missionaries, the report then summarized the catechetical effort in Goiás along the Araguaia and Tocantins Rivers.[56]

A less optimistic picture of the Christianization and aldeia program is revealed in the report of 1884, in which Minister of Agriculture João Ferreira de Moura complained that the aldeias were not prospering and that the Indians were still engaging in running attacks. In his opinion, catechesis merited a profound reorganization; but since, as he admitted, so many other projects had greater priority, finances did not permit an increase in funding. How little the imperial government had invested in the Christianization effort in Goiás in the 1880s is reflected in a survey of government-owned properties in the province: a workshop for carpentry and ironworking at the service of catechesis, valued at 1:300$000; and the Colégio Isabel, worth 4:200$000. A comparative measure of how little money was allocated to the "catechesis and civilization of Indians" in the 1870s was the expenditure of only 100$000.000, an amount that was less than that allocated to the Corps of Firemen at 180$000.000.[57]

Perhaps the most significant reason that official Indian policy was failing in Goiás is suggested by settler attitudes and attacks on Indians—not to
mention indigenous resistance. When foreign missionaries first worked
among the settlers of the Bonito River in the late 1880s, they recorded these
attitudes toward the Kayapó: "The Indian is a bad beast." In fact, the so-called
"civilized" regarded it as an act of charity to free the land of them as one
rendered service to humanity by killing a snake or jaguar.[58] The settlers of
the Claro River region, who were tired of suffering from Kayapó attacks,
organized an expedition to the Araguaia River to exterminate them. After
all the able-bodied Kayapó had fled from three aldeias, the settlers massacred
the old, the children, the sick, and those unable to flee. They spared only a
girl, who had just given birth to twins. When she later escaped to tell the
surviving Kayapó about the massacre, they exacted vengeance by plunging
the region into bitter warfare. The Indians and settlers were still at war two
years later in 1888, when a missionary visited the area.[59]

In contrast, the government's solution to the Kayapó wars in the region
of the Bonito and Claro Rivers was to send missionaries "to calm the turbu-
lence of these dangerous savages," but the missionaries actually worked first
among the settlers of the Bonito River. Since so few priests served in remote
settler communities in nineteenth-century Goiás, foreigners often ministered to the local nationals rather than to autonomous nations; hence, missionaries had limited success in pacifying hostile peoples subject to settler
invasion of their lands.[60]

A second government approach was to found a settlement of Brazilian
nationals at Macedina along the Goiás–Mato Grosso border. Its purpose was
to prevent Indian attacks, but the military post based there to guard the road
to Cuiabá had only fifteen soldiers in 1888.[61] Clearly they could do little more
than defend the people of Macedina, for they did not have the weapons to
take up offensive war against the Kayapó.

In concluding this survey of Indian policy, we should also note that both
government officials and settlers sometimes resolved what they perceived as
"the Indian problem" by "extermination" or "disinfestation." The first group,
most notable because they gave their name to the state of Goiás, were the Goyá
or Goiases, who were killed off or enslaved when the early bandeiras from São
Paulo penetrated Goiás. Also eliminated were the Quirirás (Crixás); only their
name survives for a river and a town. By 1929, at least the following peoples of
the Goiano sertão were extinct or no longer living in Goiás: the Gradau, who
had inhabited the upper sertão between the Araguaia and Tocantins Rivers;

the Akroá, who had lived in the mission of Duro; the Puxete or Patuché, or yet Tremembó of the Sono River valley; the Naraguagê (Noroguajê) of the Tocantins River valley near Boa Vista; and the Afoligé. Such individuals did not survive the onslaught of disease and frontier violence to become Christianized useful workers at the command of church, state, or settler.[62]

NOTES

1. José Rodrigues Freire, *Relação da Conquista do Gentio Xavante* [1790], 2nd. ed. (São Paulo, 1951), 19. A fuller narrative of the so-called conquest is in Mary C. Karasch, "Rethinking the Conquest of Goiás, 1775–1819," in *The Americas* 61, no. 3 (Jan. 2005): 481–85. Abbreviations used in the notes are as follows: Arquivo Histórico Ultramarino, Lisbon (AHU); Arquivo Histórico do Tribunal de Contas, Lisbon (AHTC); Arquivo Nacional da Torre do Tombo, Lisbon (ANTT); City of Goiás, Biblioteca da Fundação Educacional da Cidade de Goiás (BFEG); Biblioteca Nacional, Rio de Janeiro (BNRJ); Brazil, Ministério da Agricultura, Comércio e Obras Públicas, *Relatórios*, 1860–1888 (Rio de Janeiro) (Agricultura, *Relatório*); Goiás (Província), Presidente, *Relatórios*. 1835–1889 (Goiás) (Presidente, *Relatório*); Instituto Histórico e Geográphico Brasileiro, Rio de Janeiro (IHGB).

2. The original quotations in Portuguese of the primary sources used in writing this essay are in Mary C. Karasch, "Catequese e cativeiro: Política indigenista em Goiás, 1780–1889," trans. Beatriz Perrone-Moisés, in *História dos índios no Brasil*, ed. Manuela Carneiro da Cunha (São Paulo: Companhia das Letras, 1992), 397–412. This English version of my original essay is only slightly revised and shortened.

3. Presidente, *Relatório*, (1856), 15; and Rita Heloisa de Almeida Lazarin, "O Aldeamento do Carretão: Duas histórias" (MA thesis, Universidade de Brasília, 1985), 152. After a Canoeiro attack on a patrol, an Indian interpreter explained that the Canoeiro were still "irreconcilable" due to the attacks on them in 1819; and "they openly declared that they were not to be our slaves." BNRJ, I-28, 31, 26, Goiás (Província), Ofício de Miguel Lino de Moraes dirigido aos Snr.s do Conselho Geral da Província do Goiaz, expondo o estado econômico [e político] da província do Goiaz (Goiás, 1830).

4. AHU, Goiás, 1756–1799, cx. 17. A letter of João Manuel de Mello of 29 May 1760 complained that the two Jesuits who had worked with the Akroá and Xacriabá in the missions at Duro had let them continue "in the customs of their old barbarity" and had incited them to their uprising.

5. ANTT, Ministério do Reino, Negócios do Brasil e Ultramar, 1730–1823, maço 500; and Presidente, *Relatório* (1880) (Goiás, 1890), 38.

6. Chap. 3, "The Directorate," in John Hemming, *Amazon Frontier: The Defeat of*

the Brazilian Indians (Cambridge, MA: Harvard University Press, 1987), 40–61.
For a more detailed survey of the directorate, see Rita Heloísa de Almeida, *O Diretório dos índios: Um projeto de "civilização" no Brasil do século XVIII* (Brasília: Editora Universidade de Brasília, 1997).

7. Another translation is in Hemming, *Amazon Frontier*, 40. My translation is based on the Portuguese text in BFEG, Ofélia Sócrates do Nascimento Monteiro, "História de S. José de Mossâmedes" (Goiânia, typescript, 8 June 1951), 1.

8. Oswaldo Martins Ravagnani, "A Experiência Xavante com o Mundo dos Brancos" (PhD diss., Escola de Sociologia e Política de São Paulo, 1978), 36–37; AHTC, #4076, Livro de registo das representações da Capitania de Goyaz desde 29 de Novembro de 1784 até 31 de M.o de 1805, f. 144; and BFEG, Monteiro, "História de São José," 1.

9. Marivone Matos Chaim, *Os Aldeamentos Indígenas na Capitania de Goiás: Sua Importância na política de povoamento (1749-1811)* (Goiânia: Oriente, 1974), 61–63. Additional information on this aldeia is in Mary C. Karasch, "Damiana da Cunha: Catechist and *Sertanista*," in *Struggle and Survival in Colonial America*, ed. David G. Sweet and Gary B. Nash (Berkeley and Los Angeles: University of California Press, 1981), 102–20.

10. BFEG, Monteiro, "História de São José," 1.

11. Chaim, *Aldeamentos*, 63–64; Freire, *Relação*, 1–19; Lazarin, "Carretão," entire; AHU, Goiás, 1736–1825, cx. 4, Tristão da Cunha Menezes, Vila Boa, 10 April 1788; and AHU, Goiás, 1790–1798, cx. 35.

12. Chaim, *Aldeamentos*, 64–65; Hemming, *Amazon Frontier*, 193–94; Presidente, *Relatório* (1850), 6; and Presidente, *Relatório* (1880), 31.

13. Chaim, *Aldeamentos*, 65–66; and Karasch, "Rethinking the Conquest," 472–80.

14. AHTC, #4076, Livro de registo, 10 July 1801, ff. 142–48.

15. Karasch, "Damiana da Cunha," 102–20.

16. ANTT, Reino, maço 500.

17. Expedito Arnaud, *Aspectos da legislação sobre os índios do Brasil* (Belém: Museu Emílio Goeldi, 1973), 12–13; and Ravagnani, "Xavante," 90. See also chap. 10, "The Tocantins-Araguaia Frontier," in Hemming, *Amazon Frontier*, 181–99.

18. Julio Cezar Melatti, *Índios e criadores: A situação dos Krahó na área pastoril do Tocantins* (Rio de Janeiro: Instituto de Ciências Sociais, 1967), 32–33.

19. Dalísia Elizabeth Martins Doles, *As comunicações fluviais pelo Tocantins e Araguaia no século XIX* (Goiânia: Oriente, 1973), 35.

20. RJBN, I-31, 21, 9, Goiás (Capitania), copia da Memoria oferecida pelo Capitam d'ordenanças Francisco Jozé Pinto de Mangalhens em 3 de Janr.o de 1813. Notes by a former Tenente do Regimento de Linha of Maranhão, 1815.

21. Johann E. Pohl, *Viagem no Interior do Brasil*, trans. Milton Amado and Eugênio Amado (Belo Horizonte: Ed. Itatiaia, 1976), 213–15; and Karasch, "Rethinking the Conquest," 472–80.

22. Raimundo José da Cunha Matos, *Chorographia Histórica da Província de Goyaz* (Goiânia: Líder, 1979), 131; and Presidente, *Relatório* (1837), 16–22.
23. RJBN, I-31, 21, 9, Memoria, Mangalhens, 1813; and Hemming *Amazon Frontier*, 189.
24. Hemming, *Amazon Frontier*, 189, 395–96; Presidente, *Relatório* (1856), 13–14; Presidente, *Relatório* (1851), 14–17; IHGB, Lata 92, doc. 6, Informações relativas aos diversos serviços públicos da província de Goiás por Ernesto Vallée, inclusive presídios coloniais, 24-2-1857; and *Additamento ao relatório com que ao illm. e exmo. Sr. dr. Antonio Manoel de Aragão e Mello, fez entrega da administração da provincia de Goyaz o excellentissimo senhor doutor Francisco Januario da Gama Cerqueira* (Rio de Janeiro, 1861), 71. As late as 1879, there were only six presídios: Santa Barbara, Santo Antonio, Jurupensem, Santa Leopoldina, Santa Maria, and São José dos Martyrios. Presidente, *Relatório* (1879), 40–41.
25. RJBN, I-31, 21, 9, Goiás, Memoria, Mangalhens, 1813.
26. Ibid, note 26.
27. Ibid, note 64. Here the lieutenant accused those of trading in Indian slaves of branding them on the right wrist. IHGB, Arquivo 1.5.16, Viagem ao Rio do Tucantins em 1815, . . . pelo Major Francisco de Paulo Ribeiro, 1818, 276. See also Hemming, *Amazon Frontier*, 184–85.
28. RJBN, I-28, 24, 7, Goiás (Capitania), Noticia, que dá . . . Fernando Delgado Freire de Castilho . . . aos Senhores do Governo Interino (de Goyaz), . . . Goiás, 2 Aug. 1820; and RJBN, I-32, 13, 12, Goiás (Província), Documentos relativos a fábrica de fiação e tecelagem e malha estabelecida por João Duarte Coelho na Capital da Província de Goiás, Goiás, 1838.
29. Arnaud, *Aspectos da legislação*, 17.
30. Presidente, *Relatório* (1837, 1838, 1839, and 1842).
31. Presidente, *Relatório* (1842), 13.
32. Presidente, *Relatório* (1847), 13. See also José Oscar Beozzo, *Leis e Regimentos das Missões: Política Indigenista no Brasil* (São Paulo: Loyola, 1983), 78–79; and Hemming, *Amazon Frontier*, 385–86.
33. Arnaud, *Aspectos da legislação*, 17–18; and Agricultura, *Relatório* (1865) (Rio de Janeiro, 1866).
34. Presidente, *Relatório* (1856), 16; and Beozzo, *Leis*, 81–82.
35. The list was compiled largely from the annual reports of the Ministers of Agriculture and the Presidents of the Province of Goiás. On Kayapó expulsion from São José, see Agricultura, *Relatório* (1862), annexo, 85. For what happened to the Kayapó after their expulsion, see David L. Mead, "Caiapó do Sul: An Ethnohistory" (PhD diss. in Anthropology, the University of Florida, 2010).
36. See notes 57–60.
37. Agricultura, *Relatório* (1874), 198.
38. Ibid, 199; and Agricultura, *Relatório* (1874) (Rio de Janeiro, 1875), 298.
39. Agricultura, *Relatório* (1882), 103.
40. Agricultura, *Relatório* (1877), 483–84.

41. Ibid.
42. Presidente, *Relatório* (1880), 38–39.
43. Ibid., 40.
44. These four methods are a summary of themes developed in the nineteenth-century *relatórios* cited in this chapter.
45. Agricultura, *Relatório* (1880), 46, 59–60, 217.
46. Agricultura, *Relatório* (1884) (Rio de Janeiro, 1885), 351.
47. Agricultura, *Relatório* (1886); and Hemming, *Amazon Frontier*, 394–95.
48. Carretão: Chaim, *Aldeamentos*, 127–29; Estevão Maria Gallais, *O Apóstolo do Araguaia* (São Paulo: Revista dos Tribunais, 1942), 74–75; Ravagnani, "Xavante," 76, 78, 106–7; Lazarin, "Carretão," 58, 60, 149, 2n; Agricultura, *Relatório* (1877), 485; and Agricultura, *Relatório* (1880), 60. Aldeia de Estiva: Hemming, *Amazon Frontier*, 393–94.
49. Agricultura, *Relatório* (1881) (Rio de Janeiro, 1882), 160–61.
50. Hemming, *Amazon Frontier*, 389; Presidente, *Relatório* (1852); IHGB, Lata 92, doc. 6, "Informações . . . por Ernesto Vallée, 1857; Presidente, *Relatório* (1874), 37; Presidente, *Relatório* (1880), after p. 12 of "Catechese"; Agricultura, *Relatório* (1880), 60; Agricultura, *Relatório* (1877), 183–84, 485–86; Agricultura, *Relatório* (1881), 60–61; Agricultura, *Relatório* (1886), 45; Ravagnini, "Xavante," 78; and Lazarin, "Carretão," 207 (modern name of Tocantínia).
51. Hemming, *Amazon Frontier*, 386–89; Melatti, *Índios e criadores*, 43–45; and Agricultura, *Relatório* (1884), 351.
52. Hemming, *Amazon Frontier*, 391; Lazarin, "Carretão," 173; Presidente, *Relatório* (1851), 45; Presidente, *Relatório* (1870), 16; Presidente, *Relatório* (1875); and Agricultura, *Relatório* (1881), 160.
53. Hemming, *Amazon Frontier*, 386; Lazarin, "Carretão," 149, 164; Ravagnani, "Xavante," 78–79; Agricultura, *Relatório* (1884), 351; and Agricultura, *Relatório* (1886), 45.
54. Agricultura, *Relatório* (1877), 485; Agricultura, *Relatório* (1880), 217; Agricultura, *Relatório* (1886), 45; and Hemming, *Amazon Frontier*, 392–93, 396–97.
55. Agricultura, *Relatório* (1882), 101–12.
56. Agricultura, *Relatório* (1881), 160–61.
57. Agricultura, *Relatório* (1884), 121–22; Agricultura, *Relatório* (1877), 184; Presidente, *Relatório* (1879), 23. Spinola notes under "Catequese" that the expenditure for "*brindes a indios*" (presents for Indians) was 500$000 réis in 1878.
58. Pohl, *Viagem*, 213; Hemming, *Amazon Frontier*, 397–98; and Gallais, *Apóstolo*, 85–86.
59. Gallais, *Apóstolo*, 101–2.
60. Ibid, 77, 83–84.
61. Ibid, 86–87. Hemming, *Amazon Frontier*, 395–96, attributes "much of the failure of the Araguaia frontier to "mismanagement of the presídios."
62. Brasília, Biblioteca da Fundação Nacional do Índio (FUNAI), Serviço de Proteção aos Índios, "Relatório," (1929), 40.

8

Indigenous Resistance in Central Brazil, 1770–1890

Mary Karasch and David McCreery

The previous essay on Indian policy in Goiás provides official perspectives on indigenous peoples from the viewpoint of those who would conquer, Christianize, and enslave them. Elite images and policies, however, reveal little about the real people who resisted them with skillful war tactics or effective diplomacy. As the preceding chapter has already documented, the indigenous "nations" of Goiás often refused to become Christian captives and servants and instead fought as formidable enemies of Luso-Brazilians and their enslaved Africans. In order to demonstrate continuities in indigenous resistance, in both culture and in warfare, we will examine the history of these indigenous peoples over more than a century in the region of West Central Brazil, now the modern states of Tocantins and Goiás. One of our objectives will be to explain how and why indigenous peoples were able to resist and defy first Portuguese and then provincial government efforts to defeat, pacify, and then resettle them in Christian missions. Although we will focus on four populations, the Kayapó, Xavante, Xerente, and Canoeiro, we will also include references to the resistance experiences of other nations, such as the Akroá, Xacriabá, and Apinayé. These were not the only indigenous nations in the region, but their history of opposition to colonial and imperial Indian policy is especially notable. Mary Karasch will stress late colonial themes of resistance to about 1835; David McCreery will continue the story to the end of the

Empire in 1889. Together we hope to illustrate characteristics of indigenous resistance strategies that led to their survival as a people.[1]

THE AKROÁ AND XACRIABÁ

Our narrative of resistance begins in the north to the east of the Tocantins River in the first half of the eighteenth century (see map 5). The Akroá, a Gê-speaking people of the Timbira people, and the Xacriabá, who speak a Central Gê language, were at war with invading Portuguese and Brazilian gold miners and settlers.[2] The only way to stop the war, the Portuguese believed, was to persuade them to make peace and live in a Christian mission village (*aldeia*). According to their "conqueror," Wenceslau Gomes da Silva, he settled the Xacriabá at the mission of São Francisco Xavier and briefly separated them from their enemies, the "Acoroas." In 1753 at least six hundred Akroá joined the Xacriabá in the mission until a measles epidemic killed many, which led the survivors to flee, blaming "whites for the death of their brothers." Two years later about 250 Akroá settled in an aldeia near the first mission; it came to be called São José do Duro. There the two nations lived under the secular authority of Gomes da Silva and the spiritual authority of the Jesuits until they revolted against the cruelty and corruption of Gomes da Silva, who was treating them like slaves.[3] They took up arms in 1756 and continued to fight the Portuguese even after their Jesuits were forcibly expelled from Goiás in 1759. There was, however, a new characteristic to their method of warfare. While subject to the military authority of Gomes da Silva, they had learned how to use European firearms, a skill they now turned against the Luso-Brazilians.[4]

Since they adapted to European weaponry and fought more effectively, the Akroá and Xacriabá might have been expected to abandon the missions. However, after Gomes da Silva was arrested for corruption—he was accused of keeping the monies sent for the support of the missions for himself—some Akroá returned to São José do Duro and began to work for the Portuguese as mercenaries in the *pedestres*, the paid foot soldiers of the captaincy of Goiás. They guarded the Kayapó at São José de Mossâmedes, near Vila Boa, and hired themselves out as canoe men in the Tocantins River trade to Belém in Pará in the 1820s.[5]

In contrast to this experience, the other mission of São Francisco Xavier was abandoned, and its Xacriabá were transferred to the south of the captaincy. On their journey south, some stopped in Vila Boa de Goiás, the capital of the captaincy, to meet with the governor, who recorded that after all their years in the mission, they still did not wear clothing, and he had them covered so that they could enter the church for the baptism of their children. These Xacriabá apparently gave up armed resistance for settled life in the aldeia of Santa Anna do Rio das Velhas and eventually became so assimilated that in the last years of the colony the French traveler Auguste de Saint-Hilaire had difficulty finding anyone who could speak their language.[6]

The Akroá and Xacriabá, who were among the earliest to enter mission aldeias in the captaincy of Goiás, thus illustrate one significant pattern on this frontier: initial armed conflict, then what was described as pacification and settlement in a Christian mission, revolt over abuse by a secular director, and resolution and alliance with the Portuguese colonial power. Some, such as the Xacriabá, went even further, eventually becoming what the colonists called "domesticated Indians," who shared Luso-Brazilian culture and language.[7] Some of those who entered an aldeia and allied with the Portuguese served in subsequent conquests, or attempts at conquest, of another hostile indigenous nation. We will see this cycle of war, alliance, revolt, and resolution as we turn to other so-called contacts and conquests. One exception to this pattern was the Canoeiro, who never allied with or accepted settlement in mission aldeias, except for a few individuals, who were probably war captives. However, it is possible that some had lived in the Jesuit missions before 1759.

THE APINAYÉ

The next nation to reflect this pattern were the Apinayé, who lived in the far north at the juncture of the Tocantins and Araguaia Rivers. In the early nineteenth century, they were described as a tall and handsome people, who made hollowed-out canoes (*ubás*), with which they traveled on the rivers. In the eighteenth century, they had used their canoes to raid as far north as Cametá on the Tocantins River or to travel to Belém to trade for metal tools.[8]

According to the anthropologist Curt Nimuendajú, who lived among them in the 1930s, their "first demonstrable contact" with "civilization" occurred in 1774, when they fought against an expedition led by Antônio Luiz Tavares Lisboa at the rapids at Três Barras on the Tocantins River.

They first surrounded Lisboa's canoes with a large circle of men, some on the beach and others in canoes, and then shot arrows at Lisboa's men, who then responded with gunshots, forcing them to retreat. The next day the Apinayé attacked again with bows and arrows, but again firearms prevailed.[9]

Thus, as in the case of the Akroá and Xacriabá, the entry of the Apinayé into this history of resistance begins with an attack. Although the Portuguese built a fort at Alcobaça in 1780 to the north of modern Marabá, just over the Goiás border in Pará, the Apinayé appear to have grown in strength and prosperity, trading with their neighbors, the Karajá. They apparently lived at peace with the Luso-Brazilians until 1812, when some soldiers from a small garrison initiated conflict by raiding or destroying their fields. In retaliation, the Apinayé ambushed and killed the soldiers. The Austrian traveler Johann E. Pohl later explained how they had used their women and girls to lure the soldiers into an ambush. While the women pretended to welcome their sexual advances, the men, who were hiding, ran up and clubbed them to death. As a result, the Luso-Brazilians responded with an artillery attack on at least one of their villages, but enough survived to join the well-armed coalition of the Xavante, Xerente, Karajá, and Apinayé that attacked and destroyed the *presídio* of Santa Maria do Araguaia in 1813.[10]

The Apinayé remained a strong nation until 1817, when they were struck by smallpox. Apparently, demoralized by the disease, survivors agreed to make peace with a resident Portuguese Plácido Moreira de Carvalho in 1818, after which they helped travelers on the Tocantins River portage their goods at one of the rapids.[11] Now allies of the Luso-Brazilians, they joined a military force supporting independence organized by José Dias de Mattos and fought against a royalist force loyal to the Portuguese in the independence struggles of the early 1820s. The Apinayé also served in the pedestres and joined the expeditions that attempted to conquer the Canoeiro and Xerente.[12] Their alliance, however, did not last, and in 1824 they revolted against the commandant in Carolina, fleeing their villages on the Tocantins River. However, when the prominent soldier and politician Raimundo José da Cunha Matos met them in 1824, he reported that they were then at peace with 4,200 people living in four villages.[13]

During the early 1840s, some 1,800 Apinayé settled in an aldeia near Boa Vista, under the direction of the Capuchin friar Francisco do Monte de São Vito; an equal number were said to occupy two other villages nearby, at peace with the Luso-Brazilians but not under the direction of Frei (Friar)

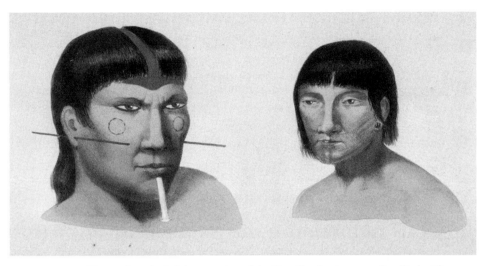

Figure 33. Pictured on the left is a warrior of the Karajá, who temporarily allied with the Xavante, Xerente, and Apinayé, securing significant military victories over Portuguese troops in the early nineteenth century. On the right is a member of the Apiaká people of Mato Grosso. Source: Castelnau, *Expedition.* Courtesy of The Catholic University of America, Oliveira Lima Library, Washington, D.C.

Francisco. Many among the men worked the river traffic to and from Belém, and others farmed, supplying food for themselves and to nearby towns.

But if these Apinayé had abandoned waging war on the Luso-Brazilians, this did not mean they necessarily lived without conflict, as events early in 1858 made dramatically clear.[14] In February the provincial president received notice that a party of Apinayé and Carijó had crossed the Tocantins River into Maranhão and attacked a settlement of Gaviões Indians, killing some and carrying off as captives one hundred children. Frei Francisco distributed these captives among the Luso-Brazilian settlers at Boa Vista to be "civilized." Both the raid and the barely disguised enslavement of the children violated imperial laws, but Boa Vista was far from the capital and the provincial president's repeated demands for an explanation of these events elicited no response from local authorities.

Such problems aside, this aldeia of the Apinayé at Boa Vista was counted among the most successful pacification efforts by the provincial government. Whereas indigenous populations brought into the typical aldeia either quickly died of disease or fled the abuses of the Brazilian directors, in the early 1880s the Boa Vista aldeia still sheltered 1,564 Apinayé. However, they remained resistant to Christianization; and in the 1930s Nimuendajú concluded that missionary influence among them was "quite imperceptible."[15]

THE KAYAPÓ

Related linguistically to the Apinayé were the Gê-speaking people that the Portuguese called the "Caiapó [Kayapó] nation." The northern Kayapó, known in the early nineteenth century as the Nhyrykwaye, were attacked by white slave hunters in 1810 between the Araguaia and Tocantins Rivers. Also known as the Gradaús, which is what the Karajá called them, they were still at this location as late as the 1840s, but by the 1850s, they had moved to an area west of the Araguaia River. In contrast to the few colonial references to the northern Kayapó, the southern Kayapó appear in most historical sources of the colonial and imperial periods; and their descendants, the Kreenakarôre or Panará, now live in the Xingu National Park in Mato Grosso.[16] During the eighteenth and early nineteenth centuries, the southern Kayapó inhabited villages in the region of the Claro and Pilões Rivers, the Serra do Caiapó, and Caiapônia (Rio Bonito) in western Goiás. They also raided along the roads to São Paulo and Cuiabá in Mato Grosso. Paulista *bandeiras* (armed expeditions) attacked them in the seventeenth and early eighteenth centuries, enslaving war captives.[17] The same bandeiras also decimated the Goyá (Goiases) about whom we know little because they did not survive, except as slaves in São Paulo.[18] In 1741, the bandeira of Antônio Pires de Campos took Kayapó heads as war trophies and enslaved a reputed eight thousand Kayapó. Those who survived fled to near Vila Boa, where they embarked on revenge raids and warfare for almost forty years. With the help of 120 Bororo from Mato Grosso, who were traditional enemies of the Kayapó, an expedition led by Pires de Campos was able to destroy an entire Kayapó village in 1742.[19]

Because of the strength of Kayapó resistance, the governor of Goiás organized a bandeira and sent José Luis Pereira to make peace with them.[20] He was accompanied by three Kayapó interpreters, thirty-six Bororo, and twelve Akroá to the Claro River region and returned with more than two hundred Kayapó in 1781. The governor confirmed his alliance and peace with them by having 113 children baptized, including Damiana da Cunha, the grandchild of their chief. Soon after, the Kayapó went to live in the aldeia of Maria I, named for the Queen of Portugal, west of Vila Boa. At its height, there may have been as many as 2,400 Kayapó living there. However, the resettled Kayapó soon abandoned the aldeia or died of diseases. Those who fled quickly resumed raiding and attacking settlers and mule teams in the southern Araguaia region. By 1813, there were so few inhabitants of the aldeia Maria I that the governor moved the remaining Kayapó to another mission, São José de Mossâmedes, founded in 1755 for the Akroá from Duro and later for the Kayapó after 1774. The population of the two aldeias combined was now only 267, and Damiana da Cunha had taken over as a leader of the aldeia of São José. In spite of her best efforts to attract more of her people to the aldeia, the numbers declined. By 1824 only 124 Kayapó remained. After her death in 1831, the Kayapó were transferred against their will and settled in Arinos, Mato Grosso, in the 1830s.[21]

While the Kayapó resided at Maria I or São José, they also served the state as soldiers in the pedestres. They accompanied José Luis Pereira, Damiana da Cunha's first husband, on a bandeira against the Canoeiro but failed to pacify them.[22] The Kayapó also participated in the expedition that made peace with the Xavante in 1788, and a Kayapó chief played a critical role in convincing the Xavante to make contact with colonial authorities. Whenever the Portuguese governors needed help, they turned to their Kayapó allies for assistance against other nations. In spite of their many services, however, they were forcibly removed from the mission lands that they had occupied since the 1780s.

For reasons that are not entirely clear, there is little news of the Kayapó in Goiás for almost a generation after they left São José. Quite likely the survivors and refugees from the settlement remained hidden in the forests across the border in Mato Grosso while they recuperated their numbers and reorganized their military forces. Suddenly, however, late in the 1850s they fell with startling ferocity upon Luso-Brazilian settlements, mining camps, and road traffic in the southwestern part of the province. Goiás's president reported in 1859 that the Kayapó, "who for a very long time have remained peaceful," had unexpectedly renewed hostilities, burning buildings and fields, destroying stock, and killing settlers and their enslaved blacks.[23] Anthropologists have argued that the Kayapó killed rather than kidnapped their victims because their form of social organization did not allow the easy incorporation of outsiders.[24] But though the Kayapó were justly feared by Goiás's rural population, they seem never to have achieved the unrelenting resistance reputation of the Canoeiro.

Year after year, with something of a break during the Paraguayan War (1864–1870), reports arrived in the capital of Kayapó raids and settler responses to these. Particularly affected were the miners along the Claro River, an area recognized as promising for gold and diamond mining since the eighteenth century. Only late in the colonial period did the state open up general access to the region. By the 1830s miners migrated each year in the dry season to work the river gravel with pans and primitive machinery. Spread out along miles of river, they were easy prey for the Kayapó and impossible for the state to defend. During the 1860s and 1870s cattle ranching developed in the Bonito River area and south around Jataí and Rio Verde, prompting more attacks; in 1881 the priest at the town of Rio Bonito threatened to abandon his parish because the violence was causing "everyone" to flee the settlement.[25] "Not in the memory of this generation," a newspaper explained, had the region experienced "such repeated attacks."[26]

Confronted by these assaults, there was little the state could do. Only in the 1870s did Goiás form a state police, and this force never employed more than a hundred agents; the presence of the regular army in the province was equally limited. Where possible, the state garrisoned key towns with detachments of ten or twelve regular troops or National Guard (militia); but these detachments were not effective in stopping raids. Instead, the common response, traditional from the colonial period, continued to be bandeiras, usually raised among a local population bent on revenge and slaving. Repeated edicts by the crown both before and after independence had in theory limited the use of violence in such instances; the 1845 codification of catechesis (religious instruction) regulations had banned violence in all instances save self-defense.[27] Nevertheless, "popular opinion has it that the legitimate and even the indispensable means of dealing with these unfortunate Indians is violence and extermination."[28] As late as the end of the 1880s when a group of local residents at São José de Mossâmedes, led by the police chief, set off to repel recent attacks on fazendas in the area, the provincial president, apparently a bit confused as to what to do, supplied them with shot and powder but at the same time warned them not to "mistreat" the Indians.[29]

As the Empire drew to an end in the 1880s, reports of abandoned properties, flight, and fear continued from Goiás's southwest. Attacks on travelers on the main road west and near the river crossing on the Araguaia River threatened communications with Cuiabá. In January of 1889 the newspaper *O Publicador Goyano* reported that during recent days groups of Indians had been seen in the Claro, Verde, and Bonito river districts and that attacks had occurred at several points along the Araguaia and as close to the capital as

São José de Mossâmedes. Although the government was sending four soldiers and an officer to the latter settlement, the writer observed dryly, this seemed unlikely to intimidate the Kayapó.[30] Most of the rural population was too isolated and too poorly armed to defend itself adequately. The state had limited forces available and competing concerns. And the Kayapó's residence in the aldeia São José de Mossâmedes had soured them on Christianity and "civilization," an experience they shared with other indigenous groups.

XAVANTE AND XERENTE

Next in reputation to the Kayapó as hostile warriors were the Xavante, who had once lived east of the Tocantins River. According to their own oral traditions, their first contact with non-Indians was "at the sea."[31] By 1751, some had crossed the Tocantins River, fleeing perhaps from the great epidemic that struck Maranhão in 1750. Settling east and northeast of Bananal Island in the Araguaia River, they soon acquired a reputation for attacking local miners and settlers. Because they were so feared, the governor organized a bandeira led by José Pinto da Fonseca to move the Xavante to a mission created for them at Pedro III do Carretão. Perhaps three thousand Xavante were initially settled at the mission, but many quickly succumbed to disease; by 1819 when Pohl visited the aldeia only 227 Indians remained.[32] Many others had fled because of the bad treatment they had received in the mission, and they turned their anger against local settlers with greater violence and ferocity, and also with greater skills in fighting learned while at the aldeia. Perhaps these Xavante joined with those who destroyed the presídio of Santa Maria in 1813.

A year later the Xavante were living on the east bank of the Tocantins River, when they were forced to move south of the Manuel Alves Grande River, a tributary of the Tocantins. According to Francisco de Paula Ribeiro, in 1815 the Xavante who had fled Carretão lived in the forests on both banks of the Tocantins River between the Manuel Alves Grande River and Porto Real (later Porto Imperial, then Porto Nacional) and as far west as the Araguaia River. Four years later, Pohl placed them between Carolina and Porto Real on the Tocantins River and as far east as Pastos Bons, Maranhão. Around Duro and nearby Formiga, however, he reported that the Xavante were called "Xerentes." In the past, the Xavante, Xerente, and Acroás-Mirim had been three distinct peoples, but the Xavante had conquered and incorporated survivors of the other two nations. Before this incorporation, they had lived in the region of Duro, including the Jesuit missions.[33]

The Xavante that Pohl met impressed him with their vigor and force and the beauty of their women. Like the Apinayé, they also used their women to lure Luso-Brazilians into an ambush. They were described as being of medium height with rounded faces and copper-colored bodies that they painted red and black, but they wore no clothing. Each warrior carried a horn to sound in battle along with bows, arrows, and war clubs of a meter in length.[34]

Although Pohl's vivid descriptions of the Xavante in 1819 suggest an almost idyllic lifestyle, the reality was that cattlemen were already invading the Tocantins River region, putting pressure on the Xavante, the Krahô, and the Canoeiro. Because of the difficulties that they experienced living so near Luso-Brazilians, there occurred a split among the Xavante sometime between the 1810s and 1840s. The A'uwê people, as they call themselves, split into two "nations" afterward known as the Xavante or Akwe-Xavante and the Xerente. The origin of the division was resistance to or living with whites.[35] The Xerente remained to live among whites along the east bank of the Tocantins River, while many of the Xavante, who rejected living with whites, moved west, eventually settling in the Rio das Mortes region of eastern Mato Grosso, where their descendants still live. Thus, the Xavante eventually abandoned the province of Goiás, but the Xerente became one of the most significant indigenous nations in the north of the province, a region that in 1988 would become the modern state of Tocantins.

According to Nimuendajú, the Xavante and Xerente are "essentially one in speech and custom," and their "history must be considered jointly." Like the Xavante, the Xerente speak a Central Gê language and have a tradition of living east of the Tocantins River, probably as far as the São Francisco River in Minas Gerais.[36] In historical sources, the Xerente were often linked with the Xavante and lived together with them in the same villages until the Xavante moved west of the Araguaia River.

In the eighteenth century, a people identified as Xerente used to live with the Xavante on the banks of the Sono and Manuel Alves Grande Rivers, eastern tributaries of the Tocantins River, northeast of Porto Real. As early as 1782, Coronel João Manoel de Braun reported that the "Xerentediquá" occupied the west bank of the Tocantins River. Another early use of the name Xerente is from the government of Fernando Delgado Freire de Castilho (1809–1820), when some "Cherentes" came in peace from the *sertão* (backlands) of Duro,

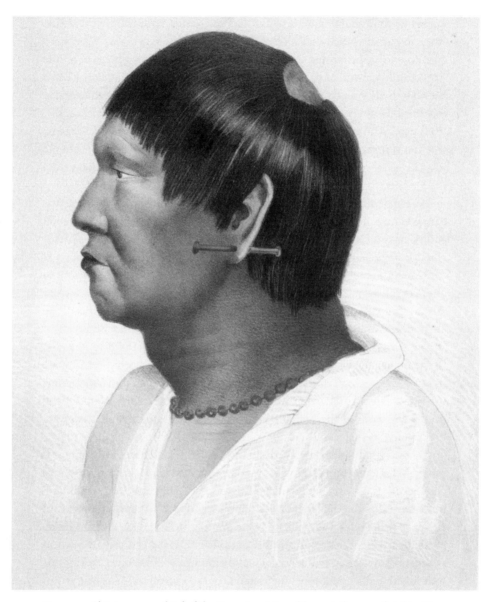

Figure 34. Chiotay was a chief of the Xerente, pictured here at the age of eighty. Over the course of his lifetime, the Xerente engaged in violent resistance to colonial settlement but also experimented with settlement in mission villages. Some were conquered and absorbed by the Xavante; others migrated west to Mato Grosso. Source: Castelnau, *Expedition.* Courtesy of The Catholic University of America, Oliveira Lima Library, Washington, D.C.

were given food, and then returned to their own lands. In the same period Luiz Antônio da Silva e Souza also identified them as "Cherentes" and "Cherentes de qua" and reported that they lived above the falls of the small lake on the Araguaia River and that their territory extended until the sertão of Duro between the Preto and Maranhão Rivers, where they had seven villages. He described them as "valiant and hardworking"; but, in his view, the "Chavantes" (Xavantes), who used the bow and arrow and who lived between the Araguaia and Tocantins rivers, were "cruel and robbers."[37] Thus, before 1812, the Xerente had already acquired a more positive reputation among Luso-Brazilians than the Xavante.

A problem for reconstructing events in these years is the continued tendency among Luso-Brazilian sources to confuse the "Cherente" (Xerente) and "Chavante" (Xavante). In contrast to Portuguese discourse, it was actually two "Chavante" who first came in peace to make contact with the "great captain" of Porto Real, Pacifico Antônio Xavier de Barros.[38] According to one of them, he had come to ask for help against the "Nations of the Cherente-dequá," the name they gave to the people who resided on the banks of the Tocantins River below them, because these had attacked them with firearms. When Xavier de Barros invited them to visit the garrison in Porto Real, the "Chavante captain" was especially interested in the weaponry there. Since the two Xavante had initiated the contact, Cunha Matos established a new Christian aldeia for them named Graciosa; it was located north of Porto Real on the left bank of the Tocantins River.[39] However, the people who were brought to the aldeia were called "Xerente by local officials."

In 1824 about eight hundred Xerente under seventeen of their captains settled in Graciosa and planted fields. They expected to receive weapons from Cunha Matos and his men to defend themselves from attacks by their enemies, the Xavante, who lived on the Sono River; but when they failed to gain adequate protection, they threatened to go to Porto Real, Carmo, or Pontal, evidently to resume attacking those towns. They also wanted the government to organize an official bandeira against their enemies, the Naraguagê. If this were all done, they proposed, they would tell the Luso-Brazilians where they could find gold.[40]

The director of the aldeia of Graciosa, Estevão Joaquim Pires, clarified in a letter who the enemies of the Xerente were. The Naraguagê were "the same Cherentes nation, who do not want peace." This nation, he continued, is "the greatest that there is in this region and the most traitorous." When they had lived in Pastos Bons, Maranhão, they had taken gifts from ranchers but then had abandoned peaceful relations and killed and robbed, taking captured women to their aldeias. He had learned the identity of the Naraguagê from the Christian women who lived among them. Significantly, Pires placed the "Cherentes" in Pastos Bons before they migrated to the Tocantins River, where they lived in 1824; the other possibility is that he was actually describing the Xavante, who used to raid for cattle in Pastos Bons and were the faction who did not want peace with whites. Pires also used the term Xerente for those living on the Gorgulho beach and asked for more troops to defend Graciosa from those living besides the Sono River (i.e., the Xavante). About 130 years later, in the 1950s, the anthropologist David Maybury-Lewis encountered the Xerente on the Gorgulho beach.[41]

The aldeia of Graciosa did not long survive because its founder and protector, Cunha Matos, left for Rio de Janeiro in 1825 to pursue his political ambitions in the Imperial Court. Without his protection, the Xerente abandoned Graciosa by 1829 because they had suffered there "more misery and privations" than when they had been autonomous.[42] By 1829 they had returned to raiding ranchers in the vicinity of Carmo, Pontal, and Porto Real, and a mere twenty-five agreed to be settled in Carretão among the Xavante. The positive image of the Xerente in late colonial official correspondence had evaporated by the 1830s, when new bandeiras were plotted against them, as well as against the Xavante. Writing in 1837, Luiz Gonzaga de Camargo Fleury referred to the "Cherentes" as "this dissembling, traitorous, cruel, and barbarous nation," words the Portuguese had applied to the Xavante in the eighteenth century. It was not the first time, he argued, that they had used the pretext of making peace, "being their principal intent to probe our forces, and dispositions, to acquire knowledge of the land. And to make us suppose that there was nothing to fear, and for this we remain unprepared."[43] As opposed to a robust and hardworking people, the Xerente had become another demonized nation at war with the new state government of the 1830s.

Like the Kayapó who experienced São José de Mossâmedes, the Xavante who had agreed to settle in Carretão profited little by the experience. Some fled and others, Cunha Matos reported in the 1820s, lived "in the most miserable poverty," drunken but peaceful. As noted in the preceding chapter, one Indian who experienced the aldeia and subsequently escaped, remembered the experience differently, emphasizing the corporal punishment liberally administered by village authorities.[44] Perhaps not surprisingly the settlement had failed to prosper, and by 1851 it had declined to a mere seventy-two who "dragged through their days in near total laziness."[45]

While the inhabitants of Carretão wasted away, much larger numbers of Xavante and Xerente resisted settlement and continued to raid the north of the province around the old mining towns of Tesouras and Peixe and to "infest" the "peninsula" between the Araguaia and Tocantins Rivers. In 1830 the newspaper *A Matutina Meiapontense* described the region north of Duro as the land of the Xerentes and the Xavantes, as well as breakaway groups such as the Xacriabá and Acroá. They dominated an area of some 70 by 100 leagues (460 by 660 km) and cultivated corn along the river banks, but each year at the beginning of the dry season they launched attacks across the north of the province, as well as into neighboring Piauí and Maranhão.

At least some among the Xavante and Xerente along with the Kayapó had a good knowledge of the Portuguese language and of settler customs, which they used to their advantage in attacks that spread terror among the rural population. The following passage describes the aftermath of one such raid:

> The body of one [settler] was found blacked with whip marks, also a girl with an arrow through the back of her neck and sticking out her throat and another woman with an arrow entering the same place and coming out her mouth, and all of them naked. Another man was propped up by a lance through his shoulder that came out between his legs and was struck in the ground; in his right hand they put another lance, on his head a crown of colored feathers and hanging from his shoulder a bow and a quiver of arrows.[46]

Sometimes they simply made fun of trapped settlers, decorating their houses with branches and laughing at them but not attacking. Survivors and refugees fled their farms and the smaller settlements to take refuge in the towns, and even here they dared not work the fields or even go to the river to draw water without an armed escort.

An effort in 1833 to negotiate with the Xavante settled along the Araguaia River failed, largely due to the incompetence and cowardice of Luso-Brazilian leaders; and Xavante and Xerente raids, often followed by ad hoc and usually unsuccessful settler retaliation, continued.[47] This prompted one of the few state-sponsored bandeiras of the post-independence period in Goiás.[48] In 1835 the Provincial Assembly proposed coordinated expeditions against the Xavante and Xerente around Porto Imperial and

Cavalcante, and against the Canoeiro in the Amaro Leite district. The following year a bandeira marched against the Xavante/Xerente with some 270 militia troops from Natividade, Carmo, and Porto Imperial. It was instructed to sweep the east bank of the Tocantins River to the Sono River, said to be the center of the lands of the Xerente. "Once those encountered there had been defeated," the bandeira was to split up and check other areas for hostile presences.

After an initial, apparently peaceful encounter with the Xerente, the militia discovered that they had been deceived. The Indians' pacific gestures were intended only to give their women and children time to escape: "The following day the Xerente suddenly appeared on a hill and shouted that they would never want peace, raising a war cry." An attack on the hill failed, as did subsequent efforts to explore the area, due to the "lack of discipline" among the government troops, most of whom clearly were intent on not finding or having to fight the Xerente. Overall, the bandeira was an expensive failure and not one the government repeated.[49]

Over the next decades Xavante and Xerente attacks continued and contributed to the final extinction of declining gold towns such as São Félix and Pontal. Such hostilities, the town council of Porto Imperial complained, were holding back the development of the whole region.[50] But ultimately, the attacks could not stop the movement of settlers and cattle ranches into the north of the province. At the same time, some two thousand Xavante were said to have settled in the aldeias of Thereza Christina and Pedro Affonso; and there were Xerente living at Boa Vista, with the Apinayé, and at São José do Araguaia, where they worked the river boats.

THE CANOEIRO

The people who best symbolized indigenous resistance in official correspondence of the nineteenth century were the Canoeiros, which in Portuguese simply means "canoers." Actually, little is known about them, since they refused to make contact with both Christians and with indigenous nations and were enemies of the Xavante. Perhaps the reason is that they spoke a language different than one of the Macro-Gê languages. In fact, some of them knew prayers in Latin and some Portuguese, suggesting that they had had some contact with Christians at some point in their history. Recent scholarship suggests that they spoke a Tupi-Guaraní language.

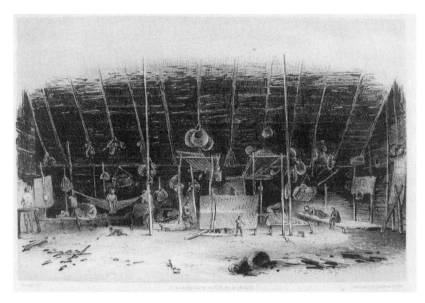

Figure 35. Well after the worst dislocations of the colonial period lay in the past, the native peoples of Goiás continued to engage in violent and nonviolent forms of resistance. The Apinayé, pictured here in a traditional great house, accepted settlement in mission villages but continued to resist conversion to Christianity and the use of clothing. Source: Castelnau, *Expedition.* Courtesy of The Catholic University of America, Oliveira Lima Library, Washington, D.C.

The quest for the historic Canoeiro begins with the basic question: where did they live? According to the anthropologist Dulce Pedroso, their traditional territory was the southern Tocantins River (or Maranhão River), from the falls of the Santa Tereza, Almas, Cana Brava, Manuel Alves, and Paranã Rivers.[51] Their villages were located near significant mining towns, such as São Félix and Cavalcante, or on gold-rich rivers, such as the Paranã. They were reputedly a large nation in the eighteenth century and had been in intense conflict with miners and their enslaved Africans since the 1720s, but especially after 1770.

According to Silva e Souza, attacks by the Canoeiros (ca. 1783–1800) had depopulated a great part of the ranches of the Tocantins River. In his view, they were a "very cruel and bellicose nation, who do not know how to flee." Although other nations sued for peace, the Canoeiro resisted to the death along with their women and fierce dogs that accompanied them. They traveled in canoes on the Tocantins, Paranã, and Manuel Alves Rivers, and to the confluence of the Palma, where they did much damage in their attacks. Besides the bow and arrow, they used long lances, "toothed on the ends," of more than twenty *palmos* (palm widths). He concluded by citing their love of horse meat, which is their "most savory food," and which was probably one motive for their raids on ranches.[52]

In 1773 an official bandeira organized by the governor of Goiás traveled to the west bank of the Tocantins River in the direction of Pontal to the Almas River. There they battled the "Xavantes de canoa," which was a name then applied to the Canoeiro. In 1789 the Canoeiro were also slaughtered, and many of their villages were destroyed in 1796. José Luis Pereira tried to contact and make peace with the Canoeiro in 1803, but in the end he "made great slaughter among them." Assisted by the Xavante from Carretão, he attacked the Canoeiro and captured fifty of them. The captives were then taken to Porto Real to be sent along with other war captives to Belém. However, Pereira did not succeed in his conquest, and the wars resumed.[53]

The next major attempt to conquer the Canoeiro was the infamous bandeira of 1819, organized by Joaquim Theotonio Segurado. This force actually entered a Canoeiro village on the Almas River, which had a large field of corn. When the bandeira proposed peace to the Canoeiro they met resistance, as usual; so the troops shot the bearded chief, torched the thatched-roofed houses, and slaughtered all those who attempted to flee. Only six children and one old woman survived. As late as 1830, the Canoeiro were still angry about the atrocities committed against them by the 1819 bandeira.[54]

The mutual warfare and raiding continued. The next expeditions sent against them were those of 1823–1825 that were organized by Cunha Matos. He justified his use of force by noting that they were "the most barbarous of the universe, whose cruelty exceeded that of the *bugres* [a pejorative word for savages] and Botocudos [the notoriously fierce fighters who inhabited the eastern forests of neighboring Minas Gerais]." Although they were not cannibals, he reported, they killed with war clubs and arrows, kidnapped Christians, and tortured their victims. Once again Cunha Matos turned to the Xavante from Carretão to help out on this expedition, while both the Canoeiro and other unpacified Xavante attacked more than eight hundred cattle ranches and plantations spread over 400 square leagues (2,600 square km), including the districts of Amaro Leite, Discuberto da Piedade, São Félix, Palma, Carmo, and Chapada dos Veadeiros, and as far south and east as the presídio at Duro. Around São Félix and Amaro Leite in particular, they had "ruined" three hundred ranches and mining camps; in 1843 the inhabitants of Palma petitioned the provincial government for funds to rebuild their church, burned down by Canoeiros who, they explained, found this the quickest way to extract the iron of the fittings.[55] Cunha Matos was having so little success that he asked for the help of Dona Damiana da Cunha and one hundred of her Kayapó warriors, and he still failed to conquer the Canoeiro.[56]

A "seventy year old" resident of a fazenda near Pilar remembered in 1833 that Canoeiro attacks had begun in the time of "Capitão [Governor] Cunha Menzes"[57] and in recent decades had become a yearly occurrence. The same year the newspaper *A Matutina Meiapontense* reported that assaults by the Canoeiro, and the Xavante, had forced abandonment of many fazendas in the Amaro Leite area, and a president subsequently lamented that "the people, intimidated by the curse, have left excellent plantings and mines and rich pasture for their cattle."[58]

The provincial regime responded by garrisoning some of the afflicted towns with small detachments of pedestres or regular troops and by creating roving militia patrols. But the garrisons were of little help to the outlying districts where most of the attacks occurred, and the patrols too often were simply cut off and wiped out. Generally, nineteenth-century Goianos lacked the forest skills of their eighteenth-century ancestors. This was clear, for example, in the 1836 state-sponsored bandeira against the Canoeiro mounted parallel to that sent against the Xavante and Xerente.[59] In this case some 181 militia soldiers from Amaro Leite and São Felix marched against the Canoeiro, but they "accomplished nothing worthwhile, apparently because of the cowardice of their commanders, [and because] of absolute ignorance of what they were supposed to do [and] of the countryside." These bandeiras had scant effect, the president feared, except to "stir up the savages, with possibly dire results."

In fact, Canoeiro attacks continued largely unabated during the 1840s and 1850s, as did petitions for help from the towns of the center north and as did retaliation by ineffectual and illegal local bandeiras. In the 1840s Francis Castelnau reported that the Canoeiro then lived along both banks of the Tocantins River, from Peixe in the north to ten leagues (66 km) to the south of Amaro Leite, on the left bank, and São José do Tocantins on the right bank of the river. Their boundary with the Xavante then coincided with the road that ran from Porto Imperial to the city of Goiás.[60] By the 1850s they had extended their arena of operations into the Chapada dos Veadeiros, north of the present Federal District of Brasília, and were attacking settler farms in the parish of Santa Luzia (Luziânia), on the road to Minas Gerais.[61] Only in the years after the Paraguayan War did attacks taper off, perhaps because settlers and their cattle were pushing aggressively back into the Amaro Leite area and ultimately forcing the Canoeiro out. Some of these moved to the banks of the Araguaia River, where they harassed river commerce, while others kept fighting in the region between the Maranhão and Paranã Rivers until the 1980s, when several were found hiding in caves from their enemies.[62] Nearly extinct, only small groups now remain in Central Brazil of this once large nation that was noted for the ferocity of its resistance to enslavement and settlement in Christian missions.

Thus far, this chapter has focused on open, armed resistance, but it is well to remember too that, like James Scott's Asian peasants, Brazil's Indians also made use of the "weapons of the weak" in their struggles against the Luso-Brazilian settlers and the state. By their very nature such activities are hard to document, but some examples do appear. As noted, the Xacriabá and the Apinayé, even while they accepted settlement in aldeias, resisted Christianity and the use of "civilized" clothing. Some of the Kayapó residents in the aldeia at São José de Mossâmedes reportedly disguised themselves as "wild" Indians to steal cattle from neighboring fazendas and attack road traffic; and they steadfastly avoided work in plantation agriculture. The Krahó, in the north, prospered for a time, raising and trading cattle into Maranhão, but they also stole cattle from ranchers, blaming it on other indigenous groups. In the 1870s the Xerente of the aldeia Thereza Christina sent representatives all the way to the imperial court in Rio de Janeiro to protest a land conflict with a neighboring fazenda. And in a bit of a reversal, inhabitants of Duro sought to revive an "Indian" identity to claim land, while their local opponents dismissed such arguments, saying, "there are no Indians here, only citizens and National Guards."[63]

In conclusion, what was critical to the survival of the indigenous peoples of the captaincy and province of Goiás was their very flexibility. On occasion, they seemed to accommodate, using the "weapons of the weak" or allying with the Luso-Brazilians; at other times they took up arms in vengeance against settler atrocities and defended their people from conquest and enslavement. In the 1830s, some were so successful at war that they almost drove the Luso-Brazilians from the north; but ultimately most were overwhelmed by the expanding agropastoral frontier of the nineteenth century and fled west of the Araguaia River to find refuge in Pará or Mato Grosso.

Figure 36. Apinayé villagers gather to dance. In the face of multiple and changing threats to their existence over the course of centuries, the Apinayé, like most of Brazil's indigenous peoples, responded with resilience and flexibility, which proved to be the key to their survival. Source: Castelnau, *Expedition.* Courtesy of The Catholic University of America, Oliveira Lima Library, Washington, D.C.

Today, the Apinayé, Krahô, and Xerente live in the state of Tocantins and send some of their young people to the federal university. The Kayapó and Xavante claim lands to the west of the Araguaia River, while remnants of the mysterious Canoeiro are subject to anthropological and linguistic investigations. Although the wars no longer occur in Goiás and Tocantins, the indigenous nations still contest local ranchers and governments and seek and secure demarcation and protection of their lands in Brasília, using the law, videotaping the "white man's promises" during the writing of a new national constitution in 1988, and appealing to the media of the twenty-first century.[64]

NOTES

1. Some themes here were also included in Mary Karasch, "Interethnic Conflict and Resistance on the Brazilian Frontier of Goiás, 1750–1890," in *Contested Ground:*

Comparative Frontiers on the Northern and Southern Edges of the Spanish Empire, ed. Donna J. Guy and Thomas E. Sheridan (Tucson: University of Arizona Press, 1998), 115–34; and David McCreery, *Frontier Goiás, 1822–1889* (Stanford, CA: Stanford University Press, 2006). Abbreviations used in the notes are as follows: Arquivo Histórico do Estado de Goiás (AHEG), Documentação (Doc.) Diversa (Div.); Arquivo Histórico Ultramarino, Lisbon (AHU); Biblioteca Nacional, Lisbon (BNL); Biblioteca Nacional, Rio de Janeiro (BNRJ); Brazil, Ministério da Agricultura, Comércio e Obras Públicas, *Relatórios*, 1860–1888 (Rio de Janeiro) (Agricultura, *Relatório*); Goiás (Província), Presidente, *Relatórios*. 1835–1889 (Vila Boa de Goiás) (Presidente, *Relatório*); Instituto Histórico e Geográphico Brasileiro, Rio de Janeiro (IHGB).

2. Greg Urban, "A História da Cultura Brasileira Segundo as Línguas Nativas," trans. Beatriz Perrone-Moisés, in *História dos índios no Brasil*, ed. Manuela Carneiro da Cunha (São Paulo: Companhia das Letras, 1992), 88, 90–91; Marivone Matos Chaim, *Os aldeamentos indigenas na capitania de Goiás: Sua importância na política de povoamento (1749–1811)* (Goiânia: Oriente, 1974), 43, 53, 99–120.

3. AHU, 995, cx. 17, Ultima carta de Venceslao Gomes da Silva, Administrador Temporal do Gentio da Natividade, Presídio de São José, 12 Feb. 1758, signed Venceslao Gomes da Sylva (copy). See also, cartas de Venceslao Gomes da Silva, Administrador contratado pelo Conde dos Arcos, Vila Boa, 1 Feb. 1757, Wenceslao Gomes da Sylva to the conde de São Miguel; Chaim, *Aldeamentos*, 114–15, 117; and John Hemming, *Amazon Frontier: The Defeat of the Brazilian Indians* (Cambridge, MA: Harvard University Press 1987), 65.

4. Odorico Costa, "Os Jesuítas em Goiaz," *Oeste*, 5–7. See also note 3 above; José Martins Pereira de Alencastre, *Anais da Província de Goiás* (Brasília: Secretaria do planejamento e coordenação, 1979 [1864]), 120–21; and Juciene Ricarte Apolinário, *Os Akroá e outros povos indígenas nas Fronteiras do Sertão Goiânia* (Goiânia: Kelps, 2006).

5. Raimundo José da Cunha Matos, *Itinerario do Rio de Janeiro ao Pará e Maranhão, pelas provincias de Minas Gerais e Goiaz* (Rio de Janeiro: Typ. Imperial, 1836), vol. 2, 164.

6. Auguste de Saint-Hilaire, *Viagem à província de Goiás*, trans. Regina Regis Junqueira (Belo Horizonte: Itatiaia, 1975), 143–47.

7. The Portuguese used the terms *índios domesticados, civilizados*, and *mansos* (domestic, civilized, and docile Indians) to describe those who adopted Luso-Brazilian culture, religion, and language. To the indigenous, however, Luso-Brazilians were "Christians."

8. BNL, Rare Books, cód. 568, "Da Viagem que se faz da Cidade de Bellem [sic] do Grão Pará, athe ás ultimas Colonias dos Dominios Portuguezes nos Rios Amazonas, e Negro Pelo Tenente Colonel de Engenharia João Vasco Manoel de Braun," 1782, f. 41; and BNRJ, 9, 2, 10, Padre Luiz Antônio da Silva e Souza,

"Memoria sobre o Descobrimento, Governo, População e Cousas mais Notaveis Da Capitania de Goyaz [1812]."

9. Curt Nimuendajú, *Apinayé*, trans. Robert H. Lowie, ed. Robert H. Lowie and John M. Cooper (New York, 1967), 2–3; and Hemming, *Amazon Frontier*, 187.

10. Nimuendajú, *The Apinayé*, 5; and Hemming, *Amazon Frontier*, 188–89.

11. Nimuendajú, *Apinayé*, 6–7; and Johann E. Pohl, *Viagem no Interior do Brasil*, translated by Milton Amado and Eugênio Amado (Belo Horizonte: Ed. Itatiaia, 1976), 248–49.

12. AHEG, Doc. Div., vol. 132, "Registro de Ofícios e Ordens Expedidos pelo Governo Provincial e Diversos, 1835–1839," various.

13. Hemming, *Amazon Frontier*, 189; and Nimuendajú, *Apinayé*, 7.

14. The following is based on AHEG, Doc. Div., vol. 308, "Correspondência da Presidência com o Ministerio do Império, 1857–1860," 21 Feb. 1858, vol. 334, "Correspondência da Presidência para as Autoridades Judiciais, 1858–1860," Juiz de Direito, Boa Vista, 6 Dec. 1858, and *Correio Official*, 12 Feb. 1858.

15. Agricultura, *Relatório* (1881) (Rio de Janeiro, 1882), 160; and Nimuendajú, *Apinayé*, 7.

16. Terence Turner, "Os Mebengokre Kayapó: História e mudança social, de comunidades autônomas para a coexistência interétnica," in Cunha, *História dos índios no Brasil*, 311–38. The newest history of the Kayapó is David L. Mead's, "Caiapó do Sul: An Ethnohistory" (PhD diss. in Anthropology, the University of Florida, 2010). See also Curt Nimuendajú, *The Eastern Timbira*, trans. and ed. Robert H. Lowie (Berkeley: University of California Press, 1946); and his map locating the Nyurukwayé (Nhyrykwaye).

17. Odair Giraldin, *Cayapó e Panará: Luta e sobrevivência de um povo Jê no Brasil Central* (São Paulo: Editora da Unicamp, 1997), 70, 80–81.

18. Horieste Gomes and Antônio Teixeira Neto, *Geografia Goiás-Tocantins* (Goiânia: CEGRAF, UFG, 1993), 41.

19. Giraldin, *Cayapó*, 55–81.

20. Mary Karasch, "Rethinking the Conquest of Goiás, 1775–1819," *The Americas* 61, no. 3 (Jan. 2005): 469.

21. Mary Karasch, "Damiana da Cunha: Catechist and *Sertanista*," in *Struggle and Survival in Colonial America*, ed. David G. Sweet and Gary B. Nash (Berkeley and Los Angeles: University of California Press, 1981), 103–5. Saint-Hilaire visited Maria I in 1819, which was abandoned, although there were remnants of the governor's house. Saint-Hilaire, *Viagem à província de Goiás*, 75. The total of 2,400 is from Giraldin, *Cayapó*, 95. On the removal of the Kayapó, see Karasch, "Interethnic Conflict," 131; and Mead, "Caiapó do Sul," on their history after removal.

22. Goiânia, AHEG, cx. 11, correspondence of João Vieira de Carvalho, Palacio do Rio de Janeiro, 7 Apr. 1823, regarding the petition of Damiana da Cunha, "viuva do Sargento de Pedestres, Jozé Luis Pereira."

23. Presidente, *Relatório* (1859), 54–55; and *Correio Official*, 16 Oct. 1858 and 19 Jan. 1859.

24. Giraldin, *Cayapó*, 122–23.

25. AHEG, Restaurar, "1879–1883, Livro de Editais, Termos, etc.," Presidente de Goiás-Ministerio de Agricultura, 21 Feb. 1881.

26. *Correio Official*, 9 Aug. 1884.

27. Decree 426, 24 July 1845, Brazil, *Colecção das Leis do Império*, vol. 3, part 2, section 25a.

28. AHEG, Doc. Div., vol. 340, "Registro de Correspondência do Governo com o Ministerio de Justiça, 1858–1862," 21 Feb. 1859; and box 337, "Correspondência da Presidência com Autoridades Policiais, 1858–1860," Deputy, Rio Claro, 16 Mar. 1859.

29. *Correio Official*, 2 Mar. 1889.

30. Ibid, 12 Jan. 1889.

31. Aracy Lopes da Silva, "Dois séculos e Meio de História Xavante," in Cunha, *História dos índios no Brasil*, 362–64; Chaim, *Aldeamentos*, 43.

32. Rita Heloisa de Almeida Lazarin, "O aldeamento do Carretão: Duas histórias" (MA thesis, Universidade de Brasília, 1985); Karasch, "Rethinking the Conquest," 481–85; and Pohl, *Viagem*, 237–38.

33. Oswaldo Martins Ravagnani, "A Experiência Xavante com o Mundo dos Brancos" (PhD diss., Escola de Sociologia e Política de São Paulo, 1978), 91–92; IHGB, Arq. 1.5.16, Goiás [Francisco de Paula Ribeiro], "Viagem ao Rio do Tucantins [sic] em 1815, pelos sertoens do Maranham . . . 1818," f. 262; and Pohl, *Viagem*, 236–42.

34. Sereburã et al., *Wamrêmé Za'ra: Mito e História do Povo Xavante: Nossa Palavra* (São Paulo: Senac, 1998), 15, 109, 111.

35. Silva, "Dois Séculos," 364–65.

36. Curt Nimuendajú, *The Serente*, trans. Robert H. Lowie (Los Angeles: [The Southwest Museum], 1942; reprint New York, 1979), 1–2, 4; and Urban, "História da Cultura Brasileira," 88.

37. BNL, Braun, "Da Viagem," 1782, f. 41; Nimuendajú, *Serente*, 5; and BNRJ, Silva e Souza, "Memoria," ff. 31, 43–44.

38. AHEG, Doc. Div., no. 69, Pacifico Antônio Xavier de Barros to Cunha Matos, Porto Real, 18 Apr. 1824, ff. 182–85; Felizardo de Nazarethe Bitancourth, Cabo de Esquadra de Dragoens to Xavier de Barros, Porto Real, 7 May 1824, ff. 213–17.

39. Matos, *Itinerario*, vol. 2, 5.

40. AHEG, Doc. Div., no. 69, Estevão Joaquim Pires to Cunha Matos, Graciosa, 1 Sept. 1824, ff. 237–38.

41. AHEG, Doc. Div., no. 69, João Manoel de Meneses, Cadete, to Cunha Matos, 18 Aug. 1824, f. 236; and AHEG, Cunha Matos, no. 18, no. 77, Ofício a Secretaria de Estado sobre o ataque dos Noraguajés, Traíras, 4 Nov. 1824, ff. 114–15. See also

Nimuendajú, *Timbira*, 36; and David Maybury-Lewis, *The Savage and the Innocent* (Cleveland, OH: World Publishing, 1965), 39.

42. Goiânia, Instituto Histórico e Geográphico de Goiás, pasta 2, doc. 51, Lino de Moraes, to Pereira, Goiás, 25 Aug. 1829, f. 18.

43. AHEG, cod. 136, Luiz Gonzaga de Camargo Fleury to the justice of peace of Porto Imperial, 1 Apr. 1837.

44. Matos, *Itinerario*, vol. 1, 179–80; and Presidente, *Relatório* (1856), 15.

45. Presidente, *Relatório* (1851), 45.

46. *A Matutina Meiapontense*, 25 Dec. 1830.

47. Ibid., 10 Apr. and 14 Aug. 1833; Presidente, *Relatório* (1835), 37.

48. The following is based on: Presidente, *Relatório* (1837), 16–18, and (1838), 12–18; AHEG, Doc. Div., vol. 108, "Livro de Registro de Propostas Apresentadas ao Conselho Geral, 1829–1838," 27 July 1835.

49. Presidente, *Relatório* (1837), 16–18, and (1838), 12–18; AHEG, Doc. Div., vol. 108, "Livro de Registro de Propostas Apresentadas ao Conselho Geral, 1829–1838," 27 July 1835.

50. AHEG, Municípios, Porto Nacional (Porto Imperial), Câmara, 15 Feb., 1848; "Índios: Assuntos Diversos," Comissão da Cathequese e Força Pública, 1850.

51. Dulce Madalena Rios Pedroso, "Avá-Canoeiro: A História do Povo Invisivel—Séculos XVIII e XIX" (MA thesis, Federal University of Goiás, 1992); Dulce Madalena R. Pedroso et al., *Avá-Canoeiro: A terra, o homem, a luta* (Goiânia, 1990); Andre A. Toral, "Os índios negros ou os Carijó de Goiás: A história dos Avá-Canoeiro," *Revista de Antropologia*, 27–28 (1984–1985); Karasch, "Rethinking the Conquest," 485–92; and Gomes and Teixeira Neto, *Geografia*, 42.

52. BNRJ, Silva e Souza, "Memoria," ff. 28, 43. An English version is in Robert Southey, *History of Brazil*, vol. 3 (1822; reprint New York: Franklin, 1970), 677–78.

53. Karasch, "Rethinking the Conquest," 486–87; and Southey, *History of Brazil*, 678.

54. Karasch, "Rethinking the Conquest," 488; and Pohl, *Viagem*, 212–15.

55. AHEG, Documentação (Doc.) Avulsa (Av.), box 32, petition, n/d [1843].

56. Karasch, "Rethinking the Conquest," 489–90.

57. *A Matutina Meiapontense*, 12 June 1833. Either Luís da Cunha Meneses (1778–83) or Tristão da Cunha Meneses (1783–1800).

58. *A Matutina Meiapontense*, 25 Sept. 1833; and Presidente, *Relatório* (1839), 24.

59. Presidente, *Relatório* (1837), 16–18, and (1838), 12–18.

60. Francis Castelnau, *Expedição às Regiões Centrais da America do Sul*, trans. Olivério M. de Oliveira Pinto (Belo Horizonte: Itatiaia, 2000), 245–46.

61. AHEG, Doc. Div., vol. 202, "Secretaria de Justiça," 22 July 1850; Presidente, *Relatório* (1853, 2d report of this year), 9, and (1854), 4; and *Correio Official*, 25 May 1853.

62. Karasch, "Interethnic Conflict," 134.

63. James C. Scott, *Weapons of the Weak: Everyday Forms of Peasant Resistance* (New Haven, CT: Yale University Press, 1985). On the Kayapó: Saint-Hilaire, *Viagem à província de Goiás*, 87, 4n. On the Krahó: Júlio Cezar Melatti, *Índios e criadores: A Situação dos Krahô na Area Pastoril do Tocantins* (Rio de Janeiro: Instituto de Ciências Sociais, 1967). On the Xerente: AHEG, Doc. Av., box 266, Ministerio de Agricultura-Presidente de Goiás, 2 July 1877; and Duro: AHEG, Dianôpolis (Duro), Deputy-Chief of Police, 17 Mar. 1874.

64. Silva, "Dois Séculos," 359, 377 (photos). See also Seth Garfield, *Indigenous Struggle at the Heart of Brazil: State Policy, Frontier Expansion, and the Xavante Indians, 1937–1988* (Durham, NC: Duke University Press, 2001); and Marlene Castro Ossami de Moura, ed., *Índios de Goiás: Uma Perspectiva Histórico-Cultural* (Goiânia: UCG/Kelps/Vieira, 2006).

Glossary

administração, administrado legal guardianship of Indians by colonists during periods of religious instruction, often tantamount to slavery; an Indian kept captive by this system

agregado household dependent

aldeia or aldeamento village, esp. an Indian village, either autonomous or overseen by missionaries or after 1757 by state officials

bandeira, bandeirante an armed expedition, expeditionary, cf. entrada

bugre derogatory term for non-Christian or uncivilized Indian, savage

Cabanagem (1835–1840) peasant rebellion affecting much of the Brazilian Amazon, named for the *cabanos* or shacks in which some of the poor lived

caboclo pejorative term for detribalized indigenous or mestizo rustic

capitão-mor militia commander

carijó originally a member of one of the Guarani peoples of southern Brazil that first encountered Europeans, the term came to be used generically to refer to a detribalize Indian

carta régia royal edict

catequese catechism, catechesis, instruction in Roman Catholic doctrine

coartação manumission contract allowing a slave to gain freedom under specific conditions through self-purchase

comarca jurisdiction roughly equivalent to a county

cruzado Portuguese coin, made first of gold (fifteenth–sixteenth centuries), later silver (seventeenth–nineteenth centuries)

curiboca pejorative term for Afro-native mestizo

descimento expedition that "descended" or brought out indigenous captives from the interior to labor on the coast

Diretório dos índios [Indian Directorate] (1757–1798) assimilationist legislation first issued in 1757 subjecting Amazonian village Indians to supervision by state-assigned lay directors; extended to all of Brazil in Direção legislation (1759); the term also refers to the period during which the legislation prevailed.

dízimo tithe, royal tax assessed on agricultural production

Emboaba perjorative term referring to an outsider, especially a Portuguese colonist who arrived in Minas Gerais soon after the discovery of gold by Paulistas

encomienda in Spanish America, a grant of native labor and tribute to a beneficiary of the crown, usually a conquistador or soldier

entrada armed expedition of conquest, cf. bandeira

fazenda, fazendeiro farm, ranch, plantation; large landholder

frei friar

gentio da terra lit. "heathen of this land"; pejorative term used to describe non-Christian Indian, cf. negro da terra

Inconfidência Mineira (1789) foiled nativist plot in Minas Gerais whose leaders hoped to found an independent republic

juiz dos órfãos local judicial official

língua lit. "language" or "tongue"; native interpreter

língua geral either of two Tupi-based linguae francae. A southern or Paulista language became extinct after it was officially proscribed in the mid-eighteenth century. A northern or Amazonian language, now known as Nheengatu, is still spoken along the upper Negro River in northern Brazil, Venezuela, and Colombia.

llanos plains

madeira de lei state-controlled forests or timber

manso lit. "tame," a docile Indian; also "domesticado" (domesticated) and "civilizado" (civilized), as opposed to "bravo" (wild) *mata atlântica* Atlantic forest

mercê appointment, pension, or other royal grant that produced income

mestiço mestizo, racially mixed

negro da terra lit. "black of this land"; derogatory term used to describe Indians, cf. gentio da terra

oca multifamily lodge used by Tupi Indians

ouvidor superior judge

pajé shaman

pau-brasil Brazilwood (caesalpinia echinata), tropical hardwood yielding red pigment used as dye

Paulista resident of São Paulo

pedestre salaried infantryman or foot soldier

pelourinho pillory

poaia active ingredient in ipecac, a widely used nineteenth-century emetic

Pombaline pertaining to the rule of Sebastião José de Carvalho e Melo, marquis of Pombal, first minister of King José I (r. 1750–1777)

presídio small garrison, fort

principais (s. principal) Amazonian village headmen comprising hereditary native nobility

Reconquista the centuries-long Christian reconquest of the Iberian Peninsula from Islamic invaders (718–1492)

reduccion Indian settlement in Spanish America created by relocating scattered indigenous groups to a central location to be supervised by missionaries and state officials

réis (s. real) basic unit of currency in colonial Brazil. One mil-réis, written 1$000, equaled one thousand réis. One conto de réis (or simply one conto), written 1:000$000, equaled one thousand mil-réis.

repartimiento in Spanish America, a crown-sanctioned system of forced indigenous labor

resgate lit. ransom, rescue, redemption; practice whereby Indians deemed to be held captive by other Indians could be "rescued" and enslaved by settlers

rotina slash-and-burn agriculture

santidade messianic movement combining elements of indigenous, Christian, and possibly African beliefs

sertanejo inhabitant of the sertão

sertanista adept of the sertão, backwoodsman, frontiersman

sertão wilderness, wilds, hinterland, backlands

sesmaria, sesmeiro royal land grant, land-grant recipient

taipa adobe

Tapuia savage, wild Indian, derogatory term appropriated by colonists from the Tupi, used to refer to non-Tupian peoples

tropa troop

ubá Tupi term for canoe

Bibliography

A Matutina Meiapontense. 1830, 1833.

Abbeville, Claude d'. *Histoire de la mission des pères capucins en l'isle de Maragnan et terres circoncoisines, où est traicté des singularitez admirables et des moeurs merveilleuses des Indiéns habitans de ce pays, avec les missives et advis qui ont esté envoyez de nouveau*. Paris: F. Huby, 1614.

Acuña, Christoval de. "A New Discovery of the Great River of the Amazons." In *Expeditions into the Valley of the Amazons, 1539, 1540, 1639*, edited by Clements R. Markham, 41–142. London: Hakluyt Society, 1859.

Alden, Dauril. "Changing Jesuit Perceptions of the Brasis during the Sixteenth Century." *Journal of World History* 3 (1992).

———. "Indian Versus Black Slavery in the State of Maranhão During the Seventeenth and Eighteenth Centuries." *Bibliotheca Americana* 1, no. 3 (1983): 91–142.

———. *The Making of an Enterprise: The Society of Jesus in Portugal, Its Empire, and Beyond, 1540–1750*. Stanford, CA: Stanford University Press, 1996.

Alencastre, José Martins Pereira de. *Anais da província de Goiás*. Reprint, Brasília: Secretaria do planejamento e coordenação, 1979 [1864].

Almeida, Eduardo Castro e, ed. *Inventário dos documentos relativos ao Brasil existentes no Archivo da Marinha e Ultramar*. Rio de Janeiro: Bibliotheca Nacional, 1913–1936.

Almeida, Maria Regina Celestino de. "Índios e mestiços no Rio de Janeiro: Significados plurais e cambiantes." *Memoria Americana* 16 (2008): 19–40.

———. *Metamorfoses indígenas: Cultura e identidade nos aldeamentos indígenas do Rio de Janeiro*. Rio de Janeiro: Arquivo Nacional, 2003.

———. "Os índios aldeados no Rio de Janeiro colonial: Novos súditos cristãos do Império Português." PhD diss., Universidade de Campinas, 2001.

———. "Política Indigenista e Etnicidade: Estratégias indígenas no processo de extinção das aldeias do Rio de Janeiro. Século XIX." *Anuario IEHS* (2007): 219–33.

———. "Tierras y recursos económicos de las aldeas indígenas de Rio de Janeiro: Conflictos y negociaciones (siglos XVII–XIX)." *Nuevo Mundo Mundos Nuevos* (2011), http://nuevomundo.revues.org/60531.

Almeida, Rita Heloísa de. *O Diretório dos índios: Um projeto de "civilização" no Brasil do século XVIII*. Brasília: Universidade de Brasília, 1997.

Amoroso, Marta Rosa, and Nádia Farage, eds. *Relatos da fronteira amazônica no século XVIII: Documentos de Henrique João Wilckens e Alexandre Rodrigues Ferreira.* São Paulo: NHII-USP; FAPESP, 1994.

Anchieta, José de. *Cartas, informacoes, fragmentos historicos e sermões do padre Joseph de Anchieta, S.J. (1554–1594)*. Rio de Janeiro: Civilização brasileira, 1933.

———. *De Gestis Mendi de Saa*. Translated by Armando Cardoso. Rio de Janeiro: Arquivo Nacional, 1958.

———. *Textos históricos*. São Paulo: Edições Loyola, 1989.

Apolinário, Juciene Ricarte. *Os Akroá e outros povos indígenas nas Fronteiras do Sertão Goiânia.* Goiânia: Kelps, 2006.

Aquinas, Thomas. *Summa theologica*. Translated by Fathers of the English Dominican Province. 3 vols. New York: Benziger Bros., 1947.

Arens, W. *The Man-Eating Myth: Anthropology & Anthropophagy*. New York: Oxford University Press, 1979.

Arnaud, Expedito. *Aspectos da legislação sobre os índios do Brasil*. Belém: Museu Emílio Goeldi, 1973.

Azevedo, João Lúcio d', ed. *Cartas do Padre António Vieira*. 3 vols. Coimbra: Imp. da Universidade, 1925.

Barman, Roderick J. *Brazil: The Forging of a Nation, 1798–1852*. Stanford, CA: Stanford University Press, 1988.

Barros, André de. *Vida do apostolico padre Antonio Vieyra da Companhia de Jesus, chamado por antonomasia o Grande, acclamado no mundo por principe dos oradores evangelicos, prégador incomparavel dos augustissimos reys de Portugal, varao esclarecido em virtudes, e letras divinas, e humanas, restaurador das misoes do Maranhao, e Pará*. Lisbon: Sylviana, 1746.

Barth, Frederick. "Os Grupos étnicos e suas fronteiras." In *O Guru, o iniciador e outras variações antropológicas*, edited by Tomke Lask, 25–67. Rio de Janeiro: ContraCapa, 2000.

Beozzo, José Oscar. *Leis e regimentos das missões: Política indigenista no Brasil*. São Paulo: Loyola, 1983.

Bergad, Laird W. *Slavery and the Demographic and Economic History of Minas Gerais, Brazil, 1720–1888*. Cambridge: Cambridge University Press, 1999.

Betendorf, João Felipe. "Chronica da missão dos padres da Companhia de Jesus no Estado do Maranhão [1699]." *Revista do Instituto Histórico e Geográfico Brasiliero* 72, part 1 (1909): 1–697.

Bieber, Judy. "Cannibalism or Commerce? Economic Relations among Indians and Settlers in Minas Gerais, Brazil, 1808–1850." Paper presented at the Latin American Studies Association Congress, Washington, D.C., September 2001.

Boccara, Guillaume. "Mundos nuevos en las fronteras del Nuevo Mundo: Relectura de los procesos coloniales de etnogénesis, etnificación y mestizaje em tiempos de globalización." *Nuevo Mundo Mundos Nuevos* (2001), http://nuevomundo. revues.org/426.

Bonavides, Paulo, and Roberto Amaral, eds. *Textos políticos da história do Brasil.* 3d ed. Vol. 1. Brasília: Senado Federal, 2002.

Boxer, Charles R. *The Golden Age of Brazil, 1695–1750: Growing Pains of a Colonial Society.* Berkeley: University of California Press, 1969.

Braun, João Vasco Manoel de. "Roteiro Corographico." *Revista do Instituto Histórico e Geográfico Brasileiro* 12 (1849).

Brazil. *Colecção das leis do Imperio do Brazil.* 64 vols. Rio de Janeiro: Typ. Nacional, 1826–1889.

Brazil. Ministério da Agricultura, Comércio e Obras Públicas. *Relatórios,* 1860–1888. Rio de Janeiro.

Brito, Joaquim Marcellino de. *Relatório da repartição dos Negocios do Imperio apresentado á Assembléa Geral Legislativa na 4ª. sessão da 6ª. legislatura, pelo respectivo ministro e secretario d'estado, Joaquim Marcellino de Brito.* Rio de Janeiro: Typ. Nacional, 1847.

Burmeister, Hermann. *Landschaftliche Bilder Brasiliens und Portraits einiger Urvölker als Atlas seiner Reise durch die Provinzen von Rio de Janeiro und Minas Geraës.* Berlin: Druck und Verlag von Georg Reimer, 1853.

Cadena, Marisol de la. "Are Mestizos Hybrids? The Conceptual Politics of Andean Identities." *Journal of Latin American Studies* 37 (2005): 259–84.

Callier-Boisvert, Colette. "Captifs et esclaves au XVIe siècle: Une diatribe contre la traite restée sans echo." *L'Homme* 145 (1998): 109–26.

Cambraia, Ricardo de Bastos, and Fábio Faria Mendes. "A colonização dos sertões do leste mineiro: Políticas de ocupação territorial num regime escravista (1780–1836)." *Revista do Departamento de História—FAFICH/UFMG* 6 (July 1988): 137–50.

Carvajal, Gaspar de. *The Discovery of the Amazon According to the Account of Friar Gaspar de Carvajal and Other Documents.* Translated by Bertram T. Lee. Edited by H. C. Heaton. New York: American Geographical Society, 1934.

Castelnau, Francis de. *Expedição às regiões centrais da America do Sul.* Translated by Olivério M. de Oliveira Pinto. Belo Horizonte: Itatiaia, 2000.

———. *Expedition dans les parties centrales de L'Amérique du Sud, de Rio de Janeiro a Lima, et de Lima au Para; exécutée par ordre du gouvernement français pendant les années 1843 à 1847*, Part 2, *Vues et Scènes*. *(Les Planches Lithographiées par Champin)*. Paris: Bertrand, 1853.

Castelnau-L'Estoile, Charlotte. *Les ouvriers d'une vigne stérile: Les jésuites et la conversion des Indiens au Brésil, 1580–1620*. Lisbon: Fundação Calouste Gulbenkian, 2000.

Castro, Aluisio Fonseca de. "Manuscritos sobre a amazônia colonial: Repertório referente à mão-de-obra indígena do fundo Secretaria do Governo (Colônial e Império)." *Anais do Arquivo Público do Pará* 2, no. 1 (1996): 9–121.

Castro, Celso Falabella de Figueiredo. *Os sertões de leste: Achegas para a história da Zona da Mata*. Belo Horizonte: Imprensa Oficial, 1987.

Chaim, Marivone Matos. *Os Aldeamentos Indígenas na Capitania de Goiás: Sua importância na política de povoamento (1749–1811)*. Goiânia: Oriente, 1974.

Coaracy, Vivaldo. *O Rio de Janeiro no Século XVII*. Rio de Janeiro: José Olympio, 1944.

Coelho, Duarte. *Cartas de Duarte Coelho a El Rei*. Edited by José Antonio Gonsalves de Mello and Cleonir Xavier de Albuquerque. Recife: Imp. Universitária, 1967.

Coelho, Mauro Cezar. "O Diretório dos índios e as chefias indígenas: Uma inflexão." *Campos* 7.1 (2006): 117–34.

Cohen, Abner. "Introduction." In *Urban Ethnicity*, edited by Abner Cohen. London: Tavistock Publications, 1974.

———. "Organizações invisíveis: Alguns estudos de caso." In *O homem bidimensional: A antropologia do poder e o simbolismo em sociedades complexas*. Rio de Janeiro: Zahar, 1978.

Cohen, Thomas H. *Fire of Tongues: António Vieira and the Missionary Church in Brazil and Portugal*. Stanford, CA: Stanford University Press, 1998.

Conklin, Beth A. *Consuming Grief: Compassionate Cannibalism in an Amazonian Society*. Austin: University of Texas Press, 2001.

Correio Official. 1858–1859, 1884.

Couto, Jorge. *A construção do Brasil: Ameríndios, portugueses e africanos, do início do povoamento a finais de quinhentos*. 2d ed. Lisbon: Cosmos, 1997.

Couto, José Vieira. *Memória sobre a Capitania das Minas Gerais: Seu território, clima e produções metálicas*. Reprint, Belo Horizonte: Fundação João Pinheiro, 1994 [1799].

Cronon, William. *Changes in the Land: Indians, Colonists, and the Ecology of New England*. New York: Hill and Wang, 1983.

Cunha, Manuela Carneiro da, ed. *História dos índios no Brasil*. São Paulo: Companhia das Letras, FAPESP/SMC, 1992.

———, ed. *Legislação indigenista no século XIX: Uma compilação (1808–1889)*. São Paulo: Universidade de São Paulo, 1992.

Dahlberg, Frances, ed. *Woman the Gatherer*. New Haven, CT: Yale University Press, 1981.

Dean, Warren. "Indigenous Populations of the São Paulo–Rio de Janeiro Coast: Trade, Aldeamento, Slavery, and Extinction." *Revista de História* 117 (1984): 3–26.

———. *With Broadax and Firebrand: The Destruction of the Brazilian Atlantic Forest.* Berkeley: University of California Press, 1995.

Debret, Jean Baptiste. *Voyage pittoresque et historique au Brésil, ou Séjour d'un artiste français au Brésil, depuis 1816 jusqu'en 1831 inclusivement.* 3 vols. Vol. 1. Paris: Firmin Didot frères, 1834.

Dias, Carlos Malheiro, Ernesto de Vasconcelos, and Roque Gameiro. *História da colonização portuguesa no Brasil.* 3 vols. Porto: Litografia Nacional, 1921–1924.

Diffie, Bailey W., and George D. Winius. *Foundations of the Portuguese Empire, 1415–1580.* Minneapolis: University of Minnesota Press, 1977.

Dippie, Brian W. *The Vanishing American: White Attitudes and U.S. Indian Policy.* Lawrence: University of Kansas Press, 1991. First published 1982 by Wesleyan University Press.

"Directorio que se deve observar nas Povoaçoens dos Indios do Pará, e Maranhão em quanto Sua Magestade não mandar o contrario" (Pará, 1757). Facsimile reprint in Moreira Neto, Carlos de Araújo, *Índios da Amazônia: De maioria a minoria (1750–1850),* by Carlos de Araújo Moreira Neto (Petrópolis: Editora Vozes, 1988), 165–203.

Doles, Dalísia E. M. *As comunicações fluviais pelo Tocantins e Araguaia no século XIX.* Goiânia: Oriente, 1973.

Domingues, Ângela. *Quando os índios eram vassalos: Colonização e relações de poder no Norte do Brasil na segunda metade do século XVIII.* Lisbon: Comissão Nacional para as Comemorações dos Descobrimentos Portugueses, 2000.

Duffy, Eve M., and Alida C. Metcalf. *The Return of Hans Staden: A Go-Between in the Atlantic World.* Baltimore: Johns Hopkins University Press, 2012.

Eisenberg, José. *As missões jesuíticas e o pensamento político moderno: Encontros culturais, aventuras teóricas.* Belo Horizonte: Ed. UFMG, 2000.

———. "Cultural Encounters, Theoretical Adventures: The Jesuit Missions to the New World and the Justification of Voluntary Slavery." *History of Political Thought* 24 (2003): 375–96.

Eschwege, Wilhelm Ludwig von. *Jornal do Brasil, 1811–1817, ou relatos diversos do Brasil, coletados durante expediçõs científicas por Wilhelm Ludwig von Eschwege.* Translated by Friedrich E. Renger, Tarcísia Lobo Ribeiro, and Günter Augustin. Belo Horizonte: Fundação João Pinheiro, 2002.

———. *Pluto brasiliensis.* Translated by Domício de Figueiredo Murta. 2 vols. Belo Horizonte: Ed. Itatiaia, 1979.

Espindola, Haruf Salmen. *Sertão do Rio Doce.* Bauru: Universidade do Sagrado Coração, 2005.

Farage, Nádia. *As muralhas dos sertões: Os povos indígenas no rio Branco e a colonização.* Rio de Janeiro: Paz e Terra, ANPOCS, 1991.

Faria, Sheila de Castro. *A colônia em movimento: Fortuna e família no cotidiano colonial.* Rio de Janeiro: Ed. Nova Fronteira, 1998.

Fausto, Boris. *A Concise History of Brazil*. Cambridge: Cambridge University Press, 1999.

Ferguson, R. Brian, and Neil L. Whitehead. "The Violent Edge of Empire." In *War in the Tribal Zone: Expanding States and Indigenous Warfare*, edited by R. Brian Ferguson and Neil L. Whitehead, 1–30. Santa Fe: School of American Research Press, 1992.

Fernandes, Florestan. *Organização social dos Tupinambá*. São Paulo: Instituto Progresso, 1948.

Fernández-Armesto, Felipe. *Amerigo: The Man Who Gave His Name to America*. London: Weidenfeld and Nicolson, 2006.

Ferreira, Alexandre Rodrigues. *Viagem Filosófica pelas capitanias do Grão Pará, Rio Negro, Mato Grosso e Cuiabá*. Rio de Janeiro: Conselho Federal de Cultura, 1974.

Ferreira, M. T. C. da R. "Os aldeamentos indígenas no fim do período colonial." MA thesis, Universidade de São Paulo, 1990.

Figueiredo, Luciano Raposo de Almeida, and Maria Verônica Campos, eds. *Códice Costa Matoso: Coleção das notícias dos primeiros descobrimentos das minas na América que fez o doutor Caetano da Costa Matoso sendo ouvidor-geral das do Ouro Preto, de que tomou posse em fevereiro de 1749, & vários papéis*. 2 vols. Belo Horizonte: Fundação João Pinheiro, 1999.

Formisano, Luciano, ed. *Letters from a New World: Amerigo Vespucci's Discovery of America*. Translated by David Jacobson. New York: Marsilio, 1992.

Freire, José Ribamar Bessa, and Márcia Fernanda Malheiros. *Aldeamentos indígenas do Rio de Janeiro*. Rio de Janeiro: Programa de Estudos dos Povos Indígenas, Universidade do Estado do Rio de Janeiro, 1997.

Freire, José Rodrigues. *Relação da Conquista do Gentio Xavante*. 2d ed. São Paulo: Universidade de São Paulo, 1951.

Fritz, Samuel. *Journal of the Travels and Labours of Father Samuel Fritz in the River of the Amazons between 1686 and 1723*. Translated by George Edmundson. London: Hakluyt Society, 1922.

Gallais, Estevão Maria. *O Apóstolo do Araguaia*. São Paulo: Revista dos Tribunais, 1942.

Gandavo, Pero de Magalhães. *História da província Santa Cruz a que vulgarmente chamamos Brasil*. Edited by Hue Sheila Moura and Ronaldo Menegaz. Lisbon: Assírio and Alvim, 2004.

Garcia, Elisa Frühauf. *As diversas formas de ser índio: Políticas indígenas e políticas indigenistas no extremo sul da América portuguesa*. Rio de Janeiro: Arquivo Nacional, 2009.

Garfield, Seth. *Indigenous Struggle at the Heart of Brazil: State Policy, Frontier Expansion, and the Xavante Indians, 1937–1988*. Durham, NC: Duke University Press, 2001.

Giraldin, Odair. *Cayapó e Panará: Luta e sobrevivência de um povo Jê no Brasil Central*. Campinas: UNICAMP, 1997.

Goiás (Província). Presidente. *Relatórios*. 1835–1889. Goiás.

Gomes, Horieste, and Antônio Teixeira Neto. *Geografia Goiás-Tocantins*. Goiânia: CEGRAF, UFG, 1993.

Gonzaga, Tomás Antônio. *Cartas Chilenas*. Edited by Tarquínio J. B. De Oliveira. São Paulo: Ed. Referência, 1972.

Goslinga, Cornelis C. *The Dutch in the Caribbean and on the Wild Coast, 1580–1680*. Assen: Van Gorcum, 1971.

Gravesande, Laurens Storm van 's. *Storm van 's Gravesande: The Rise of British Guiana*. 2 vols. London: Hakluyt Society, 1911.

Greenlee, William Brooks. *The Voyage of Pedro Álvares Cabral to Brazil and India: From Contemporary Documents and Narratives*. London: Hakluyt Society, 1938.

Gruzinski, Serge. *The Mestizo Mind: The Intellectual Dynamics of Colonization and Globalization*. Translated by Deke Dusinberre. New York: Routledge, 2002.

Hackel, Steven W. "The Staff of Leadership: Indian Authority in the Missions of Alta California." *The William and Mary Quarterly* 3d ser., 54, no. 2 (1997): 347–76.

Hair, P. E. H. "Portuguese Documents on Africa and Some Problems of Translation." *History in Africa* 27 (2000): 91–97.

Harlow, Vincent T. *Colonising Expeditions to the West Indies and Guiana, 1623–1667*. London: Hakluyt Society, 1925.

Harris, Mark. *Rebellion on the Amazon: The Cabanagem, Race, and Popular Culture in the North of Brazil, 1798–1840*. Cambridge: Cambridge University Press, 2010.

Hemming, John. *Amazon Frontier: The Defeat of the Brazilian Indians*. Cambridge, MA: Harvard University Press, 1987.

———. "Indians and the Frontier." In *Colonial Brazil*, edited by Leslie Bethell, 145–89. Cambridge: Cambridge University Press, 1987. Reprint, 1991.

———. *Red Gold: The Conquest of the Brazilian Indians, 1500–1760*. Cambridge, MA: Harvard University Press, 1977.

Hill, Jonathan D. "Indigenous People and the Rise of Independent Nation-States in Lowland South America." In *Cambridge History of the Native Peoples of the Americas*, edited by Frank Salomon and Stuart B. Schwartz, vol. 3, pt. 2, 704–55. Cambridge: Cambridge University Press, 1999.

———. "Introduction." In *History, Power, and Identity: Ethnogenesis in the Americas, 1942–1992*. Edited by Jonathan D. Hill. Iowa City: University of Iowa Press, 1996.

———, and Fernando Santos-Granero, eds. *Comparative Arawakan Histories: Rethinking Language Family and Culture Area in Amazonia*. Urbana: University of Illinois Press, 2002.

José, Oiliam. *Indígenas de Minas Gerais: Aspectos sociais, políticos e etnológicos*. Belo Horizonte: Imp. Oficial, 1965.

———. *Marlière, O Civilizador: Esboço biográfico*. Belo Horizonte: Ed. Itatiaia, 1958.

Kantor, Iris. "Um visitador na periferia da América Portuguesa: Visitas pastorais, memórias históricas e penegíricos episcopais." *Vária História* 21 (July 1999): 436–46.

Karasch, Mary C. "Catequese e cativeiro: Política indigenista em Goiás, 1780–1889." Translated by Beatriz Perrone-Moisés. In *História dos índios no Brasil*, edited by Manuela Carneiro da Cunha, 397–412. São Paulo: Companhia das Letras, FAPESP/SMC, 1992.

———. "Damiana da Cunha: Catechist and Sertanista." In *Struggle and Survival in Colonial America*, edited by David G. Sweet and Gary B. Nash. Berkeley: University of California Press, 1981.

———. "Interethnic Conflict and Resistance on the Brazilian Frontier of Goiás, 1750–1890." In *Contested Ground: Comparative Frontiers on the Northern and Southern Edges of the Spanish Empire*, edited by Donna J. Guy and Thomas E. Sheridan, 115–34. Tucson: University of Arizona Press, 1998.

———. "Rethinking the Conquest of Goiás, 1775–1819." *The Americas* 61, no. 3 (2005): 463–92.

Kelly, Arlene Marie. "Family, Church, and Crown: A Social and Demographic History of the Lower Xingu Valley and the Municipality of Gurupá, 1623–1889." PhD diss., University of Florida, 1984.

Kicza, John E. *Resilient Cultures: America's Native Peoples Confront European Colonization, 1500–1800*. Upper Saddle River, NJ: Prentice Hall, 2003.

Kiemen, Mathias C. "The Indian Policy of Portugal on the Amazon Region, 1614–1693." PhD diss., Catholic University of America, 1954.

La Condamine, Charles-Marie de. *Relation abrégée d'un voyage fait dans l'interieur de l'Amérique méridionale: Depuis la côte de la mer du Sud, jusqu'aux côtes du Brésil & de la Guiane, en descendant la riviere des Amazones; lûe à l'assemblée publique de l'Acdémie des Sciences, le 28. avril 1745*. Paris: Veuve Pissot, 1745.

Langfur, Hal. "Colonial Brazil." In *A Companion to Latin American History*, edited by Thomas H. Holloway, 89–105. Oxford: Blackwell Publishing, 2007.

———. *The Forbidden Lands: Colonial Identity, Frontier Violence, and the Persistence of Brazil's Eastern Indians, 1750–1830*. Stanford, CA: Stanford University Press, 2006.

———. "Moved by Terror: Frontier Violence as Cultural Exchange in Late-Colonial Brazil." *Ethnohistory* 52, no. 2 (2005): 255–89.

———. "The Return of the Bandeira: Economic Calamity, Historical Memory, and Armed Expeditions to the Sertão in Minas Gerais, Brazil, 1750–1808." *The Americas* 61, no. 3 (2005): 429–61.

———. "Sources of Conflict: The Evidence of Indian Resistance in Eastern Minas Gerais, 1760–1808." Paper presented at the Latin American Studies Association Congress, Washington, D.C., September 2001.

———. "Uncertain Refuge: Frontier Formation and the Origins of the Botocudo War in Late-Colonial Brazil." *Hispanic American Historical Review* 82, no. 2 (May 2002): 215–56.

Lazarin, Rita Heloisa de Almeida. "O Aldeamento do Carretão: Duas histórias." MA thesis, Universidade de Brasília, 1985.

Leite, Serafim. *História da Companhia de Jesus no Brasil*. 10 vols. Rio de Janeiro and Lisbon: Livraria Portugalia and Civilização Brasileira, 1938.

———. *Monumenta Brasiliae*. 5 vols. Rome: Monumenta Historica Societatis Iesu, 1956.

———. "Os 'Capitulos' de Gabriel Soares de Sousa." Ethnos 2 (1942): 217–48.

Léry, Jean de. "De seer aanmerklijke en vermaarde reys van Johannes Lerius na Brazil in America. Gedaan Anno 1556 . . ." In *Naaukeurige versameling der gedenk-waardigste zee en land-reysen na Oost en West-Indiën . . . beginnende met het jaar 1246, en eyndigende op dese tijd*, edited by Pieter van der Aa, vol. 15, plate Y. Leiden: Pieter van der Aa, 1707.

———. *Histoire d'un voyage faict en la terre du Brésil*. Edited by Frank Lestringant. Paris: Livre de Poche, 1994.

———. *History of a Voyage to the Land of Brazil, Otherwise Called America*. Translated by Janet Whatley. Berkeley: University of California Press, 1993.

Lorimer, Joyce. *English and Irish Settlement on the River Amazon, 1550–1646*. London: Hakluyt Society, 1989.

MacLachlan, Colin. "The Indian Directorate: Forced Acculturation in Portuguese America." *The Americas* 28, no. 4 (1972): 357–87.

Marchant, Alexander. *From Barter to Slavery: The Economic Relations of Portuguese and Indians in the Settlement of Brazil, 1500–1580*. Baltimore, MD: Johns Hopkins University Press, 1942.

Marques, A. H. de Oliveira, and João José Alves Dias. *Atlas histórico de Portugal e do ultramar português*. Lisbon: Universidade de Lisboa, Centro de Estudos Históricos, 2003.

Matos, Raimundo José da Cunha. *Chorographia Histórica da Província de Goyaz*. Goiânia: Líder, 1979.

———. *Itinerario do Rio de Janeiro ao Pará e Maranhão, pelas provincias de Minas Gerais e Goiaz*. Rio de Janeiro: Typ. Imperial, 1836.

Mattos, Izabel Missagia de. "Descanibalização e Expropriação da Língua 'Botocuda': Vale do Mucuri, século XIX." Paper presented at the Latin American Studies Association Congress, Washington, D.C., September 2001.

Mauro, Frédéric, ed. *Brésil au XVIIe siècle: Documents inédits relatifs à l'Atlantique portugais*. Coimbra: n.p., 1961.

Maxwell, Kenneth R. *Conflicts and Conspiracies: Brazil and Portugal, 1750–1808*. Cambridge: Cambridge University Press, 1973.

Maybury-Lewis, David. *Akwe-Shavante Society*. Oxford: Clarendon Press, 1967.

———. *The Savage and the Innocent*. Cleveland, OH: World Publishing, 1965.

McCreery, David. *Frontier Goiás, 1822–1889*. Stanford: Stanford University Press, 2006.

Mead, David L. "Caiapó do Sul: An Ethnohistory." PhD diss., University of Florida, 2010.

Melatti, Julio Cezar. *Índios e criadores: A situação dos Krahó na área pastoril do Tocantins*. Rio de Janeiro: Instituto de Ciências Sociais, 1967.

Mercadante, Paulo. *Os sertões do leste: Estudo de uma região: A mata mineira*. Rio de Janeiro: Zahar, 1973.

Metcalf, Alida C. "AHR Forum: Millenarian Slaves? The Santidade de Jaguaripe and Slave Resistance in the Americas." *American Historical Review* 104 (1999): 1531–59.

———. "Disillusioned Go-Betweens: The Politics of Mediation and the Transformation of the Jesuit Missionary Enterprise in Sixteenth-Century Brazil." *Archivum Historicum Societatis Iesu* 77 (2008): 283–319.

———. *Go-Betweens and the Colonization of Brazil, 1500–1600*. Austin: University of Texas Press, 2005.

Meyerson, Mark D. *The Muslims of Valencia: In the Age of Fernando and Isabela, between Coexistence and Crusade*. Berkeley: University of California Press, 1991.

Monteiro, John M. "The Crises and Transformations of Invaded Societies: Coastal Brazil in the Sixteenth Century." In *Cambridge History of the Native Peoples of the Americas*, edited by Frank Salomon and Stuart B. Schwartz, vol. 3, pt. 1, 973–1023. Cambridge: Cambridge University Press, 1999.

———. "Escravidão indígena e despovoamento na América portuguesa: S. Paulo e Maranhão." In *Brasil nas vésperas do mundo moderno*, edited by Comissão Nacional para as Comemorações dos Descobrimentos Portugueses, 137–67. Lisbon: Comissão Nacional para as Comemorações dos Descobrimentos Portugueses, 1992.

———. "The Heathen Castes of Sixteenth-Century Portuguese America: Unity, Diversity, and the Invention of the Brazilian Indians." *Hispanic American Historical Review* 80, no. 4 (Nov. 2000): 697–719.

———. *Negros da terra: Índios e bandeirantes nas origens de São Paulo*. São Paulo: Companhia das Letras, 1994.

———. "Os Índios na história do Brasil: Bibliografia comentada." IFCH-Unicamp, http://www.ifch.unicamp.br/ihb/bibcom.htm.

———. "Rethinking Amerindian Resistance and Persistence in Colonial Portuguese America." In *New Approaches to Resistance in Brazil and Mexico*, edited by John Gledhill and Patience A. Schell, 25–43. Durham, NC: Duke University Press, 2012.

———. "Tupis, tapuias e historiadores: Estudos de história indígena e do indigenismo." Tese de Livre Docência [post-doctoral thesis], UNICAMP, 2001.

Moreira Neto, Carlos de Araújo. *Índios da Amazônia: De maioria a minoria (1750–1850)*. Petrópolis: Editora Vozes, 1988.

Motta, Márcia. "Terra, nação e tradições inventadas (uma outra abordagem sobre a Lei de Terras de 1850)." In *Nação e poder: As dimensões da história*, edited by Sônia Mendonça and Márcia Motta, 81–92. Niterói: EDUFF, 1983.

Moura, Marlene Castro Ossami de, ed. *Índios de Goiás: Uma Perspectiva Histórico-Cultural*. Goiânia: UCG/Kelps/Vieira, 2006.

Muniz, João de Palma. "Limites Municipaes do Estado do Pará." *Annaes da Biblioteca Pública do Estado do Pará* 9 (1916): 247–319.

Murr, Christoph Gottlieb von. *Reisen einiger Missionarien der Gesellschaft Jesu in Amerika*. Nuremberg: Johann Eberhard Zeh, 1785.

Naud, Leda Maria Cardoso, ed. "Documentos sôbre o índio Brasileiro (1500–1822)." *Revista de Informação Legislativa* 8 no. 71 (1971), 2: 250–52.

Nazzari, Muriel. "Da escravidão à liberdade: A transição de índio administrado para vassalo independence em São Paulo colonial." In *Brasil: Colonização e escravização*, edited by Maria Beatriz Nizza da Silva, 28–44. Rio de Janeiro: Nova Fronteira, 2000.

Nimuendajú, Curt. *The Apinayé*. Translated by Robert H. Lowie. Edited by Robert H. Lowie and John M. Cooper. New York: Oosterhout, 1967.

———. *The Eastern Timbira*. Translated and edited by Robert H. Lowie. Berkeley: University of California Press, 1946.

———. *The Serente*. Translated by Robert H. Lowie. Los Angeles: [The Southwest Museum], 1942. Reprint New York, 1979.

Nóbrega, Manuel da. *Cartas do Brasil (1549–1560)*. Rio de Janeiro: Officina Industrial Graphica, 1931.

Novaes, Adauto, ed. *A outra margem do ocidente*. São Paulo: Companhia das Letras, 1999.

O'Brien, Jean M. *Firsting and Lasting: Writing Indians out of Existence in New England*. Minneapolis: University of Minnesota Press, 2010.

O'Callaghan, Joseph F. *Reconquest and Crusade in Medieval Spain*. Philadelphia: University of Pennsylvania Press, 2003.

Oliveira, Roberto Cardoso de. "Identidade étnica, identificação e manipulação." In *Identidade, etnia e estrutura social*, edited by Roberto Cardoso de Oliveira, 1–31. São Paulo: Pioneira, 1976.

———. "Pardos, mestiços ou caboclos: Os índios nos censos nacionais no Brasil (1872–1980)." *Horizontes Antropológicos* 6 (1997): 60–83.

———. "Uma Etnologia dos 'índios misturados': Situação colonial, territorialização e fluxos culturais." In *A viagem de volta: Etnicidade, política e reelaboração cultural no nordeste indígena*, edited by João Pacheco de Oliveira, 11–36. Rio de Janeiro: ContraCapa, 1999.

O'Malley, John W. *The First Jesuits*. Cambridge, MA: Harvard University Press, 1993.

Ottoni, Theophilo B. "Noticia sobre os selvagens do Mucury, em uma carta do Sr. Theophilo Benedicto Ottoni." *Revista do Instituto Histórico e Geográfico* 21 (1858): 173–218.

Paraíso, Maria Hilda Baquiero. "O tempo da dor e do trabalho: A conquista dos territórios indígenas nos Sertões do Leste." PhD diss., Universidade de São Paulo, 1998.

———. "Os Botocudos e sua trajetória histórica." In *História dos índios no Brasil*, edited by Manuela Carneiro da Cunha, 413–30. São Paulo: Companhia das Letras, FAPESP/SMC, 1992.

Pedroso, Dulce Madalena Rios. "Avá-Canoeiro: A história do povo invisivel—séculos XVIII e XIX." MA thesis, Federal University of Goiás, 1992.

——, Eliana Granado, Ester Silveira, Hélio Madalena, and Monica Pechincha. *Avá-Canoeiro: A terra, o homem, a luta.* Goiânia: Universidade Católica de Goiás, 1990.

Perrone-Moisés, Beatriz. "Índios livres e índios escravos: Os princípios da legislação indigenista do período colonial (séculos XVI a XVIII)." In *História dos índios no Brasil,* edited by Manuela Carneiro da Cunha, 115–32. São Paulo: Companhia das Letras, FAPESP/SMC, 1992.

——. "Inventário da legislação indigenista, 1500–1800." In *História dos índios no Brasil,* edited by Manuela Carneiro da Cunha, 529–66. São Paulo: Companhia das Letras, FAPESP/SMC, 1992.

Petrone, Pasquale. *Aldeamentos paulistas.* São Paulo: EDUSP, 1995.

Pinto, Renato Venâncio. "Os últimos carijós: Escravidão indígena em Minas Gerais: 1711–1725." *Revista Brasileira de História* 17, no. 34 (1997): 165–81.

Pohl, Johann Emanuel. *Viagem no interior do Brasil.* Translated by Milton Amado and Eugênio Amado. Belo Horizonte: Ed. Itatiaia, 1976.

Pompa, Cristina Auteur. *Religião como tradução: Missionários, Tupi e Tapuia no Brasil colonial.* Bauru: EDUSC, 2003.

Porro, Antonio. "Social Organization and Political Power in the Amazon Floodplain: The Ethnohistorical Sources." In *Amazonian Indians: From Prehistory to the Present: Anthropological Perspectives,* edited by Anna C. Roosevelt, 79–94. Tucson: University of Arizona Press, 1994.

Prudhomme, Louis Marie S. M. H. *Voyage à la Guiane et a Cayenne: Fait en 1789 et années suivantes; contenant une description géographique de ces contrées, l'histoire de leur découverte; les possessions et etablissemens des Français, des Hollandais, des Espagnols et des Portugais . . .* Paris: Chez l'éditeur, Rue des Marais, No. 20, F. G., 1798.

Queiroz, João de São José. "Viagem e visita do sertão em o Bispado do Gram-Pará em 1762 e 1763." *Revista do Instituto Histórico e Geográfico Brasileiro* 9 (1847): 43–107.

Raleigh, Walter, Sir. *The Discoverie of the Large, Rich, and Bewtiful Empyre of Guiana.* Transcribed, annotated, and introduced by Neil L. Whitehead. Norman: University of Oklahoma Press, 1997.

Ravagnani, Oswaldo Martins. "A Experiência Xavante com o Mundo dos Brancos." PhD diss., Escola de Sociologia e Política de São Paulo, 1978.

Resende, Maria Leônia Chaves de. "Brasis coloniales: Índios e mestiços nas Minas Gerais Setecentistas." In *História de Minas Gerais. As Minas Setecentistas,* edited by Maria Efigênia Lage de Resende and Luiz Carlos Villalta, 221–51. Belo Horizonte: Autêntica, 2007.

———. "Brasis coloniales: O gentio da terra nas Minas Gerais setecentista (1730–1800)." Paper presented at the Latin American Studies Association Congress, Washington, D.C., September 2001.

———. "Devassa da vida privada dos índios coloniais nas vilas de El-Rei." *Estudos Ibero-Americanos* 30, no. 2 (2004): 49–69.

———. "Gentios brasílicos: Índios coloniais em Minas Gerais setecentista." PhD diss., Universidade de Campinas, 2003.

———. "Minas dos Cataguases: Entradas e bandeiras nos sertões do Eldorado." *Vária História* 33 (Jan. 2005): 186–202.

———, and Hal Langfur. "Minas Expansionista, Minas Mestiça: A resistência dos índios em Minas Gerais do século do ouro." *Anais de História de Além-Mar* 9 (2008): 79–103.

———, and Hal Langfur. "Minas Gerais Indígena: A resistência dos índios nos sertões e nas vilas de El-Rei." *Tempo* 12, no. 23 (2007): 15–32.

Reys-boeck van het rijcke Brasilien, Rio de la Plata ende Magallanes, daer in te sien is, de gheleghentheyt van hare landen ende steden. . . . [Dordrecht?]: n.p., 1624.

Ribeiro, Núbia Braga. "Cotidiano e liberdade: Um estudo sobre os alforriados em Minas no século XVIII." MA thesis, Universidade de Sao Paulo, 1996.

Rivière, Peter G. *Absent-Minded Imperialism: Britain and the Expansion of Empire in Nineteenth-Century Brazil.* London: I. B. Tauris, 1995.

Rocha, Rafael Ale. "Os oficiais índios na Amazônia Pombalina: Sociedade, hierarquia e resistência (1751–1798)." MA thesis, Universidade Federal Fluminense, 2009.

Roosevelt, Anna C. *Amazonian Indians: From Prehistory to the Present: Anthropological Perspectives.* Tucson: University of Arizona Press, 1994.

———. "Arqueologia Amazônica." In *História dos índios no Brasil,* edited by Manuela Carneiro da Cunha, 53–86. São Paulo: Companhia das Letras, FAPESP/SMC, 1992.

Ross, Eric. "The Evolution of the Amazonian Peasantry." *Journal of Latin American Studies* 10 (Nov. 1978): 193–218.

Russell-Wood, A. J. R. "Identidade, etnia e autoridade nas Minas Gerais do século XVIII: Leituras do Códice Matoso." *Vária História* 21 (July 1999): 100–118.

Sá, Mem de. *Documentos relativos a Mem de Sá, governador geral do Brasil.* Rio de Janeiro: Biblioteca Nacional, 1906.

Saint-Hilaire, Auguste de. *Viagem à província de Goiás.* Translated by Regina Regis Junqueira. Belo Horizonte: Itatiaia, 1975.

———. *Viagem ao Espírito Santo e Rio Doce.* Translated by Milton Amado. Belo Horizonte: Itatiaia, 1974.

———. *Viagem pelas províncias do Rio de Janeiro e Minas Gerais.* Translated by Vivaldi Moreira. Belo Horizonte: USP/Itatiaia, 1975.

Salomon, Frank, and Stuart B. Schwartz, eds. *The Cambridge History of the Native Peoples of the Americas.* Vol. 3, pts. 1–2. Cambridge: Cambridge University Press, 1999.

Santos, Francisco Jorge dos. *Além da Conquista: Guerras e rebeliões indígenas na Amazônia pombalina*. 2d ed. Manaus: Universidade do Amazonas, 2002.

Schmidl, Ulrico. *Derrotero y viaje al Río de la Plata y Paraguay 1534–1554*. Edited by Roberto Quevedo. Asuncion: Biblioteca Paraguaya, 1983.

Schwartz, Stuart B. "The Historiography of Early Modern Brazil." In *The Oxford Handbook of Latin American History*, edited by Jose C. Moya, 98–131. Oxford: Oxford University Press, 2011.

———. "Indian Labor and New World Plantations: European Demands and Indian Responses in Northeast Brazil." *American Historical Review* 83, no. 1 (1978): 43–79.

———. *Sugar Plantations in the Formation of Brazilian Society: Bahia, 1550–1835*. Cambridge: Cambridge University Press, 1985.

———, and Hal Langfur. "Tapanhuns, Negros da Terra, and Curibocas: Common Cause and Confrontation between Blacks and Natives in Colonial Brazil." In *Beyond Black and Red: African-Native Relations in Colonial Latin America*, edited by Matthew Restall, 81–114. Albuquerque: University of New Mexico Press, 2005.

Scott, James C. *Weapons of the Weak: Everyday Forms of Peasant Resistance*. New Haven, CT: Yale University Press, 1985.

Sereburã, Hipru, Rupawê, Serezabdi, and Sereñimirãmi. *Wamrêmé Za'ra: Mito e História do Povo Xavante: Nossa Palavra*. São Paulo: Senac, 1998.

Shostak, Marjorie. *Nisa: The Life and Words of a !Kung Woman*. New York: Vintage, 1983.

Silva, Aracy Lopes da. "Dois Séculos e Meio de História Xavante." In *História dos índios no Brasil*, edited by Manuela Carneiro da Cunha, 357–78. São Paulo: Companhia das Letras, FAPESP/SMC, 1992.

Silva, D. A. Tavares da. *O Cientista Luso-Brasileiro: Dr. Alexandre Rodrigues Ferreira*. Lisbon: n.p., 1947.

Silva, Joaquim Norberto de Souza. "Memória histórica e documentada das aldeias de índios da província do Rio de Janeiro." *Revista do Instituto Histórico e Geográfico do Brasil* 17, 3ª série, no. 14–15 (1854): 109–552.

Simón, Pedro. *The Expedition of Pedro de Ursua and Lope de Aguirre in Search of El Dorado and Omagua in 1560–1*. Translated by William Bollaert. London: Hakluyt Society, 1861.

Sommer, Barbara A. "Colony of the Sertão: Amazonian Expeditions and the Indian Slave Trade." *The Americas* 61, no. 3 (2005): 401–28.

———. "Cracking Down on the *Cunhamenas*: Renegade Amazonian Traders under Pombaline Reform." *Journal of Latin American Studies* 38, no. 4 (2006): 767–91.

———. "Negotiated Settlements: Native Amazonians and Portuguese Policy in Pará, Brazil, 1758–1798." PhD diss., University of New Mexico, 2000.

Southey, Robert. *History of Brazil*. Vol. 3. Reprint, New York: Franklin, 1970 [1822].

Souza, Laura de Mello e. *Norma e conflito: Aspectos da história de Minas no século XVIII*. Belo Horizonte: UFMG, 1999.

Spalding, Karen. "The Colonial Indian: Past and Future Research Perspectives." *Latin American Research Review* 7, no. 1 (1972): 47–76.

———. "Social Climbers: Changing Patterns of Mobility among the Indians of Colonial Peru." *Hispanic American Historical Review* 50, no. 4 (1970): 645–64.

Spix, J. B. von, and S. F. P. Martius. *Viagem pelo Brasil.* São Paulo: Melhoramentos, 1976.

Staden, Hans. "De voorname Scheeps-togten van Jan Staden van Homburg in Hessen, na Brazil gedaan Anno 1547 en 1549." In *Naaukeurige versameling der gedenk-waardigste zee en land-reysen na Oost en West-Indiën . . .*, vol. 15, edited by Pieter van der Aa, 1–106. Leiden: Pieter van der Aa, 1707.

———. *Hans Staden's True History: An Account of Cannibal Captivity in Brazil.* Translated and edited by Neil L. Whitehead and Michael Harbsmeier. Durham, NC: Duke University Press, 2008.

———. *The True History of His Captivity, 1557.* Translated by Malcolm Letts. London: Routledge, 1928.

———. *Warhaftige Historia und Beschreibung eyner Landtschafft der wilden, nacketen, grimmigen Menschfresser Leuthen, in der Newenwelt America gelegen, vor und nach Christi Geburt im Land zu Hessen unbekant, biss uff dise ij. nechst vergangene Jar, da sie Hans Staden von Homberg auss Hessen durch seine eygne Erfarung erkant, und yetzo durch den Truck an Tag gibt. : mit eyner Vorrede D. Joh. Dryandri . . . Inhalt des Büchlins volget nach den Vorreden.* Marburg: Andres Kolben, 1557.

Steains, William John. "A Exploração do Rio Doce e seus afluentes da margem esquerda." *Revista do Instituto Historico e Geografico do Espírito Santo* 35 (1984): 103–27.

Sweet, David Graham. "A Rich Realm of Nature Destroyed: The Middle Amazon Valley, 1640–1750." PhD diss., University of Wisconsin, 1974.

Thevet, André. *Le Brésil d'André Thevet: Les Singularités de la France Antarctique.* Edited by Frank Lestringant. Paris: Éditions Chandeigne, 1997.

Toral, Andre A. "Os índios negros ou os Carijó de Goiás: A história dos Avá-Canoeiro." *Revista de Antropologia* 27–28 (1984–1985): 287–325.

Turner, Terence. "Os Mebengokre Kayapó: História e mudança social, de comunidades autônomas para a coexistência interétnica." In *História dos índios no Brasil*, edited by Manuela Carneiro da Cunha, 311–38. São Paulo: Companhia das Letras, FAPESP/SMC, 1992.

Urban, Greg. "A História da Cultura Brasileira Segundo as Línguas Nativas." Translated by Beatriz Perrone-Moisés. In *História dos índios no Brasil*, edited by Manuela Carneiro da Cunha, 87–102. São Paulo: Companhia das Letras, FAPESP/SMC, 1992.

Urban, Greg, and Joel Sherzer, eds. *Nation-States and Indians in Latin America.* Austin: University of Texas Press, 1991.

Vainfas, Ronaldo. *A heresia dos índios: Catolicismo e rebeldia no Brasil colonial.* São Paulo: Companhia das Letras, 1995.

Vasconcellos, Simão de Gil d'Aravio Francisco. *Vida do veneravel Padre Ioseph de Anchieta da Companhia de Iesu . . .* Lisbon: João da Costa, 1672.

Vasconcelos, Diogo [Luís de Almeida Pereira] de. *História antiga das Minas Gerais.* 4th ed. Belo Horizonte: Ed. Itatiaia, 1974.

———. *História média de Minas Gerais.* 4th ed. Belo Horizonte: Ed. Itatiaia, 1974.

———. *Breve descrição geográfica, física e política da Capitania de Minas Gerais.* Reprint, Belo Horizonte: Fundação João Pinheiro, 1994 [1807].

Vilas-Bôas, Crisoston Terto. "A questão indígena em Minas Gerais: Um balanço das fontes e bibliografia." *Revista de História* (Ouro Preto) 5 (1995): 42–55.

Wade, Peter. "Rethinking Mestizaje: Ideology and Lived Experience." *Journal of Latin American Studies* 37 (2005): 239–57.

Wallis, Helen, ed. *The Maps and Text of the Boke of Idrography Presented by Jean Rotz to Henry VIII.* Oxford: Oxford University Press, 1981.

Warren, Jonathan W. *Racial Revolutions: Antiracism and Indian Resurgence in Brazil.* Durham, NC: Duke University Press, 2001.

Weber, Max. *Economia e sociedade.* Brasília: Editora da Universidade de Brasília, 1994.

Wied-Neuwied, Maximilian, Prince of. Travels in Brazil in the Years 1815, 1816, 1817. London: Henry Colburn, 1820.

———. *Viagem pelo Brasil.* Belo Horizonte: Itatiaia/USP, 1989.

Whitehead, Neil L. "The Ancient Amerindian Polities of the Lower Orinoco, Amazon and Guayana Coast: A Preliminary Analysis of Their Passage from Antiquity to Extinction." In *Amazonian Indians: From Prehistory to the Present: Anthropological Perspectives,* edited by Anna C. Roosevelt, 33–54. Tucson: University of Arizona Press, 1994.

———. "Black Read as Red: Ethnic Transgression and Hybridity in Northeastern South America and the Caribbean." In *Beyond Black and Red: African-Native Relations in Colonial Latin America,* edited by Matthew Restall, 223–44. Albuquerque: University of New Mexico Press, 2005.

———. "Indigenous Slavery in South America, 1492–1820." In *The Cambridge World History of Slavery,* edited by David Eltis and Stanley L. Engerman, vol. 3, 248–74. Cambridge: Cambridge University Press, 2011.

———. *Lords of the Tiger Spirit: A History of the Caribs in Colonial Venezuela and Guyana, 1498–1820.* Dordrecht: Foris, 1988.

———. "Native Peoples Confront Colonial Regimes in Northeastern South America (c. 1550–1900)." In *Cambridge History of the Native Peoples of the Americas,* edited by Frank Salomon and Stuart B. Schwartz, vol. 3, pt. 2, 382–441. Cambridge: Cambridge University Press, 1999.

———. "Native Americans and Europeans—Early Encounters." In *The Oxford Handbook of the Atlantic World, c.1450–c.1850,* edited by Nicholas P. Canny and Philip D. Morgan, 55–57. New York: Oxford, 2011.

―――. "Tribes Make States and States Make Tribes: Warfare and the Creation of Colonial Tribes and States in Northeastern South America." In *War in the Tribal Zone: Expanding States and Indigenous Warfare*, edited by R. Brian Ferguson and Neil L. Whitehead, 127–50. Santa Fe, NM: School of American Research Press, 2000.

―――, ed. *Histories and Historicities in Amazonia*. Lincoln: University of Nebraska Press, 2003.

―――, ed. *Nineteenth Century Travels, Explorations and Empires: Writings from the Era of Imperial Consolidation, 1835–1910*. Vol. 8, South America. London: Pickering & Chatto, 2004.

―――, and Robin Wright, eds. *In Darkness and Secrecy: The Anthropology of Assault Sorcery and Witchcraft in Amazonia*. Durham, NC: Duke University Press, 2004.

Williamson, James A. *English Colonies in Guiana and on the Amazon, 1604–1668*. Oxford: Clarendon Press, 1923.

Wilson, John. "The Relation of Master John Wilson . . . into England from Wiapoco in Guiana 1606." In *Hakluytus Posthumus: Or Purchas His Pilgrimes: Contayning a History of the World in Sea Voyages and Lande Travells by Englishmen and Others*, edited by Samuel Purchas, vol. 16, 338–51. Glasgow: J. MacLehose, 1906.

Wolney, Maria Jovita Valente, ed. *Coletânea: Legislação agrária, legislação de registros públicos, jurisprudência*. Brasília: Ministério Extraordinário para Assuntos Fundiários, 1983.

Wright, Robin, and Manuela Carneiro da Cunha. "Destruction, Resistance, and Transformation—Southern, Coastal, and Northern Brazil (1580–1890)." In *Cambridge History of the Native Peoples of the Americas*, edited by Frank Salomon and Stuart B. Schwartz, vol. 3, pt. 2, 287–381. Cambridge: Cambridge University Press, 1999.

Contributors

Maria Regina Celestino de Almeida, associate professor of history at the Universidade Federal Fluminense, completed her doctorate at the Universidade Estadual de Campinas. She is the author of *Metamorfoses indí- genas—Identidade e cultura nas aldeias coloniais do Rio de Janeiro* (Rio de Janeiro: Arquivo Nacional, 2003) and *Os índios na história do Brasil* (Rio de Janeiro: Fundação Getúlio Vargas, 2010), as well as many articles. She coedited (with Rachel Soihet, Cecília Azevedo, and Rebeca Gontijo) *Mitos, projetos e práticas políticas—Memória e historiografia* (Rio de Janeiro: Civilização Brasileira, 2009).

Judy Bieber, associate professor of history at the University of New Mexico, did her doctoral work at the Johns Hopkins University. Her books include *Power, Patronage and Political Violence: State Building on a Brazilian Frontier, 1822–1889* (Lincoln: University of Nebraska Press, 1999) and an edited volume, *Plantation Societies in the Era of European Expansion* (Brookfield, VT: Ashgate, 1997). Her research focuses on the dynamics of frontier societies in Brazil with an emphasis on race, ethnicity, and the articulation of localized forms of power and authority. She is currently completing a book manuscript about the contested settlement of indigenous territories in eastern Minas Gerais during the nineteenth century.

Mary Karasch, professor of history emerita at Oakland University, received her doctorate from the University of Wisconsin. Her principal publication is *Slave Life in Rio de Janeiro, 1808–1850* (Princeton, NJ: Princeton University

Press, 1987). Her recent articles include "Construindo comunidades: As irmandades dos pretos e pardos," *História Revista* 15, no. 2 (2010): 257–83, and "Quality, Nation, and Color: Constructing Identities in Central Brazil, 1775–1835," *Estudios Interdisciplinarios de América Latina y el Caribe* 19, no. 1 (2008): 1–12. She is completing a book manuscript titled "Frontier Life in Central Brazil, 1780–1835."

Hal Langfur, associate professor of history at the University at Buffalo (SUNY), earned his PhD at the University of Texas at Austin. He is the author of *The Forbidden Lands: Colonial Identity, Frontier Violence, and the Persistence of Brazil's Eastern Indians, 1750–1830* (Stanford, CA: Stanford University Press, 2006) and many articles published in the U.S., Brazil, and Portugal. His present research focuses on wilderness expeditions and the projection and subversion of Portuguese power in the Brazilian interior during the late colonial period.

David McCreery, professor of history emeritus at Georgia State University, received his PhD from Tulane University and a Diploma in Social Anthropology from University College, London. His works include *Rural Guatemala, 1760–1940* (Stanford, CA: Stanford University Press, 1994); *The Sweat of their Brow: Work in the History of Latin America* (Armonk, NY: ME Sharpe, 2000); and *Frontier Goiás, 1810–1890* (Stanford, CA: Stanford University Press, 2006); as well as many articles. His current research is on Brazilian maritime history.

Alida C. Metcalf, Harris Masterson Jr. Professor of History at Rice University, completed her doctorate at the University of Texas at Austin. She is the author of *Family and Frontier in Colonial Brazil* (Berkeley: University of California Press, 1992) and *Go-Betweens and the Colonization of Brazil* (Austin: University of Texas Press, 2005), and coauthor (with Eve M. Duffy) of *The Return of Hans Staden: A Go-Between in the Atlantic World* (Baltimore, MD: Johns Hopkins University Press, 2012). Her current research focuses on cartographers of the sixteenth-century Atlantic world and (with Farès el-Dahdah and Verena Andreatta) the social and architectural history of Rio de Janeiro.

Maria Leônia Chaves de Resende, associate professor of history at the Universidade Federal de São João del Rei, did her doctoral work at the

Universidade Estadual de Campinas and postdoctoral studies at the Centro de História de Além-Mar, Universidade Nova de Lisboa, with which she is also affiliated. She is the coeditor (with Sílvia Maria Jardim Brügger) of *Caminhos Gerais: Estudos históricos sobre Minas, séc. XVIII–XIX* (São João del-Rei: UFSJ, 2005) and (with Júnia Ferreira Furtado) *Travessias inquisitoriais das Minas Gerais aos cárceres do Santo Ofício: Diálogos e trânsitos religiosos no império luso-brasileiro, sécs. XVI–XVIII* (Belo Horizonte: Fino Traço, forthcoming), and the author of many articles.

Barbara A. Sommer, associate professor of history at Gettysburg College, earned her PhD in history with a minor in anthropology at the University of New Mexico. Her articles on Portuguese Amazonia have appeared in *Slavery & Abolition, Journal of Latin American Studies, The Americas*, and *Colonial Latin American Historical Review*. Her essays in edited collections include "Wigs, Weapons, Tattoos, and Shoes: Getting Dressed in Colonial Amazonia and Brazil" in *The Politics of Dress in Asia and the Americas*, edited by Mina Roces and Louise Edwards (Portland: Sussex Academic Press, 2007).

Neil L. Whitehead was a professor of anthropology at the University of Wisconsin, Madison, until his death in 2012. He completed his DPhil at the University of Oxford. He authored *Lords of the Tiger Spirit: A History of the Caribs in Colonial Venezuela and Guyana, 1498–1820* (Providence, RI: Foris Publications, 1988) and *Dark Shamans: Kanaimà and the Poetics of Violent Death* (Durham, NC: Duke University Press, 2002). His many edited and coedited volumes include (with M. Harbsmeier) *Hans Staden's True History: An Account of Cannibal Captivity in Brazil* (Durham, NC: Duke University Press, 2008) and (with Michael Wesch) *Human No More: Digital Subjectivities, Unhuman Subjects, and the End of Anthropology* (Boulder: University Press of Colorado, 2012).

Index

Page numbers in italic type indicate illustrations. The letter *c*, *t*, or *n* following a page number indicates a chart, table, or note on the cited page(s). The number following the *n* refers to the note number.

Spanish America, 9; mestiços and, 85n53;
   Treaty of Madrid and, 20–21
"Spanish Arawaks," 99
Staden, Hans, 32, *43*, 56n16
sugar plantations, 95
Sweet, David, 110

Taggia, Rafael de, 216
Taggia, Segismundo de, 199
Tapojoso, 92
Tapuia Indians (enemies of the
   Tupinambá), 15–16, 91–92, 156, 172
Teixeira, Pedro, 88, 91
territorial jurisdictions, boundary commissions and, 103
Tocantins River region, 200, 203, 205, 206,
   208, 211, 227, 234
Torres, Miguel de, 42
traditional scholarship, 99–101; anachronism and, 14–15; Brazilian Indians
   and, 7, 8; chronicle of extinction and,
   136; "colonial Indians" and, 109–10;
   context, scope and, 14–15; demograph-
   ics and, 9; indigenous history and, 7;
   indigenous resistance, adaptability
   and, 17, 19; Luso-Brazilian Indian policy and, 199; Minas Gerais and, 132–33;
   Tupi-Guaraní, Tapuia and, 15–16; vanishing Indian and, 133
Treaty of London of 1814, 104
Treaty of Madrid of 1750, 20–21, 97, 99, 112
Treaty of Tordesillas of 1794, 87, 88
Tupi-Guaraní languages, 15–16, 33, 46. *See
   also* Guarani Indians/languages
Tupinambá Indians, 89, 108, *111*, 169
Tupi-speaking Indians, 7, 15–16, 30, *49*, 167,
   169–70, 172; aldeias and, 171; economic
   rationality of, 170; extractive activities
   and, 170

Valadares, José Luís de Meneses
   Abranches Castello Branco, count of,
   137, 138, 141, 155, 158
Vale, Leonardo do, 48, 51, 53
Vasconcellos, José de Almeida, 202–3
Vasconcelos, Diego de, 163n33

Veiga, Manoel Francisco da Silva, 71–72
Venezuela, 104
Vespucci, Amerigo, 2, 4–5
Vianna, André Alves Pereira, 71, 83n23
Vieira, António, *3*, 109, 113
Vila Velha, 29

Waldseemüller Map, 4
washerwomen in Rio de Janeiro, *73*
Weber, Max, 79
Whitehead, Neil, 19
Wilckens, Henrique João, 117, 128n50
Wilson, John, 88
women: agriculture and, 18, 171–72; attire
   and, 128n35; as captives, *15*; as colonial
   Indians, *20*; combat and, 234; as domestic servants, 18, *73*; as hereditary
   nobility, 113; marriage and, 34, 36, 117;
   mestiço children and, 18; nursing and,
   194n58; Paulistas and, 148; slavery and,
   40, 154, 225; Tupi men and, 34;
   Vespucci landing and, 4–5

Xacriabá Indians, 203, 226–27
Xavante Indians, 23, 208, 216, 233–39; agriculture and, 187; aldeia of Carretão
   and, 203; autonomy and, 23; conquest
   of, 198; "conquest of," 203; description
   of, 234; field work and, 187; locations
   of, 233–34; Luso-Brazilian Indian policy and, 198–99; military challenges
   and, 100; Pedro Affonso aldeia and,
   239; reciprocity and, 187; ritual practices and, 196n95; Thereza Christina
   aldeia and, 239; warfare and, 208;
   Xerente Indians and, 233–34
Xavier, Francisco, 153
Xavier, Inácio, 158–59
Xerente Indians, 23, 186, 208, 216, 233–39;
   aldeia of Graciosa and, 236; attacks of,
   238; demonization of, 236–37; locations
   of, 234, 236; Naraguagê Indians and,
   236–37; Xavante Indians and, 233–34

The War for Mexico's West: Indians and Spaniards in New Galicia, 1524–1550
—Ida Altman

Damned Notions of Liberty: Slavery, Culture, and Power in Colonial Mexico, 1640–1769
—Frank Proctor

*Irresistible Forces: Latin American Migration
to the United States and its Effects on the South*
—Gregory B. Weeks and John R. Weeks

Cuauhtémoc's Bones: Forging National Identity in Modern Mexico
—Paul Gillingham

Slavery, Freedom, and Abolition in Latin America and the Atlantic World
—Christopher Schmidt-Nowara

A History of Mining in Latin America: From the Colonial Era to the Present
—Kendall W. Brown

Modernizing Minds in El Salvador: Education Reform and the Cold War, 1960–1980
—Héctor Lindo-Fuentes and Erik Ching

Masculinity and Sexuality in Modern Mexico
—Edited by Víctor M. Macías-González and Anne Rubenstein

Emotions and Daily Life in Colonial Mexico
—Edited by Sonya Lipsett-Rivera and Javier Villa-Flores

SERIES ADVISORY EDITOR:
**Lyman L. Johnson,
University of North Carolina at Charlotte**